BELOVED COMMUNITY

CULTURAL
STUDIES
OF
THE
UNITED
STATES

—

Alan Trachtenberg,
editor

BELOVED COMMUNITY

The

Cultural Criticism of

Randolph Bourne,

Van Wyck Brooks,

Waldo Frank, &

Lewis Mumford

CASEY NELSON BLAKE

The University of North Carolina Press
Chapel Hill and London

Library of Congress Cataloging-in-Publication Data

Blake, Casey Nelson.
Beloved community : the cultural criticism of Randolph Bourne, Van
Wyck Brooks, Waldo Frank, and Lewis Mumford / Casey Nelson Blake.
p.   cm.—(Cultural studies of the United States.)
Includes bibliographical references.
ISBN 0-8078-1935-2 (alk. paper).—ISBN 0-8078-4296-6 (pbk. :
alk. paper)
1. United States—Civilization—20th century.   2. United States—
Intellectual life—20th century.   3. Bourne, Randolph Silliman,
1886–1919.   4. Brooks, Van Wyck, 1886–1963.   5. Frank, Waldo David,
1889–1967.   6. Mumford, Lewis, 1895–1990.   7. Community.   8. Self-
realization.   9. Personality.   I. Title.   II. Series.
F169.1.B597   1990
973.9—dc20   90-50013
                                                                                      CIP

Permission to reproduce quoted matter can be found on page 366 of this book.

FOR ARLENE

Contents

Illustrations

Foreword

O ne of the effects of the recent upsurge of cultural studies in United States universities—an extraordinary expansion of scholarly and critical horizons to embrace cultural activity in all spheres of contemporary life—has been a revived interest in American precursors, in earlier efforts and projects to achieve a specifically American cultural criticism. There are risks in pursuing such an interest, risks of parochialism, of surrender to the seductions of cultural nationalism and an exceptionalist theory of America. In its present state academic cultural studies seems to immunize itself against such risks and compromises by drawing its inspiration and its agenda chiefly from recent European sources, from theoretical writings not only wary of nationalisms but resolutely focused on dissolving all ideologies, on uncovering and denying all structures of power hidden within cultural symbologies. The great theme of recent cultural studies is complicity: how, within the American field, writers and critics commonly studied as figures within a national tradition entrap themselves and undercut their own often-dissenting criticism by implicit consent to nationalist ideology. The study of past cultural criticism in America seems more likely to produce object lessons in unconscious compliance than models of engagement—less likely to deliver precursors than self-victimized failures.

Casey Blake's *Beloved Community* could not be more timely, for the book appears at a time when the terms of a significant debate both about and within American cultural criticism have been maturing. His book gives us something new and compelling to talk about. He is concerned here with learning why several young American intellectuals in the early twentieth century turned to or, better put, felt obliged to *invent* cultural criticism as a personal discourse of rebellion, vocational aspiration, social criticism, and political vision. It is not a univocal or homogenized usable past that Blake is after, but a legacy in the best sense of the word: a legacy, recovered here with both sympathy and detachment, of intensely youthful and intensely committed confrontation with industrial society and its cultural reflexes. It is a legacy we can no longer accept in its entirety; Blake is as severe in his critique as he is empathic toward the passionate commitments of his figures, Randolph Bourne, Van Wyck Brooks, Waldo Frank, and Lewis Mumford. But it is a critique we cannot ignore without further impoverishing our historical sense. Not special pleading but critical evaluation with an eye on the present—this is Blake's purpose in his collective portrait of the first generation of self-defined cultural critics in twentieth-century America.

The book is not only a study of "cultural criticism," but an example of it, for Blake's achievement here is to remake his subject into a study of American intellectual culture itself in the 1910s and 1920s. Not exactly a prosopography, the book nevertheless provides a strong biographical context, not for the sake of biography itself but for the sake of grounding ideas within actual lived experience. Biography is the link between the various projects of the members of this group and their historical moment; biography connects us with historical agents rather than abstract figures, disembodied authors of ideas. The drama enacted on these pages begins with the personal but reaches toward the historical: Progressivism, immigration, world war, metropolitan popular culture, the beginnings of mass consumer culture, all play a role in setting the pace and the agenda of the intellectual labors of this group. Ideas are situated within both private and collective life.

Blake treats his figures as a group, the "Young Americans," but nicely discriminates among them, tracking each as a separate but related story of personal struggle and intellectual development. Other figures of moment appear—John Dewey most significantly. The result is a texture of arguments and debates, set within the rhythm of personal relations. Intellectual drama appears as personal drama, treated with skill and tact.

One of the book's most important revelations is the profound role played by the belief in the essential importance of personal experience to any program of cultural renewal. *Beloved Community* represents its four figures as voices in a continuing dialogue about democracy and culture in modern America. And the book projects Casey Blake's own voice into the dialogue. Behind the voices he orchestrates we can hear his own, arguing that in the legacy of these four cultural critics we can find elements for a heritage, a tradition of communitarian vision based on "cultural citizenship," a pregnant phrase to which this book will give new currency. And adding strength and confidence to Blake's revival of these figures is the fact that he does not hold back his dissent when Bourne or Brooks or Frank or Mumford veer, as they too often do, dangerously toward vague mysticism or elitism or aestheticism—when they seem to betray their own standards by forgetting the communitarian core of their cultural criticism.

Beloved Community speaks to its own contemporary situation. It brings the past forward as a lesson, as a legacy that helps us see the present in a different light. Certain American responses to the same or similar issues engage cultural criticism today, especially the political character of cultural production and cultural criticism and the nexus between criticism and a program for change. The Young Americans inaugurated American Studies; they were exact precursors, acknowledged by academic scholars like F. O. Matthiessen. They recognized that the study of the past and criticism of the present obliged the critic-scholar to clarify goals, to articulate social ends, to discern possibilities for change in the present state of culture. Casey Blake helps us identify their shortcomings, to sift through their legacy in the light of our own quest for a criticism committed as much to justice as to self-realization. They were the first generation to adopt the stance of "Americanists," and *Beloved Community* provides us with major insights into the meanings of that undertaking.

Alan Trachtenberg
Yale University

Acknowledgments

Academic life may not be a Beloved Community, but sometimes it comes pretty close. In writing this book I have been blessed with more assistance and support than any reasonable person has a right to expect. My chief intellectual debt is to Christopher Lasch, who followed the progress of this project from its inception. By encouraging me to explore the full implications of the Young Americans' work for a critical understanding of modern culture, and by his own example, he reminded me time and again of the necessary connection between historical scholarship and public discourse. I also thank him for his careful reading of this work and his advice as to its improvement. I am grateful, too, for the advice, criticism, and education in intellectual fellowship I received from Richard Wightman Fox. Fox's comments on my work proved invaluable, as did our joint venture in what Bourne called "the excitement of friendship." Alan Trachtenberg shared his views of the Young American circle and offered priceless suggestions and encouragement as I revised my manuscript. This book also benefited from a close and careful reading by John L. Thomas, who brought to it his inestimable knowledge of the American adversary tradition. In addition, I am indebted to Everett Akam, John Bodnar, Peter Kelley, Mark Krupnick, Michael Meranze, Robert Poss, David Roberts, Joan Shelley Rubin, Arlene Shaner, Lisa Steinman, David Thelen, Stewart Weaver, Robert Westbrook, and Richard Yeselson for their comments on various versions of this manuscript. My editors at the University of North Carolina Press, Iris Tillman Hill and Kate D. Torrey, played an essential role in shepherding this project to completion. Not all of these people liked everything they read here, so I hasten to add the usual disclaimer that I alone am responsible for any errors of fact or interpretation. They can share the credit for those things I got right.

In addition, I am deeply grateful to Peter Stimson Brooks, Jean K. Frank, and Sophia Mumford for helping me to locate unpublished sources and granting me permission to quote from them in this book. In the final stages of completing the book, Diane Cooter, Vincent DeMattio, James Hoopes, Donald Miller, Jane Morley, and Raymond Nelson all graciously offered assistance in finding visual and photographic materials. My special thanks also to the Special Collections librarians at Van Pelt Library, University of Pennsylvania—particularly Neda Westlake, Kathleen Reed, Nancy Shawcross, and Daniel Traister—and to Kenneth A. Lohf, Bernard R. Crystal, and the staff at the Rare Book and Manuscript Library at Butler Library, Columbia University, for their help with unpublished materials by the four main subjects of this study. I am also indebted to the staffs at the Beinecke Library, Yale University, the Newberry Library, the Library at the American Philosophical Society, the Office of Special Collections at the New York Public Library, the Indiana University Library, the Reed College Library, and the University of Rochester Library.

For their financial support for this project, I thank the New York State Higher Education Services Corporation, the Newberry Library, the Charlotte W. Newcombe Foundation, the Provost's Office of Reed College, and the Office of Research and the University Graduate School at Indiana University.

This book has made all too many demands on members of my family. I can hardly begin to acknowledge their contributions here. Each of my parents taught me in different ways that ideas matter, a family blessing (or curse) I hope to pass on to my children. I thank my mother, Petty Nelson Blake, for her constant care and good humor during my seemingly endless education. I thank my father, Peter Blake, for his encouragement with this and other endeavors, including the wrongheaded ones. My greatest personal debt is to my wife, Arlene Shaner, who read through the many drafts of this manuscript, found excellent reasons for further revision, and still kept faith with its author. "The little utopia of the family is the enemy—indeed the principal enemy—of the beloved community," Mumford wrote in *The Story of Utopias*. Not the least of Arlene's contributions was her demonstration that great men (and lesser ones too) are often just plain wrong. Hannah Ruth Blake, another Young American, made no tangible contributions to this book—no stylistic revisions, no suggestions for changes—except to keep alive the sense of possibility that inspired me to write it in the first place.

BELOVED COMMUNITY

Introduction

*All our idealisms must be those of future social
goals in which all can participate,
the good life of personality lived in the
environment of the Beloved Community.*
—RANDOLPH BOURNE,
"Trans-national America"

This book traces the development of the critique of industrial American culture made by the "Young American" critics—Randolph
Bourne, Van Wyck Brooks, Waldo Frank, and Lewis Mumford—
during the first four decades of this century. It is by no means the first
study of their thought. If there exists a canon of writings by twentieth-
century American intellectuals, the work of Bourne, Brooks, Frank, and
Mumford surely belongs there. Treatments of their criticism appear
in virtually every survey of modern American thought, and historians
have called upon these writers to serve as exemplary characters in one
or another crucial episode in the transition from Victorian to modernist culture. Bourne's evocation of a youth culture in the early 1910s,
Brooks's attacks on literary gentility in *America's Coming-of-Age*, the
founding of the *Seven Arts* in 1916 as a forum for Greenwich Village
radicalism, the Young Americans' polemics against John Dewey and the
"pragmatic acquiescence" during and after World War I, and the efforts
by Frank and Mumford to articulate a radical vision of organic community in the 1930s: such events have become familiar benchmarks in the
history of American intellectuals during the early twentieth century.

Nonetheless, the familiarity of this history has had the unfortunate
effect of obscuring the continuities in the cultural criticism that engaged
Bourne, Brooks, Frank, and Mumford from their earliest youth through
the 1930s. Too often, historians have separated their essays in cultural
criticism from their political writings or from their autobiographical
musings, choosing to emphasize one element of their criticism at the
expense of others. It is commonplace, for example, to view the Young
Americans as "cultural nationalists" and to deride their politics as "lyrical" or sentimental. Similarly, the synthesis of cultural, political, and

personal themes in their writings invites charges that their fundamental preoccupations were personal, not political. As a result, the persistent quest for "personality" that marked all these writers' work loses any connection to their political and cultural concerns. More recently, historians have depicted the Young American critics as representatives of a cultural transition from Victorian values of character building and self-reliance to a consumer ethos emphasizing therapeutic growth within the structures of a corporate capitalist society. Cultural historians have cited these critics' interest in the fostering of personal growth as emblematic of a more generalized remapping of the standards of success in bourgeois society at the turn of the century, once ascetic self-discipline gave way to the privatistic hedonism of consumer capitalism. Such an argument again distorts the Young Americans' enterprise by severing their ideal of personality from the broader political and cultural themes of their criticism.

This book, by contrast, takes these writers seriously as radical critics of modern culture and holds that the unifying theme in their work was not a therapeutic conception of the self, or cultural nationalism, but a communitarian vision of self-realization through participation in a democratic culture. It places particular emphasis on the intersection of questions of self, culture, and society in their work. It is the joining of these themes, I believe, that gives their criticism its power as a source of insight into modern American life. Although this is not a collective biography, I do examine the roots of the Young Americans' work in their own crises of personal identity: crises that took the form of a collapse of confidence in the symbols and meanings that we now associate with Victorianism and that these critics labeled the "genteel tradition." The Young Americans' reflections on their own moral and spiritual predicament in a corporate society prompted their explorations of the conflicts at work in their country and their culture. But in their best work they did not subordinate cultural and political issues to personal concerns. Instead, they insisted that the search for self-fulfillment was a search for communities that engaged the self in the language and civic association of a democratic culture. "All our idealisms must be those of future social goals in which all can participate," Bourne wrote in 1916, "the good life of personality lived in the environment of the Beloved Community."[1]

Instead of the conventional view of the Young Americans as cultural nationalists, I give special attention to their radical critique of the industrial division of labor and its cultural consequences. Bourne, Brooks,

Frank, and Mumford were undeniably advocates of an indigenous modern culture, but they viewed such a development as one component of a far broader assault on the culture of industrialism. In their writings, calls for cultural renewal were joined with attacks on the factory system, which by undermining craftsmanship had deprived men and women of the cultural resources necessary to participation in a democratic community. Their generous ideal of a revitalized American culture could only be realized, they argued, in a society that returned aesthetic experience to the center of everyday life by reversing the industrial division of labor. The interpretation of the Young Americans as latter-day Emersonians misses the social and political implications of their work.

The political perspective of the Young Americans' criticism has proved so perplexing to many commentators because its roots lie in traditions that are far removed from the categories of conventional liberal and socialist politics in the twentieth century. At the risk of oversimplification, it is fair to say that Bourne, Brooks, Frank, and Mumford generally borrowed from two different sources for their critique of modern culture. The first was a romantic critique of capitalism that found its most coherent expression in the work of the English radicals John Ruskin and William Morris but which had significant parallels in the American Transcendentalism of Ralph Waldo Emerson, Henry Thoreau, and Walt Whitman. The second was a radicalized variant of civic republicanism, the tradition of public humanism reaching back to Aristotle, which in the late nineteenth century inspired a series of populist attacks on industrial capitalism, most notably in the work of Henry George. In the twentieth century, John Dewey would emerge as the preeminent heir to this tradition and the foremost republican critic of American social and political institutions. What marked both of these traditions off from conventional progressivism—whether of the liberal or Marxist variety— was their relative inattention to the public sphere as an arena of conflict and their subordination of questions of class or rights to an ideal of community. Both the romantic and the republican indictments of modern industrial society stressed the need for personal fulfillment in small-scale communities knit together by shared cultural traditions, mutual aid, and a sense of the common good.

In contrast to a radicalism that defended natural rights or liberties, or which denounced the economic conditions that drained such rights and liberties of meaning, the Young Americans launched a critique of modern society that was moral, aesthetic, and, above all, personal. It was the personal failure of modern industrial life—its inability to give meaning and satisfaction to individuals—that was its most damning feature from the perspective of those raised on a republican conception of citizenship and a romantic belief in the authority of the creative imagination. "We were all sworn foes of Capitalism," Frank later recalled, "not because we knew it would not work, but because we judged it, even in success, to be lethal to the human spirit."[2]

This synthesis of romantic and republican anticapitalism was not unique to the Young American critics. Such a combination can be found among many communitarian thinkers within pragmatic and Progressive circles at the turn of the century in the United States, including figures as diverse as Edward Bellamy, Josiah Royce, Jane Addams, Charles Horton Cooley, and Mary Parker Follett. All these thinkers defended an often vague ideal of community that linked the republican ideal of participation in civic life with such romantic virtues as shared religious faith, handicraft traditions, and face-to-face interaction. Nor was such an argument purely American, the product of this country's Puritan and revolutionary founding myths. European thinkers inspired by the promise of a scientific analysis of society also drew heavily on romantic and republican perspectives on industrial life. A distinction between an organic *community* and industrial-capitalist *society*, *Gemeinschaft* and *Gesselschaft*, was central to the first generation of European social scientists, as Max Weber, Emile Durkheim, and Ferdinand Tönnies attempted to make sense of the consequences of industrial capitalist development for modern social relations. Not only did their portraits of premodern societies rely on romantic and republican images of organic mutuality, their very methodologies often called on these earlier currents of social and political philosophy to counter the mechanistic bent of mid-nineteenth-century thought. As H. Stuart Hughes has argued, such European critics of positivism turned to idealist traditions that gave priority to individuals' ability to apprehend and master their environment. "Far from being 'irrationalists,'" Hughes writes, "they were striving to vindicate the rights of rational inquiry. Alarmed by the threat of an iron determinism, they were seeking to restore the freely speculating mind to the dignity it had enjoyed a century earlier."[3]

What distinguished Bourne, Brooks, Frank, and Mumford in the early years of this century was their relentless attempt to find a home for "the freely speculating mind" in the social practices of a revitalized democratic community. Whereas many Progressive intellectuals drew on vitalistic and idealist currents of thought to revive conventional liberalism, the Young Americans believed that a politics of personal growth had to start from radically different premises. Their keenest insights into modern culture derived from their commitment to the capacities of ordinary men and women for aesthetic creativity and self-government, which they believed were stunted or restricted in an impersonal bureaucratic society. By simultaneously invoking romantic themes of self-transcendence through art and republican ideals of participatory politics, these critics kept a steady pressure on the underlying assumptions of their country's institutions. In the process, they moved far beyond the familiar terrain of modern politics.

In my view, the Young Americans were most successful when they drew on the romantic critique of industrial civilization to reaffirm and deepen the republican project they shared with John Dewey. The most promising tendency in their cultural criticism was their aesthetic or subjectivist variant of pragmatism, which supplemented Dewey's theory of a democratic culture of experience with an artisanal critique of the industrial separation of art and labor they learned from Ruskin and Morris. The key terms of the Young Americans' criticism—*personality*, *experience*, *values*, and *culture*—reflected their immersion in Deweyan pragmatism and Morrisite radicalism. Along with Dewey and Morris, they believed that democratic radicals had to put questions of personal identity and creativity at the center of their politics and in the process offer an alternative to the traditional discourse of progressive politics. Linking self-fulfillment to participation in a public culture, they hoped to defend the resources of the human imagination from the corporate organization of work and leisure in an industrial society. They sought to foster communal practices that mediated between the self and social institutions, promoting a mutual process of social and self-reformation through the medium of a public culture.

This perspective on modern industrial society found its clearest elaboration in the 1920s and 1930s in Mumford's theory of symbolic interaction and in his hopes for a revival of regional culture and local politics. By giving citizens the opportunity to participate in the use and reshaping of a shared vocabulary of symbolic form, Mumford's cultural politics gave an aesthetic dimension to the republican understanding of "civic life as a form of personal self-development." William M. Sullivan describes this ideal of citizenship: "Self-fulfillment and even the working out of personal identity and a sense of orientation in the world depend upon a communal enterprise. This shared process is the civic life, and its root is involvement with others: other generations, other sorts of persons whose differences are significant because they contribute to the whole upon which our particular sense of self depends. Thus mutual interdependency is the foundational notion of citizenship." Mumford would have agreed with Sullivan, adding that this spirit of interdependency can take hold as a practice—as opposed to a set of civics-text pieties—only if it first takes shape in the forms and symbols of a local environment. Once embodied in the human-made world of symbolic language, such cultural interdependency serves individuals as a way of strengthening their community's identity and as a resource for its criticism and reconstruction. A public culture provides a setting for personal growth, in this view, by allowing the human aspiration to transcendent meaning to take form, literally, as artistic achievement. The Young Americans' aesthetic revision of pragmatism was a reminder to Dewey and his followers that civic life must engage personalities in the creation of cultural form, as well as in the open-air debates of a participatory democracy.[4]

When the Young Americans veered toward a romantic defense of spirit, intuition, and artistic prophecy in their critique of modern culture, however, they gave up the most important insights of their aestheticist pragmatism. Bourne, Brooks, Frank, and Mumford often skillfully employed notions of mystical "wholeness" and "organic experience" to reaffirm the full potential of creative personalities and to expose the moral and psychological thinness of contemporary political creeds. This romantic indictment of capitalist modernity was invaluable as a source of cultural criticism, but it proved altogether unhelpful as a guide to a politics of democratic renewal and cultural revitalization. Too often, calls for a holistic understanding of culture gave way to demands that prophets of transcendental "wholeness" take the leading role in social and political change. Too often, the recognition that political issues had cultural and psychological manifestations issued in programs that substituted artistic leadership and spiritualistic therapies for a sustained project of civic reconstruction. At times, this meant that the Young Americans flirted with utopian schemes for technocratic social engineering that mirrored the worst features of modern progressivism. On other occasions, such visions of cultural prophecy led to purely aesthetic solutions to political problems. In either case, the central ideal of an interactive, cultural self—of personality refashioning its environment and itself through culture—was lost. Once unhinged from its roots in a republican theory of citizenship, the use of romantic values as a source of critical insight on industrial practice could degenerate into strategies that unleashed the imperial powers of private intuition to remake the world in its own image.

"Modern society," writes philosopher Charles Taylor, "is Romantic in its private and imaginative life and utilitarian or instrumentalist in its public, effective life." At their most romantic, the Young Americans asserted the claims of the private self against those of a commercialized public world. Hence the charge that theirs was an autobiographical, therapeutic criticism divorced from politics. Viewed in the context of their critical project as a whole, however, such moments appear more properly as lapses in an enterprise that was deeply opposed to the stark divisions Taylor describes in industrial society. Their calls for a democratic culture of personality were meant, above all else, to challenge the relegation of imagination and self-expression to private consumption and the enthroning of a bureaucratic rationality at the center of our common public sphere. One aim of this book is to salvage that worthy goal from the romantic wreckage that has absorbed the attention of this group's detractors.[5]

Throughout this study, I keep a tight focus on the lives and work of Bourne, Brooks, Frank, and Mumford, although I do expand my scope at times to include important secondary figures, such as Dewey, and such occasional Young Americans as James Oppenheim, Paul Rosenfeld, and Harold Stearns. I maintain a close watch on these four central figures in order to probe the central assumptions that unite their very diverse experiments in cultural criticism. In stressing the importance of themes of personal renewal and communitarian democracy in their work, I undoubtedly neglect other issues deserving of attention and spend less time than some might wish tracing the connections between these thinkers' work and that of some of their contemporaries.

Nonetheless, I believe this close study of a small group of important cultural critics does have broader significance for the history of the first decades of this century and for contemporary debates about modern culture and politics. First, the Young Americans' search for personality through participation in a democratic culture poses an important challenge to the view that the sole modern successor to the Victorian character ideal was a therapeutic notion of personal adjustment and privatistic growth. Thanks to a growing literature on nineteenth-century ideals of personal identity, we know that aspirations to character could take very different forms, legitimizing both paternalistic theories of elite leadership and populist dreams of self-government by virtuous artisans and farmers. There is a great deal of evidence that the twentieth-century culture of personality has been equally diverse, spawning resistance as well as accommodation to consumer capitalism. The Young Americans' radical understanding of personality belies any monolithic interpretation of the shift from Victorian to modern notions of selfhood. Their dissenting view alone suggests the need to pay closer attention to the variety of perspectives on the meaning of personal fulfillment in this century. It may make more sense to view personality as a contested terrain than as a quietistic counsel of adjustment.

Moreover, the political sources of the Young Americans' criticism reveal a complexity and depth to Progressive-era political debates that often elude their historians. The heady mix of social-scientific pragmatism, civic republicanism, prophetic religion, and romantic radicalism that made up the political culture of reformers and radicals alike at the start of this century demands our respect and careful scrutiny. Neither the softheaded victims of "status anxiety" once parodied by liberal realists nor the "corporate liberals" derided by New Left historians, most progressive intellectuals of note in this period combined a Deweyan enthusiasm for the critical power of "science" with a desire for the moral regeneration of political life. Theirs was a program of "social hope," as the theologian Walter Rauschenbusch called it, that sought to join ethics and social science in new forms of political practice. We still need a careful exploration of the different strains of political and moral reasoning within twentieth-century progressivism.[6]

For those seeking to understand the unfolding of an indigenous radical tradition in the United States, the connection between the Young Americans' work and that of John Dewey has some important lessons. Bourne, Brooks, Frank, and Mumford may have savaged Dewey and "pragmatic liberals" time and time again after 1917, but they were far more indebted to Deweyan pragmatism than they cared to admit. In the exchanges between Dewey and his critics on the Left there exists a tradition of critical thinking about the prospects for republican democracy in industrial society that deserves further study. Given the confusion of liberals and radicals in our own time, we ought to approach the political controversies of this period with some humility: we still have a great deal to learn from their participants.

We may especially learn from the Young Americans' early awareness of the limitations of modern liberalism as a public culture. At their best, the Young Americans challenged progressives to confront the moral and aesthetic impoverishment of liberal politics, and they urged them to place the reconstruction of selfhood and the revival of creative experience at the forefront of a new democratic politics. They encouraged the Left to uphold a decentralized politics of regional communities instead of relying on the centralized state as the sponsor of social reforms. Their challenges were never fully answered; it proved easier for liberals and many radicals to ignore the disturbing implications of their work than to address its questions about culture, community, and the crisis of personal identity in advanced industrial societies. More than a half-century later, such questions can no longer be avoided. They reappear in virtually all discussions of the collapse of welfare liberalism, even among those who have never heard of the Young Americans or their work. The scholarly interest in populism, republicanism, communitarianism, poststructuralism, and various antimodernist and romantic critiques of contemporary society throughout the 1980s reflects a growing sense that the usual rhetoric of progressive politics is exhausted, or at the very least in need of some rethinking. Such complaints echo those made by Bourne, Brooks, Frank, and Mumford at the start of this century. I have been convinced in writing this book that a careful exploration of the strengths and weaknesses of the Young Americans' thought would illuminate current debates about modern American culture and politics. But I have made every effort to resist the temptation to resurrect these critics as heroic forebears of my own position in such debates. As dissenting members of the progressive intelligentsia, Bourne, Brooks, Frank, and Mumford probed the fault lines of their own intellectual tradition. I have tried to do the same: to vindicate their achievement by holding their work to its own critical standards and in turn make those standards my own.

1
The Malady of the Ideal

What I knew . . . did not make sense. . . .
Nothing real made sense.
—WALDO FRANK,
Memoirs of Waldo Frank

Walking alone in Central Park, Quincy Burt, the protagonist of Waldo Frank's autobiographical novel, *The Unwelcome Man*, felt himself "swept back from life in the city to the rural setting that preceded it." As Frank's title made obvious, the book's hero was an "unwelcome" child, unexpected by his parents and ill at ease in the middle-class world he shared with them. At age fifteen, the boy was already too sensitive, too quiet, too intellectually curious for his parents and siblings, who resisted "with all their powers" Quincy's "zealous efforts" at self-expression. On a walk from his family's brownstone in New York's Upper West Side, Quincy recalled his infancy in rural Long Island, and, "as if a long restraint on a long hunger had suddenly been lifted, he dashed into the thick woods" of the park. Quincy's "vague and therefore easily idealized" memories of his youth gave him his only hope of escaping the emotional and cultural barrenness of his parents' home. "Man will have his happiness," Frank wrote, "though he distort childhood, fabricate history, to attain it," citing "the usual happy conception, in man's mind, of childhood" as an example. "Quincy, miserable with the present, had been forced back in his search of that mystic Eden each man and each race must cherish, to make of it a goal and pattern for the future." Frank completed *The Unwelcome Man* in 1915 and moved on to other literary pursuits, but his early concern with memory as a source of alternatives to a "miserable" present remained central to his cultural criticism in later years. Just as Quincy's treasured recollections of the past—however "distorted" or "fabricated"—allowed him to imagine future happiness, the mature Frank grounded his critique of present realities in a historical memory that raised the possibility of their transcendence.[1]

When Frank, Van Wyck Brooks, and Lewis Mumford looked back on their youth in later life, they often did so in the spirit of Frank's Quincy Burt recalling his rural childhood. Having lived through two world wars, the dashing of their early socialist hopes, and the tensions of the cold war, Frank, Brooks, and Mumford thought anew of the middle-class culture into which they had been born at the end of the nineteenth century and portrayed it in their memoirs with a fondness unimaginable in the 1910s and 1920s, when they had led the youthful revolt against Victorian gentility. "How safe, with all its fictions, this world seemed," Brooks wrote in retrospect. Its internal contradictions and hypocrisies aside, the Victorian ethos in which they had been raised at least attempted to lend human activity a sense of place and of belonging to a wider culture that Americans coming of age in the 1950s, 1960s, and 1970s—the years in which these critics turned to autobiography—would never know. The genteel culture of the educated middle class, Brooks recalled, "seemed to be a stable world, permanently supported by cast-iron customs, by a ritual of living that was immemorial, or assumed to be, and that extended into every corner of existence." Cultural radicals who undermined that culture by attacking its "vital lies" discovered later that they had "condemned themselves to playing lone hands against the universe, with no underlying sense of security whatever." If the Young Americans' memories of the world that ended with the outbreak of war in 1914 were as "vague and easily idealized" as Quincy Burt's apotheosis of childhood—and, in Brooks's case, a good deal more sentimental—this reflects their desire to present readers with an alternative to the individual rootlessness and bureaucratic organization they believed had supplanted Victorian self-reliance, pride in work, and loyalty to place and family.[2]

Nonetheless, the portrait of late nineteenth-century Victorianism that emerges in the Young Americans' autobiographical writings is far from monolithic. Frank may have most fully captured the ambivalence that he, Brooks, and Mumford shared "about that now lost green world" of their youth when he wrote, "it was green, but it was also brown. It was full of a sap of love, a flowing and a flowering, but hard as the tough oak." The bourgeois culture in which Frank's family lived was "brown" not only because it was "hard" in its discipline and self-restraint but because it was already dying by the time Frank was born. When Brooks and Frank joined Randolph Bourne in attacking genteel culture in the 1910s, they knew they were rejecting a way of life that had lost its claim on the allegiance of a younger generation. As the memoirs Brooks,

Frank, and Mumford wrote years after Bourne's death make clear, American Victorianism was already in crisis by the time these critics reached adolescence. Bourne and Brooks were born in 1886, Frank in 1889, and Mumford in 1895. All four knew the civilization of the nineteenth century only in its senescence. Though the surviving Young Americans came to appreciate the stability of genteel culture, they spent much of their youth feeling as unwelcome in that culture as Quincy Burt.[3]

In writing about the culture of their families and their class in the 1890s and 1900s, Brooks, Frank, and Mumford could not avoid the tensions and faults that ran through Victorianism. They did not have to look hard to find them: the lives of their own parents were evidence of the doubt and disarray that increasingly plagued the once stolid certainties of bourgeois culture. New developments in scientific theory leveled the theological foundations of religious belief, making faith an ever more elusive goal of the educated bourgeoisie. Similarly, the ethos of individual competence and republican self-government that upheld entrepreneurship and democratic institutions was under attack from all sides by the 1890s, not only by populist and socialist movements but by the presence of huge corporations and political machines seemingly immune to challenges from small businessmen or enlightened reformers. Personal identification with a particular city or region had grown problematic once the industrial market began shifting crucial decisions about production and consumption far from the realm of most people's personal experience. Nor could the domestic sanctuary of Victorian folklore resist signs of strain and internal collapse when the religious, moral, and political creeds that had legitimated the authority of the patriarchal family lost their hold on wives, children, and fathers themselves. Together, these developments left middle-class Americans with the feeling, as Richard W. Fox and T. J. Jackson Lears put it, that their "sense of selfhood had become fragmented, diffuse, and somehow 'weightless' or 'unreal.' "[4]

The growing "unreality" of their parents' culture did not escape the Young Americans as they achieved maturity. When, as an undergraduate at Yale, Frank brought his music teacher home to New York to meet his mother, he noted with pleasure his professor's praise for his mother's singing; "she must be a good musician, not merely a good mother," Frank thought. But as he remembered years later, the compliment could not compensate for the revulsion he felt at the life his parents led. "The house and home must be abandoned! and the security," he concluded.

"The language of Schubert and Brahms must be jettisoned. Yale must be discarded. It didn't make sense, this doom, and I did not ask that it make sense. What I *knew* ... did not make sense.... Nothing real made sense." "Nothing real made sense" anymore because the ideas and values that had once structured middle-class life had no meaning, while the yearnings and rebelliousness of young people of Frank's generation remained inchoate and unrealized in practice.[5]

As Brooks, Frank, and Mumford came to value their childhood memories as a source of comfort in a culture that dismissed the past as irrelevant to present concerns, they also came to believe that the promises of bourgeois culture, however vitiated by their denial in practice, still had much to offer those left homeless and confused by the violent upheavals of the twentieth century. Yet they never lost their early recognition that nothing real made sense in the world they confronted, from an early age, as outsiders, as "unwelcome men." Their memories of their own past left them with the uneasy sense of having been born somewhere "in between" the nineteenth and twentieth centuries, and they were comfortable in neither one of them. While they deplored the hypocrisy that attended the waning of Victorian values in the 1890s and 1900s, they also recognized that those very values were resources that had once sustained character and community and might yet do so again. A memory of cultural coherence, of a certainty of identity in a larger framework of loyalties and values, was as much a part of the Young Americans' early years as their rebellion against gentility and a crucial inheritance from an era that had ceased to make sense.

In 1918, when Randolph Bourne looked back on the "old tyrannies" that had ensnared even the most rebellious youth, he noted with particular bitterness "the three sacred taboos of property, sex, and the State" that constituted the Victorian credo. From the first, Bourne wrote of childhood in such a culture, "you are a hapless victim of your parents' coming together," with as much significance "as a drop of water in the ocean, and against which [you] can about as much prevail." Such a child is "merely an accident, unintentional, a species of catastrophe in the life of your mother, a drain upon the resources that were none too great already." Worst of all, parents did nothing to equip their children to master and refashion their world; not only have they not "conceived you as a work of art," Bourne complained, "but they are wholly incapable after you are born of bringing you up like a work of art."

Beneath the Victorians' sentimentality about childhood lurked the old tyrannies, which left their victims as unconscious in life as "a drugged girl who wakes up naked in a bed, not knowing how she got there." This indictment of his parents' generation was among the most severe that Bourne ever wrote, reflecting his disillusionment and pessimism about the prospects for political change after World War I. In many respects, however, it was a departure from the earlier satires of bourgeois culture that won Bourne fame as an advocate for youth in the prewar years. Bourne faulted his elders in 1918 for their devotion to middle-class proprieties in sexuality, economics, and government, but his most penetrating criticisms have to do with their bewilderment as parents, which prevented them from bringing up their children as "works of art." What was unique about the adults of the late nineteenth century, in Bourne's analysis, was not so much their acquiescence in the "sacred taboos of property, sex, and the State" as their inability to give meaning to childhood. Their children grew up with the grim suspicion that they were "accidents" or "catastrophes," rather than the embodiments of their parents' unfulfilled hopes or the heirs to a vibrant culture. Bourne's complaint that his generation had not been nurtured "like a work of art" is far more suggestive of the changes in family life among the late Victorian bourgeoisie than is his more predictable lament about the imposition of a stifling moral code on young children. Childhood had lost its purpose as a time of training in character and faith, Bourne recognized, because his parents' culture was riven with conflicts that undermined its authority. Those conflicts were most evident in the home and the local environment—in a waning sense of place, in a domestic life enervated by the growing rift between equally sterile male and female roles, and in a larger crisis of spiritual meaning and identity— where they affected young people less as a restrictive straitjacket of cultural repression than as an assault on their integrity as individual beings. If parents could not give their children the well-crafted framework of meaning associated with great works of art, they also failed to give them any sense that their own selves were more unique than "a drop of water in the ocean." The tyranny of late Victorian culture, then, was only partly one of outmoded conventions. The past exercised a much more powerful hold over Bourne's contemporaries when it left them feeling that their very existence was arbitrary and devoid of larger purpose.[6]

For Bourne and Brooks, children of "Wall Street Suburbs," as Brooks called his hometown of Plainfield, New Jersey, the most obvious indication of the crisis of nineteenth-century culture was the loss of local identity in the towns in which they had grown up. Brooks remarked in his autobiography that "it was in the nature of our suburban world that everybody had come from somewhere else," a description that characterized his own family, which had moved to Plainfield from New York. "The unloved state of New Jersey" had always been "depolarized" by New York and Philadelphia, Brooks wrote, but its lack of a coherent regional character became particularly evident in the last quarter of the nineteenth century, when aggressive suburbanites working in New York overrode the provincial qualities of small towns like Plainfield. Brooks, who would grow up to be a major interpreter of New England's literature, always felt a "foreigner" when he encountered people from that area because they displayed "local atmospheres" and "flavors" that had long vanished from suburban New Jersey. When Bourne wrote about his own hometown, Bloomfield, New Jersey, he shared Brooks's disdain for the suburban life that had displaced local customs in small towns. Bourne described the new commuting inhabitants of that town as "nomadic," "sinking no roots" in Bloomfield before they picked up and moved elsewhere. Like Brooks, Bourne feared that the contingent nature of suburban culture—always dependent on importing culture from the metropolis for its sustenance—threatened "the cultivation of that ripening love of surroundings that gives quality to a place, and quality, too, to the individual life."[7]

As the distinct civilizations of town and country gave way to nomadic settlements of commuters clustered around large cities, the notion of a stable, secure residence grew increasingly difficult to maintain. That notion became even more tenuous, in the minds of the Young American critics, once it became apparent that their childhood homes were subject to the workings of a larger political and economic order beyond their parents' control. Frank and Mumford, New Yorkers who never shared firsthand Bourne's and Brooks's experience of suburbanization, understood by early adolescence that their families' home life on Manhattan's Upper West Side existed in an impersonal landscape of wealth and power. "For the life of the house," Frank wrote later, "was carried on within the rules of a fierce competition, within the laws of a jungle defending the rightful booty of the strong against the disorderly weak." Mumford recalled the "diagrammatic neatness" of the Upper West Side at the turn of the century, where the poor were consigned to the tenements of Amsterdam and Columbus avenues, segregated from the wealthy inhabitants of Central Park West and Riverside Drive and from the middle-class families whose brownstones lined the neighborhood's side streets. Even Bloomfield, in Bourne's portrait, revealed class and ethnic tensions only slightly concealed by the social isolation of its working class. When Polish and Italian immigrants entered that town to work in its textile mills, Bourne noted, their "fearful squalor" marked the end of Bloomfield's cultural homogeneity and relative social equality. An immigrant working class and a nomadic new middle class of commuters together undermined an older bourgeois ideal of stability and localism, best represented in the United States by the mythology of the New England village, and replaced it with cultural rootlessness and a naked geography of power. For middle-class young people growing up in such an environment, identification with a particular place lacked the moorings of custom or dialect, becoming instead a function of chance and social class. Of all these writers, only Mumford developed a strong loyalty to his birthplace, even after urban development transfigured the New York of his youth. For the others, a sense of homelessness persisted in their personal lives and in their criticism, the product of a widening gap between ideals and practice in modern life.[8]

The conflict between the official culture of late Victorian America and its rapid disintegration had its greatest emotional repercussion when it entered the domestic realm. In middle-class ideology, the home functioned according to a rigid sexual division of labor, offering a feminine sanctuary of love and culture in a masculine universe of contention and competition. The bourgeois father, drawing his authority from his status as breadwinner and representative of a dominant male culture, might yet defer to his wife on questions of childrearing, domestic life, and religion. Husbands subject to the tempests of the marketplace during the working day would return home at night to the moral guidance of their wives and the consolations of the family routine. At the same time, children would find in the home a cloistered realm of peace that protected them from the harsh social order outside until they were prepared to assume their rightful place in it as adults. This coexistence of male and female spheres within the home was the foundation for the synthesis of "premodern modes of thought" and "attitudes specifically linked to the modernization process" that Daniel Walker Howe has described in American Victorianism. The Victorian family not only reflected the divided world of industrial capitalism but promised to assuage some of its meanness by protecting one area of human life, the home, from the arbitrary fortunes of a modern, market-oriented society.[9]

On the surface, the family lives of the young Brooks and Frank conformed to these expectations. Brooks's father was a businessman who worked in New York, while his mother raised her children in the bland mixture of watered-down Protestantism, moralism, and sentimentality that constituted the domestic culture of Victorian America. Brooks's father never had any "real doubt that life was based on laws" of personal conduct and belief, among which was the "automatic Republicanism" he passed on to the young Van Wyck and his brother, who made their opinions about the 1892 presidential race known by burning in effigy a stuffed pillow they named "Grover Cleveland." As for his mother, her "natural taste was all for the frivolous and gay," though she readily came to the defense of her husband's pronouncements by telling the children that these were "so considered," though, as Brooks recalled, "the question never arose, considered by whom?" The elder Brookses made sure to impress their children with "the regularity of everything around us," from "the winding of clocks on Sunday mornings" to "the universal parade to church and the ceremony of 'lying down' in the middle of the day." Frank depicted the official regimen of his own family in a similar light. His house was "a warm fortress" in which the "three nations" of parents, children, and servants had carefully assigned places. Frank's father, a successful Wall Street lawyer and reform Democrat, governed his affairs with a "moral rectitude" that extended to "rules about food, about study and entertainment, about saving electricity, and phone calls . . . about the hours and minutes." Although such rules established the contours of the daily routine, Frank found the emotional atmosphere of his home suffused by the presence of his mother, whose fondness for classical music made a lasting impression on Frank and his siblings. Her position within the Frank household derived from her authority over her children as a guardian of culture, and Frank's recollection that the family home "expressed itself more through music" than through the leather-bound books and oil paintings that lined his father's library testifies to her command over the imaginative life of her family. In this neat scheme of his father's "moral rectitude" and his mother's cultural influence, Frank's autobiography echoes Brooks's memories of an apparently stable family life.[10]

The difficulty was that their parents' efforts to structure relations within the family constantly fell short of what was required to make the home a true fortress against insecurity. As Brooks explained in his memoirs, and as his biographers have since confirmed, neither one of his parents could adequately play the roles prescribed by the bourgeois cult of domesticity. For Brooks, as for the other Young Americans, the contradictions of the late Victorian family revealed themselves most fully in the financial and emotional failure of fathers to provide for their wives and children. If Brooks later gave his fictional alter ego Oliver Allston the maxim that "American mothers are always more potent as parents than American fathers," he did so because his own father, Charles Edward Brooks, had played a largely negative role in his upbringing, which added to Van Wyck's feeling of homelessness the burden of being fatherless. Charles Brooks had begun his career as a junior partner in a mining company in the 1870s. He traveled throughout Europe and the American West, but this part of his life always remained a mystery for Van Wyck. By the time Van Wyck was born in 1886, his father was already a "semi-invalid," who put in his time at a "fictitious" firm but no longer supported his family or exercised much authority over its members. Charles Brooks's disgrace began in the early 1880s, when he traded ownership of an Arizona copper mine (which would later earn millions supplying the U.S. Mint) for title to a worthless nickel mine in Nevada. Ceding economic support of his family to his wife, Sallie Bailey Brooks, and her relatives, Charles ended his life as an obscure clerk in a Wall Street brokerage firm. Sallie Brooks maintained a cheerful facade in the face of her family's economic misfortunes, almost convincing her children by her bravado when she asked, "What's *money*!" but it was obvious to Van Wyck that his family was "poor, more or less," in prosperous Plainfield and that his mother was capable only of keeping up the appearance of a genteel life-style that her finances could never support.[11]

In Brooks's mind, his father's business failure and his impotence within the family revealed the threat posed by commerce to the certainties of middle-class culture. In 1904, he confided to his diary his growing conviction that "the basis of our age is wrong." "Business," he wrote, "is the one profession which is wholly sordid," since the businessman does not "give his own personal service to some higher cause" but instead pursues wealth for its own sake. Charles's stories of his European travels always impressed Van Wyck, but his son soon came to associate the magic of European culture with feminine qualities, an identification undoubtedly strengthened when his mother took Van Wyck and his brother Ames to Europe in 1898 but left their father behind in Plainfield. What came to mind most readily when the mature Brooks thought of his father were Charles's experiences out West, which had resulted in his ruin. Brooks found his father's memory haunting him when he visited ghost towns in Colorado and Wyoming, with their broken-down mines and furnaces built to unearth and smelt metal "that was never found"—the very towns he later decried in a 1916 essay for their "morbid" quality of a "bloodless death-in-life," a phrase that might well have characterized Charles's place in the Brooks household during Van Wyck's childhood. Brooks's fear of the dangers of commerce could only have been aggravated, as his biographers point out, when, during the Depression, his brother Ames took his own life after having forsaken poetry for an unhappy business career. The elder Brooks, whom Van Wyck remembered living by strict laws of conduct, lived to see all those laws overthrown by the chance workings of the market-place. No wonder, then, that Charles's fate seared his son with the image of business as a devouring Moloch that destroyed "whatever was best in the American mind." The American Moloch had done exactly that to Brooks's father, leaving him a parody of the patriarchal ideal, a ghost-boarder who shared the Brookses' quarters in expectation of death.[12]

In Waldo Frank's case, fatherlessness was not so much a product of failure in business enterprise as it was of his father's inability to win his son's affections at home. In recollection, Frank put far less emphasis on his father's role in his development than he did on his mother's. Julius J. Frank, a second-generation German Jewish immigrant, earned enough money as a Wall Street lawyer to raise his children in upper-middle-class style on New York's Upper West Side, but he seems always to have been a remote figure to his son. Waldo did all he could to win the attention of his mother, Helene Rosenberg Frank, the daughter of a wealthy Alabama Jewish family. Almost thoroughly assimilated into a secular culture, Julius Frank came to symbolize for Waldo the loss of transcendent religious belief in modern industrial societies. The books stored in Julius's library gave Waldo "a sanctuary of Europe," a secluded refuge in busy New York, but the portraits of Washington, Lincoln, Napoleon, and Beethoven that hung on the library walls revealed a side of the elder Frank's personality that betrayed the room's serenity and quiet. These figures represented "the will of the ego" in Frank's father, a driving force that made Julius a business success at work while alienating his precocious younger son at home. "Poor Waldo," Frank wrote later, "with these giants of will looking down upon him!"[13]

Whatever the precise reasons for Frank's estrangement from his father, he clearly never felt comfortable with the masculine role exemplified by Julius Frank. Frank opens his memoirs with a "little episode of no importance" that nevertheless indicates the distance between his father's values and his own. Sometime during Waldo's childhood, his father "ordered" a carpenter to come to the Frank house to make an estimate for the construction of new bookshelves. But when the carpenter arrived, the Franks were at dinner, and Julius had him wait in the kitchen while he slowly finished his meal. The incident made Frank nervous and guilty, though he could not decide whether his guilt came from his father's rudeness or his own "failure to take his superiority for granted, which would have made the discourtesy to the carpenter a small matter."[14]

Frank's break with his father came out into the open when, as a fifteen-year-old, he ran away from home while his mother was on vacation in Europe. The break obviously had deeper roots, but Julius's affair with "a woman of the breed then called 'adventuress'" was the immediate precipitant for Waldo's decision to leave. After a day spent wandering in Long Island and Central Park, Waldo returned home to find "Mrs. X" in the library with his father. By the next morning, the woman had disappeared, and the decision of Julius's brothers to have her followed by detectives probably did much to hasten the end of the affair; but Julius's brief "intrigue" permanently damaged him in his son's eyes. Afterward, as Julius lapsed into an "amnesia" about the incident, and as "the home with its romantic music and stern stoical regime went on," Waldo retained the memory of his father's retreat from "moral rectitude." "The strange crisis in the life of that upright man, Julius J. Frank, had deep effects on me, his son," Frank remembered years later. "My father seems to have got by his syndrome; the rest of his life was as unitary and transparent as its beginnings." But for Waldo, his father's betrayal of his own "upright" morality revealed the invidious effect of the will on human relations and of masculine enterprise generally. "My crisis never ended."[15]

Fatherlessness was a physical as well as an emotional reality in Bourne's and Mumford's childhoods. Little is known about Charles Bourne, the "handsome gay blade" and real estate salesman who was Randolph's father, except that "alcohol got the better of him and his business fell apart," as one of his daughters put it. If Charles's financial problems and drinking undercut his authority in the Bourne family, his situation further deteriorated when a trolley car in New York pulled him down and permanently injured his back. By the mid-1890s, Charles's inability to support his family became obvious to all concerned, prompting his brother-in-law to step in as benefactor for Charles's wife and four children on the condition that he leave them for good. Although Randolph's friends remembered his referring to his father at different times with sympathy or with a dismissal of the family "disgrace," he plays no role in the autobiographically inspired essays Bourne wrote as an adult. Halsey Barrett, the brother of Randolph's mother, Sarah Barrett Bourne, apparently had much more influence over the boy's upbringing than Charles Bourne ever did, though his role was almost entirely economic.[16]

The divorce between masculine business and the sentimental culture of the feminine household could not have been more absolute than it was in Bourne's childhood. Sarah Bourne drew her sense of genteel satisfaction and family pride from her Anglo-Saxon roots and membership in Bloomfield's Presbyterian church. But such traditions apparently did not serve her well in confronting her adult family life. Not only was her marriage a failure, she had to contend with the physical disabilities of her eldest child. Disfigured at birth by a forceps delivery and further deformed by the spinal tuberculosis he contracted at age four, which left him hunchbacked and nearly dwarfed, Randolph naturally was a source of concern and preoccupation for his mother. She appears in his later autobiographical writings as a distracted and confused figure, overwhelmed by the circumstances of her adulthood. By contrast, her brother Halsey Barrett seems to have figured in the family as a representative of economic power and masculine self-assertion untempered by emotional or moral concerns. In the rumors and reminiscences associated with Randolph's early life, his uncle's mercenary approach is typified by his patronizing remark to his deformed nephew that someone like "*you*" would have no place in college—a devastating rejection of Bourne's pleas for funds to attend Princeton. Aside from his uncle and younger brother, Bourne grew up in a wholly feminine environment, moving with his family into his grandmother's home after his father's shameful expulsion. The savage sarcasm that Bourne later turned on Victorian models of masculine propriety in his cultural criticism reflects, in part, his early encounters with a male business world divided between besotted failure and callous calculation, extremes that offered little comfort to an acutely sensitive, intellectual young man.[17]

Lewis Mumford's childhood follows the pattern of fatherlessness that marked the youth of his fellow critics, but as he was an illegitimate child, the contrast between his actual family life and official Victorian mores was particularly stark. Mumford began his autobiography with the announcement, "I was a child of the city," explaining later that "New York exerted a greater and more constant influence on me than did my family," because "I was orphaned, as it were, even before my birth." As the offspring of a brief liaison between his mother, Elvina

Conradina Baron Mumford, a divorced housekeeper, and Lewis Mack, the nephew of her employer, Mumford felt his father had been irrelevant to his early development. "I still find it as hard to acknowledge him as my biological progenitor as if I had been the product of an artificial insemination from an anonymous donor," he later wrote. Until his mother told him the truth of his parentage in 1942, when Mumford was forty-seven years old, he believed that his father was his mother's former employer—his real father's uncle. That employer, Jacob Mack—referred to as "J.W." in Mumford's autobiography—had been the object of Elvina Mumford's unrequited affection, and his family established a "niggardly" trust fund for Elvina and her son after Lewis's birth. It is therefore not surprising that Mumford pieced together a story in which "J.W." assumed the role of an absent father. In his memoirs, Mumford warned a future "psychoanalytic biographer" against attaching too much importance to this story of his origins, insisting that his "shadowy awareness of my dubious parentage" never troubled him until he himself married and raised children. Maybe so, but it is difficult to imagine Mumford's growing up without encountering children and adults who pressed him about his origins, thereby bringing the question to the forefront of his imagination. Mumford's own hints of later difficulties in marriage and childraising suggest that the mystery of his father's identity may yet have troubled him, as does his comment that he was an orphan at birth. Much like Sallie Brooks, Mumford's mother maintained "a self-deluding gentility" in her household but with even fewer material resources than Brooks's mother, Elvina Mumford was forced to take in boarders to support her efforts at respectability. The absence of a visible father whose failure left him subject to his mother's genteel pretenses may have spared Mumford the thorough disillusionment with masculine practical life that so embittered Bourne, Brooks, and Frank in their youth. "Since my father's family did not 'exist' for me," he wrote, "their wealth aroused no hopes and their indifference promoted no resentments"—a far cry from the situation of Bourne and Brooks, who suffered the humiliation of relative poverty in an affluent suburban milieu and had to rely on the public largess of their mothers' relatives to compensate for lack of paternal support. For the latter Young Americans, the coexistence of an official code of familial behavior and a family life that clearly contradicted it left them with a deep distrust of the dual realms of masculine business and feminine domesticity that had failed to order their early lives.[18]

Mumford also differed from Bourne, Brooks, and Frank in having the constant company of his mother's stepfather, Charles Graessel, who took Lewis on long walks through New York. Graessel "introduced" the boy to New York, taking him to neighborhoods far removed from the familiar West Side and making him feel "at home" in the Metropolitan Museum of Art and the American Museum of Natural History—two institutions whose "marriage" Mumford would advocate in an early essay on the reconciliation of art and science. In the New York education he received from his grandfather, Mumford found a release from whatever anxieties he felt about his origins, making him truly a "child of the city."

Mumford's grandfather is a singular figure in the early biographies of the Young Americans. He was a male family member who commanded young Mumford's respect without recourse to naked economic power or a sheer expression of personal will. As a former headwaiter at Delmonico's restaurant, Graessel typified for Mumford an early nineteenth-century ideal of success, that of "being fortunate enough to retire in middle life on a 'competency,' as they called it—enough to enable them to enjoy their leisure and their good health before their bodies became enfeebled." Graessel had not been dragged down to defeat by involvement in the masculine world of practical activity; on the contrary, he had managed to subdue the destructive tendencies of that world by following a standard of personal conduct that subordinated economic achievement to an ideal of the good life. Graessel's way of life combined hard work and leisure, the gentlemanly comportment appropriate to the high-society clientele at Delmonico's and a kindly solicitude for his young grandson. The New York he showed Mumford "married" science and art, commerce and culture, and luxury and destitution. In his walking tours of the city, Graessel impressed Mumford with the possibility of finding a way out of the equally sterile alternatives of endless accumulation and a "self-deluding gentility." Graessel's authority in the Mumford household was legitimate, in Lewis's eyes, because it derived from a life of physical vigor and intellectual curiosity immersed in the myriad social institutions of a vibrant urban culture. Years later, when Mumford confronted an intellectual "father" in the writings of urban theorist Patrick Geddes, he must have experienced a moment of déja vu. Geddes's urban surveys began with a technique long familiar to Mumford: walks through the city.[19]

Betrayed by a masculine realm that divorced the pursuit of success from any moral meaning, the Young American critics grew
to maturity in the feminine environment of middle-class domestic culture. Not only did Bourne, Brooks, Frank, and Mumford come of age in
households dominated by their mothers or other female relatives, they
also developed their own identities as intellectuals in confrontation with
the cultural pursuits of the late Victorian bourgeoisie, a sphere of society formally overseen by women. Their encounters with turn-of-the-
century feminine culture proved disillusioning. That culture made no
more sense than the masculine world of the will, and in comparison to
that masculine world at its most robust, feminine values appeared ema-
ciated and lifeless. The stifling formalities of their mothers' gentility—its
endless rounds of church services and moral instructions disregarded in
everyday life, its sterile notion of cultural excellence as the acquisition, if
not the mastery, of classical canons of knowledge, and its grotesqueries
of interior decoration and domestic entertainment—served no better as
a model of conduct than did their fathers' destructive will to power.
Nevertheless, these four young men all perceived an ideal of femininity
that retained validity and meaning, despite the shallowness of woman's
cultural sphere. Identification with that ideal, dimly associated in their
minds with infantile union with the mother, permitted the spiritual
reinvigoration of cultural life and the transcendence of both the actual
world of religion, morality, and art in which their mothers lived and
their fathers' egoistic world of commerce. The Young Americans interpreted that ideal in different ways, evoking visions of a return to the
mother, of merging souls, of mystical unity with the physical environment and ultimately the cosmos, and of the dissolution of the self into a
loving community of friends. Their cultural criticism in the 1910s and
after retained the tension between the ideal of spiritual and psychological union and the realities of a modern society divided between equally
empty realms of male and female endeavor. That tension had personal
roots in the Young Americans' quest for union and meaning amid a
decaying culture—a quest that Brooks would later term "the malady of
the ideal."[20]

Of all the Young Americans, Mumford's sense of fatherlessness was
the most extreme, and his adolescent disenchantment with his mother's
social milieu and with traditional feminine culture generally was the
most intense. Elvina Mumford "consecrated her life" to him, reserving
for her tombstone only her name, the years of her life, and the epitaph
"Mother of Lewis Mumford." Still, Mumford seems to have felt a good

deal of ambivalence about such devotion. Elvina's nervous temperament and her passion for "card games, social visits, afternoon family kaffee-klatsches, or dinner parties, along with horse races and matinees," put some much-needed distance between Lewis and his mother. According to Mumford, that distance saved their relationship from a near-suffo-cating closeness—or worse, if Mumford's belief that "we were peril-ously near the same kind of familiarity that Melville's hero, Pierre, exhibited towards Mrs. Glendinning," is accurate. Mumford's wife, So-phia Wittenberg, would later see the "otherwise too tightly tied knot" between Elvina and Lewis as an early difficulty in their marriage. The young Mumford also enjoyed the constant attention of his nurse, Nellie Ahearn, or "Nana," who became his "second mother." An Irish Catho-lic with an earthy sense of humor, Nana introduced Lewis, who had been baptized an Episcopalian, to the mysteries of the Catholic mass, which captured his imagination in a way that Protestant services never had. Between the joint affection of his mother and Nana, Mumford "had a sense of being constantly surrounded by love," giving him a security that lasted into adulthood as a "deep inner confidence." In his memoirs, Mumford repeated Sigmund Freud's remark that "a man who has been the indisputable favorite of his mother keeps for life the feeling of a conqueror, that confidence of success which often induces real success." The darling of two mothers, Mumford believed that his result-ing self-esteem more than compensated for any doubts he had about his father's identity.[21]

At the same time, however, Mumford thought that "I could not have found myself in a more foreign human environment" than that of his mother and her family, and his fond memories of the maternal love that "surrounded" him in youth contrast sharply with his harsh criticism of his family's routines. His mother's humdrum life was matched by that of her relatives, who exhausted themselves in idle "dissipation." "Never touched by an idea or purpose, however narrow, that might have lifted them above their aimless round," Mumford's maternal relations lived a "treadmill existence filled with empty amusements, empty excitements, empty quarrels—anything for distraction!" From an early age, Lewis felt very much alone amid the tedious chatter of his relatives' Sunday gatherings, where "life itself . . . oozed away" from the participants. For a young man with a sharp mind, the trivial preoccupations of his moth-er's circle must have been difficult to endure. Mumford's reaction took the form of an extreme bookishness, a minor rebellion in a family whose reading consisted mostly of the society page. "A self-contained, unassertive boy," Donald L. Miller writes, "Lewis Mumford rejected the world of his mother's family by withdrawing from it. And because his mother sheltered him at home and took him with her almost everywhere she went, his withdrawal and rebellion was almost entirely psychological. He built a mental wall between his family's world and his own fast-developing inner world." The combination of intense maternal love and a frustrating superficiality of mind was a jarring reminder of the contradictions within a feminine culture grown overripe with sentiment and amusements.[22]

Bourne also drew a distinction between maternal love and the shortcomings of the "serious puckered women" whose duty it was to pass on the fundamentals of gentility to a new generation. Given Randolph's physical deformity, it is not surprising that he drew a good deal of his mother's care and attention. Sarah Bourne may well have considered Randolph the favorite of her four children, but she too found it difficult to hold the allegiance of her young son once he acquired a certain degree of intellectual sophistication. Sarah's oversolicitous concern grated on Randolph, especially as it became clear that she had little understanding of his emerging character. In an essay titled "The Handicapped," Bourne ruefully recalled "the exhibitions of my musical skill that I had to give before admiring ladies" as humiliating performances by an unwilling boy for an uncomprehending audience. Bourne was intellectually isolated in a home "innocent of current discussion," where unread classics remained "stiffly enshrined between glass doors that were very hard to open." Randolph's sister Natalie summed up Bourne's plight at home when she wrote years later that "our relatives did not understand Randolph, classed him as a 'Radical,' decided he was queer," although they were "proud to claim him" once they learned of his fame after his death in 1918.[23]

In a posthumously published autobiographical sketch, Bourne took his revenge on a feminine culture that had both coddled and ignored him. There, the divorce between maternal love and his mother's inability to accept him on his own terms reemerged as a conflict between two separate characters, the narrator Gilbert's grandmother Garna and his mother. "Gilbert liked to have Garna all to himself," spending long afternoons stroking his grandmother's hair and rubbing "the expanse of cool flesh" on her bare arms. Or the boy sat high up at Garna's secretary-desk—"one of the most satisfactory spots in the whole world"— which filled him with a sense of "delicious privacy" and childish omnipotence. If Gilbert was truly lucky, he would get to sleep in Garna's bed, a privilege that made sleeping far more "solemn" than it normally was. These were pleasures to be guarded from the intrusion of Gilbert's sister Olga and his mother. The latter, at any rate, was too preoccupied with her own misfortunes to give the boy the love he needed. "She did not seem to know what she wanted," Bourne wrote. "Every incident was a crisis," and Gilbert often found her crying to herself over some personal trouble. Soon he learned how easy it was to pretend to obey her commands "with a certain chilly haughtiness" and wear out her patience; then, "he would be left alone to follow his own desires." The only conceivable ally the boy might have found in such a family was his Aunt Nan, whom Bourne depicted as a progressive New Woman who taught school in New York and read William James. Otherwise, Gilbert's grandmother, a mute figure of undemanding affection, and his mother, a bundle of nerves unable to reach or control her son, defined the boundaries of the domestic sphere for the young Bourne.[24]

The strains and divisions within the feminine world were manifest even in its physical setting, the interior of the family home. Bourne captured the sticky sentimentality of the age in his description of the pictures hanging in the bedroom that Gilbert shared with his sister: "one representing a donkey in the midst of illimitable and ineffable summer pastures, and marked, 'Everything Lovely,' the other showing him in the blizzard before a locked stabledoor, with 'Nobody loves me!'" Mumford recalled that it was "a point of honor" among housewives to "cover every square foot available" on their walls with such kitschy reproductions, not to mention various layers of wallpaper and obscure, faded oil paintings. Victorian women enclosed house windows in shutters and adorned them with curtains and drapes that "screened out the light" from public rooms. Such lugubrious decoration was a constant symbol of the decrepitude of late nineteenth-century gentility in the essays and memoirs that the Young Americans wrote about their childhoods. Bourne painstakingly recreated the "musty dining-room" of Gilbert's family home, "with its old frayed chairs, its uncertain carpet, its stained brown walls," and the "dull squalor" that "nobody ever did anything to take away . . . and for which perhaps nothing could be done." Gilbert walked through the gloomy darkness of the front parlor in a "subdued" mood, "involuntarily" lowering his voice when he spoke, "as if someone had died there." Those "dusky domestic interiors," those "Egyptian tombs," as Brooks called them, epitomized the obsolescence of the feminine sphere for these critics, just as they did for so many intellectuals who looked back in anger in the 1910s on the middle-class "tombs" in which they had been raised. All that remained of a once-robust bourgeois culture were the incongruous trappings of domestic life: a ragtag collection of objects that cluttered rooms and gathered too much dust. When Bourne wanted to describe the effects of such a life on the youthful imagination in a 1913 essay, he consciously chose a metaphor from his own memory of the Victorian home as an overdecorated prison. "Too many minds," he explained, "are stuffy, dusty rooms into which the windows have never been opened—minds heavy with their own crotchets, cluttered up with untested theories and conflicting sympathies that have never got related in a social way." Twentieth-century modernists who finally decided to "clear out the rubbish," as Mumford put it, were thinking of more than just interior design. In reorganizing the family home along sparse, functional lines, they responded to widespread dissatisfaction with a moribund feminine culture among children of the Victorian middle class.[25]

Outside of the home, religion was the area of social life in which women of the nineteenth-century bourgeoisie had the greatest influence, and its institutions fared no better, in the Young Americans' recollections, than did the other constituents of woman's sphere. Bourne most succinctly summed up the decline of religious faith when he wrote that "the old Puritan ethics," with its moral torments and personal soul-searching, had given way to "a mere code for facilitating the daily friction of conventional life." The best that could be said for the American middle class was that "it does not disbelieve," though this was a far cry from the impassioned sectarianism of its ancestors. Troubled by their own spiritual yearnings for meaning and identity, Bourne, Brooks, Frank, and Mumford found the churches of their parents especially frustrating and superficial. In a wickedly ironic passage in his autobiographical fragment, Bourne recalled the Sunday afternoons he had spent as a child reading the Bible and trying to envision the faces of God and Jesus. There was "something cold and repellent" about the bearded, white-haired God he modeled after his paternal grandfather, and Gilbert's uneasiness about the apparition intensified once he associated him with his minister's sermons about punishing sin. Jesus, on the other hand, presented a more appealing picture, "a young man in an archaic blue robe, holding a lamb in one arm, and followed by others." But "Gilbert had never seen young men carrying lambs" and so his enthusiasm for his idealized Jesus quickly faded.[26]

It had been a long journey from Puritanism when a child's crisis of faith expressed itself in bored cynicism about a picture-book deity. In

Bourne's Presbyterian family, the Bible had become nothing more than "a magical book that you must not drop on the floor," though no one had adequately explained why. Brooks and Mumford left behind no comparable portraits of their first encounters with Protestantism, but the only faith that held young Van Wyck's attention for very long was Catholicism, which he absorbed through the filters of Ruskin and his own 1898 trip to Italy. Mumford and his mother also wore their religion lightly. The trips Lewis made with Nana to a Catholic church were far more important to him than his formal baptism as an Episcopalian or his absent father's Judaism. An official creed that eased the transactions of everyday life, late-Victorian Protestantism offered little spiritual nourishment to any of these three young men. Their parents' religion proved unsatisfying not because it imposed conformity upon its adherents but because it had become meaningless even to those who upheld its tenets.[27]

In Frank's case, the failure of the family faith took the form of a crisis in Judaism among assimilated Jewish immigrants and their children—a subject he would return to again and again during his career as a cultural critic. Frank saw his own religious predicament as emblematic of that of an entire generation of American Jews, the "solitary sons and daughters" of second-generation immigrants who could not stomach their parents' compromises with a half-secular, half-Christian culture. While the first generation of immigrants maintained the old faith, observed the Sabbath, and obeyed traditional religious laws, its children bowed to the pressures of scientific theories that undermined religious doctrine. The "Jewish paradox" throughout history, Frank wrote in Our America in 1919, was the coexistence of "seemingly antagonistic motives: the will-to-power, the need of mystical abnegation, the desire for comfort on the sensuous and mental planes." Conforming to the mores of nineteenth-century America, with its tepid blend of Christian pieties and faith in technological progress, had taken its toll on the child of Jewish immigrants, requiring "the suppression of the mystical in his heart." The assimilated Jew denied the otherworldly, prophetic currents in Judaism and moved on to eliminate virtually all of Jewish religion itself. Third-generation Jewish children grew up ignorant of their own cultural heritage; they were, as Frank sarcastically noted, "altogether 'free.'"[28]

The experience of Frank's family bore out these generalizations. Though Frank's mother, Helene, seems to have had little or no religious influence on Waldo, Julius Frank's path away from Judaism paralleled that of other second-generation German Jews who adopted the culture of their new home. The elder Frank belonged to the Society for Ethical Culture, an "adulterate religion," as Waldo called it, that served well-to-do Jewish professionals like Julius as a way station on the road to secularism. Felix Adler had founded the Ethical Culture movement in 1876 on the principles of sexual self-discipline, charity, and a Kantian conception of intellectual enlightenment. Ethical Culture's liberal approach to personal morality was too weak a brew for Waldo; he quickly came to feel the need for more demanding spiritual loyalties. To Frank, Ethical Culture represented everything that was wrong with the watery moralism of second-generation immigrant Judaism, right down to its refusal to specify a belief in any particular deity as a condition of adherence. In his early twenties, Frank expressed his contempt for Adler's pseudo-religion in an aphorism he jotted down in his diary: "The Ethical Society for the culture of soul-less men and breast-less women." By 1919, Frank's critique was more focused and more political. Adler had created "a completely commercialized religion," he wrote in *Our America*; he had substituted a "moral code destined to make good citizens of eager pioneers" for "all the mystery of life, all the harmony of sense, all the immanence of God." The feminine sphere of religion had fallen victim to the male world of business, just as the mystical Jewish tradition had given way to a Jewish will to power. As a result, Jewish men had grown cold and spiritless and Jewish women lost their femininity and became "breast-less."[29]

In middle age, Frank described himself as an "ignorant Jew," whose knowledge of Judaism came only after he had turned thirty. Up to that age, Frank admitted, he could read five languages, but "Hebrew and Yiddish were not among them"; he knew Catholic, Greek, and Indian religious doctrine far better than he knew the Bible. Though he had been to services in "scores of churches and cathedrals," Frank had "never set foot in a synagogue!" Throughout his youth, Frank was a "Jew who is a Jew because he cannot help it"—a situation he came to see as "shameful." Frank's parents and their friends never denied that they were Jewish, and they prided themselves on "their Jewish values," but "none belonged to a synagogue or a temple." The closest that Waldo ever got to a Sabbath service was the weekly Friday night dinner at the Frank home, which all of Julius's relatives attended. But even there, "not a word, not a ritual act, ever reminded anyone that this was the Sabbath meal," Frank remembered. As in Ethical Culture meetings, a meaningless ritual lingered on long after the religious culture in which it had once flourished had been discarded as an impractical anachronism. " 'Friday night' was to me simply a family gathering, held at my father's house since he was head of the family; and the dinner was a feast representing my mother's culinary genius."[30]

The Young Americans did not criticize religion as a superstition that deluded the masses. Rather, their early contact with religion—as with the entire feminine cultural sphere—indicates that their attacks on official religion grew out of a reaction against the spiritual impoverishment of their parents' faiths. The ideal of the religious life as a collective experience of moral discipline, a life simultaneously lived in the world and yet devoted to standards the world constantly violated, was never an object of their criticism. If anything, they constantly sought to rehabilitate that ideal as a way of understanding and challenging modern culture. "We must somehow comprehend a world where both the cold, mechanical facts of the physical plane exist and the emotional and conscious life of desires and ideals and hopes," Bourne wrote a friend in 1913. The faith of their parents had grown so feeble precisely because it had forsaken the realm of "desires and ideals and hopes" for a pliant gospel of getting by in the "cold, mechanical" world. Bourne found in Emerson, Thoreau, Whitman, and William James "a sense of background, mystical, inscrutable, but healing and beneficient [sic],—my idea of religion," a conviction that would unite Brooks, Frank, and Mumford in their exploration of America's "usable past" in the 1920s. In their youth, however, these four men were largely unaware of the idealist currents in American thought—though Waldo David Frank had been named for Ralph Waldo Emerson and Henry David Thoreau, unusual namesakes for a Jewish boy—and their disdain for their parents' religions led them to try on an array of spiritual identities that ultimately left them unsatisfied. At different times, they were drawn to an aestheticist Catholicism, the idealized medieval culture depicted in the writings of John Ruskin, William Morris, and Walter Pater, the Christian anarcho-pacifism of Leo Tolstoy, and the European romantics' cult of artistic imagination—a representative sample of the antimodernist, spiritual preoccupations of turn-of-the-century American intellectuals. Meanwhile, their own heritage from American and Judeo-Christian cultures remained a mystery to them. Their fathers had failed them, giving them neither a firm sense of place nor a confidence in their origins. Now their mothers offered no acceptable culture or religious inheritance. As Frank recognized, he was "a Jew without Judaism, an American without America."[31]

The religions of the Young Americans' parents had been tried and found wanting, but another religion proved more nourishing, one associated with the "oceanic feeling" of personal boundlessness that Sigmund Freud described in *Civilization and Its Discontents*. The "feeling of an indissoluble bond, of being one with the external world" that Romain Rolland suggested to Freud as the original source of religious belief struck Freud as an unconscious recollection of infantile dependence on the mother. The oceanic feeling contained both an illusion of warmth and endless love and a primitive aggression directed against a real mother who frustrated the child's sense of omnipotence by refusing to meet its every demand. In troubling dreams, psychic experiences, and moments of mystical reconciliation with the universe, the Young Americans glimpsed the existence of an ideal state of maternal union that lay beyond the superficialities of feminine culture. Childhood memories of that ideal retained their potency into adulthood because they provoked such intensely ambiguous reactions. On one hand, psychological recovery of the mother raised the exhilarating possibility of release from the confines of gentility and of the reconstruction of a truly spiritual cultural realm. On the other hand, the feminine ideal unleashed terrifying visions of unchecked violence, which might turn against the self and destroy it.[32]

In their attempts to explore the unconscious currents of their own minds, the Young Americans were part of a larger transvaluation of values among members of the Western bourgeoisie that ranged from the discoveries of psychoanalysis to mind-cure fads and experiments in Eastern occultism. In their public and private writings, these authors returned again and again to an image of maternal union because it alone seemed real in an age of illegitimate ideologies. The feminine ideal of union may have been a "malady," as Brooks later claimed, but it appeared to offer the only direct, unmediated expression of one's inner being in a society that had corrupted practice through commerce and culture through cheap sentiment.[33]

The belief that the best hope for cultural renewal lay in a return to maternal union inspired Frank's first published novel, *The Unwelcome Man*, which drew heavily on psychoanalysis for its depiction of the subjective world of its protagonist. Like all of Frank's subsequent fiction, *The Unwelcome Man* suffers from a heavy-handed use of social-psychological theory, and its characters are such obvious products of a preconceived conceptual apparatus that they rarely become anything more than stereotypes in the reader's mind. Frank was never able to move beyond cultural criticism cast in a literary mode to fictional themes that worked as literature, and his 1917 novel exhibits all the weaknesses that would plague his entire career as a novelist. Nonetheless, *The Unwelcome Man* is a fascinating document of the mind of the young Waldo Frank as he tried to understand the origins of his crisis of personal identity. As one of the first American novels to employ both psychoanalytical categories and a stream-of-consciousness technique, *The Unwelcome Man* deserves more attention than it has received so far from literary historians. Its present value, however, lies in its brutally honest portrayal of the psychology of a young man adrift in a decaying Victorian culture and its interpretation of the infantile roots of the feminine ideal.

Frank's novel clearly draws on his own life, and in many scenes it is plainly autobiographical. Quincy Burt is a child of upper-middle-class parents in New York who feels no ties to his father's business dealings and is frustrated in his attempts to win his mother's affection. As a youth, he has moments of mystical awakening that resemble those Frank would later describe in his memoirs. Quincy goes off to college at a university very much like Frank's Yale, where he is ostracized by the student elite of prep school graduates and fraternity members. During his college years, a series of encounters with women, with a sympathetic professor and his wife, and with an aesthetically inclined roommate reinforce the young man's sense of difference and encourage him to make a minor rebellion against the staid world of his parents, the university, and business. In the end, though, Quincy calls off his revolt, suppresses the mystical side of his nature, and assumes the rightful place in society of a young man of his class and family background. Realizing that he has betrayed some essential part of his personality, Quincy contemplates suicide only to reject even this negative act of self-assertion. A different kind of suicide awaits him in New York's business world, where "he is one more molecule" in a "blind level of mass and flow, of clinging death and leaping restlessness"; and Quincy chooses to annihilate his soul by giving in to the suffocating conformism of industrial society. Until his final failure, Quincy's life closely parallels Frank's, and his depiction in *The Unwelcome Man* reveals a wealth of information about the role of maternal union in Frank's quest for a newly revived feminine culture.[34]

Quincy's distance from his family, his classmates, and the social milieu represented by an inhuman urban landscape takes the form of an extreme melancholia, which torments the boy with "a dull regret, as for something he had never had, yet something perpetually desired and observed." Its deepest source was Quincy's infantile trauma of separation, to which Frank attributed the most profound significance. Before Quincy can make the simplest distinction between himself and the objective world embodied in his mother, "he is still All," enjoying a "wealth of sensation" in which "everything that he absorbs, he absorbs literally. All of it becomes the stuff of himself, as surely as the milk he sucks. In his own world, he is omniscient and omnipresent." That infantile fantasy of total power, of being "All," is the first casualty of the painful process by which Quincy recognizes the existence of objects and persons not amenable to his will. Nevertheless, the unconscious memory of that early state of union with his mother and of the sense of boundlessness and satisfaction that accompanied it weighs on Quincy's mind throughout the novel.[35]

One indication of the force of that memory is the boy's idealization of his mother, whose image dominates his psyche into adulthood. In infancy, everything but his father "was a note in his own harmony, a weave of his own texture." Quincy began to realize his mother's separate identity, but she was "always within the bounds of a strong empire—that empire, himself." His father was completely different; he alone failed to submit to the child's imperial will. "He was not only apart in his movements and effects; he seemed connected by no bond whatever to the dominion that was Quincy!" There was something "entirely fortuitous" about this man's place in Quincy's life, and Quincy would fantasize in adolescence that his real father was someone else altogether. The feminine ideal of early union with his mother was far more attractive to the boy than the masculine models his family encouraged him to assimilate. His brother, who mimicked their father's behavior in every way, mocked Quincy as a "molly-boy" who loved his mother. And as Quincy grew up, he came to despise the male world of commerce and industry. "To be like a man was to be moved by ugly things—like business and money and machinery. To be like a man was to be edified by things not only ugly but wrong,—like pain, and that murder of self called sacrifice." Separation from the mother began a course of personal disintegration, of "murder of self," as Frank termed it, that ended with induction into an impersonal male bureaucracy.[36]

Frank's response to the industrial system of "business and money and machinery" had more to do with personal self-transformation than political resistance. The adult's recovery of the psychological state of maternal union would release his essential being, returning him to a state of childlike innocence of inherited social conditions. "He who clears the eyes of one child toward itself does more for truth than the leader of a national rebellion," Frank wrote. "And until there be a nation made up of men who were just such children, all reform and all revolt must be a romantic variant upon some theme of falsehood." The idea that spiritual regeneration must precede—or even displace—social revolution had many precedents by the time Frank wrote his novel, including the transcendental reformism of Emerson and Thoreau and the romantic radicalism of Blake and Tolstoy, but Frank's elaboration of this theme was distinctive in its emphasis on the recovery of maternal union and infantile omnipotence. In Frank's novel, the latent psychological currents in romantic and mystical theories of self-renewal became explicit. The way to escape the process of decline and fall that trapped Quincy after his separation from primal unity was mysticism, which resurrected the subjective dimension of infantile union as an adult experience of spiritual "oneness."[37]

Frank was very clear about the psychological connection between mystical consciousness and buried memories of maternal love. At age fifteen, Quincy tried to protect himself from his mocking and alien family by erecting an emotional barrier around himself. "He made of himself a world, and a society. And they who came upon him were the intruders!" But this attempt at psychic self-sufficiency failed, and in a fit of rage at his relatives' insensitivity, he left his home for a few moments of solitude. As he wandered through Central Park, the memory of his childhood in rural Long Island seized him, and he began to feel an intuitive unity with the landscape around him. "It was as if the trees had bent down, of a sudden, and possessed him; as if their acrid juices had been shot within him; as if their leaves were brushing upon his face like amorous fingers. The woods were a vibrant, sinuous form against his body, pressing it to a sweet numbness like a mother's breast. Quincy's blood tingled. A madness gripped him, mounted him, spurred him into flight. He ran. There was nothing else. The woods were in him. And they were an ecstasy. So, sustaining it, he ran." Mysticism recreated the early state of omnipotence that had eluded Quincy in his feeble efforts at building a walled fortress of the self. In both cases, Quincy sought to recover a childlike sense of being "All." The same year, Quincy tried to run away from his family for good (just as Frank himself had at fifteen), and as he walked through the Rambles of Central Park he daydreamed of "living in a miraculous family, a group of persons who would respect him, leave him alone, and welcome with attentive eagerness his least advance." Fantasies of replacing his family with a loving community of friends were but another side of his desire for boundlessness, a state of being that would overcome all distinctions between subject and object, bathing him in effusions of warmth and total devotion. In Quincy's second major mystical experience, during a walk along a country road near his college, this psychological journey came to its logical conclusion. Quincy felt his very soul breaking out of "the bonds of body" and entering "in tremulous unison with the earth and the other stars." The incident ended with a spoken promise from God: "I keep you until the time that you seek Me. Then, shall you come forth and receive." In his infancy, Quincy's mother had promised him a limitless power, only to break that promise when she removed him from her breast. Now, that promise would be redeemed in a compact with God.[38]

Quincy's fall from grace began, in Frank's mind, when he broke that compact, choosing to submit to the ways of a decadent social order instead of opposing it with the knowledge he had gained from mystical experience. The problem was that Frank offered no real possibility of waging such a battle on Quincy's terms. From the standpoint of infantile omnipotence, virtually any overt act of political rebellion was likely to appear fruitless. When compared with the ideal of maternal union, every expression of consciousness in culture was doomed to fall short of Quincy's expectations. Frank appears to have understood this, at least in part: he wrote that "there was no happy mean in Quincy's nature" because "he had suffered through too wide a surface of fine feeling." Quincy's mother, for example, always disappointed him because she could not live up to his idealized perfect mother, who existed as an extension of the boy's will and responded to his every desire with love and encouragement. She could not make sense of his brooding, his rebellion against convention, and his refusal to share in the fruits of her husband's material success. In reality, Quincy felt, his mother was the female representative of the "vast, impersonal machine to which he mattered nothing save as a conforming cog. Of course, that part of his mother was also such a cog. It had no right to exploit the bonds of the real mother who knew and cared for no machine." Similarly, the domestic sphere of culture was just another snare that manipulated the child's memories of union to force him back to his place within the social machine. The "real mother" of Quincy's memory recognized no such feminine culture; her loyalties were to no machine but to the infant's all-powerful self.[39]

Quincy's difficulty was in maintaining the sense of "oneness" beyond a few minutes of mystical epiphany. Too often, his longings for union led in a dangerous direction, to thoughts of death. While on his way to college, Quincy experienced "a desire not to go on—a yearning to cease altogether." The young man longed for "non-existence," for "a state without time" and "an endless truce to goal and striving." Mysticism provided release from the turmoil that followed on early separation, but its pleasures were fleeting and nearly impossible to sustain. A far easier release was available in death—if not through suicide, then through the mutilation of the self that Quincy suffered in business.[40]

Frank later termed *The Unwelcome Man* "a tale of the seed that rotted and did not rise," a parable of wasted promise and decline. But in many respects, Quincy's psychological self-effacement at the novel's end was the only coherent conclusion to the longings for nonexistence that accompanied his desires for reunion with his mother. The line dividing ecstatic communion with nature and Quincy's later decision to abandon himself to the workings of an inhuman society was a thin one, and, in Quincy's case, it may not have existed at all. Ironically, Waldo Frank, who as a young boy detested his father's restless will to power, held up a cultural alternative of intuitive union that was simply the obverse side of the infant's imperial will. At one point, toward the novel's end, Quincy again reflected on the disparity between his mother's conduct and that of his maternal ideal. "If only his mother had had less to ask him! How he longed for a more humble mother, one to respect his silence, to be mute before his ecstasy. How he would have cherished such a one!" Unfortunately, the objective existence that Quincy first recognized in his separation from his mother proved recalcitrant and indifferent in the face of such demands. Union with the mother was impossible when the external world she represented refused to be "humble" and "mute before his ecstasy." The illusion of the limitless self ran up against the very real limits of individuals, institutions, and objects that defied the claims of pure subjectivity. In that situation, the only chance of merging self with nonself was in the murder of the former, whether in suicide or in craven conformity. A rebellion premised on the feminine ideal ended in death, that final removal of the barriers separating the soul from its surroundings.[41]

The feminine ideal was no less ambiguous in Frank's life than it was for Quincy Burt, prompting violent impulses alongside "oceanic" fantasies of blissful repose. Frank's very first recollections of childhood were of aggression—"my own or nature's"—and "the fear of it," and he recalled that "war" was "never far away" in his relations with his siblings. "I let fly a hairbrush at my brother, which crashes on his cheek. I hurl an iron fireman at sister Enid which barely misses her eyes and leaves a scar forever." Intertwined in his memory with such scenes was an incident that took place when Frank was about seven years old. It was then that Frank became "the high priest—and the body—of a religion," a "Waldean" religion of which Waldo Frank was the sole prophet, follower, and supreme being.

> Friday is bath night for me. I luxuriate in the hot soapy water. I lie stretched out in it, on my back (the tub longer than my stripling length), all immersed except my penis. It stands up, erect, the island apex of a continent which a pressure of hands and foot on the bottom of the tub reveals above the water. This is the Waldean continent, with the male organ as its center. . . . So far as I can recall, that is all there was to it: no dogma to this religion, no ritual: solely the fact of the continent of my body to be contemplated and that has my name, Waldea, and is centered at my member.

Frank's phallic cult was a religion of his own self, now inflated beyond its bodily limits into a "continent"—a new Eden or Walden—and into a new God.[42]

Frank's allegiance to "Waldea" may have lasted only briefly, but its heady illusion of potency and omnipotence persisted in other forms. The young boy fantasized about being a Lincolnesque president, "delivering a long speech, standing before the mirror," or he imagined himself an "intrepid hero," like a fireman, whose exploits won him popular acclaim. As a child, Waldo began keeping a notebook, the first of many he would have throughout his life, which he inscribed to "Mama" and filled with tales of his "surprising intimacy with God whom I was going to help run the world." By seventeen, that intimacy became a sacred pledge in his notebook: "All the books that I shall write shall be proofs of God." The prophet of Waldea had entered into a covenant with God, in which he would use his writing to search for truth for as long as God permitted.[43]

The "Waldean continent" first revealed to Frank the existence of a divine world of truth beyond the phenomena of appearances, but Frank's interest in mysticism began in earnest with an experience he had when he was about ten. Walking down his street in New York on a snowy winter afternoon, Waldo noticed a small black cat sitting by a lamppost. "He stopped to look at it, while the snow, muffling the white street, welded together the houses patched with lights, his body and the little beast." At that very moment, Frank claimed, he first understood the unity of all things. If he and the cat had somehow exchanged identities at that instant, *"nothing would have changed"*; his own consciousness, that of the cat, the existence of the street and its houses would all "be as they were!" This experience did not last for long, but Frank soon had others like it, including one that inspired the Central Park episode of *The Unwelcome Man*. Frank remembered how, during a walk through the woods, he felt the need to reach out to the trees around him "as a child embraces its embracing mother." Frank thrilled to this "revelation," with "its apparently absolute freedom from the relations that weave the tissues of life," and he consciously associated it with a feminine ideal that transcended his mother's particular identity. "Most men realize God, sometime during their lives," Frank wrote in his notebook while a student at Yale, "only they have contracted the evil habit of calling it 'the foolishness.' All women realize God save those that have never laid sincerely in their hearts—I am a woman."[44]

Frank's feminine ideal erased all distinctions based on gender, on the division between subject and object, and on the separation of sacred and profane. Its male prophet, heir to an infantile cult of his own phallus, could also be a woman because this meant only an identification with a disembodied ideal. Similarly, he could also be his religion's sole deity, dissolving his self into those of cats and gods alike. In Frank's mind, the feminine ideal reigned supreme, unrestrained by any conventions, and he would devote himself to its propagation in literature, criticism, and politics. As a mystic, he would explore the depths of his own personality with a passionate zeal for self-knowledge. As a cultural critic, he would insist on the recovery of the "oceanic" state of maternal union—of "oneness"—as a prerequisite to a new radical politics and a new community life. The hold of his early fantasies of maternal love, omnipotence, and primitive aggression over his imagination never lessened as Frank reached adulthood, nor did his obsession with their meaning. When he first prepared to write his memoirs in 1958, he considered "The Boy Outside" as a possible title. "I've always felt myself as an *outsider*—yearning, struggling to *get in*," he confessed to his journal.

"*Into* my own home, *into* N.Y. of the people, *into* France (later Spain), *into* literary America (7 *Arts*, *Our America* & the 1920s), *into* the Revolution (the People)." But his attempts to find unity in such endeavors—with his family, with other writers, with "the People"—paled in comparison with the brief communion with the world he had achieved as the high priest of Waldea. "I've never succeeded," Frank admitted, "whence my growing stress and importance of *into* the Cosmos."[45]

Frank was not alone in seeing himself as the youthful herald of a new faith. Sometime in his teens or early twenties, Brooks wrote an imaginary sermon he thought he might deliver at Grace Church in his hometown of Plainfield. There, before the assembled congregation of local worthies, friends, and his own family, Brooks would take his vengeance on the hypocrisy of the genteel middle class, daring it to live by the Christian morality it piously invoked but never practiced. "I have heard many say that these words of Christ have no meaning now-a-days," Brooks said, baiting his shamed listeners; "*they are so ill-adapted to our present-day conditions!*" In his unpublished fantasy "A Little Sermon," Brooks spoke the good news of a true faith with "no set of traditions," taking "no part of priests & dogmas," but which "*is* spirit, pure, active, faith filled." Such a religion could not be dismissed as irrelevant to "present-day conditions" because it "would be too deep, too universal, too catholic, too independent of any place or any time."[46]

The gap dividing spirit and the religious and cultural institutions of the American bourgeoisie obsessed Brooks in his youth, plunging him at one moment into a melancholic despair about the shortcomings of the material world and then intoxicating him with the dizzying possibility of inhabiting an ideal world "independent of any place or any time" through art and mysticism. Years later, after his recovery from the mental breakdown of the late 1920s that nearly cost him his sanity and his life, Brooks deliberately repressed the elements of his personality that had sought fulfillment in otherworldly spirituality. Publicly, he described the sentiments expressed in writings such as his imaginary sermon as products of youthful hubris and fin-de-siècle aestheticism. "What an ass I was at the age of 22!" he wrote in 1952 inside the cover of a notebook dating from the same period as his Grace Church sermon. Perhaps he was right, but there was more than insolence in such fantasies. The young Van Wyck Brooks was not just a precocious crank. He was also an avenging prophet in his mother's house of worship, who would destroy the feminine temple of gentility with the pure fire of the feminine ideal.[47]

In his autobiography, Brooks recalled that as a youth he had "never been at home" in Plainfield "or anywhere but in my own mind," where he constructed a refuge from "business." The desire for sanctuary led Brooks to take up a career in writing, which he called "my retreat into a world in which, without it, I would have foundered." He traced his longings to a childhood dream of flight from "a Hindu" dressed in "a coat of many colors," who pursued him with "a glittering knife that he held in his outstretched hand." Just as his assailant drew near, Brooks "soared into the air and floated away, free, aloft and safe." In other dreams of persecution, Van Wyck "was not even anxious" when he saw his would-be attacker, "for I knew I possessed the power to float away." To Brooks, the dreams revealed his early terror of his father's aggressive business milieu and his own belief that there existed a safe haven to which he could escape and live free of his father's torments. The dreams may have a more complex significance, however, one that becomes evident in Brooks's later psychological development, in which fantasies of floating and refuge coexist with fears of violence directed against himself. Brooks's dreams introduced images of self-destruction into his conscious mind at the very moment that they held out the hope of effortless flight into freedom.[48]

In Brooks's adolescence, these impulses took the form of two different fantasies—one, of a mystical religion of mingling souls, the other of death as an idyllic refuge from the conflicts of life—which fused in his mind with a feminine ideal centered on Eleanor Stimson, whom Brooks would marry in 1911. At seventeen, he composed a poem based on the legend of Parsifal, which he gave to Eleanor. Van Wyck identified with his hero, who was "ignorant of his origin or his destination, but overflowing with his love ideal, yearning for his soul, whom he feels is existing for him." Brooks copied the crucial verses of his poem, which also appeared in his high school's literary magazine, into his diary.

> Herefore were we made mortal;
> That passion-drawn our human hearts may mingle
> Involving so the souls to weld them into single.
> All is for love;
> The green below, the blue above;
>   And every cloud
> Filled with the essence of its God.

At about this same time, Brooks began sending Eleanor poems about how, after death, they would share a heavenly afterlife of pure love.

There is nothing very unusual in such poems, especially given Brooks's adolescent infatuation with literary romanticism (and particularly with the Pre-Raphaelite movement in England), which had used similar language to express its hatred of the spiritual emptiness of a commercial civilization. Yet the intensity of these images in Brooks's mind and their continued hold over his adult consciousness suggest that they involved more than a teenage aesthete's self-indulgence.[49]

The association of Brooks's fantasy world of spirit with the feminine ideal explored in Frank's *Unwelcome Man* is evident in the syncretic religion that Brooks drew up and tried to impress upon Eleanor in 1903 and 1904. In a long 1903 diary entry, replete with charts and diagrams, Van Wyck elaborated a complicated system of religious rebirth that wove "the principle of evolution," platonic love, and the human passions into a purified Christianity without "contradictions" or "absurdities." Believing that *"every soul is created for one other and* [that] the whole purpose of our incarnation into mortality is that we may come into contact with that destined co-partner," Brooks described an evolutionary process whereby souls would unite in love ("weld . . . into single," as he wrote in "Parsifal") and then survive the death of their bodies to reach a higher "moral plane." Death, in this scheme, was "the bursting-forth of our souls from the bounds which prevent God in us from growing big" so that they may merge again in other lives, culminating in a final union "on the plane of complete moral perfection, which is the plane of Jesus Christ." At last, the soul would "step off into the infinite, the *bosom of God*," enveloped in "the complete and all-annihilating comprehensiveness" of love.[50]

At this point, Brooks's religion fused with his cult of an idealized Eleanor. He believed that since "the best of what we know of human nature is what woman preeminently has," Jesus had "all the qualities of the woman," much as Eleanor was "the incarnation of all good to me— a very near image of the Christ." Van Wyck's evolutionary faith of merging souls ended, then, in union with the feminine ideal: a Christlike Eleanor. But he admitted, "all this I believe, but do not feel," because there was "no religion in it—nothing which appeals to the emotions."[51]

This difficult entry in Brooks's diary is riven with contradictions: between the otherworldliness of souls and the passions of human love that bring them together; between images of death and of loving union; between a male Jesus and his female qualities; and between the emotionally charged feminine ideal and Brooks's insistence that his religion did not inspire him to belief because it lacked anything "which appeals to the emotions." These conflicted themes persisted in other entries in which Brooks dwelled on his rarefied vision of a renewed faith. "We must fight our intellect," Van Wyck wrote in February 1904, and he held up Jesus as a suprarational model who "had gone *through mind to the truth*." The greatness of religion and poetry lay in their ability to surpass the intellect and reach directly into an "atmosphere" of emotion and spirit by putting "us into *moods*." Two years later, in an "imaginary letter" from a "victim of the Literary Temperament to an Artist," Brooks wrote in his journal of his own "excessive self-consciousness," which threatened to destroy all unity in the world with its penchant for analysis and classification. Those addicted to the "literary temperament" risked losing the "perception of the whole" that was the goal of all religion and art.[52]

In 1906 Brooks wrote Eleanor Stimson of a "*wild dream*" that displayed all the warring tendencies in his inner life. Brooks dreamed that "my nature had split up into so many motives & furrows, which ran along quite independently that I had become incapable of any action or feeling which was absolutely whole-souled." In the dream, Eleanor grew so "confused & disgusted" with his internal divisions and subsequent paralysis that she fell in love with another man, "whose whole life was simple & obvious." Brooks's "superiority of intellect" made him look down on his rival for his "puerile" simplicity, but he was incapable of winning back Eleanor. "If one desire or feeling ran along one furrow," he complained, "its opposite must run along the next." In the end, Brooks decided to put an end to this "interesting state of affairs" by chasing Eleanor's lover with a pistol ("I only loved you in a fierce mad way," he told her), but he woke up just as he was at the point of "blowing out my own brains" instead.[53]

These divided impulses haunted Brooks throughout the years of his education at Harvard and his trip to Europe in 1907–8, during which time they overlapped with his interests in Catholicism, Italian culture, and a neomedieval aesthetic. At times, he returned to his adolescent religion of merging souls in his flirtation with Catholicism, which he claimed "asserts *everything*, everything in so mystical a way that it means everything or nothing according to one's mood." Unlike Protestant churches, where "certain families have their regular pews" and social inequality divides the congregation, "in a Catholic church everyone gives up his outside position and simply becomes a soul." Fantasies of merging his soul with those of others in a "mood" of Catholicism coexisted with others that upheld the monastic life as the most appropriate means of safeguarding spiritual integrity. Brooks compared the "quiet garden" of monasticism to the "conflict of ideas" in the modern world, which prohibits the individual from withdrawing to a personal "dwelling-place." "We see all sides of questions, we feel and we believe everything, we forgive everything—the soul loses form and outline and becomes a vague shadow, a drifting chord, a something which exists only in its connotations."[54]

Yet neither a religion of joined souls nor an ideal of personal sanctuary offered Brooks much comfort. How could orthodoxy displace the conflicting tendencies in human thought when it consisted only of moods? Brooks's Catholic fantasies sought to retrieve the stable, unquestioned world of his parents' Victorian ideology, but because that mythical world had been undermined by social changes it could not control, it persisted only as an imagined realm of pure subjectivity. The cloistered self, subject to endless shifts in mood, could be as divided and troubled as the world outside. "I seem to exist in sentiments which have not even the vitality to assert themselves," Brooks confessed. And the experience of transcending one's body in an otherworldly communion of souls could lead as much to feelings of personal insignificance as to delusions of power. During the same period that he was indulging in the attractions of the monastic life, Brooks underwent a "strange adventure" in which he saw himself "from the outside, like another person, perfectly, distinctly standing there." But the sense that he was "entirely free" of his identity saddened him. "I'm sure you would never had chosen *him* to live in if you'd had your wits about you!" Brooks came to pity "this figure standing there without a soul in his body and before I knew it I was inside of him again."[55]

The feminine ideal produced both images of a limitless self fusing with the world (or its mother) and primitive rages against that objective world that often awakened fears of death. In Brooks's conscious life, these impulses manifested themselves in wild mood swings from unqualified egomania (in 1906, Brooks noted that he had written all of his letters during the past five years under the assumption that they "would eventually be published; yes, and edited with footnotes") to self-hatred and a fear that he was nothing more than a cipher. Even within its cloistered shell, "the soul" could fade into "a vague shadow . . . a something which exists only in its connotations," and that possibility forced Brooks into long periods of deep depression. In his unconscious mind, he oscillated between visions of an autonomous, omnipotent self suspended in "moods" of emotive reverie (whether in isolation or in harmony with the cosmos) and nightmares of death, soullessness, and self-disintegration. Brooks recoiled from the violence associated with his oceanic fantasies of union, insisting that his "excessive self-consciousness" threatened his psychic well-being; but it seems clear that it was not so much Brooks's critical intellect that threatened him as the potential for self-annihilation inherent in the feminine ideal. Parsifal had a blood brother, a Hindu wielding a glittering knife, who gave him no rest.[56]

Frank and Brooks embraced the feminine ideal in its most extreme, otherworldly form, and its illusion of boundless freedom and loving union spurred their interest in mysticism and religious spirituality. Bourne and Mumford were more conscious of its dangers. Though beguiled by the promise of self-transcendence, they also recognized the aggressive impulses that accompanied their encounters with the feminine ideal. In Bourne's autobiographical piece on Gilbert and his family, such an experience interrupted the conscious life of the young protagonist with ambiguous sensations of both reassurance and anxiety. A strong undercurrent of dread pervaded Gilbert's flirtation with omnipotence. The same boy who loved to spend hours secluded in his grandmother's room, where he surveyed the world from the heights of her secretary-desk, lapsed into fantasies of escaping time and space to reign as a triumphant God—fantasies that soon slid over into nightmares of emptiness and death.

On hot summer afternoons, Bourne wrote, Gilbert's mother would keep him and his sister in the house's "darkened black parlor," where he would fall into a drowsy stupor and "the tedium vitae would overwhelm in a great drenching wave." Gilbert had the sensation of being "alive in a tomb," of having survived into an era in which time itself had stopped. "The world was a great vacuum with nothing to experience and nothing to do." As the sultry hours passed, the "vacuum" of the parlor fused in his mind with the "colossal ennui of heaven," and Gilbert indulged himself in daydreams of eternity that simultaneously attracted and repelled him. There he was, "seated infinitely high above the earth," as if on the very "white clouds on which God rode," far removed from the earth below. He had left the darkness of the tomblike parlor and was "floating in the clearest, most luminous light." Yet there was something truly horrifying about this vision, despite its fulfillment of the boy's longings for godlike power; "what seized Gilbert's imagination was the vast emptiness of the space around him, the disorientation of everything." And when he recalled these sensations on later occasions, "a vague feeling of homelessness and of fear" would sweep over him and interrupt his play with troubling thoughts.[57]

Although he admired mystics for their insights into human psychology, Bourne never succumbed to the temptations of mysticism that attracted Frank and Brooks. If union with the cosmos opened up new ways of conceiving the self's relation to its surroundings, it also endangered the integrity of the self at a time when little remained to shore up its autonomy. The "colossal ennui of heaven" was good reason to avoid the mystical pursuit of maternal union, but Bourne would attempt to salvage some of the oceanic spirit of the feminine ideal in his writings on friendship, which advocated the creation of a "community of sentiment" among peers as an alternative to the traditional family. In his political writings during the 1910s, Bourne's feminine ideal would reappear in a social incarnation, substituting a democracy of friends for the mystical apprehension of cosmic unity. A social unity of equals, based on shared emotions and intellectual goals, was Bourne's answer to the visions of boundlessness and union that haunted him in his youth.[58]

Like Bourne, Lewis Mumford also shunned mysticism for another route to the recovery of the feminine ideal. In Mumford's childhood, memories of maternal love provoked equally ambivalent feelings of fear and excitement, but as an adult he was able to sublimate the feminine ideal into a concrete vision of personal achievement. Mumford chose to forego a return to infantile omnipotence for the challenge of intellectual mastery of the external world—not its dissolution into sheer sentiment. The feminine ideal that inspired him sprang from the same sources that motivated the other Young Americans in their search for an answer to the deadlock of Victorian civilization. But in Mumford's case, that ideal developed beyond its primitive origins, prompting less the hope of returning to the ideal mother than of reasserting her neglected contributions to a shared world of practical activity. For Mumford, the way out of the opposition of bankrupt male and female spheres was not a retreat to an abstract feminine realm beyond time and space but the integration of love, nurture, and the artistic imagination into social life.

In 1962, Mumford recorded "the one dream I can truly recall from infancy, a dream that was almost a nightmare." He interpreted it as an "oceanic dream," a "direct reminiscence of the prenatal life one spent surrounded by the amniotic fluid in the womb," which released a sense of a limitless self blurring into its watery surroundings. There was "an unbearable pressure of emptiness," Mumford remembered, and he had the feeling "of existing in the midst of empty space, with infinity pressing in upon me from every direction." The "dream that was almost a nightmare" did not lead him to mysticism or to the hyperaesthetic sensibility of the young Brooks when Mumford compared its memory of union to the shallowness of his mother's sham gentility. His experience of the feminine ideal raised the possibility of a new culture that resolved the crisis of modern identity by engaging the self in the reconstruction of the public world. Self-renewal and cultural regeneration had to be conceived as mutual processes; otherwise, the feminine ideal of union threatened to deepen the sense of isolation and emptiness that plagued the individual in an era of crumbling creeds and desiccated traditions. Once again, Mumford's grandfather Charles Graessel had provided a living example of how the extremes of masculine will and feminine sentiment might be overcome. Thanks to Graessel, Mumford's feminine ideal would take root in a living culture instead of drifting in the liquid of a remembered womb. Mumford had no need for a "Waldean continent," when his grandfather had given him New York.[59]

In a Whitmanesque passage of real lyric beauty, Mumford wrote in his autobiography of a twilight walk across the Brooklyn Bridge during his adolescence. Waldo Frank had used similar experiences in *The Unwelcome Man* to describe Quincy Burt's struggle to bring a mystical conception of oneness to bear on the practical life of modern New York. As a college friend advised Quincy, "Knowing a city is being open to the vibrance of its crowds and buildings." But Quincy's moment of transcendence on the bridge unwittingly betrayed the chasm between his spiritual aspirations and the world around him. Although the bridge "seemed an arbiter," a means into the "city's soul," which it literally "bound" together into a single force, Frank's narrator always remained distanced from the "swarm" of people and the brutal landscape he surveyed from above. Frank never gave up the central focus of his novel on Quincy's self-conscious striving for union, which even in passages like this one overcame any appreciation for the particulars of his environment. The failure of this moment to bind Quincy to either the people or the structures of New York helps explain his spiritual defeat at the novel's end.[60]

By contrast, Mumford's moment of epiphany on the bridge gave him a profound respect for the city's otherness—for its physical presence outside his consciousness—even as it infused him with an expansive sense of his own self. As he crossed the bridge on his way to Manhattan,

Mumford saw sunlight break through the clouds, "forming a halo around the jagged mountain of skyscrapers, with the darkened loft buildings and warehouses huddling below in the foreground." "Here was my city," Mumford wrote, "immense, overpowering, flooded with energy and light"; and he reveled in its magnificence—the huge sweep of New York Harbor, the "relentless tide" of trains and trolleys, and the "dazzling mass" of buildings "against the indigo sky." The scene is unique in Mumford's memoirs, a moment that recalls Frank's descriptions of mystical euphoria but surpasses them in Mumford's profound love for the particulars of his urban environment. He found himself "drinking in the city and the sky, both vast, yet contained in me, transmitting through me the great mysterious will that had made them and the promise of the new day that was still to come."[61]

For Mumford, union with his city and the world meant something very different than a return to an infantile ideal. His experience of spiritual unity never violated the natural and human world that lay beyond the self. Self-transcendence was a way of contributing to that external world, of fusing one's subjectivity with the artifacts and cultural traditions that survived beyond one individual's existence. The "exultation" of that moment "was like the wonder of an orgasm in the body of one's beloved," Mumford wrote, an ecstatic experience of union in tension with difference. Mumford's lifelong engagement with the city had begun, at once critical and analytical as well as affectionate and exuberant. "The world, at that moment, opened before me, challenging me, beckoning me, demanding something of me that it would take more than a lifetime to give, but raising all my energies by its own vivid promise to a higher pitch." Here was the ideal of union at its most creative and visionary, stemming "not from my isolated self alone but from the collective energies I had confronted and risen to": "a fleeting glimpse of the utmost possibilities life may hold for man."[62]

2
The Soul and Society

The world has nothing to lose but its chains—
and its own soul to gain.
—RANDOLPH BOURNE,
"Youth"

The suggestion that personal distress and psychological conflict may have played a role in the intellectual development of political and cultural radicals elicits predictable responses across the ideological spectrum. For conservatives, evidence of inner turmoil in the lives of modern leftists simply confirms their suspicion that radicalism is an intellectual's malady, a disorder afflicting those whose education and temperament alienate them from traditional communities and institutions. To most liberals, the appearance within radical circles of individuals who seek personal identity and self-definition through opposition to the status quo illustrates the need to temper "adolescent" fantasies with a more modest "realism" so as to avoid the dangers of blurring distinctions between public and private life. Adults, presumably, do not suffer from the flights of fancy that deliver the immature and troubled into the hands of fanatics and extremists. Even the orthodox Left takes a negative view of such individuals. Leftists often share with liberals a belief that political realism (in this case "class consciousness") demands adherence to a pure ideology, untainted by emotional or psychological issues.[1]

The history and biographies of turn-of-the-century American radicalism do not bear out any of these conclusions. Instead, they indicate that widespread psychological disorientation was intrinsic to the shift in cultural standards in that period and that radical activists and intellectuals may have differed from their contemporaries only insofar as they gave a particularly political and ethical interpretation to changes in their public and private lives. Complaints about "modern nervousness," full-fledged nervous breakdowns, experiments with occultism, mystical experiences, and a generalized longing for a comprehensive framework of meaning not available in traditional religious faiths were the conditions of emotional and spiritual life for more than a handful of isolated intellectuals. Jane Addams, Charlotte Perkins Gilman, William James, and John Dewey were among the leading turn-of-the-century thinkers who joined social criticism with a personal search for identity in a period when older ideals lacked potency and authority. Eugene Debs, the towering figure of American radicalism, became popular in part because he identified the prevalent crisis of "manhood" among skilled male workers like himself with the changing conditions of industrial capitalist social relations. Like his more intellectual contemporaries on the Left, Debs saw that public, collective activity provided the only solution to this loss of personal meaning.[2]

Nor were radicals alone in participating in a cultural transformation centered on the reconstruction of the self. In a provocative essay on the "culture of personality," Warren I. Susman discovered an extraordinary concern for the changing nature of selfhood in the popular culture of the 1900s and 1910s. American films, self-help guides, advice literature, and novels all articulated a new ideal of "personality" in opposition to the nineteenth-century notion of "character." If *character* carried with it assumptions of self-reliance, moral self-restraint, and instinctual renunciation, the emerging culture of *personality* emphasized the traits necessary to attract, maintain, and then conform to one's peer group. A successful personality cultivated personal magnetism, charm, sincerity, and other intangible qualities that made one popular and "well-liked." Whereas the Victorian bourgeoisie saw character as the end result of a long process of hard work, religious training, and self-education that would separate the worthy from the morally unfit, modern proponents of personality recommended the measured exposure of one's "soul" as the way to win friends and influence people. Character, like Puritan election, was attainable only by the few. Personality, however, was available to all who knew how to display their inner resources in public. One radio critic, himself a proponent of literary knowledge as a means of achieving social success, summed up the promise of personality in a 1934 broadcast. "Not every person can become a personage," he told his listeners, "but every person can become a personality."[3]

The popular preoccupation with cultivating personality may have helped legitimate the new consumer culture made possible by mass-production industries, as Susman and other historians suggest. A shifting sense of selfhood defined in terms of magnetic exchange between the individual and his or her social environment created insecurities and self-doubts that advertisers exploited to sell their products. The dialectic of personal anxiety and the creation of new desires that could be fulfilled only through the consumption of manufactured goods worked hand in hand with a therapeutic ethos that promoted "adjustment" and psychic contentment over loyalties to family or place, religious belief, or political participation. The irony of the culture of personality, then, was that in the name of releasing Americans' inner beings it subjected their very identity to advertisers and corporations. Self-liberation meant in practice harnessing personality to images, slogans, and social pressures existing outside the self.

Yet at the same time, the turn to personality could also provide the basis for a radical critique of capitalist society, one framed in the very terminology that came to legitimate that society in an age of consumption. The belief that personality lay dammed up and imprisoned, a restricted soul trapped behind a shell of class and social position, could lead to a new vision of political change. This was the case in Brooks's and Bourne's earliest writings on culture, society, and youth, in which they upheld an ideal of egalitarian communities where men and women defined themselves freely in communion with one another. By advocating personality and the liberation of the soul as alternatives to business and domestic gentility, Brooks and Bourne may have been participants in a cultural transformation that ultimately fueled an ethos of consumption as the ideal of a good life. Yet their own version of this general appeal to personality led them to criticize fundamental aspects of the consumer ethos. Their concern for questions of selfhood was not, in the end, antipolitical. On the contrary, it deepened the political content of their cultural criticism by providing insights into the psychological costs of modern industrial life that more traditional political polemicists would have missed. That such insights owed much to Brooks's and Bourne's youthful explorations of the feminine ideal does not lessen its interpretive force as an analysis of American culture, nor does it make either man pathological or irrational. Rather, their concern for the social imprisonment of the soul in late Victorian society indicates that, in the minds of two of the most perceptive critics of their generation, the rhetoric that eased the transition from a culture of character to one of personality could also fashion a radical challenge to the social organization of corporate industrialism.[4]

In the early writings of Brooks and Bourne, true self-fulfillment lay beyond Victorian character and a personality mortgaged to the shifting fads of a consumer culture. The liberation of personality would occur

only in communities that resonated with the spiritual and aesthetic richness of music and fine art or in small groups structured by the egalitarian give and take of long-established friendships. The critique of capitalist society in the name of free personalities could degenerate into
sentimentality, oblivious to the realities of power and economics. A
program for personal fulfillment ran the risk of neglecting the tension
between intellect and environment necessary to a thorough social criticism. Nevertheless, a discourse of emancipated personality could also
become sharply politicized, once Brooks and Bourne realized that the
feminine ideal of maternal union—now recast as the reconciliation of
the soul and society—required the democratic reconstruction of social
life. "The modern radical opposes the present social system not because
it does not give him his 'rights,' " Bourne wrote in 1912, "but because it
warps and stunts the potentialities of society and of human nature."
Liberation of the soul required a liberation of society, with personalities
achieving their full emancipation in the construction of democratic
communities.[5]

Van Wyck Brooks signaled his move from the private contemplation of the feminine ideal to public advocacy of a revolution in
American culture in a 1904 commencement address at his high school
in Plainfield. Describing "the mission of American art," Brooks praised
the growing interest in art among his countrymen. "There is no longer
a market for gilt vases. Our schools, once timbered barns, are now
picture galleries." But Brooks was not satisfied. Americans had not done
enough to bridge the gap separating art from other activities, particularly science and commerce. These latter occupations had come to define a way of life that must be "harmonized, softened, idealized." Masculine enterprise and feminine culture could no longer remain separate
spheres, he told his audience. "We have a mighty slough of Commercialism that only Art can reconcile with Ideal. For Art always makes for
righteousness and cleanness, drawing forth directly the nobilities of the
character." The mission of American culture, then, was to "combine a
Lincoln and a Raphael. We shall have eloquent Beauty and sturdy Manhood." A new union of art and morality, culture and politics, and aesthetic and practical sensibilities would rescue American life from the
extremes of commercialism and gilt vases.[6]

Brooks's desire to reconcile commerce with the "Ideal" indicates that,
even in 1904, his vision of cultural transformation was far more ambi

tious than a simple program of improving schools and elevating middle-class taste. He believed that art could "purify our national failings" because it expressed "the great soul which exists behind all." It was this "great soul," this unity of spirit beyond the phenomenal world, to which Brooks appealed for help in remaking American life. Art was simply its instrument. Brooks made a similar argument in his imaginary sermon before Plainfield's Episcopal congregation, returning to the roots of Protestantism to challenge the sentimental Christianity of his family and neighbors. Comparing pure faith to justification by the law, Brooks told his imagined listeners that "religion comes only after we can grow so lofty that we can despise the mere literary demands of the words, and find in them the living voice of God." As with art, the "mere literary demands" of religious law had significance only insofar as they opened up the believer's soul to the divine.[7]

Brooks began his career as a critic with the understanding that the renewal of "mere" literature was not sufficient in and of itself. Art and literature had a role in the moral regeneration of American life because they tapped a spiritual force—a "great soul"—that might overcome the dual reign of masculine enterprise and feminine gentility. Brooks was right to call his program for American culture a "mission" and thereby to see himself as a cultural missionary, for his vision had deeply religious overtones. The danger in such a mission, of course, was inherent in the very notion of a cultural revolution that disdained "mere" art and literature except when they revealed a spiritual ideal. It was a danger familiar to students of religion, who know the perpetual conflict between church institutions and religious faith. In Brooks's own psyche, the unchecked cult of maternal union threatened the possibility of self-disintegration. In his criticism, the cultural ideal of union with pure spirit hinted at the future elimination of the very artifacts of culture. A religion of the one "great soul" behind art and literature might dispense with the icons and liturgy of its own church.

Brooks's religious-aesthetic mission preoccupied him throughout the years he spent at Harvard (1904–7) and after, up through the publication of *The Malady of the Ideal* in 1913. This was the period of Brooks's greatest infatuation with literary Bohemianism, when as a student in Cambridge or as a struggling part-time journalist, critic, and teacher in London, New York, and California, he immersed himself in the writings of nineteenth-century romantics and the fin-de-siècle pessimists among the European avant-garde. As an undergraduate, Brooks indulged in "the Pre-Raphaelite aestheticism and the dilettantish Catholicism that flourished at Harvard" in the early 1900s. Its formal center, or shrine, was the home of Charles Eliot Norton, who presided over "Dante evenings" every Sunday, reading out loud from the poet's work beneath a Rossetti portrait *Dante Meeting Beatrice*. As a member of Norton's Dante cult, Brooks shared the group's affection for Walter Pater, John Ruskin, William Morris, Matthew Arnold, Henry Adams, and other critics of modern—and especially American—civilization. The last traces of the New England Renaissance had long since disappeared from Harvard, and what little its students knew of contemporary arts and letters in the United States struck them as thin, superficial fare, unworthy of serious study.[8]

Brooks and his friends believed that "we lived in a uniquely unlovely and degenerate age in which it would have been far better not to have been born at all," a sentiment he later associated with his classmate and literary bête noir, T. S. Eliot. But Brooks's deep distrust of business and his reading of such radicals as Ruskin and Morris prevented him from following Irving Babbitt and other conservative antimodernists at Harvard in calling for a restoration of "the old European rigidities of the medieval order." Brooks's critique of modern culture would take a distinctly social, and socialist, turn in the mid-1910s. His first book, *The Wine of the Puritans*, published in 1908, foreshadowed many of the arguments in *America's Coming-of-Age* about the social roots of American cultural backwardness. More representative of his early intellectual development, however, are his first essays on art and personality and such books as *The Soul* (1910) and *The Malady of the Ideal* (1913). In these, his most obscure writings, Brooks honed the vague antimodernism of Harvard aestheticism and his own notion of cultural mission into a radical variant of the conservative critique of industrial culture. Drawing on his own inner turmoil and his reading in romantic criticism, Brooks envisioned a movement for cultural renewal that went far beyond fantasies of medieval revival or the mere literature of bourgeois gentility.[9]

At first, this critique of American culture took shape as a neoromantic defense of youth and women against the presumptions of an adult, male world. In a 1906 piece for the *Harvard Advocate*, he chastised the old for suppressing the young poets within themselves in order to pursue the "grosser joys" of business. "The whole world is against us," he wrote of young writers and artists, "trying to make us like other men,—jealous of other worlds." Among those other worlds was the one inhabited by "all sensitive women," as he noted in his journal two years later.

Brooks believed that he shared with such women a "normal mood" of "melancholy, sadness, and regret" because, like them, he harbored feelings that were too "fine" for ordinary expression. In another essay for the *Advocate*, he described the predicament of art in similar terms, stressing its utter incompatibility with the "reason or dialect of any particular age." Art at its best "is evolved from the infinite, and to the infinite it returns, happy indeed to bring men glimpses of what they may never understand." Aside from occasional appearances in the public world of language, craft, and intellect, art flourished in a realm uncontaminated by contact with the particular.[10]

Dante's great achievement, according to Brooks, was his ability to dissolve the barriers that separated intuition and personal life from language and public expression. In *La Vita Nuova*, Dante's ode to Beatrice Portinari, Brooks found a model for the future reconciliation of emotional and practical life and of art and society. Writing for the *Harvard Monthly* in 1906, Brooks celebrated "the spirituality, the intensity of Dante," who felt it impossible to "divorce experiences and emotions from the literary expression that is instinctive in them." Brooks argued that "the consummate artists of this world"—Dante, Shakespeare, Virgil, Sophocles, and Browning—had all been "sane men" because they joined emotional experience to literary creation. For such writers, "literature becomes their life, and life literature. . . . This rises so far above vulgar note-taking that life itself becomes expression: and this is the quality of all supreme literature."[11]

This distinction between "vulgar note-taking" and an art mingling expression with experience echoed Brooks's early contrast of the ideal realm of spirit to mere literature. His conviction that what was at stake in cultural criticism was a renovation of American life and not simply a transformation of style or taste deepened as he came into contact with the work of French critic Charles Augustin Sainte-Beuve and the aesthetics of the Irish portraitist John Butler Yeats. In describing his own critical method, Sainte-Beuve had written that "the study of literature leads me naturally to the study of human nature," which in turn involved considering a writer's personality, family background, social milieu, and nationality. The nineteenth-century romantic critic saw literature as an avenue to a much broader knowledge of culture and society, much as Brooks would come to see writing as a window on personality and national spirit. Yeats pushed Brooks in a similar direction, warning him against subordinating values to craft in literature. "Don't worry so much about technique," he told Brooks. "When life takes a deeper hold on you, it will find for you its own technique." By 1910, Brooks had taken this advice to heart and was writing Eleanor Stimson of "a glimmering . . . in me—somewhere—a something is stirring, the first breath of a view of life that is not mere literature—but a statement of something absent in American life." What Brooks had in mind was "not a fine art" but "in some vague and minor degree, a mission, a significance, a personality."[12]

In 1910 and 1911, Brooks devoted himself to these aspirations in an essay on English critic Vernon Lee and a highly personal short book titled *The Soul*. In the first of these Brooks laid out the "questions with which creative criticism will have to occupy itself": "In what manner is art to be made to contribute to conduct? How are the types of experience that have hitherto found expression only through art to be drawn into the service of life, to be given the chance of expressing themselves in conduct? Under what conditions, to be attained how, can the artist reach normality? How, in brief, is the pulse of the world to be made to beat as fast as the pulse of the artist?" In answering these questions, Brooks turned to Lee's claim that a work of literature had significance only "in the degree to which it possesses personality." A society in which art was more than an adornment to commercial life, in which those who shared the literary temperament had forsaken marginality to "reach normalcy," would be one that had recaptured the state of "perfect intuition" in which personality flourished. The rift between artistic and social experience would disappear once life itself became a work of art, partaking of the intuitive qualities of uninhibited personality. "We must have passed through organization," Brooks wrote, "back into the disorganization which is the only human attitude, considering the whole universe, that is not positively impudent."[13]

The Soul provided the background for Brooks's discussion of Lee by exploring a question of great personal and intellectual urgency: "How does the soul . . . become walled about, local, definitely and awkwardly formed?" The book drew together Brooks's youthful religion of merging souls, his infatuation with medieval Catholicism, and his general dissatisfaction with a social order dedicated to commercial exchange. It is Brooks's most lyrical and idiosyncratic book, as well as the clearest statement of his insights into his own personality, which may explain why in later life he tried to ignore its existence. In the years after his recovery from mental illness in the late 1920s and early 1930s, Brooks omitted *The Soul* from lists of his published work and failed to mention the book in his autobiography. Nevertheless, *The Soul* deserves a close reading for the view it gives of Brooks's initial attempts to shape the feminine ideal into a more concrete indictment of modern civilization.[14]

The human predicament, Brooks explained in *The Soul*, consisted of the loss of childhood illusions that "the destiny of man is to experience the whole of life." If it survived at all, this belief persisted into maturity as a nostalgic memory of a golden age, "a consolation for what cannot be." The child who once intuitively "experienced all modes of being" later confronted a society that "requires of us an economy of morals, a singleness of aims." Adulthood demanded an inevitable fall from grace, but Brooks, no matter how fatalistic his tone, could not bring himself to accept the limitations of such an existence. At best, adult life offered "a multitude of objects upon which we can expend ourselves" in a vain effort to make individuals "forget that we desire all, all, all." Growing up and conforming to social expectations meant neglecting the "inner eye," replacing "the mood of wonder in the presence of immense and undiscovered forces" with "a mood of lesser possibilities, probabilities, and what we call facts." Socialization, in short, was the incarceration of the soul.[15]

Brooks admitted that his first responses to the denial of intuitive, personal life were resignation and a craving for death. He imagined humanity as "a vast ocean which contained all things known and un-known," upon which sailed the ships of individual lives. "Then I said, I will be this ocean: and if I have to be a ship I will be only a raft for the first wave to capsize and sink." But Brooks quickly rejected his impulses toward self-destruction. "Existence could not be wrong," he wrote, "for existence is all there is to give us the meaning of right and wrong." The reason for the internment of souls must be "what is made of life," social conditions, and not the very fact of life itself. As he surveyed the ways of modern society, however, there seemed little reason to believe that those conditions could be alleviated or reversed: "Everything on earth stands like a flaming sword between a man and the intimacy of his own soul."[16]

The only moments of happiness available to the individual were those in which he dimly remembered the primal unity of his soul with the universe. In language reminiscent of his private writings on Catholicism, Brooks explained that "it is only moods that we remember, only moods in which we live, only moods that one heart offers to another." In a rare burst of Proustian passion, Brooks invoked the power of memory as a force that could shatter the hold of adult conventions over childhood insights into the nature of the soul: "Something in us reverberates and

rolls away over the whole wide world of human life, and we find ourselves reaching out, groping out among remembered sounds, remembered sights, above, beside, behind, sound beyond sound, wave beyond
wave . . . and in dizziness and confusion we feel that we have for an
instant had our two hands upon the whole current of significant things."
In these "electric fantasies," men and women transcended their individual experiences and joined other souls in joyous communion. The
division of life into separate categories, the reduction of persons into
specific functions, and even the alienation of human beings from one
another would all cease, at least briefly, as repressed memories of wholeness flooded their conscious minds. At such times, the individual grasped
something precious that Brooks believed "might be truth," namely that
the goal of living was "to be in solution, in perpetual readiness, to be as
responsive as mercury . . . to be conscious of ourselves only in moments
of growth." Brooks counseled his readers "to wait and hope and dream
until the whole world has become vibrant with sense and the apparency
of things has melted away and we see in everything a connection with
everything else, meaning within meaning."[17]

Religion had always been the traditional means of reconciling such
intuitive glimpses of the universal with the limitations of everyday life,
but Brooks took a dim view of its role in the modern world. With few
exceptions, the history of organized religion—or at least of Christianity—was that of "the infinite imposing itself upon the finite by finite
means." As its institutions compromised with secular authorities, Christianity lost its fiercely antisocial loyalty to the life of the soul, becoming
yet another prop of the established order. Brooks looked back fondly to
medieval Catholicism, praising its fusion of mysticism and science, and
he saw in both St. Francis's moral intransigence and Thomas à Kempis's
monasticism promising examples of opposition to worldly demands. But
the Protestant religion Brooks had inherited was dead set against the
"electric fantasies" that ignited individuals' awareness of their own
souls. Martin Luther, the consummate realist in politics, and John Wes-
ley, who confused piety with "commerce and social regeneration," symbolized for Brooks the alliance of Protestantism with the European
bourgeoisie. The history of Christianity followed the pattern of socialized decadence that Brooks had uncovered in individual development.
An early awareness of the primacy of spirit over matter, of wholeness
over functional parts, had given way to an idolatry of the existing social
order and a suppression of human essence, the soul.[18]

One other road to the spiritual life remained open to Brooks. "In literature I seemed to see a refuge," he wrote. The life of the writer attracted him because it "had no barriers, no moralities, asked no questions, reconciled all modes of being with each other simply because the human heart dreamed of them." The writer chose his or her career less out of a desire to find satisfaction in literary craftsmanship than out of a hope that writing might liberate personality. Yet Brooks acknowledged that the same process of socialization that had imprisoned the soul in every adult and had reduced Christianity to a doctrine of acquisitive pursuits could also turn literature into "propaganda" because "expression here too implied an audience" that evaluated writing according to social criteria.[19]

Since "the history of poetry may be taken as a parallel of the soul's history in the midst of life," Brooks looked to memory to return the writer to the primitive origins of his art. The earliest sources of poetry lay in primitive man's recognition of his own mortality and in his refusal to accept that mortality as the sum of his existence. His frustration that the "feeling of something infinite in him" could find no outlet in life grew sharper and harder to endure as he contemplated "the immense freedom of the universe" around him. Finally, in an inarticulate outburst of joy and sorrow, he chose "to cry out his heart. In doing so he found relief." Primitive poetry captured for Brooks an existential tension between a longing for transcendence and the biological confines of human life. The writer who wished to challenge the social constraints of language and thereby make literature a force for social transformation would have to recover the outpouring of the soul at the heart of poetry, with its anguished acceptance and protest of the limitations of life.[20]

Brooks identified his own spiritual aspirations with a widespread movement to return culture to its roots in the direct expression of the soul. "Today society is endeavouring to bind itself together in a moral programme," he wrote with uncharacteristic confidence. "It assumes that this programme will defeat the rhetoric of civilization by placing more and more individuals in a state where they can become more conscious of themselves." Brooks singled out the novels of Tolstoy, Turgenev, and Dostoevsky as examples of how the unconscious origins of primitive speech might be reintegrated with modern literature. The Russian novelists were the voices of "the most inarticulate people of the world," writers who were "dragging their dreams out of the soil." The emotional intensity of their work had prompted European authors such as Henrik Ibsen, Emile Zola, and Gerhart Hauptmann to plumb "the mysterious forces of heredity, of sex, of race, of the soil" for subject matter. In Russian fiction and the early works of European modernism, Brooks discovered a "literature without style in its traditional sense as an independent aspect of the literary art. These are not literary men, in the proper sense, at all."[21]

Brooks had come to a crucial point in his critical theory. He could suggest that a literature of the unconscious depths of personality was the most appropriate means of divulging the needs of the soul in a modern, secular age. Or he could follow the implications of his thesis to its logical conclusion, insisting that literature itself had become an impediment to his "moral programme." Instead, Brooks wavered and chose neither route. He praised Tolstoy for recognizing that "the refuge of literature" was finally "inadequate" as a source of spiritual regeneration. But he could not go so far as to endorse Tolstoy's decision to take up a life as a latter-day St. Francis, choosing peasant asceticism and revolutionary pacifism over the social position of a literary intellectual. Brooks had come to the understanding that writing alone could not lessen the torments of the soul in the modern age, but his strict separation of spirit and society left him no satisfactory alternative in either literature or politics.[22]

Brooks's coda to the main text of *The Soul* revealed his inability to heal the rift between ideals and practice in modern society. He lyrically announced his decision to live a double life: one, a mask of cold plaster to present his social self to the world; the other, a private life of the soul. Beneath the protection of his mask, all was possible: "I release my lips. I open my eyes. Oh the silence! oh the dark solitude! and all that whirls within me." But as James Hoopes has observed, this image of silent solitude resembled nothing more than a death mask hardening over the face of a corpse. Brooks's hasty resolution of the conflicts he had discovered in contemporary culture and within his psyche rang strangely false. Soul and society remained as estranged as ever. Brooks could not fashion a vibrant cultural life out of the materials he prized most dearly for their closeness to the soul: a literature free of social language, a religion uncontaminated by practical life, and a politics without institutional manifestation. His work had reached an impasse that he refused to confront. *The Soul*'s conclusion was less a celebration of subjectivity than an admission of its impotence in the face of a hostile world.[23]

By 1913, Brooks had decided that cultural revolution meant pressing far beyond purely literary concerns to a whole new conception of the relationship between art and everyday life. Once art had been defined as an unhappy compromise between the soul and society, it followed that a thorough reconciliation of these realms in a soulful society would end in the destruction of art itself. This was Brooks's program in "The Twilight of the Arts," the most ambitious of his early attempts to define his mission of cultural renewal. "True art is never satisfied with anything short of its own annihilation," he announced. Stressing idealist content over artistic form, Brooks advocated a passive, meditative approach to an art of pure spirit. Insofar as music, Impressionist and abstract painting, and the romantic poetry of Blake and Yeats refused any concessions to the "collective mind," they raised the possibility that the public would shake off conventions and "accept the point of view that lies behind" such artistic works. Art itself would then become superfluous. Personality would be liberated once men and women engaged in the direct apprehension of spirit. "Art as an institution," Brooks predicted, "dissolves toward the pure soul."[24]

Here again Brooks looked to Tolstoy for inspiration, but in this essay he had no qualms about describing that Christian radical as a "first rough sketch" of the role of "the artist of the future." Brooks made no mention of Tolstoy's ideology, his anarchism, or his critique of industrial technology; instead, he saw Tolstoy as a revolutionary saint who had dedicated his life to bringing social conditions in line with the spiritual ideals of his novels. In such a life, everyday existence gained a meaning previously found only in art and religion. A Tolstoyan society could easily dispense with artists and with art because it had realized their deepest purpose in social reality. As Brooks put it, an "art that springs from the soul . . . is willing to sacrifice even itself for the life of the soul."[25]

This was by no means a straightforward solution to the separation of soul and social life. When Tolstoy took up the life of a radical, he sought more than a society of pure intuition. Tolstoy's was a social and political response to the divorce of ideals and practice, not a return to a transcendent soul. His Christian communitarianism promised the great majority of people the opportunity to make and enjoy artistic works, an opportunity denied them under the conditions of poverty and the mechanization of crafts. If anything, the eradication of art that Brooks proposed might hinder such a project because the mind absorbed in spiritual reverie might well withdraw from the challenge of abolishing a class society. By

looking beyond art to pure spirit, Brooks had neglected the social function of art as a craft, which Tolstoy had seized upon as a way of returning creativity to labor and subjectivity to everyday life.

In *The Malady of the Ideal*, Brooks confronted the possibility that a
purely intuitive reconciliation of soul and society might fall short of his
goal of revitalizing modern culture. The book was a summation of his
explorations of the promise of personality, but it also revealed his ambivalence toward the writings of Henri Amiel, Etienne de Sénancour,
and Maurice de Guérin, who shared many of the mystical assumptions
behind *The Soul*. At times, Brooks reiterated their call for a literature in
which "personality projects itself beyond finite conditions," insisting
that criticism must help locate "the obstructions that exist in the world"
and remove them. Writers and critics had to create a society in which
"every personality can be free to realize itself." But Brooks also showed
an uneasiness about that ideal, as if the suggestion that art itself were
one of those obstructions might prove counterproductive as a program
of cultural renewal.[26]

The faith in free personality on the part of these French writers was
also their "malady." Brooks described Amiel, Sénancour, and Guérin
not as the sane men of Dante's model but as "abnormal souls" who "see
nothing but the infinite and fall back upon existence with immense
weariness." These were men who saw their own craft as illegitimate, as a
corrupt deal struck with an alien social world. As a result, they were
unable to express themselves except in private journals and letters.
Brooks clearly had misgivings about this particular reunion of art and
life. In Amiel, he saw a writer for whom "only the ego and the subjective existed"; "he sat like a spider in some kind of cosmic web spun
from his own body, unable to find himself because he could not lose
himself." Far from ushering in a society of soulful communion, an art of
pure personality might never transcend the merely personal. Instead of
laying the groundwork for a mission to reshape daily life, it could end in
trivia and gossip, the literary wreckage of routinized introspection.[27]

The Malady of the Ideal and "The Twilight of the Arts" had taken the
feminine ideal—or the culture of the soul—as far as it could go as a
strictly spiritual force. The monastic life of withdrawal that had attracted Brooks as an adolescent now struck him as a morbid symptom,
a malady that had prevented Amiel, Sénancour, and Guérin from creating a significant body of literary work or contributing to social change.
A purely ethereal synthesis of soul and society had left both realms
unchanged. Tolstoy's route implied a break with Brooks's early vision of

an ideal culture as a disembodied, unworldly retreat from life. It did not mean, however, a repudiation of Brooks's concern for the subjective anguish of life in a society devoted to mindless practice. Instead, to follow Tolstoy, Brooks would have had to identify his cultural mission with a larger program of political and social transformation, one that would give the soul a place in everyday activity instead of seeing it as a refuge from worldly affairs. Within a few years, Brooks would come to argue exactly along these lines, insisting that a Tolstoyan social revolution, and not the life of pure intuition, held out the greatest promise for a revitalized American culture.

Between 1909 and 1913, while still an undergraduate at Columbia, Randolph Bourne gained a national reputation as a spokesman for an emerging youth culture. In essays for the *Atlantic* and the *Columbia Monthly*, collected in 1913 in *Youth and Life*, Bourne took aim at the decaying values of his parents' generation, developing themes of cultural criticism that paralleled many of Brooks's early arguments about personality and the soul. But where Brooks lapsed into fatalism and otherworldly despair, Bourne integrated his critique of middle-class socialization with a new morality of sexual equality, social reform, and progressive education. Along with Walter Lippmann's *Preface to Politics*, Bourne's early work was one of the first attempts by an American to join political radicalism to the Continental social philosophy of Henri Bergson, Friedrich Nietzsche, Arthur Schopenhauer, and Freud. Condemning "the timidity and laziness of the old, who sit in the saddle and ride mankind," Bourne challenged socialists, Progressives, and other reformers to broaden their aspirations to envision a cultural revolution engaging the deepest issues of personal and psychic life. "The social movement," he explained, could not be satisfied with a humanitarian interest in the weak or a condescending pity for the impoverished. Radicals had to move beyond such sentiments to a "delight in a healthy, free, social life, to an artistic longing for a society where the treasures of civilization may be open to all, and to our desire for an environment where we ourselves will be able to exercise our capacities, and exert the untrammeled influences which we believe might be ours and our fellows'." Bourne's was as much a radicalism of the unconscious and private life as it was a protest against unjust political and economic structures. His published work had a highly personal flavor and confessional style that mixed moral passion with incisive rational criticism. Struggling over each of his sentences, Bourne deliberately gave his readers the impression of a mind literally drunk with ideas and of an author whose lived experience was one with his intellectual work. Bourne's distinctive voice is present in all his essays, but it is nowhere stronger than in his early writings on youth, friendship, and the "life of irony."[28]

Unfortunately, the exuberance of those early essays has obscured the issues that connect *Youth and Life* with Bourne's later analyses of education and politics. Bourne was not a cultural innovator turned political radical. His interest in creating a new politics of radical dissent informed his work from the start. A narrow focus on the theme of youth rebellion in Bourne's first essays ignores their political content, as well as the nature of Bourne's intellectual development. As Olaf Hansen has noted, "Bourne was at no time merely a prophet of a youth cult." The ideal of youth was for Bourne "a metaphor expressing the necessity of a socio-critical, intellectually unyielding attitude toward reality." Nor do Bourne's discussions of friendship and his critique of the bourgeois family constitute an endorsement of the peer group as the primary agency of socialization in a modern industrial society. Bourne's vision encompassed far more than a protest of youth against its elders. In his first critical writings, Bourne was groping toward a decentralized radicalism of self-organized communities that would persist well beyond the approach of middle age, combining individual self-realization with a democratic reconstruction of social life.[29]

Aside from youth, the chief metaphor in Bourne's early work is that of the imprisoned personality. In his autobiographical essay on the handicapped, Bourne claimed that "the doors of the deformed are always locked, and the key is on the outside." The image recurs throughout his work: souls are imprisoned, locked in dark rooms, trapped in the cells of conventional activity. Bourne argued that the forced enclosure of the soul had social causes. An ethos of individual self-control may have made sense in the early nineteenth century, when economic conditions and the opportunity of making a life on the frontier rewarded the autonomous entrepreneur willing to delay gratification for economic independence. By the early twentieth century, however, such opportunities had dwindled. With the rise of a corporate economy, self-control had degenerated into an ideological cover for the induction of youth into oppressive, bureaucratic organizations. "The only choice for the vast majority of young men to-day," Bourne complained, "is between being swallowed up in the routine of a big corporation, and experiencing the vicissitudes of a small business, which is now an uncertain, rickety affair." The more sensitive members of Bourne's generation harbored "a vague desire to expand, to get out of our cage, and liberate our dimly felt powers." The liberation of the soul was at the very center of Bourne's political radicalism. Correcting Karl Marx, he proclaimed that "the world has nothing to lose but its chains—and its own soul to gain!"[30]

Freeing the soul from its prison would require more than a change in political leadership or a redistribution of wealth, though Bourne clearly saw these as indispensable to any thoroughgoing social reform. A politics of personality—a radicalism of the soul—would have to prefigure in the present the very society it sought to create in the future so as to ensure that social reconstruction did not reproduce current cultural patterns. It could not simply wait for the future abolition of exploitation or the coming to power of a radical party. "The strength and beauty of the radical's position is that he already to a large extent lives in that sort of world which he desires." In friendship and the "life of irony," Bourne saw the possibility of anticipating the experience of living in a radically transformed society. The free expression of personality, a life of stimulating friendships, a critical intelligence engaged in the ironic analysis of social realities: these were not just the attributes of youth but the cultural prerequisites to the creation of a newly democratic society. In exploring these themes, Bourne not only vented his anger against outmoded social conventions, he was also instructing radicals in the fundamentals of cultural revolution.[31]

Like Brooks, Bourne wished to reassert the demands of the soul in daily life as an integral part of cultural renewal. Bourne also resembled Brooks in occasionally succumbing to the temptation to live in two worlds, one of social labor and another of private personality. Much as Brooks had argued in the closing passage of *The Soul*, Bourne wrote in "The Dodging of Pressures" that those who nurture their inner selves may escape the burdens of commerce by "letting the routine work lie very lightly on our soul." Even here, though, Bourne was less than optimistic about the prospects for separating life into public and private compartments. He considered it "doubtful" whether the prevailing standards of success in business or the professions could be achieved "without a certain betrayal of the soul." The aesthetic-intuitive sensibility that he and Brooks associated with personality would wither if it were secluded in a purely private realm. In the end, that sensibility would have to challenge and remake the public world, substituting "living effectiveness" for "mechanical efficiency."[32]

Whereas Brooks identified the health of the soul with an inevitably passing youth, Bourne preoccupied himself with the problem of maintaining the restless curiosity of youth into adulthood. It was essential to prevent the "huge bundle of susceptibilities" he associated with youth from hardening into a thoughtless routine. "To keep one's reactions warm and true is to have found the secret of perpetual youth," he wrote, "and perpetual youth is salvation." A commitment to the life of critical inquiry—what Bourne called the "life of irony"—became his surrogate religion, promising to nurture the youthful spirit in every adult. Such a religion would combine a Socratic method of dialectical inquiry with pragmatism in an effort to heighten and thereby understand the contradictions of life. Bourne equated irony with the "sense of being spiritually alive which ceaseless criticism of the world we live in gives us, combined with the sense of power which free and untrammeled judging produces in us." The ironist saw life whole, as both a participant and a critical observer. By constantly probing the social environment and subjecting its underlying assumptions to uncompromising criticism, the ironist "rubbed out the line that separates his personality from the rest of the world." An ironic personality would unite the individual with his or her social environment, but that union would always be one of tension because intellect would freely respond to irrational social conditions.[33]

With his conception of irony, Bourne had avoided the sterile opposition of personality and social life that had plagued Brooks in his early work. Brooks could join the soul and society only by positing a future life of intuitive moods or by withdrawing from the public world to an omnipresent "great soul." In the early 1910s, Brooks never managed to reconcile his love of art and literature with his nagging suspicion that they existed only as obstructions to the direct expression of personality. At its best, Brooks felt, the writer's life was a grudging compromise with society and a slight to the full realization of the soul. In identifying the vigor of youthful idealism with the development of a critical intellect, Bourne had indeed found "the secret of perpetual youth," as well as a way of reintegrating the intuitive personality with social practice. Bourne's "life of irony" remade Brooks's literary compromise into a relationship of constant tension between the soul and society, which were bound together by the rational workings of a restless mind. "Things as they are, thrown against the background of things as they ought to be—this is the ironist's vision." By constantly exposing the personal and the public to their opposites, the ironist would practice "the photography of the soul."[34]

For those who, like Bourne, believed that a career in corporate America would strangle their souls, the ironist's life offered an attractive alternative. Disdaining the unfulfilling occupations open to the educated children of the Victorian middle class, Bourne called on his peers to become a self-consciously critical intelligentsia. An intellectual class dedicated to the life of irony would finally escape the spiritual emptiness of masculine activity without retreating to the otherworldly isolation or pursuit of mystical union that overcame the young Brooks. Moreover, unlike Brooks's early conception of a life of the soul, Bourne's critical irony was distinctly social. Brooks had clung to his adolescent fantasy of a communion of souls, but he found it unimaginable that such a community could actually exist in organized society. Since to him virtually all organization was suspect, Brooks could envisage spiritual union among individuals only as a kind of afterlife. Bourne, on the other hand, saw in friendship and the quick-witted conversation of ironists concrete examples of social groups bound by shared experience, love, and a commitment to the life of the mind.

Bourne's theory of friendship derived from his own experience at the center of a clique of young radicals during and after his years at Columbia. One friend recalled years later how Bourne "wanted desperately a free-flowing channel between himself and other people." Their conversations lasted for hours, touching on "an almost endless range of subjects," as she and Bourne felt themselves filled with "a heady sense of exploration and discovery." Bourne was the catalyst of the long exchanges that took place among his friends, challenging them with satire and pointed humor to question the unexamined assumptions that guided their lives. As his friend remembered, Bourne "seemed able to draw out of his listeners more than they knew, and to endow them with an unaccustomed gift of speech. Then his response lifted the talk to a new level." Bourne himself wrote an acquaintance of his delight in such intellectual sparring and repartee. "I love people of quick, roving intelligence, who carry their learning lightly, and use it as weapons to fight with, as handles to grasp new ideas and situations with, and fuels to warm them into a sympathy with all sorts and conditions of men." "Good talk" among friends was the terrain on which the ironist engaged the public world. It allowed ideas to take on an emotional, even "personal" quality, as the conversation grew more animated, while still preserving the ironic stance of personality as something not totally immersed in the give and take of social relations.

> The good talker . . . takes the world quite seriously, but he takes himself quite flippantly. He talks of himself quite frankly, of his interests and points of view, but he does it all objectively, presenting himself as a type of human nature, poking fun at his idiosyncracies [sic], smiling at his failings, and failures, but yet strongly insisting on the fact of his personality. Even his most serious opinions he offers as something rather detached from himself, which he is perfectly willing to examine with you at your leisure; he will be interested but not angered, if you reject them. It is this calm insistence on their personality, but with a sort of amused commentary running along beside it, that makes the talk of great talkers like Holmes, Stevenson and France so delightful.

Such "good talk" was the perfect example of Bourne's conception of irony, making intellectual exchange personal and yet objective, just as friendship itself united individuals in an emotional bond that still preserved their integrity as separate persons.[35]

That emotional bond, or "sympathy," provided the necessary foundation for the sharp intellectual exchange that Bourne yearned for in friendship. Friendships rested on a shared sensibility and on intangible qualities that had more in common with aesthetic than with purely rational understanding. Bourne wrote ecstatically of the "golden moments" he spent at Columbia playing the piano for a friend "with whom I . . . felt absolute musical sympathy." "There was a sort of rapture about being thoroughly musically understood and it would give me at times a feeling that the material keys had dissolved away and one was evoking pure spirit without effort and simply by the movement of one's appreciating will." Such occasions inspired Bourne to write "The Excitement of Friendship," in which he celebrated "those golden hours" of shared experience "when thought and feeling seemed to have melted together." In the exhilaration of common interests, stimulating conversation, and joined sensibility, Bourne discovered an avenue for the release of the soul from its prison. Friendships founded on mutual delight in art and argument offered the individual both independence and intimacy, autonomous selfhood and communion with others. The paradox of the Trinity, in which the Holy Spirit animated both the heavenly Father and His earthly Son, reappeared in the ironic union of friends.

No wonder, then, that Bourne believed that if there were a God, He existed in "the closeness of friendships."[36]

In evoking the ideal of friendship as the model for a radically transformed society, Bourne's essays demanded more than a cult of interpersonal relations. In fact, Bourne's theory of friendship may be read as a direct response to the cultivation of friendliness as a form of social affability that developed alongside the bureaucratic order of the modern corporate economy. Impatient with the superficial friendliness demanded of those who wished to be well liked and successful, Bourne explored a communal alternative of friendship that he hoped would provide the basis for a participatory democracy. That alternative recalled an older philosophy of friendship and democratic self-government with origins in the fifth-century Athenian polis and in Aristotle's *Nicomachean Ethics*. As Alasdair MacIntyre explains, the Aristotelian tradition saw friendship as "the sharing of all in the common project of creating and sustaining the life of the city, a sharing incorporated in the immediacy of an individual's particular friendships." Bourne did give greater weight to the affectionate bonds of friendship and to a romantic ideal of communion through love and aesthetic experience than did the Aristotelian tradition, but he agreed with Aristotle's central premise that true friendship grew out of a shared commitment to the common good. Good talk among friends was aimed at discerning that common good, and it was this moral and political project that raised genuine friendship above the chitchat of socially enforced friendliness. By grounding democratic politics in an egalitarian republic of friendship, Bourne was searching for a third way between the atomism of nineteenth-century capitalism and the corporate order he saw taking form around him. Love and mutual respect would support the dialogue about the common good that Bourne believed was integral to a democratic community life. The social fabric of friendship would make decision making a form of mutual consensus, giving unity to political argument without coercing ideological conformity.[37]

Bourne's discussion of friendship recalled an ideal of unitary democracy with roots in classical moral and political philosophy. In Jane J. Mansbridge's description, the consensual model of unitary democracy built on Aristotle's observation that "friendship [*philia*] appears to hold city-states together."

The face-to-face interaction of friends helps to create and to maintain their common interests. Friends enjoy the drama of each other's existence and value the time they spend together rather than
resenting it. They come to respect and know one another by piecing
together, over time, informal cues derived from intimate contact.
Without such contact, friendship usually withers. Thus, for a polity
built on friendship face-to-face assemblies are a benefit as well as a
cost. These four central features of friendship—equal status or respect, consensus, common interest, and face-to-face contact—recur
in unitary democracies throughout history.

Despite the ascendancy of adversarial democracy in Western political
thought with Thomas Hobbes and John Locke, Mansbridge notes that
unitary models of self-government have still engaged the imagination of
modern theorists, especially in periods of crisis and political instability;
she finds in Jean-Jacques Rousseau, Ferdinand Tönnies, and much of the
American New Left a persistent strain of democratic theory favoring
localized, participatory forms of citizenship. Bourne's name belongs on
this list as well. In his writings on irony and friendship, Bourne was
groping toward a unitary model of democratic community in which
the bonds of friendship reinforced citizens' devotion to the common
good.[38]

Bourne's objection to classical liberal politics—what Mansbridge
would call the tradition of adversary democracy—grew out of his belief
that its negative conception of freedom provided no other basis for
authority or agreement than sheer force, whether economic or military.
At Columbia, he had imbibed the social-scientific indictment of laissez-
faire capitalism expounded by John Dewey, Charles Beard, and other
Progressive intellectuals, and he shared their contempt for a formalist
equation of personal liberty with economic self-interest. These thinkers'
insistence on the social character of all human activity and beliefs, including those described as "individualist," dovetailed in Bourne's mind
with the communitarianism of Henry George and Jean-Jacques Rousseau, two theorists of republican democracy who had already shaped
his thinking about liberal individualism. In a 1912 essay "The Doctrine
of the Rights of Man as Formulated by Thomas Paine," Bourne borrowed from recent anthropological theory to vindicate George's and
Rousseau's assumptions. He argued that collective tradition and social
groups, not a natural state of unfettered individualism, had characterized the earliest stages of human history. Bourne sought to revive the
group ideal that liberals ignored, and he offered "the ideal of *social*

justice" as an ethical doctrine to give both a positive content and a communal context to personal freedom.[39]

However attractive it may have been as an alternative to adversarial forms of politics, Bourne's unitary democracy of friendship and social justice was hardly free of ambiguities. Bourne's reliance on friendship and group unity had disturbing implications, which threatened to sacrifice his ironic independence to the demands of the group. The danger of a politics of friendship was the possibility that one's critical spirit might dissipate in the ebb and flow of camaraderie and group pressure. For Bourne, in particular, there existed the additional threat that the emotional bonds of friendship might undermine, rather than nourish, the intellectual exchange he associated with good talk. He admitted that "I find myself hopelessly dependent on my friends, and my environment." There was "one weak spot" in the intellectual "armor" of the ironist. "He fears to be cut off from friends and crowds and human faces and speech and books, for he demands to be ceaselessly fed." In a telling image, Bourne likened this dependence to that of the modern city on the "steady flow of supplies from the outside world." Just as the self-sufficient rural society of yeomen and artisans had given way to the interdependence of town and country, so too had the autonomous individual of liberal legend disappeared, replaced by a figure who voraciously consumed the emotional experiences of friendship. "He lives in a world of relations, and he must have a whole store of things to be related. He has lost himself completely in this world he lives in."[40]

This was a far more ambiguous formulation of the relationship between personality and society than that of a mind critically engaged with its social surroundings. The collapse of competitive individualism in an age of large-scale bureaucracies and corporations had led Bourne to develop his own theory of a personality that gained independence and self-knowledge in exchanges with friends. Yet Bourne also seemed to suggest that the independence necessary to the life of irony was finally impossible because there existed no irreducible core of personality free of the pressures of group life. Friends "are a true part of our widest self," he wrote; "we should hardly have a true self without them." But privately, he confessed to a friend that he might have exaggerated the importance of friendship in the socialization of critical thinkers. "People with that inner command of moods do not need friends so keenly as I do; they are more self-sufficing. What would seem to me 'a prison with a life of penal solitude' is to them simply the four walls of their own home, where they dwell among their interesting moods and ideas. I lack this and I generalized far too sweepingly on my own poverty of inner resources."⁴¹

In the years after he graduated from Columbia, Bourne felt himself cast adrift without any communal support from his old friends. His group of college classmates quickly moved away, married, or otherwise dispersed. During that period, Bourne admitted his deepest self-doubts in letters to Alyse Gregory, a feminist, suffrage activist, and later a member of the editorial staff of the *Dial*. Bourne's letters to Gregory reveal all that was confused in the ideal of a soul evolving toward self-consciousness in the company of friends. Envying Gregory her commitment to a definite cause, as well as her secure position within a political movement, Bourne still recoiled from the demands that such a movement made on intellectuals. By necessity, the social role of the critical thinker was one of lonely isolation. The dialectic of soul and society was easy enough to imagine in the abstract, but how could one reconcile their competing claims in real life?

This was the question Bourne returned to again and again in his correspondence with Gregory between 1913 and 1915, the years in which he graduated from Columbia, left for Europe under the aegis of the university's Gilder fellowship, and returned to Greenwich Village and a position at the *New Republic*, only to find his college friends bickering and at odds with one another. Gregory's role as a feminist activist seemed to make her the committed intellectual par excellence and the very opposite of Bourne's own status as a marginal critic. "You don't know how much I envy you your activity and the chance to reach people with a vital message and in such a direct way," he wrote her in June 1913. "I seem to be merely mooning along the wayside of life, helpless and unachieving, while you are on the battle-line expressing yourself, expressing your convictions and ideals in the most effective, and—I should think—soul-satisfying way." As befit the author of "The Life of Irony" and "The Excitement of Friendship," Bourne conceived of effective intellectual activity as necessarily taking place within the context of a supportive group. "I would give almost anything for that feeling of *participation*, something that you must wonderfully have." Without it, critical thought flickered in a rootless limbo, and "one's mind is constantly unsettled." Divorced from the social setting of the group, criticism faded into irrelevance, much as Bourne felt his own personality emptying into a void as his friends left him. "What is cold writing in comparison with direct campaigning?" he asked pathetically.⁴²

The disparity between his own life of isolated criticism and Gregory's activist involvement was the constant theme of later correspondence. In a letter from Paris, Bourne lashed out at "the artificiality of my life and ideas" and at his career as "a feeble little artist," whose work consisted only of an "indigestion of myself." "Writing without the contact of some definite movement, some definite demand, some definite group, must lack real vitality as I feel all mine does." In another letter, he compared "this dilettante life of mine" to Gregory's "splendid work," again suggesting that the ironist's life and the life of the group were ultimately irreconcilable. The plight of the unemployed filled him with loathing for his inability to effect social change. "How I hate my smooth writing when such urgencies are about to be dealt with! And what weapons have we?"[43]

Returning to New York from Europe in the summer of 1914, Bourne watched as his circle of friends dissolved "into individual units, each of whom is more and more absorbed in his work and, if he marries, somebody else, and thus passes out of that free, inexhaustible, spendthrift atmosphere that we used to know." He asked Gregory for advice on how to "fortify one's self" in the face of "such a doom of isolation." Still craving the friendship he had known at Columbia, he wrote of his urge "to be 'in' something," to be "connected up with something or somebody to whom you were important and even necessary." The most fleeting and voluntary of social groups, friendships, faded or ended abruptly over real or imagined slights, leaving Bourne an ironic prophet without an established audience.[44]

Gradually, Bourne came to terms with this situation. In his essay on the life of the disabled, he described his condition as far more difficult psychologically than that of the individual whose handicap or deformity precluded any social activity. With his disfigured face, his dwarfed and twisted body, Bourne felt himself "truly in the world, but not of the world." This was the uncomfortable stance he would finally adopt as a social critic. By 1915, he had apparently come to accept the disintegration of his Columbia circle. In addition, he had recognized that his independence as a thinker precluded the complete subordination of his personality to the life of a group. If a circle of friends, however sympathetic, demanded that the soul bend to its pressures, then the critical mind would have to "give up clamoring to be 'in' things and 'do' things," as he wrote Gregory. "It used really to worry me, to be filled with so much reforming spirit, and to be so detached from the machinery of change," he told her. Now he saw that he had "unsuspected powers of incompatibility with the real world" and that some "deep destiny" presided over his position as a "lonely spectator" in but not of society.[45]

Bourne had never hoped to free young people from family and tradition so that they might indulge their own eccentricities. As a critic of individualism, he had no naive faith in the completely unrestrained self, free of all social obligations or loyalties. But he also recognized, as he wrote in one of his essays, that his generation had found no substitutes for the "family cohesion and authority" it rejected. "The youth of today cannot rest on their liberation," he warned, for "the emancipation of the spirit is insufficient without a new means of spiritual livelihood" to orient the development of a new community life. Friendship was to provide just such a spiritual livelihood in Bourne's early work, offering a supportive space in which personality might reach full expression. The political promise of an egalitarian democracy of friendship still retained its original force. But, as Bourne's own experience indicated, groups of friends alone could not create the basis for a new community.[46]

The Victorian culture of family, place, and religion that Bourne's peers had rejected was composed of far tougher and more durable elements than the transitory friendships among youth. Bourne and Brooks turned against that culture because it had become so thoroughly corrupted by the adversarial individualism of the market, which had hollowed out its claims to loyalties and obligations beyond sheer self-interest. But young Americans had not yet found an adequate spiritual livelihood—or "cultural mission" in Brooks's words—to take its place. A participatory democracy of citizen-friends would require social roots at least as deep as those that had originally nurtured bourgeois culture. Radicals intent on creating a decentralized democracy of small groups would have to build on values and institutions that closely engaged the conditions of American life, or at least did so more effectively than had Bohemian circles of students and intellectuals. For Bourne and Brooks, this meant that dissenting thinkers had to delve more deeply into the very heart of their country's traditions, retrieving and renewing those aspects of the national heritage that nourished the intuitive values of the soul rather than the cold calculation of commerce.

At the same time that a radicalism of the soul required a new attention to the social and cultural fabric of the United States, it also demanded an unyielding independence of mind on the part of its intellectual representatives. Paradoxically, the future reunion of the soul and society rested on the extent to which radicals could shore up the integrity of the two realms of critical thought and community. Group life would benefit from a strengthening of social resources of fraternity and mutual aid that endured beyond the warm glow of friendship. Intellectual inquiry would flourish once social critics gave up their contempt for "mere" literature or "dilettantish" theoretical work and embraced their positions as "lonely spectators" of the American scene. Having passed through otherworldly religions of unitary souls and through a cult of friendship that threatened to smother the critical mind in the emotional intensity of the group, Bourne and Brooks entered the second half of the 1910s with a new understanding of the proper relationship between the soul and society.

That relationship would take the form of mutual criticism, sustained by a self-conscious striving for independence on the part of critical intellectuals and dissident groups. More specifically, it would take the form of two equally significant, though not equivalent, projects for the renewal of national thought and politics: an American cultural renaissance and participatory democracy.

3

The Politics of Cultural Renewal

One cannot have personality, one cannot have the
expressions of personality so long as the end of society
is an impersonal end like the accumulation of money.
—VAN WYCK BROOKS,
America's Coming-of-Age

As Bourne and Brooks turned their attention from personal and spiritual issues to larger questions of political and cultural criticism, they discovered that the tensions between ideals and practice that ran through their private lives had deeply social causes. Just as the divorce of feminine gentility from the workaday world of masculine enterprise had deprived the socialization of youth of a structure of meaning or purpose, so too had the separation of cultural traditions from the realities of industrial production degraded both these realms of American life. Culture had become mere artifice, while work had lost the skill and creativity associated with craftsmanship. Everywhere moribund traditions persisted as genteel fashions in a marketplace that, in and of itself, provided few spiritual rewards.

Though it was essentially personal concerns that led Bourne and Brooks to their critique of the culture of industrialism, it would be wrong to suggest that they turned to socialist politics to address purely private problems. Bourne and Brooks moved so easily between discussions of personal identity and the politics of culture because their own self-scrutiny had convinced them of the social and political issues at stake in matters that often took the most personal forms. The joining of the personal, the political, and the cultural in their early work reflected their understanding of the profound transformations wrought in these spheres during a century of industrialization and of the revolution in consciousness and community required to democratize American politics and culture. An intellectual project that began with the emancipation of the soul led in the mid-1910s to a call for the full-scale renovation of American life, a project that would necessarily entail the reorganization of the workplace. As Bourne wrote in 1914, modern industrial labor was objectionable precisely because it hindered personal development and sapped "the vitality of the worker." As a result, "the clerk dulled and depressed by the long day, and the factory worker—his brain a-whirl with the roar of the machines—must seek elation and the climax which the work should have given them, in the crude and exciting pleasures of the street and the dance and the show." The crisis of personality was at the heart of the devaluation of work and leisure, of culture and practical life. The soul could flourish only in a culture that once again rejoined these realms of social life. The shared experience of renovating and renewing their culture would enable Americans to participate fully as "true personalities and full-grown citizens, instead of the partially handicapped persons that society makes them now."[1]

The difficulty that plagued Bourne and Brooks in the early and mid-1910s was how to envision such a project of cultural renewal. How might American culture be brought to bear on the new conditions of industrial society and thereby transform them? A culture detached from social realities was meaningless, they believed, but a cultural life organized in accordance with those realities would lose its critical character. In this regard, the predicament of culture was identical with that of religion in an urban-industrial age. Bourne and Brooks shared with their contemporaries in the Protestant Social Gospel movement an awareness of the precarious position of idealist and spiritual traditions of thought in a society that had embraced an ideology of practicality and production. Walter Rauschenbusch, the most penetrating of the Social Gospel theologians, recognized that the prophetic religious tradition had to find a way of entering into the mainstream of modern industrial life without succumbing to its assumptions. The growing belief that religion was a private affair—a belief captured in the expression "Don't mix business and religion"—had detrimental effects for both religion and public affairs. A public life devoid of moral reasoning, bound to no higher spiritual principles, would devolve into exploitation of the weak by the strong. Rauschenbusch argued in 1907, "The more churchly Christianity is, the more will the Church be the only sphere of really Christian activity." Rauschenbusch identified the division of spirit and practical life as the central ethical problem of an industrial-capitalist civilization. "Thus life is cut into two halves, each governed by a law opposed to that of the other, and the law of Christ is denied even the opportunity to gain control of business." Bourne and Brooks did not speak the same Protestant language Rauschenbusch did, but they shared his fear that modern life lacked a moral center and his desire for a new cultural vision to shape high ideals and everyday practice.[2]

In the early 1910s, the promise of *science* figured in their work—as it did in that of many liberal and socialist Protestants, including Rauschenbusch—as a way out of this debilitating division of spirit and society. During this period, Bourne and Brooks often echoed such Progressives as Thorstein Veblen, Herbert Croly, Walter Lippmann, and—most important—John Dewey in arguing that art and ideas should reflect the new social arrangements and techniques of industrial capitalism. In this view, intellectuals would look to applied science and professional specialization as models for the practical implementation of culture in social reform. Part of the ambiguity in this argument derived from the Progressive notion of science, which often equated technical and critical reason and confused the work of the efficiency expert with the experimental spirit of the scientific community. As a result, Progressives could in one breath endorse the liberating potential of rational discourse within the scientific professions as an antidote to the factory system and in the next hail the technological and organizational achievements of industrialization. In Bourne's essays on Progressive education and Brooks's study of Fabian socialist H. G. Wells, an emphasis on technique undermined the democratic implications of their quest for a new scientifically organized community. In these writings, Bourne and Brooks joined their Progressive and socialist contemporaries in calling for the extension of industrial administration and efficiency to all realms of public life. Radicals would reconcile theory and practice by making ideas themselves a reflection of industrial technique.[3]

Bourne and Brooks quickly moved away from this functionalist vision of cultural renewal. By the mid-1910s, they had parted company with the majority of their peers on the Progressive Left. In Brooks's *America's Coming-of-Age* and Bourne's "Trans-national America," both critics rejected their earlier belief that applied science, large-scale organization, and technical expertise promised a restoration of community life. In these works, Bourne and Brooks turned back to their previous interest in traditional communities—the Catholic church, the household system, and folk cultures—but now used them as standards by which industrial life might be criticized, instead of arguing for their reconstruction on scientific lines. They now abandoned the idea that industrial social arrangements alone provided a new cultural unity. If anything, the industrial system stood in the way of a genuine cultural democracy because its separation of planning and execution deprived most people of the knowledge and skills necessary to cultural production or appreciation. In so doing, the factory system also prevented most Americans from full citizenship in a democratic polity. Progressives who sought to assimilate culture and politics to the corporate organization of industry were only deepening these trends. They were not fulfilling the promise of American life but betraying it.

The most glaring failure of the Progressive cultural ideal, Bourne and Brooks now realized, was its inability to provide men and women with a meaning to life. Americans lacked the shared moral conscience and intellectual discipline that these two critics found in European cultures. European nations had preserved such an ethos from the ravages of industrialization; they spawned a community life in which a rough consensus on moral values and cultural traditions informed vigorous public debate. Such communities promoted free personalities instead of stifling them. To create comparable communities in the United States, intellectuals would have to retrieve and renew those elements of American culture that challenged the undemocratic assumptions of the new industrial order. In the process, they would have to look for examples of popular resistance to that order in languages and forms of association outside the boundaries of elite culture. Culture itself would take on a new meaning, not by becoming an adjunct to industrial relations but by forming the basis for a new communal life of democratic self-realization. "On the economic plane," Brooks wrote, "that implies socialism; on every other plane it implies something which a majority of Americans in our day certainly do not possess—an object in living."[4]

"Socialism and the Catholic Ideal," an essay Bourne published in the *Columbia Monthly* in 1912, while still an undergraduate, illustrates the influence of his personal, spiritual musings on his political and cultural criticism. The article also reveals Bourne's attempt to combine the antimodern and mystical tendencies of his writings on youth with the belief in scientific expertise that was the hallmark of Progressive social thought. Bourne's interest in linking the spiritual fellowship of the Catholic religious ideal with socialist politics persisted throughout his later work and found echoes in the critical writings of the other Young Americans. But his hope that the spiritual succor that the medieval church once offered believers would again be nurtured in the modern community of scientific socialists would prove a far more ambiguous legacy to his colleagues' work, one that would provoke utopian fantasies of a scientific priesthood of intellectuals interpreting a modernist Kingdom of Heaven to a new congregation. Bourne's student essay prefigured two strains of thought that were to remain intertwined and often confused in the Young Americans' vision of a revived community. The first looked to a morally grounded consensus as the foundation for a renascent American culture and participatory democracy; the second foreshadowed an elitist role for radical intellectuals as the new priests of a hierarchical community.[5]

Reflecting his disillusionment with middle-class liberal Protestantism, Bourne devoted almost as much energy to attacking his old "sectarian" faith as he did to promoting a modern revision of the Catholic ideal. In his essay, he argued that the Protestant emphasis on the believer's personal relationship with God created congregations of atomistic individuals held together by no bonds of spiritual or emotional sympathy. "A Protestant 'church,'" Bourne noted sarcastically, "is thus a social club with a religious leader," merely "an aggregation of convenience." Modern Protestants mocked the Roman church as a feudal anachronism, but Bourne found the Protestant notion of "individual responsibility and allegiance to a master, without any relation to the other vassals," far more medieval than the communitarian ethos of Catholicism. Protestant believers congregated solely on the basis of "intellectual agreement," Bourne complained. No true community could thrive on such a thin diet of rationalism; its members would soon give in to "worldly standards and measurements" as means of self-definition. This attitude led to the Protestant belief in election, which Bourne rejected as undemocratic. "The attitude of the elect towards the rest of the world is one of frosty charity, when it is not one of contempt." Bourne obviously had Bloomfield's congregations in mind, not the Calvinist theology that had sought to preserve faith from the very worldly demands Bourne abhorred. His argument had an internal logic that bore little resemblance to the actual history of Protestant doctrine. Bourne believed that a community of loosely bound individuals, whose association derived from rational agreement, could not resist the disintegrating tendencies of capitalist social relations. Society would inevitably triumph over spirit in the haughty disdain of the Protestant bourgeoisie toward its inferiors and the identification of spiritual election with financial success.[6]

In response, Bourne looked longingly to "the Catholic ideal of a living, universal Church, founded on a rock of historical and spiritual community, and embracing in a mystical union all those who believe efficaciously in the divine Christ and his sacrifice for men." Throughout the essay, Bourne invoked images of the church that recalled the moments of mystical union that he and the other Young Americans had found so compelling in their youth. Bourne's Catholic church was a "mother" that "nourishes" its followers. The individual believer found an inviting place as "a cell in the vast organism" of the church, which provided personal identity through "participation in the glorious company of saints and apostles." Catholicism offered the "organic cohesion" absent in Protestant sects, and Bourne noted approvingly the traditional metaphor of the church as the living body of Christ. "To the Catholic, the ecclesiastical organization is the bony structure of the Church, the laity the flesh and muscle, and the priesthood the life-blood bringing nourishment to all the cells and organs of the body." Bourne's Catholic community was no intellectual abstraction, no congregation of isolated individuals. The church was an organic whole brought to life by the intuitive knowledge of a people and sustained by deeply felt loyalties to the sacraments.[7]

Paradoxically, Bourne found the greatest promise for a vital church in two opposing theological trends from the nineteenth century: the Oxford movement within the Anglican church and Catholic modernism. The former resurrected High Church ritual as a defense against scientific rationalism, whereas the latter worked to reconcile Catholic doctrine to many of the assumptions of its liberal critics. Bourne waved away the contradictions between the two positions, seeing in both an elevation of "the real Church" as "an invisible, a spiritual body" over institutional traditions. Bourne's belief that the Oxford movement's recourse to faith and ritual in no way contradicted the emerging Catholic openness to modern science that was crucial to his argument. His own synthesis of socialism and the Catholic ideal followed along similar lines: the spiritual community of the Catholic church would reach full efflorescence once faith was wedded to the progressive spirit of scientific socialism.[8]

Bourne's references to socialism displayed a dual impulse toward an egalitarian community and a scientifically directed social order. The inclusiveness of the Catholic ideal prefigured the classless society envisioned by socialists, and his interest in the tightly knit fabric of faith and tradition that made up the universal church suggested that socialism too would need spiritual commitments and loyalties absent in a Protestant, capitalist society. But Bourne's socialist enthusiasm also pointed toward "a civilization . . . with all the resources of modern science and with a new insight into human nature." Here was a new holism, a new world church founded on the rock of natural and social science, permitting "a far more perfect realization" of spiritual ideals "than could have been true in any other era of the world's history." Intellectuals would have a key role in that process, forming a new priesthood modeled after "modern heroic medical scientists." If the socialist church was a living organism, then intellectuals were its doctors, ministering to believers' spiritual and bodily needs.[9]

Bourne's fascination with the priesthood as a Catholic and now socialist ideal for intellectuals revealed the darker side of his vision of cultural renewal. Although the modern Protestant minister seemed to Bourne little more than an ordinary professional, the Catholic priest was "a Vicar of the divine" mediating between his parishioners' desires and God's will. Science provided the new priests of socialism with similar possibilities for commanding specialized knowledge inaccessible to the average believer. Bourne undermined the communitarian elements of the Catholic ideal by calling on a scientific priesthood to implement it. The notion that the new priests would again bring "life-blood" to the "cells and organs" of the socialist body did not augur well for the creation of a democratic community. In fact, Bourne's scientific church verged on a dangerous authoritarianism, viewing its congregants as largely nonrational organs of a political body controlled by progressive intellectuals. The most promising aspects of liberal rationalism—its belief in a public sphere for rational debate, its potential for informed political participation by all citizens, and its recognition of the place of power and conflict in public affairs—had virtually no place in Bourne's Catholic socialism. Instead there was a vague mysticism and the jargon of scientism, which wedded technocratic reform to the unquestioned authority of the medieval church.[10]

This tension between an intuitive communitarianism and a far more hierarchical vision of social unity persisted in Bourne's later work and colored his perceptions during his postgraduate tour of England, France, Italy, Germany, and Denmark in 1913–14. Traveling on a fellowship from Columbia, Bourne met with European students, intellectuals, and reformers, many of whom shared his optimism about an emerging scientific civilization. In writing about his impressions of Europe, Bourne returned to the polarities evident in "Socialism and the Catholic Ideal" and gave them a specifically nationalistic orientation. Recoiling from the "hard inhumanity" and "crusted hypocrisy" of the English, whose lack of introspection reminded him of America's Anglophile middle class, Bourne divided his sympathies between the French and Germans, whose cultures came to symbolize, respectively, the intuitive and technical dimensions of his own radicalism. Bourne was well aware that he might be finding in the Old World the very qualities of experience he had been searching for at home, that he might be engaged in "some gigantic flattery" in his depiction of European life. "To cross the seas and come upon my own enthusiasms and ideals vibrating with so intense a glow seemed an amazing fortune," he wrote in "Mon Amie," a 1915 portrait of a young Frenchwoman. Bourne's year abroad confirmed his hostility toward Anglo-American bourgeois culture, but it also gave him a glimpse of more welcome alternatives. The comparison of France and Germany left in his mind a constant tension between an aesthetic sensibility and a more positivist focus on scientific rationality. Bourne would return from Europe in the summer of 1914 committed to transfusing American culture with Germany's cold, masculine intellect and France's warm, feminine soul.[11]

Bourne's romance with French culture pervades his letters and essays about his tour. French civilization was organic, he believed, in its union of intellectual and emotional experience. The French, he wrote a friend, "do not slice their souls up as we Anglo-Saxons do." Instead, they loved the very combination of playful wit and intellectual passion that Bourne cherished as the quintessence of the free personality. "I would sit almost helplessly and listen to her sparkle of talk," he wrote of his French friend in "Mon Amie." The "world of school-children and tired business men" he had left behind in the United States had no place for such a woman, for "the sensual delight which she took in thinking, the way her ideas were all warmly felt and her feelings luminously expressed." The woman's rural background and Catholic upbringing especially appealed to Bourne. "And if I had fallen in love, I know it would not have been with her. It would have been with the Frenchness of her," he confessed.[12]

What distinguished Bourne's love affair with French culture from the inferiority complex before European civilization that had so long characterized American letters was his sense that the French people's spiritual qualities largely accounted for their intellectual achievements. Rationality and intuition were in no way opposed for Bourne; rather, it was France's preservation of a religious background for ideas that explained its position at the forefront of modern thought. The French university system, with its intensely vital student culture and its extension programs in working-class districts, was the embodiment of what Bourne and his friends had yearned for at Columbia and the very antithesis of Oxbridge stuffiness. Bourne was fascinated by the new theater of the Vieux Columbier and the circle of writers around Jules Romains, whose *unanimisme*—a literary movement dedicated to the expression of French folk-consciousness in an urban-industrial setting—struck him as "a sort of Gallicized Whitman."

These two groups of French modernists would also remain lifelong influences on Waldo Frank, who wrote at length about their work and tried to incorporate its innovations in the portrayal of a collective consciousness into his novels and criticism. What Bourne admired in the new French culture was its evocation of a "group-mind," which provided the necessary soil for the growth of true personalities. Forged in the country's peasant Catholicism, France's "group-mind" had a tenacity that enabled it to resist the ravages of industrialization. Like the Italians, the French stood much closer to the socialist future than did the Germans, English, or Americans, despite the latter nations' obvious economic advantages. The atomistic individualism of American life ensured that its communities would cohere only on the basis of external force. By contrast, France's organic, collective spirit created free personalities by providing their intuitive beliefs with a larger framework of loyalty and meaning. And the inclusiveness of French culture, reaching down into the peasantry for inspiration and extending into the new working class, marked it off from the priggishness and snobbery that Bourne hated in English society. "Class-distinctions, which hit you in the face in England and America," seemed hardly to exist in France. Instead, there was "a democracy, where you criticized everything and everybody," and "the distinction between the 'intellectual' and the non-intellectual seems to have quite broken down." France had managed to spawn whole men and women who maintained "the directest connection" between their innermost thoughts and feelings and their "outer expression in speech, gesture, writing, art." These were the characteristics of a people on the cutting edge of Continental radicalism, and these were the qualities of sentiment and social life so obviously lacking in the United States. "It was a new world," Bourne breathlessly reported upon his return, "where the values and the issues of life got reinstated for me into something of their proper relative emphasis."[13]

The other leading center of European radicalism left Bourne a good deal more ambivalent. If France thrilled him with the giddy promise of an organic fusion of emotion, intellect, and conduct, German culture both attracted and repelled him. Bourne arrived in Dresden at the end of

July 1914, and the sight of "crowds of youths parading the streets . . . cheering for Austria and the War" sickened him. But he was deeply impressed by the German penchant for administrative efficiency and urban order. "I do like very much the clean and massive lines of the new German architecture and the boldness and versatility of the household art and decorative work; and I am enthusiastic about their municipal science, and their sense of efficiency and their instinct for machinery which makes their factories and workshops look almost like laboratories or hospitals, so professional are they." But as he wrote a friend, the outbreak of militaristic nationalism and a certain "thickness and sentimentality" and "lack of critical sense" among the Germans made him wary of their "soul."[14]

Nonetheless, Bourne was confident that a new radicalism could unite the intuitive organicism of French culture with the mechanistic marvels of German science. As he wrote Alyse Gregory, "My social philosophy is working around to a paradoxical desire for Tolstoyan ends through Nietzschean means; socialism, dynamic social religion through the ruthless application of scientific materialism." As in his essay "Socialism and the Catholic Ideal," his "paradoxical" goal took the form of combining an aesthetic-intuitive sensibility with modern reason in his criticism and a preindustrial loyalty to community with scientific administration in his vision of a new socialist democracy. That paradox received its first test in the mid-1910s, when Bourne turned to the movement for educational reform, which he saw as an American counterpart to European radicalism and the best hope for uniting spirit and science in the creation of free personalities.[15]

In his 1912 sketch of a newly scientific church, Bourne singled out education as "the Socialist sacrament" by which each citizen entered into the cultural heritage of his or her community. In the two years after his return to the United States, Bourne championed Progressive education in the pages of the New Republic. While Bourne was still in Europe, his former professor Charles Beard had made arrangements with Herbert Croly for Bourne to join Croly's new journal of opinion as a regular contributor. But Bourne soon found that his pieces on education, urban planning, and cultural criticism were peripheral to the magazine's brand of political commentary. The New Republic's arrival, he wrote Alyse Gregory, "always gives my proud spirit the awareness that I am having nothing to say about its policy, and that I am an insignifi-

cant retainer of its staff." Bourne's writing for the magazine reflected
in the end less an encounter with its editors Croly, Walter Lippmann,
and Walter Weyl than it did with John Dewey, the foremost philosopher of Progressivism. Though Dewey had played only a minor role in
Bourne's undergraduate education, his ideas on education soon became
virtually indistinguishable from Dewey's. Bourne's essays on the Progressive school, collected in *The Gary Schools* in 1916 and *Education
and Living* the following year, were saturated with Dewey's influence.
"The point-of-view of these papers," Bourne confessed in the preface to
the latter collection, "will be recognized as the product of an enthusiasm for the educational philosophy of John Dewey." In turning to
Dewey for a philosophy for his new church, Bourne began an encounter
with pragmatism that lasted throughout his life and became a central
feature of all of the Young Americans' subsequent work. It would not be
an exaggeration to say that John Dewey was *the* contemporary thinker
of significance for the Young Americans, first as an ally in the campaign
for democratic community and then as the symbol of the betrayal of
democratic promise by modern liberals. An understanding of Dewey's
strengths and weaknesses as a democratic theorist, then, is crucial not
only to any reading of Bourne's educational writings but to that of the
Young Americans' work as a whole.[16]

Bourne's thoughts on educational reform owed much to five principal
currents of Dewey's philosophy. The two most important of these had to
do with Dewey's ideal of democracy. First and foremost was Dewey's
theory of a democratic community grounded in critical discourse and
free communication. Dewey's valuation of modern science and its role in
dissolving the bonds of tradition stemmed from his belief in the scientific community as a collectivity governed by rational inquiry. A new
democratic politics would have to take as its starting point the creation
of a free community of informed discourse if its citizens were to participate fully in self-government. Second, Dewey shared Bourne's belief that
self-transformation and the creation of a democratic social order were
inextricably linked. In the years before World War I, Dewey defended
democracy as "a form of moral and spiritual association" that would
release individuals from the constraints of class and superstition and
allow them to become masters of their own destiny. As historian Robert
Westbrook writes, "For Dewey, democracy would always be inseparable
from the ethics of self-realization; democracy would always mean the
universalization of the opportunity for an individual to develop his par-

ticular capacities and powers as an active participant in the life of the community."[17]

Dewey had written early in his career, "In one word, democracy means that *personality* is the first and final reality," and Bourne obviously saw in Dewey's philosophy a way of liberating personality within the context of a democratic community. This linkage of personal growth to the democratization of public life was the most powerful aspect of Deweyan pragmatism and its most important contribution to Bourne's thought. Throughout his life, Dewey argued for a "new individualism" that would avoid the extremes of competitive individualism and bureaucratic organization. Prospects for communitarian democracy, in Dewey's view, rested on a new understanding of the cultural nature of the self, an idea he shared with his fellow pragmatists George Herbert Mead and Charles Horton Cooley. In *Democracy and Education*, he rejected the "conception of mind as a purely isolated possession of the self," arguing instead that "the self *achieves* mind in the degree in which knowledge of things is incarnate in the life about him." Self-knowledge derived from an active process of interaction with the environment and from the advances of a social intelligence. It followed, then, that personal growth could occur only when men and women had full access to the intellectual and artistic resources of their society and the opportunity to participate in the fashioning of their own civic culture.[18]

Bourne enthusiastically embraced Dewey's vision of democratic self-fulfillment. "Professor Dewey has given us a whole new language of meanings," he wrote in a 1915 tribute to the pragmatic philosopher. "After reading him, you can see nothing again in the old terms." Dewey's ideal of self-realization through participation in a community of free inquiry was so attractive to Bourne because it dovetailed with his own thinking about a republic of friendship, in which enthusiastic conversation, mutual respect, and affection fostered solidarity. Essentially, Bourne and Dewey both conceived of democracy as a process of collective inquiry into the conditions of civic participation and the means by which such participation might allow individuals to lead a good life.[19]

A third tenet of Dewey's pragmatism held additional appeal for Bourne. In an attempt to reform philosophy, Dewey sought to transcend the endless debates between empiricists and idealists by emphasizing *lived experience* as the central concept of philosophical inquiry. For Bourne, who had long held that ideals removed from social practice fortified artificial conventions while leaving everyday realities untouched, the pragmatic notion of experience was an invaluable insight. One can see Bourne groping for a comparable category in his essay "Socialism and the Catholic Ideal." There, he had dismissed the lifeless rationalism of liberal Protestantism and looked instead to Catholics' fuller appreciation of emotional and intuitive understanding to complement the discoveries of modern science. Dewey's notion of experience as consciously informed social practice might yet free American society from the extremes of feminine sentimentality and masculine utilitarianism. Experience preserved the intuitive spirituality of French culture alongside the free spirit of scientific investigation that guided German social engineering. If a rich and heightened experience replaced empty moralism and commerce as the goal of a rewarding life, then American culture would escape its status as genteel adornment. Culture would no longer be marginal to social life; on the contrary, as integral parts of conscious experience, art and literature would become the basis of a renascent American democracy.

A culture of conscious experience would proceed along the lines of scientific inquiry. Dewey's enthusiasm for science was the fourth tenet of his philosophy to shape Bourne's understanding of pragmatism. For Dewey, a philosophy of experience would proceed according to the experimental methods of modern science, thereby reopening moral and political debates that had been sealed shut in ossified intellectual categories. This critical function of science would ensure the free and rational communications that Dewey saw as the heart of a democratic community. Moreover, it would make it possible to reestablish qualitative judgments of value on a more secure, consensual basis by removing them from their foundationalist setting in idealist and religious metaphysical systems. In his efforts to reconstruct philosophy as a public language of lived experience, Dewey hammered away at the Platonist currents within the philosophical tradition for substituting a priori notions of truth for practical wisdom and for seeking absolute certainty instead of provisional understanding of the world. His polemics against idealism and foundationalism returned again and again to the promise of science—understood as a collective process of inquiry, consensual reasoning, and practical experiment—as an alternative to the fruitless attempts to make philosophy a source of knowledge about timeless, unconditioned truths.

Yet Dewey's turn to the example of experimental science in his assaults on idealist metaphysics had ambiguous consequences for his pragmatism that may have confused many readers, including Bourne.

Dewey understood science as a modern successor to Aristotle's idea of practical wisdom, but his writings often assimilated the critical content of scientific reason to the technical achievements of industrialization, as if the workings of practical wisdom were equivalent to the application of scientific knowledge in the mastery of nature. Dewey never intended to endorse science as a purely technical, value-free activity limited to the sole purpose of adapting means to ends. If anything, his vision of founding a democratic culture on conscious experience opened up scientific inquiry to a dialogue with such value-laden processes as art, ethics, and religion. Nevertheless, his attacks on idealism often left the impression that he equated the critical inquiry he admired in scientific activity with an instrumentalist view of knowledge as applied science and technique.[20]

Dewey's belief that scientific method provided the materials for a rational, consensually understood ethics and democratic polity often slid too easily into an assertion that industrial conditions provided the basis for a new culture of participatory democracy. In *The School and Society*, published in 1899, Dewey identified two irreversible trends as the causes for the demise of the preindustrial household: first, "the increase in toleration" made possible as a rationalized social order replaced arbitrary, patriarchal authority; and second, the industrial transformation of the earth, which had "lifted man from his precarious subjection to nature." Both trends had enormous significance for Dewey's democratic ideal. The first disqualified traditional communities, ordered as they were by premodern forms of loyalty and obedience, as models of consensual democracy. It seemed to follow from Dewey's argument that the precondition for the reorganization of such communities along democratic lines was their virtual destruction by the modernizing forces of scientific industry. The second trend apparently identified the critical rationality of modern science with its technical application in the subjugation of nature, making the two processes indistinguishable. The implication of this line of reasoning was that the reconciliation of thought and practice in experience would follow the guidelines of applied science. In all of this, Dewey was maddeningly vague about how the critical content of reason would guide the construction of democratic communities if its chief manifestation in modern life was in institutional arrangements that Dewey himself regarded as undemocratic. *The School and Society* asserted that "the industrial history of man is not a materialistic or merely utilitarian affair" but "an ethical record as well" and "a matter of intelligence," but Dewey was obscure about how industrial civilization could generate the ethical and intellectual aims of a regenerated democracy.[21]

This vagueness about the relationship between industrialization (and especially the industrial application of scientific technique) and the construction of a scientific culture of community placed Dewey's entire project in jeopardy. The irrelevance of traditional moral and intellectual categories to modern industrial practice had first led Dewey, Bourne, and other Progressive intellectuals to give up abstract theorizing for a philosophy of practice. "Reason is not a divinely appointed guide to eternal truths," Bourne wrote of pragmatism, "but a practical instrument by which we solve problems." But Dewey's blurring of practical wisdom and scientific technique endangered the critical content of culture that alone might raise human experience above thoughtless drudgery. Dewey saw a pragmatic philosophy of experience as the appropriate intellectual grounding for democracy because it had as its end the intelligent mastery of self and society by free and rational citizens. Yet it is difficult to see how ideas would inform a democratic order if they were first to reflect the hierarchy of specialization endemic in industrial societies. How would a culture organized in accordance with the technological control of nature nurture a critique of industrial society? Dewey's use of science to convey both critique and technique opened up the possibility that philosophy would end up as a gloss on existing social arrangements. Self-realization would become its opposite, as pragmatism freed individuals from patriarchal authority only to subject them to the technical authority of industrial organization.[22]

Dewey's idiosyncratic terminology, particularly his use of the term *adaptation* to explain the proper relationship between an individual's values and aspirations and his or her environment, further complicated the issue. Many critics and admirers of pragmatism understood Dewey to be urging that individuals adapt their own ways of thinking to the demands of their time and place. In less sophisticated versions, this argument could take the form of a crude harangue against "cultural lag" and a call for bringing cultural traditions and individual habits in line with industrial progress. But as Westbrook notes, this reading of Dewey as a positivist advocate of bending qualitative values to practical exigencies and of subordinating the individual to society was profoundly mistaken. Dewey's dialectical understanding of *adaptation*—as opposed to what he called *accommodation*—gave priority to making the social environment responsive to individual needs and to shaping practical life in accordance with humans' ethical and aesthetic aspirations. Still, the very use of the term *adaptation*, in conjunction with passages extolling the advantages of scientific technique over idealism, led to confusion about Dewey's evaluation of the opportunities for critical reasoning, moral deliberation, and creative expression in an industrial society.[23]

Dewey's rhetorical conflation of practical wisdom and scientific technique pervaded much of his work on education, which provided the fifth and ultimately most significant source of contact between Bourne and Dewey in the mid-1910s. As Westbrook writes, Dewey hoped to "establish schools as powerful adversarial institutions in the heart of American culture." A school should be "a miniature community, an embryonic community," Dewey argued, and in particular an embryo of a society that had overcome the industrial division of labor. Bourne echoed these sentiments exactly, portraying the ideal school as "an embryonic community life, where the child would sense the occupations and interests of the larger society into which he is to enter and so have his curiosity and practical skills awakened to meet and conquer them."[24]

Preparing students to conquer their society meant challenging the industrial division of labor, beginning with the specialized categories and procedures of traditional education. Though Dewey welcomed the material and intellectual benefits of an industrial society, he was always uncomfortable with "the division into 'cultured' people and 'workers,' the separation of theory and practice" that resulted from the rise of the factory system. The factory's fragmentation of practice into routinized work found its intellectual counterpart in the classical school curriculum, which separated knowing from doing and classified experience into disciplines that had little relation to the child's process of learning and self-reflection. As education became a tedious matter of memorization and recitation divorced from practice, and as knowledge devolved into the command of formal abstractions, children lost their intuitive sense of play in learning about their world.[25]

In arguing for the centrality of practical experience in education, Dewey was often accused of promoting a purely vocational form of education. But in *The School and Society*, Dewey carefully differentiated education for an occupation from narrow training for a trade. "By occupation," he wrote, "I mean a mode of activity on the part of the child which reproduces, or runs parallel to, some form of work carried on in social life." Dewey was quick to add, however, that this did not mean that training for an occupation involved the subordination of knowledge to "external utility." Rather, an occupation differed from a trade "because its end is in itself." Unlike manual training, Dewey's education for an occupation would maintain "a balance between the intellectual and the practical phases of experience," stressing excellence in both realms so as to achieve mastery of a given occupation. Dewey's educational ideal appears much closer to an older notion of work as a calling, or to what Alasdair MacIntyre has called a "practice," than to strictly utilitarian training. For Dewey, the new school would foster self-realization among its students and the attainment of a moral end—in this case, democracy—by educating children in the internal discipline of occupations.[26]

While pursuing educational reforms, Dewey came into conflict with business reformers who sought to apply the principles of scientific management to the school system, separating academic curricula from industrial education. Dewey's response to one such proposal is revealing: "The kind of vocational education in which I am interested is not one which will 'adapt' workers to the existing industrial regime; I am not sufficiently in love with the regime for that. It seems to me that the business of all who would not be educational time-servers is to resist every move in this direction, and to strive for a kind of vocational education which will first alter the existing industrial system, and ultimately transform it." Industrial production promoted "unconscious and mechanical" work, the aim of which was always external—the greatest production at the lowest cost. The aim of an occupation was precisely the opposite: "to put the maximum of consciousness into whatever is done."[27]

Yet this generous conception of education for democratic citizenship also foundered on Dewey's use of applied science as an example of how theory and practice could be reconciled in a culture of experience. Dewey often suggested that the Progressive school was an "inevitable" response in the realm of education to the "changes in modes of industry and commerce" of the previous half-century. His fuzzy formulations of the fit between the school and its surrounding environment paralleled his ambiguous resolution of the divorce of culture and social life through science, leaving his ideas open to appropriation by the very industrial reformers he opposed. If the traditional school was obsolete because it failed to engage the conditions of industry and commerce, if the classical curriculum lacked an appropriate grasp of modern social arrangements, and if scientific technique provided the best means for bringing ideas to bear on experience, then it followed that the school should not only prepare students for life in industrial society but also should mirror it in its internal organization. Moreover, Dewey's insistence that school learning be reintegrated with the processes of child development often took on a manipulative cast, as when he claimed that "it is possible to lay hold upon the rudimentary instincts of human nature" so as to "control their expression." Like Bourne's new church, Dewey's embryonic community often appeared to be populated by nonrational citizens open to new techniques of psychological control. This element of Progressive educational theory held enormous appeal for efficiency experts and scientific managers, who saw in it a means of socializing children into the industrial working class. Once again, Dewey's ambiguous invocation of science as critique and technique eroded the democratic content of his philosophy, providing a theoretical language appropriate to either self-realization or manipulation. The theory Bourne turned to for support in constructing his own vision of democratic community was as riven with tensions as was his early ideal of a socialist church.[28]

Bourne's educational writings lack Dewey's philosophical sophistication, but they exhibit many of the contradictions inherent in the pragmatic theory of culture and social change. Bourne differed from Dewey in his aesthetic sensibility, which led him to place far more emphasis on students' acquisition of independent taste in cultural appreciation than Dewey ever had. Bourne's essays on the Progressive school movement veered between two poles that were in many respects analogous to Dewey's critical and technical conceptions of scientific method but took a distinctive form in Bourne's work. On one hand, Bourne looked to the experimental school as a way of freeing Americans for participation in the shared culture and intellectually grounded democracy that he imagined the French enjoyed. Education would have to produce graduates who were capable of autonomous judgment in cultural affairs and willing to challenge Matthew Arnold's definition of culture as "the best that has been thought and said in the world." On the other hand, Bourne took Dewey's injunction to harmonize the curriculum with social experience to mean that the school should instruct its students in the technical and scientific knowledge required to administer modern industry. Lurking behind this duality of aesthetic and technical training was that of French and German culture, and Bourne's essays demonstrate a persistent, if unsuccessful, effort to bring together the best of these two civilizations in a movement for American cultural renewal.

Bourne's work on education, however, lacked Dewey's stress on rational discourse and free debate as the prerequisites for a full democracy. In all of his early work, Bourne had emphasized the necessity of good talk and a shared culture in democratic communities, but these often took the form of intuitive understanding rather than a consensus derived from vigorous debate. As in the case of his socialist church, a common culture required the existence of a mediating figure who articulated the inchoate sentiments of the group. Bourne himself had played such a role among his friends at Columbia, and his removal to Europe after graduation played no small part in the disintegration of that group into petty squabbles and infighting. In his essays for the *New Republic*, Bourne reconceived the Catholic priest who figured so prominently in his socialist church; he now became a "new type of teacher-engineer-community worker," who would draw on modern educational methods to refashion American society. As Bourne wrote his friend the anthropologist Elsie Clews Parsons in 1915, "I cannot see how any resolute social program can ever be put through without some strong party which has a professional attitude towards government and a will towards the Great State." He combined his French and German models in a new politics of technical expertise and avant-garde culture, to be directed by a priesthood of artist-administrators. "I begin to wonder whether there aren't advantages in having the administration of the State taken care of by a scientific body of men with a social sense, or perhaps rather an aesthetic-scientific idea of a desirable urban life. There really may be something in the German claim that this liberates energies for real freedom of thought."[29]

"A Moral Equivalent for Universal Military Service," Bourne's 1916 coda to William James's famous proposal for an "army enlisted against Nature," brought to a head Bourne's Progressivism and revealed its dangerously undemocratic tendencies. In Bourne's mind, the self-realization of young Americans would require their conscription into an educational army spreading the gospel of efficiency and modern administrative techniques. If Dewey had blurred the distinction between practical wisdom and applied science, Bourne collapsed culture and industrial management in his vision of the school as an embryonic community. As a result, his interest in liberating Americans' aesthetic experiences from the constraints of genteel culture was often confused with a utilitarian theory of knowledge that threatened the existence of any culture whatsoever. Once again, an adversary education meant to erase the industrial division of theory and practice ended up reinforcing it. The critical potential of Progressive school reform—its ideal communities of rational discourse—dissolved in the rhetoric of efficient administration.[30]

Bourne's critique of the traditional school was fully in keeping with his general indictment of American cultural life. The classical school had failed to create genuine communities of children, thus paving the way for the artificial cohesion that marked American society at large. In most cases, the classroom was "a collection of things, in relation with the teacher," not "a network or a group" of active participants. The system reminded Bourne of a factory. "Children have had to be massed together into a schoolroom just as cotton looms have had to be massed together into a factory." The traditional school failed to recognize that children differed from mere instruments in their consciousness, which could "only be developed by the freely inter-stimulating play of minds in a group." Whatever Bourne's writings lacked in theoretical breadth, they more than made up for in enthusiasm. There was no reason to acquiesce in the dullness and apathy of traditional learning. "The school," he promised, "might be a place where play passed insensibly into work, and aimless experiment into purposeful construction."[31]

First, however, Americans would have to give up the "cult of the best" that governed traditional education. The Arnoldian fixation on elite culture had not produced adults capable of artistic discrimination but only an intellectual class system that left all Americans aesthetically impoverished. Art education for the wealthy "has meant to like masterpieces" and then to buy them. It was no wonder, then, that millionaires stuffed their mansions with half-understood treasures from foreign lands and that the country's architects, trained in the beaux-arts tradition, had "filled our cities with sepulchral neo-classicism and imitative debris of all the ages." The cult of the best had promoted an ideal of culture as a commodity available to all those with the requisite income and educational background to purchase it. Even more disturbing to Bourne was the tendency for an education oriented toward the acquisition of "the best" to overlook "the joyous masses who might easily, as in other countries, have evolved a folk-culture if they had not been outlawed by this ideal." Traditional education had drained both high and low culture of their vitality, substituting for one the collection of officially sanctioned masterpieces—now torn from any larger cultural context—and for the other, the outsider's distrust of a superior's possessions.[32]

As a way out of these degraded alternatives, Bourne promoted the education of a popular taste growing "naturally and spontaneously out of the experiences of everyday life." This ideal of a critical taste in art and culture served a purpose in Bourne's educational writings analogous to that of rational discourse in Dewey's philosophy. Students who learned to make their own art in Progressive schools, instead of silently following their teachers through tomblike museums, would later participate fully in the creation and appreciation of a native American culture. They would have learned not only "to appreciate a Mantegna and a Japanese print, and Dante and Debussy," but to feel "nausea at Main Street." Bourne looked to the aesthetic education of young people to generate a new American culture out of the shared experience of freely creative personalities. "Indigenous style is the only art that really means anything," he wrote. "Out of an education in taste will grow creative art as a flower from rich soil."[33]

Bourne's hopes for an American artistic renaissance clashed violently with another aspect of his critique of Arnoldian culture. In an essay titled "Class and School," Bourne denounced "the industrious proletarian and the exclusive Tory" for "joining hands" in defense of such "useless" subjects as "formal classics and mathematics." The aesthetic dimension of his educational theory upheld a vision of an indigenous "group-mind" in the United States like the one he had encountered in France, yet Bourne's praise for technical learning led him to attack high culture for its lack of practical application. His indictment of the traditional curriculum as useless suggested that only a purely utilitarian culture was worth acquiring. The critical engagement with tradition that had been Bourne's goal in artistic education—and that had characterized his own mastery of the liberal arts at Columbia—was absent in this functionalist view of culture, which swept aside the debris of traditional learning to make room for education in efficiency. Sounding very much like Thorstein Veblen, who saw the "instinct of workmanship" in engineers as an example of unalienated labor in industrial production, Bourne embraced applied science as an intellectual alternative to Arnoldian culture. Schools should "produce the type of mind perhaps most needed to-day," Bourne wrote in *The Gary Schools*, "that of the versatile engineer, the mind that adapts and masters mechanism. . . . For this type of mind, 'culture' would not be a fringe, but a more or less integral part of life." Ironically, the same critic who attacked the tradi-

tional classroom for working like a factory now looked to modern industry to liberate the curriculum from genteel elitism. No longer the
means to an independent public taste, culture would escape its degraded
status as adornment, in Bourne's functionalist view, once it was put to
use in the factory system.[34]

Bourne may always have felt an outsider at the *New Republic*, but in
this aspect of his writing he was very much in step with his editors' view
of corporate organization and efficiency as the sources for a new liberalism. The most ambitious statement of Bourne's views on education
came in July 1916, with the publication in the *New Republic* of "A
Moral Equivalent for Universal Military Service." Although it recalls
James's "Moral Equivalent of War," Bourne's essay had a somewhat
different aim than James's campaign for restoring the country's morale
by toughening up "overcivilized" youth. Here Bourne looked again to
"Nietzschean means" to achieve "Tolstoyan ends," to the scientific technique he identified with Germany to realize an organic culture along the
lines of French civilization. Bourne called for two years of compulsory
education for young people between the ages of sixteen and twenty-one
not only as "a moral equivalent to war" but as an army for cultural
improvement. Grouped in "flying squadrons" of students, Bourne's
educational troops would target the "appalling slovenliness, the ignorance of great masses in city and country as to the elementary technique
of daily life." The student conscripts would essentially be teachers,
spreading the new gospel of Progressive social science. "I have a picture
of a host of eager young missionaries swarming over the land, spreading
the health knowledge, the knowledge of domestic science, of gardening,
of tastefulness, that they have learned in school." The commanders at
the front lines of American culture would be "that new type of teacher-
engineer-community worker that our best schools are already produc-
ing." Having argued that industrial conditions demanded education for
technical professions, Bourne now recommended letting such graduates
loose on society at large to remake it in the image of the Progressive
school.[35]

With this full-blown utopian vision of national education, Bourne
betrayed both the political and the cultural promise of his critique of the
industrial division of labor. His turn to engineering and professional
administration as solutions to the separation of theory and practice
ignored the issues of power and privilege that gave rise to that separation. Bourne looked to the very groups that had benefited from the
specialization of labor in the factory to transcend it, and his proposal to

have schools train students in industrial technique represented not the rebirth of the household system—as Dewey would have had it—but its destruction. Rather than prepare students for occupations and thereby promote a standard of work as a craft or calling, Bourne's school reform would accelerate the tendency to view both labor and knowledge as technical means to a utilitarian end. Bourne might have insisted that schools train workers in the very skills that had been appropriated by management over the course of the previous half-century. Such a practical education would have represented a truly radical challenge to the culture of industrialism, reaching back to the preindustrial household for an example of apprenticeship and forward to a thorough democratization of the factory system. Instead, he tended to view the separation of thought from action in isolation from the conflicts over power that had made the industrial workplace a contested terrain.

The political naïveté of this position is even more startling in Bourne's extension of the Progressive educational movement into a larger project of cultural uplift. Having modeled education after the factory system, Bourne then proposed to reshape American society in the image of the Progressive school. This program may very well have created a community of shared ideas and culture, but it was far from a democratic community. Bourne had borrowed from the army and the factory—arguably the least democratic sectors of American life—the hierarchy of discipline and specialization that would implement a new scientific culture. This technocultural vanguard, taking command of everything from gardening to tastefulness, was the antithesis of the generous ideal of cultural democracy he had outlined in his critique of the cult of the best. In the end, Bourne's army of intellectual missionaries was not a movement for democratic community but a program for the industrialization of culture.

In their conception of culture, Bourne's educational essays marked a regression from his early hopes of transcending the separation of feminine gentility and masculine practice. Nor did they provide a theory of indigenous culture that would lead Americans out of the stalemate between the cult of the best and Main Street. Their failure to do so resulted, in part, from Bourne's ambivalence about the place of traditions in cultural life. He reveled in the peasant-bred organicism of French culture but found little in American life that might be called upon to contest the new culture of industrialism. Genteel traditions in the United States stifled new ideas instead of engaging them in any larger national project. His belief that German science and planning might recreate, in modern form, the shared culture of France, thereby giving industrial America a substitute for the organic traditions it had never enjoyed, was problematic at best. Bourne had been attracted to French culture by its combination of shared values and incisive debate. Participation in a shared culture of art and ideas, sense and sensibility, had made France the most democratic nation he had ever seen. The scientific rationality he admired in German social reform left little space for such participation. Ultimately, Nietzschean means and Tolstoyan ends (as Bourne defined them) were incompatible: Germany offered few lessons in how to realize Bourne's idealized vision of France. Technical reason and the industrial division of labor could never restore the organic unity of the old household or the Catholic ideal, nor could education in efficient administration prepare students for the discriminating taste necessary to an indigenous culture. By modernizing traditions, Bourne had effectively gutted them, calling on their authority as common ideals while emptying them of their popular, democratic content.

The conflicting claims of modernity and tradition, of applied science and aesthetics, and of intellect and intuition also marked Van Wyck Brooks's early criticism. Like Bourne, Brooks hoped to reestablish the organic unity of preindustrial cultures on a modern, democratic basis. And like Bourne, Brooks flirted with a technocratic progressivism as the best means of bridging the gap between industrial realities and cultural ideals. Brooks differed from Bourne in his deeper antipathy to cultural modernism and his far greater sympathy for the Arnoldian ideal of high culture. Even as he attacked the genteel tradition, Brooks remained firmly committed to its equation of culture and morality and its view of literary education as a form of ethical training for democratic citizenship. While Bourne looked to science and efficient administration to sweep aside the bankrupt promises of gentility, Brooks suggested in his early work that scientific technique and a gradualist socialism would fulfill, not dispel, those promises. Brooks never believed that high culture was a useless accoutrement of the privileged; rather, he searched for ways of realizing its potential for moral instruction in an urban-industrial age. No matter how close he came to embracing the progressivist faith, Brooks never abandoned his belief in culture as a process of self-culture. Mastering the heritage of Western civilization always meant for Brooks an achievement in self-mastery, without which the full development of personality was impossible. The question that he tried to resolve in his work in the late 1900s and early 1910s was how to restore to self-culture its moral and critical role in a period when culture functioned as a polite veneer to sordid commercial dealings. His attempt to answer that question led him, as it did Bourne, to confront the industrial division of labor and the stagnation of American democratic traditions, which had made a mockery of any ideal of culture as a means to a moral life. Brooks's dedication to self-culture forced him to explore issues that transcended the purely personal realm of selfhood.

Throughout this period, Brooks grappled with many of the same problems that preoccupied Bourne, but he did so on the terrain of literary culture rather than social thought. One reason why Brooks did not follow Bourne in absorbing the new currents in social science was that his ideal of cultural renewal always had a less explicitly social component than Bourne's. Brooks may have shared Bourne's fondness for the medieval church, but he was less interested in finding an institutional means of resurrecting its universal community than he was in finding a modern successor to the theological doctrine that once supported that community. Modern life required a new set of ideals, a new canon; once that existed, the forms and institutions by which men and women structured their social lives would work themselves out. A revolution in culture involved primarily a renovation of art and morals and only after that a transformation in everyday life.

Perhaps because of the emphasis he placed on high culture, Brooks found English intellectual life far more to his liking than Bourne did. His experiences in that country during 1907–8 and 1913–14 impressed him with the vitality of English cultural traditions. In particular, Brooks admired the "cultural centralization" of England, "the focussing of the general mind so that every English feeling and thought had its instantaneous effect on every other." Because they had been raised on a cultural heritage available to the nation at large, English intellectuals wrote for a wide public and even influenced the workings of government. "Centralization is the secret of all thought & art here," he wrote Eleanor Stimson in 1913; "every act & thought has its place and affects every other act and thought—like the solar system. Standing in London you can put your fingers on every shade of opinion, and as in a coherent organism nothing is lost." An American cultural renaissance would require a similar centralization of intellectual life, with writers and critics assuming the responsibility for creating a new canon of ideas and values for their countrymen.[36]

The need for a new center to American culture was the subject of two of Brooks's earliest essays, "Harvard and American Life" and *The Wine of the Puritans*, both of which were published in 1908. At the same time that his private writings showed Brooks engaged in a quest for spiritual knowledge that would culminate in the publication of *The Soul* in 1911, these first critical essays explored the absence of coherent moral and intellectual traditions in American life. The reinvigoration of American culture, in Brooks's early thinking, would involve not so much a philosophy of social experience or a science of group life—as Dewey and Bourne would have it—as it would a spiritual and intellectual project that would ultimately inform politics and social action.

For Brooks, American culture lacked focus in large part because of the demise of the classical liberal arts college, which played a role in his early criticism analogous to that of the medieval church in Bourne's. The old humanism of Harvard College, steeped in "the provincial point of view of New England," had once offered such a focus, and the college had been the ancestral home of generations of American intellectuals. Ever since the late nineteenth century, however, when President Charles William Eliot introduced the elective system and disciplinary specialization into the Harvard curriculum, the college had given up its familiar New England character and had begun to resemble industrial America at large. Harvard, Brooks charged, was now "the factory of imperialism," a center for the production of businessmen possessing a smattering of "pseudo-culture" and a "touch-and-go familiarity" with humanistic knowledge. Without the provincial stability afforded by New England culture, Harvard had become an adjunct to the administrative apparatus of modern industry. By bringing higher education in line with industrial organization, Eliot had ironically made college life less useful as a source of informed commentary about society.[37]

These criticisms of the modern university were not altogether new; Brooks was echoing defenders of the classical curriculum who preceded him by a quarter-century or more. Brooks's critique was distinguished by its concern for the university as a miniature representative of the social arrangements of American culture. Brooks complained that "in America there is no institution which, like Oxford, unites the intimate, corporate, personal quality of the college with the cosmopolitan, broadening quality of the university." The old Harvard College may have been such a place, with the "intimate" provincialism of New England serving to introduce students to the mainstream of Western civilization, but Eliot's research-oriented university was no modern counterpart. Relations between students and professors had become "German-ised and depersonalized into a pure intellectualism," with the result that any moral authority within the university appeared purely "arbitrary." Brooks's image of the new Harvard closely resembled Bourne's carica-ture of Protestant sects as random groups held together by a feeble "intellectualism." In such groups, internal standards of conduct with-ered as the "effective specialisation" of industrial society imposed itself on student life. "Year after year the Harvard type grows less and less distinct as the American type more and more defines itself," Brooks claimed; "with the College the old-fashioned humanist fades away, with the University the efficient practitioner of the future emerges."[38]

For Brooks, the intellectual and personal transformations of college life were inseparably linked. The demise of the old liberal arts curricu-lum went hand in hand with the loss of undergraduate spirit and collegiality. Changes in the canon of humanistic learning had conse-quences that reached far beyond the curriculum, sapping the social life of the college and giving the authority of faculty and administrators an arbitrary, even illegitimate quality. Without a consensus on a com-mon set of goals—in this case, the training in literary and religious culture that had characterized provincial Harvard—college society had devolved into a grim careerism, industrial specialization, and rule by force. Brooks hinted in his essay that "something wider and more cos-mopolitan, something still indistinct in its outline," was emerging to take the place of New England culture as a focus for American intellec-tuals, but such hopes rang false in the general context of his analysis. Like American society as a whole, Harvard had lost its moral and cul-tural roots, giving up its historic mission in self-culture to become a transmission belt in the "factory of imperialism."[39]

The Wine of the Puritans, written at roughly the same time as "Har-vard and American Life," addressed many of these same issues, but in it Brooks's criticism took on a sweeping, even global scale. Putting aside the political attack he had leveled against Harvard, and by implication all of industrial American culture, he turned to a broad indictment of the spiritual emptiness of the entire American experience since its Puri-tan founding. Written as an imaginary dialogue between two overly refined expatriates, "Graeling" and the narrator, *Wine* was Brooks's first major step toward the cultural criticism that would establish his career in the 1910s. Though his characters returned constantly to their own status as expatriate intellectuals—a subject of obvious personal interest to Brooks, who wrote the book in London—the essay was a much more ambitious meditation on the spiritual shortcomings of Enlightenment rationality and practically all of modern culture. Brooks's lament that "American history is so unlovable" might have been made in regard to the entire modern era, which afforded men and women little that might be honestly loved. The failure of modern thought to give love and emotional loyalties a position of comparable importance to reason had meant that people formed only a superficial attachment to their cultures and their communities. Modern culture had freed individuals from all prerational loyalties, but that did not make them free; lacking deeper commitments to people or place, they never became full personalities capable of understanding or modifying their social environment.[40]

The crisis in American culture was present at its earliest origins. Americans were rootless moderns from the start, Brooks argued, people who fled the constraints of tradition when they set sail from Europe. "Unlike any other great race, we were founded by full-grown, modern, self-conscious men," he wrote of the Puritans. As a nation, Americans lacked a childhood, a rich fund of experiences to nurture their personalities into adulthood. Expatriates like Brooks and "Graeling" had gone to England in search of a storybook childhood that could never be theirs. Their flight was emblematic of that of countless other American artists and intellectuals who sought European equivalents for the traditions missing in their own culture. As in Brooks's discussions of spirituality and the soul, childhood figured in *Wine* as a lost period of wholeness that adults might recapture in later moments of cultural appreciation or religious reverie. But since they were "the most grown-up race in the world," Americans had no such common memories to guide them in their various pursuits. Art, literature, education, and politics lived off a mindless social existence as "excrescences," never coalescing into "a background, a point of view." In short, Americans' lack of a childhood prevented them from fully becoming adults.[41]

Early nineteenth-century New England provided the one opportunity for the unification of American culture, but its arts and letters never survived the collapse of rural society. The case of Emerson symbolized the inability of provincial New England to engage the expanding commercial society around it. Emerson's Transcendentalism gave up trying to understand or criticize social conditions and retreated to the realm of pure spirit; it abandoned any hope of integrating ideas and social life in a postmedieval synthesis. The divorce of an ethereal idealism from the society of merchants and pioneers had never been resolved, to the persistent detriment of American culture. As Brooks's narrator said, " 'You put the old wine into new bottles . . . and when the explosion results, one may say, the aroma passes into the air and the wine spills on the floor. The aroma, or the ideal, turns into transcendentalism, and the wine, or the real, becomes commercialism. In any case one doesn't preserve a great deal of well-tempered, genial wine.' " The metaphor of old wine in new bottles exactly captured Brooks's meaning. Unlike European nations, America had no properly aged culture to inspire its artists and writers and give a coherence to public discourse. A society born out of a disintegrating medieval order, the United States stood for all that Brooks saw as bankrupt and decadent in the modern project: the divorce of reason from emotion, the relegation of culture to a privileged realm that sacrificed its importance in everyday life, the elevation of the present over the past, and (most important) the absence of a moral and intellectual framework for practical life. More than a dialogue about the status of expatriates, *Wine* was a condemnation of virtually all of Western culture since the Enlightenment.[42]

Given the scope of Brooks's assault, it is not surprising that he came up short with alternatives, let alone any articulated program for American cultural renewal. *Wine* ended on a surprisingly optimistic note, with Brooks predicting a future "when the names of Denver and Sioux City will have a traditional and antique dignity like Damascus and Perugia—and when it will not seem to us grotesque that they have." Still, this goal was as disembodied as Emerson's realm of transcendent spirit and Brooks's upbeat conclusion as forced as his vision of a newly united Harvard College. The difficulty, as Brooks readily admitted, was that the lack of an American childhood—as he defined it—left few choices for modern intellectuals. "It's all so vague, so difficult," said *Wine*'s narrator. "You can't deliberately *establish* an American tradition." Whitman's attempt to do exactly that on the basis of "cosmos" and "universal comradeship" was a valiant effort, but it too lacked any mooring in custom and social life; "for practical purposes it means—nothing. It means just 'Yawp.' " Brooks had stared the matter in the face and had not blinked. Americans could not build communities on the basis of artificial traditions. Utopias like Brook Farm had tried and had failed miserably. There was no substitute for traditions so long gone that they might as well have never existed. Americans could not repudiate their modernity by acting like children; they would only be acting childish.[43]

The Wine of the Puritans remained mired in a fin-de-siècle pessimism that Brooks could surmount only by radically changing the terms of his critique of modern culture. The sweep of Brooks's critique gave it a remarkable power, especially for such a short and in some ways minor essay; yet that sweep was also one of its major limitations. Brooks's indictment of modern culture was itself so far removed from political and social realities as to invite the criticism that he himself was part of the Emersonian tradition he deplored. The historical and political specificity that gave his essay on Harvard its sting was missing, as Brooks seemed to appeal to great writers (Emerson's "Representative Men") and a healthy dose of spirit to remedy problems that required more than high-minded and well-meaning individuals. Because he located the crisis of modern culture in the collapse of medieval holism and not in the nineteenth-century revolution in social organization he held responsible for the new Harvard, Brooks left his readers with little concrete understanding of the social and political afflictions of American culture. In closing, Brooks gestured emptily to the need for "great constructors, great positive forces, someone to bind together the estranged fragments of society," a suggestion as authoritarian as it was gratuitous. What vintner did Brooks expect to restore America's spilt wine and sour aroma to its new bottle? How would one or even a group of writers succeed in aging a vintage culture to his specifications? Even if such a group existed, would its work alone lift Americans as a whole out of the morass of modernity, giving them the childhood they never had? The essay ended without any answers to these questions, because Brooks had failed to weave his ideas into the historical texture of American society. *Wine*'s thesis found confirmation in Brooks's own intellectual predicament.[44]

The way out of that predicament lay in socialism, which became of increasing interest to Brooks between 1908 and 1915. Not only Tolstoy's religious anarchism but the radicalism of the American West, Fabianism, and William Morris's arts-and-crafts socialism appealed to Brooks as alternatives to the intellectual and moral poverty of American life. Moreover, they gave him a way to pull his analysis out of the dead ends of aestheticism and otherworldly spirituality that had left him despairing about any alternatives in modern culture. Brooks's engagement with socialism was purely intellectual, except for two important experiences. During a year spent teaching at Stanford University in 1911, Brooks had the good fortune to meet members of a nearby socialist local typical of those that supported the rich political culture of the Wobblies, Debsian socialists, and other western radicals. Brooks's encounter with the local's "'immigrant intellectuals,'" "ex-miners and ex-cowboys," and students left a lasting impression on him, and he would later reflect in his autobiography on its "sensitive generous young people" and on the western locals generally as "centres of light" in a region "where ideas were few." In all likelihood, this was Brooks's first experience with a nonelite cultural community, and his recollections suggest that he found its lively discussions and cosmopolitan air a refreshing surprise in torpid Palo Alto. For the members of such locals, the revolutionary ideas of world socialist movements provided the new canon Brooks was looking for, a new focus for culture and politics in the modern age. Like the old Harvard, the tiny socialist groups that dotted the American West combined the familiarity and face-to-face interaction of local communities with the openness and diversity that came from involvement in an international endeavor. Socialism provided another route to the cultural unity Brooks had been looking for, one that rooted cosmopolitan ideas in local experience even as it raised that experience out of parochialism by giving it a transcendent moral purpose.[45]

The other direct encounter Brooks had with socialist politics in this period was in London in 1913–14, where he observed with fascination the debates raging within Britain's intellectual Left between the Fabians, H. G. Wells, Morrisite radicals, Hilaire Belloc and G. K. Chesterton, and a host of other groups and figures. During his year and a half in London, Brooks taught in a school for working-class students and generally soaked up what he could of English radicalism, reworking his newly acquired knowledge in light of his own views on modern industrial culture. Given those views, it is not altogether surprising that his first forays into a socialist cultural criticism reflected the influence of not altogether congenial currents of thought. Brooks's interest in resurrecting an organic culture bore a superficial resemblance to ideas current among virtually all sectors of London's radical circles, which allowed him to claim widely divergent views of cultural renewal as his own.

One reason for Brooks's enthusiasm for the English Left was its continuity with over a century of English thought about the very meaning of culture, which had shaped Brooks's earliest ideas about the subject. That continuity allowed Brooks to think through the limitations of the Arnoldian strategy for elite culture as moral instruction and transform it into a theory of cultural preparation for socialist political change. As Raymond Williams demonstrated, the word *culture* acquired a new meaning in the nineteenth century which held within it an implicit critique of capitalist social relations. When opposed to the word *society*, *culture* emerged in English thought "as a court of human appeal, to be set over the processes of practical social judgment and yet to offer itself as a mitigating and rallying alternative." The rhetorical opposition of *culture* and *society* recognized the industrial division of theory and practice but offered three very different strategies for resolving its social consequences. In its Tory formulations, *culture* recalled a hierarchical community in which benevolent aristocrats ensured the well-being and virtue of the people as a whole. In its Arnoldian cast, *culture* provided the moral glue otherwise absent in competitive individualism, with training in elite culture socializing the working class into habits of deference and national loyalty that would stabilize a capitalist order. Whereas the Tory opposition of *culture* to *society* carried with it an explicit condemnation of a system in which the cash-nexus had eroded the paternalism of the feudal countryside, Arnold's cultural strategy was meant to plug the holes in classical liberalism, thereby shoring up the free market and the liberal polity against the tides of class conflict and "anarchy." Although the young Brooks had little use for Arnoldian culture as a reinforcement for capitalist social relations, he agreed that culture had a centralizing role to play in society, without which nations would lose their moral compass and practical activity would degenerate into philistine commercialism.[46]

The alternative view of culture that Brooks discovered in English radicalism allowed him to channel the critique of the industrial devastation of traditional communities implicit in the Tory and Arnoldian strategies into a call for a socialist cultural community. Late nineteenth-century radicals like John Ruskin and William Morris had paved the way for such a change, retaining the moral and communitarian implications of culture in Victorian thought while severing its connections with elitist social control. As a haven for pre- and anticapitalist virtues of cooperation, mutuality, and localism, the English idea of culture had influenced Brooks's discussion of childhood and tradition in *The Wine of the Puritans*; the more romantic connotations of the opposition between culture and society, which contrasted the intuitive spirituality of the former to the manipulative utilitarianism of the latter, also found obvious parallels in Brooks's dialectic of the soul and society. Even the American variants of this tradition of cultural theory, with their emphasis on self-culture and moral uplift, might be seen as containing an analogous critique of the industrial division of labor, since genteel commentary held that culture would give individuals the moral autonomy and intellectual discipline necessary to democratic self-government. For these reasons, Brooks was more than ready for the radicals' revision of English cultural criticism by the time he arrived in London in the fall of 1913.[47]

The most obvious place for Brooks to turn to understand London's left intelligentsia was the Fabian Society, which gave a focus to the exciting and stormy debates between the various factions of the English Left. Brooks seized almost immediately upon the quasi-mystical elements of Fabian rhetoric as a corollary to his own thinking about socialism and cultural renewal. Fabians such as Edward Pease and Sidney and Beatrice Webb were deeply indebted to Auguste Comte's "Religion of Humanity," and they often described socialism as a modern religion, arguing that a period of spiritual conversion would have to precede political action if social solidarity were ever to replace capitalist competition. As in Comte's positivism, this Fabian mystique of religious solidarity revealed a genuine hostility to any participatory politics, let alone the political factionalism of parliamentary liberalism. Also like Comte, the Fabians adopted industrial progress as a secularized Providence so that spiritual preparation took the form of adapting social theory to the "laws" of historical development. With economic centralization and the industrial division of labor accepted as irreversible steps toward socialism, the primacy of spirit and ideas meant in practice a political revolution from above, in which Fabian planners reconstructed society in accordance with their newly scientific religion. Despite all the talk of cultural and spiritual regeneration, Fabianism looked to the administrative state to provide the basis for a new social unity beyond competition and ideological conflict. Brooks absorbed the quasi-religious language of spiritual solidarity that pervaded Fabianism but failed to recognize that its vision of cultural centralization had nothing in common with the freewheeling community he so admired in western radicalism. In the Fabian worldview, culture would guide socialist transformation only after it took on the repressive features Brooks abhorred in society.[48]

Brooks grafted the spiritual rhetoric of Fabianism, the implications of which he only partly understood, onto the antimodernist radicalism he gleaned from reading Tolstoy, Ruskin, and most of all Morris. These thinkers also saw the revival of a communal ethos as central to socialist politics, but they entirely rejected the specialization of knowledge, the scientistic cant of progress, and the statism that were so integral to the Fabian mind. Morris's radicalism had as its goal the abolition of the industrial division of labor and the restoration, on a cooperative basis, of the artisanal mode of production. Invoking the critical content of culture in English discourse, Morris predicted that "one day we shall win back Art, that is to say the pleasure of life; win back Art again to our daily labour." In his political and cultural criticism of the 1880s and 1890s, Morris insisted that the craft tradition, which "used the whole of a man for the production of a piece of goods, and not small portions of many men," would have to inform a qualitatively new organization of labor if socialism were to mean more than a change in administrators. By making the reintegration of art and labor, of culture and society, his highest goal, Morris offered Brooks a radical lineage that both sought an organic synthesis of aesthetic, moral, and practical experience and challenged the fundamental premises of industrial capitalism.[49]

What Brooks was slower to see, however, was that Morris had formulated his radicalism in opposition to what he called the "quasi-machinery of socialism" in the Fabians' statist reform. Morris consistently argued against turning over political power to social planners, who substituted "business-like administration" for "the old Whig muddle of *laissez-faire* backed up by coercion," a project that ran directly counter to his own vision of a conscious association of producers skilled in craft knowledge. For Morris, a radical politics would have to begin by encouraging ordinary people to recover the skills that had been usurped by administrators and use them to construct a socialist community. Where the Fabians looked to social science and a technical elite to restore the unity of preindustrial cultures, Morris held that such unity had to come from below as workers reclaimed their own heritage as craftsmen and citizens. In turning to Morrisite and Fabian ideas to give his criticism a political dimension it previously lacked, Brooks was drawing on movements with fundamentally divergent strategies in politics and culture.[50]

These unresolved contradictions in Brooks's socialism found expression in his 1915 study *The World of H. G. Wells*. Despite Wells's stormy relationship with the Fabian Society, his administrative socialism was fully in keeping with the main tenets of Fabianism. If anything, Wells took Fabian principles to their logical conclusion, proposing that the state collectivize the family and use eugenics to organize reproduction along scientific lines. Brooks's reading of Wellsian socialism was idiosyncratic, to say the least. In Brooks's book, Wells emerged as the heir to both the Tory and Arnoldian traditions in English cultural criticism, and his political theory took on a decidedly Morrisite cast. *The World of H. G. Wells* told more about Brooks's confused political position, with its amalgam of antimodernist and technocratic radicalisms, than it did about Wells's own ideas. Brooks may have praised "the remarkable tendency in Wells to find good in the old humanistic Tory, as distinguished from the modern, bureaucratic Liberal, view of life"; he may have seen Wellsian socialism as "a natural outgrowth of those 'best things that have been thought and said in the world' "; but he never successfully reconciled Wells's thought to his own suspicion of cultural modernity. Even as he took up the progressivist cause, Brooks's doubts resurfaced in his text, revealing his own ambivalence about his new-found political faith.[51]

Wells's importance for Brooks lay in his voluntarist defense of ethics and consciousness in the transition to socialism, which Brooks preferred to the economic determinism of the orthodox Left. Moreover, Brooks saw in Wellsian socialism "a personal and mystical conception of life" that gave priority to moral conduct and "a special religious attitude" in politics. Brooks noted approvingly Wells's interest in religion as a means of social integration, and he praised Wells's novels for reintroducing the traditional religious problem of sin as a conflict between society and the individual, with sin now defined as "any sort of voluntary self-isolation" from the social good. Much like Bourne, Wells and Brooks adopted an idealized religious universalism as the model for a socialist community, while relinquishing the conflict between sacred and secular realms that had historically afforded the individual a safe haven from the claims of social authority. It followed, then, that the prophetic role of the clergy would find a counterpart in the socialist future, and Brooks was quick to see Wells's aristocratic ideal of a "Samurai, or New Republican," as a successor to Nietzsche's Superman, Carlyle's Hero, or Confucius's Superior Man. Wells had escaped economic determinism by investing socialist hopes in a prophetic nobility whose moral righteousness already embodied the folkways of a new society.[52]

Brooks was notably silent about the undemocratic nature of this theory of socialist transformation. Nor was he aware of its close affinities with the technocratic collectivism he criticized in Fabian thought. Brooks agreed with Wells that the "excessive conservatism" of the Fabians "toward the existing machinery of government," without any compensatory mobilization of popular support, "has tended to throw the whole force of the socialist movement into a bureaucratic regime of small-minded experts." Sounding less like Wells than Morris, Brooks condemned Fabianism for tending toward "a socialization of the poor without a corresponding socialization of the rich; toward a more and more marked chasm between the regimented workers and the free employers." In these passages, Brooks echoed Morris and other radical critics of Fabianism such as Hilaire Belloc and G. K. Chesterton, who saw in the Fabians' vision of an administrative politics the ascendancy of the "Servile State." Wells was far closer to Fabianism than Brooks allowed, and Brooks's unwillingness to confront the authoritarian tendencies of Wells's thought suggests that he too had not fully assimilated the radicals' critique of Fabianism. The prophetic ideal that he admired in Wells's socialist aristocracy appeared as a professional elite of technicians and engineers in Wells's novels. The message Brooks took away from those books was that "democracy, as we know it, will pass away," once a new class of mechanics, engineers, doctors, and other professionals restructured society according to "a self-wrought scientific education and view of life." The lost community of religiously grounded societies would revive after "the power of society" fell into the hands of "the only indispensable element" in modern society: "the scientifically trained, constructive middle class." Brooks's unstable mixture of Morrisite and Fabian ideas had found a peculiar convergence in Wells, whom Brooks used first to attack the Fabians' "Servile State" only to resurrect that state in an aesthetic and spiritualized form.[53]

Nevertheless, the careful reader could not miss the undertow of caution that swept through Brooks's book, especially in the passages in which he discussed Wells as a literary artist. "Wells is devoid of historical imagination," he wrote at one point, with the result that Wells's characters lacked any relation to the concrete world of human experience and interactions. "We live in two worlds—the primary world of vivid personal realities and the secondary world of our human background. It is the secondary world that anchors us in time and space; the primary world we carry with us as part of ourselves. In Wells there is no secondary world, no human background, no sense of abiding relations. It is his philosophy of life and the quality of his men and women to be experimental in a plastic scheme. His range is very small: the same figures reappear constantly." In the context of Brooks's thinking since *The Wine of the Puritans*, this critique of Wells was devastating. If Wells failed to engage "the secondary world that anchors us in time and space," then he had abandoned all tradition, including that of culture, as understood in English criticism. It was that "secondary world" that Brooks had looked to socialism to provide, and it was that "human background" and "sense of abiding relations" that had been lost to the factory system and the bitter aroma of a stale idealism. Brooks's book contained an indictment of Wellsian socialism that Brooks himself did not grasp: Wells—like his Fabian rivals—had sacrificed culture and tradition to the "primary world" of scientific technique and expertise.[54]

Instead of pursuing this promising line of argument, Brooks ended his book with the claim that it was the very absence of a historical dimension to Wellsian socialism that made it so relevant to American conditions. Because Wells's mind was, like that of Americans, "a disinherited mind, not connected with tradition," it could provide them with the critical self-consciousness absent in American culture. Wells could serve as a mirror to the United States, giving American society a reflection of itself in literature. For this reason, Brooks wrote, "there is, I think, a special sort of connection between Wells and America." At this point, Brooks retreated from *Wine*'s conclusions about the consequences of modernity for American life. In *Wine* he had denounced the absence of collective traditions as the source of the superficiality and rootlessness that afflicted both high and low culture. Now he saw in Wells's future-oriented socialist novels, with their engineer prophets and scientific utopias, a surrogate for American traditions. The answer to the emptiness of modern life would be a politics and culture of the future, a science-fiction socialism that would crystallize American consciousness in awareness of itself. Like Dewey, Wells and Brooks looked to the very social forces that had undermined organic cultures to resurrect them on a progressive basis. The "new spirit" that Wells expressed in his novels may be "entirely irrelevant to the values of life as we know them," Brooks admitted, but "it may in the end prove to have contributed to an altogether fresh basis for human values." Modernity would prove its own remedy.[55]

In the closing pages of his book, Brooks returned to his goal of overcoming the atomism of American life. "Society must be brought into some kind of coherence before morality, art and religion can once more attain any real meaning," he explained, repeating his persistent hopes for an organic synthesis of culture and social experience. Only now Brooks put less stock in a great writer like Whitman to achieve that synthesis than he did in "an enlightened individualism, outside the recognized institutions," which would foster an oppositional culture in an organized intelligentsia. "The rudiments of the Socialist State," however "falsely based," were to be found "in the Rockefeller Institute, the Carnegie and Russell Sage Foundations, the endowed universities and bureaus of research, and in the type of men they breed." Having reconciled himself to the Enlightenment's destruction of premodern cultures, Brooks now found the first glimmers of American cultural renewal in the research-and-development wing of modern industry. Wells's mirror to the American mind had become a distorted funhouse mirror, where Brooks saw the Rockefeller Institute reflected as a socialist community.[56]

Although he drew on very different intellectual traditions, Brooks had arrived at a program of cultural renewal that anticipated Bourne's "Moral Equivalent for Universal Military Service." Both men recognized in their own lives and in those of their countrymen the effects of a divorce of traditional ideals from modern social practice, and both men located the source of that divorce in the repudiation of premodern cultures that began in Enlightenment thought and climaxed in the nineteenth-century factory system. A chasm separated spirit and society in their personal experience, just as it did culture and practical life in the experiences of most Americans. Although their reverence for tradition could lead to a dreamy aestheticism coupled with pessimism—as in Brooks's *Wine*—their turn to pragmatism and Fabianism for modern substitutes for organic traditions undermined the historical dimension of their criticism, once the discourse of "progress" and "efficiency" replaced any serious consideration of how past traditions might inform new values in culture and everyday life. In their early work, Bourne and Brooks oscillated between extremes of traditionalism and progressivism that obscured their search for historically grounded alternatives to a degraded culture and community. History too often gave way to the brooding nostalgia of *Wine*; a visionary sense of new opportunities became the futuristic prophecy of Bourne's educational essays and Brooks's study of Wells. In their early work, these critics lost track of the subtle dialectic between historical understanding and critical vision that William Morris articulated when he answered the charge that he was a backward-looking romantic. "As for romance, what does romance mean?" he asked his critics. "I have heard people miscalled for being romantic, but what romance means is the capacity for a true conception of history, a power of making the past part of the present."[57]

In Brooks's *America's Coming-of-Age* and Bourne's "Trans-national America," these two critics finally marshaled the "power of making the past part of the present" and put it to work in their most coherent statements of cultural criticism. After a period of confusion, both men found their voices as writers and articulated an ambitious project of American cultural regeneration. In retrospect, their achievements—now familiar staples of American intellectual history—are remarkable, given that they so closely followed works that revealed their authors' weakness for an unthinking Progressivism. *America's Coming-of-Age* appeared the same year as Brooks's book on Wells. Bourne published "Trans-national America" in the *Atlantic* in July 1916, the very month "A Moral Equivalent for Universal Military Service" appeared in the *New Republic*. Nonetheless, the two essays were marked advances over these other works, as well as over their predecessors. Along with Whitman's *Democratic Vistas*, they stand as the foremost documents of a radical canon of American cultural criticism, wedding a call to revive native traditions of cultural democracy to a promise of a new community of rational discourse and fellowship. Brooks and Bourne heightened the tension between history and vision in their analyses, maintaining a taut energy in their writing that they hoped would jolt American life out of its modern slump. Acquiescence in present realities would give way to a new appreciation of future possibilities, once tradition and imagination endowed the American mind with the potential for critical self-reflection. Culture would lose its identification with privilege as it became the very stuff of a democratic community life. Most important, personality would flourish, and the soul would be released from its social tomb, once men and women began to live in a conscious fellowship with one another. The future had finally taken shape in Brooks's and Bourne's thought as something more than a mirror of modernity. "All our idealisms must be those of future social goals in which all can participate," Bourne proclaimed, "the good life of personality lived in the environment of the Beloved Community."[58]

Both essays began with the premise that a "focal centre" was "the first requisite of a great culture," as Brooks put it in *America's Coming-of-Age*. That assumption led Brooks and Bourne to their now familiar critique of American culture as rootless and decentered, though they had never made their case as eloquently as they did now. "America is like a vast Sargasso sea," wrote Brooks, "a prodigious welter of unconscious life, swept by ground-swells of half-conscious emotion." Its art and ideas had never "been worked into an organism" so that Americans experienced life as "an unchecked, uncharted, unorganized vitality like that of the first chaos." The problem was not that American society lacked energy, but rather that, lacking any consistent body of critical thought, its energy exploded in a destructive commercialism that ravaged the human mind as much as it did the natural landscape.[59]

Bourne picked up this theme, arguing that the ideal of assimilating immigrants into the "melting pot" of American culture had resulted in reality in a "centrifugal, anarchical" society, one that divested immigrants of their cohesive traditions only to cast them off into the fringes of American life. "America has as yet no impelling, integrating force," Bourne wrote, that would have given immigrants and Anglo-Saxons alike a meaning to life. The result was a nation without either high or folk cultures, where consciousness survived as an adjunct to commerce.

> Just so surely as we tend to disintegrate these nuclei of nationalistic culture do we tend to create hordes of men and women without a spiritual country, cultural outlaws, without taste, without standards but those of the mob. We sentence them to live on the most rudimentary planes of American life. . . . Those who came to find liberty achieve only license. They become the flotsam and jetsam of American life, the downward undertow of our civilization with its leering cheapness and falseness of taste and spiritual outlook, the absence of mind and sincere feeling which we see in our slovenly towns, our vapid moving pictures, our popular novels, and in the vacuous faces of the crowds on the city street. This is the cultural wreckage of our time, and it is from the fringes of the Anglo-Saxon as well as the other stocks that it falls.

Culture, as understood in English criticism and in the sense of spiritual wholeness Bourne admired in France, had become its opposite in industrial America. Instead of safeguarding the values of spirit and mutuality from industrial society, culture now mirrored the mindless frenzy of social life. Industrialism had manufactured a commercial substitute for America's missing cultural center. Mass culture—with its "leering cheapness and falseness of taste and spiritual outlook"—had taken hold so easily in the United States because there existed no residue of pre-industrial culture to resist it.[60]

Industrialization, in this argument, had widened the gap between culture and practical life that dated back to Puritan New England. The first Anglo-Saxon settlers remained "slavishly imitative of the mother country" in cultural tastes even as they devoted their energies to "the objective conquest of material resources." That split between an increasingly archaic Anglophile culture and the pioneers' assault on nature is what Brooks sought to capture in his celebrated opposition of "Highbrow" and "Lowbrow" in the opening pages of *America's Coming-of-Age*. Brooks was neither contrasting high and low cultures nor calling attention to a division within American literature between "paleface" effeminate novelists and robust, masculine "redskins," as later commentators have argued. Nor was he simply echoing the categories of George Santayana's 1911 address on the "genteel tradition," which in any case dealt with a dichotomy in American thought, not within American society. Indeed, Santayana was influenced by Brooks's *Wine*, which had been published three years before. Rather, Brooks's antithesis of "Highbrow" and "Lowbrow" grew out of his exposure to Morris's critique of the division of culture and practical life under capitalism. For Brooks, the separation of theory and practice was a social, as well as an intellectual, phenomenon, which had degraded both realms of modern life: "on the one hand, a quite unclouded, quite unhypocritical assumption of transcendent theory ('high ideas'), on the other a simultaneous acceptance of catchpenny realities." There existed no "genial middle ground" of cultural experience, no alternative to the extremes of "desiccated culture" and "stark utility," that might serve a centered and democratic community life.[61]

Yet Brooks and Bourne did not attribute all of Americans' cultural failings to the social division of theory and practice. Intellectuals, especially the genteel critics of the late nineteenth century, were to blame for fostering a cult of Anglo-Saxon elite culture and for ignoring the two currents that might have coalesced into a vibrant American tradition— the indigenous renaissance of New England thought, which found its fullest expression in Whitman, and the folk cultures of the "new immigrants" from central and eastern Europe. The Arnoldian ideal of elite culture as a means of social control and moral uplift had lost its appeal for Brooks and Bourne, even as they continued to adhere to its theory of self-culture as ethical training. The Mugwump hope of "somehow lifting the 'Lowbrow' elements to the level of the 'Highbrow' elements" could not comprehend, Brooks charged, "that Tammany has quite as much to teach Good Government as Good Government has to teach Tammany." The tyranny of Anglophile conventions "unconsciously belittled" what little there existed of a "distinctively American spirit," which Bourne found in Whitman, Emerson, and William James. Genteel culture had so removed itself from the main currents of American life as to become an impediment to genuine cultural expression. By doting on the relics of aristocratic England, genteel critics had doomed their own project of moral regeneration to irrelevance.[62]

When Brooks and Bourne turned to their own programs for cultural renewal, they borrowed liberally from the pragmatic theory of knowledge as experience, which they now stripped of the associations with scientific technique it had in Dewey's work. A critical intellect would have to shape and inform practice, thereby ending the opposition of Highbrow and Lowbrow, but that intellect would itself have to explore existing social conditions. "Let us work with the forces that are at work," Bourne wrote of America's immigrant cultures. "Already we are living this cosmopolitan America. What we need is everywhere a vivid consciousness of the new ideal." A similar understanding of the need for a new relationship between theory and practice shaped Brooks's analysis of the achievements and failures of Whitman, the writer who first "gave us the sense of something organic in American life." Unlike Bourne, Brooks had little use for Emerson, whose Transcendentalism he used to illustrate—as he had in *Wine*—the philosophical consequences of the divorce of theory and practice. Whitman was another case altogether, the only poet whom Brooks felt had conveyed a middle range of American experience: "Whitman—how else can I express it?—precipitated the American character. All those things that had been separate, self-sufficient, incoordinate—action, theory, idealism, business—he cast into a crucible; and they emerged, harmonious and molten, in a fresh democratic ideal, based upon the whole personality." But Whitman had only partly captured the ideal of experience Brooks was searching for. He was too "catholic and passive" before his immediate environment; his "instinct was to affirm everything," rather than subject the world to rational criticism. Whitman's yea-saying mysticism gave him an insight into the flesh and blood of American life that Transcendentalism never achieved, but it lacked the element of critique that would make culture a transformative force in society.[63]

Brooks and Bourne had taken from pragmatism its emphasis on critical discourse, while jettisoning its fascination with technical rationality. This was a substantial advance over their previous work, as was their new sensitivity to the ways in which traditional cultures had as much—if not more—to offer as examples of consensual democracy as did the scientific community. "Tammany Hall" had so much to offer "Good Government" because the ethnic cultures that supported machine politics had a substantive rationality of their own, which Brooks and Bourne now saw as resources for a renewed democracy. Like Whitman's holistic view of American life, ethnic communities anticipated a new center to American culture, one in which traditional bonds of shared experience reinforced modern ones of rational inquiry. Bourne's ideal of a "Beloved Community," a phrase he borrowed from Josiah Royce but adapted to his own purposes, fully captured the vision he shared with

Brooks of a regenerated American society: one in which all could participate in the creation of "future social goals." Here was a community that Americans could rationally shape and also love, a form of experience that engaged their capacities as moderns while fulfilling the functions of tradition.

The Beloved Community ideal harked back to Bourne's and Brooks's interest in a revived universal church, with one essential difference. In "Socialism and the Catholic Ideal" and *The World of H. G. Wells*, the modern socialist church integrated spirit and society, giving a scientifically organized society the religious authority of the medieval church. By equating spiritual fellowship with a culture of expertise, these works subsumed the free expression of personality in an undemocratic hierarchy of technical elites. A technocratic *Gemeinschaft*, combining the most authoritarian tendencies in traditional and modern cultures, lurked behind these earlier portraits of a new church. Now Brooks and Bourne reintroduced the tension between spirit and social conditions within which personality might flourish. Though they still held to their goal of bridging the gap between culture and society, they now recognized the friction between thought and social practice as a source of creativity and personal growth. The relationship between Morris's writings and the artisanal culture of the English working class was for Brooks a perfect example of the "muscular and earthy sense of opposition under which personality becomes aware of itself and grows with a certain richness." Morris had found in the artisanal experience a fund of resistance to the factory system; once his ideas on the subject took shape in literary works saturated with his own personality, they then shaped the consciousness of English workers "and gave them how rich and how adequate a reason to turn over this world of ours, as a spade turns over a clod of earth." If culture were immediately equated with community life, as in Bourne's and Brooks's modern church, it would have little to contribute to personalities engaged in reshaping their world. Theory and practice would be joined, in this new formula for cultural renewal, only after intellectuals exploited the tensions between the two, honing their ideas into a critical discourse of social transformation.[64]

This new understanding of the relationship between culture and society had significant political implications for both critics. In the past, they had flirted with a Progressive politics in which intellectuals assumed power as a professional priesthood. The reconciliation of theory and practice had taken place, in their minds, on the terrain of an administrative socialism, with technical expertise replacing the self-governing democratic polity. Now both men took care to distinguish between cultural renewal and socialist change, even while they insisted that both were part of the quest for a Beloved Community. The creation of a "middle plane between vaporous idealism and self-interested practicality" in culture would have to precede any political transformation. "It is of no use to talk about Reform," Brooks warned. "Society will be very obedient when the myriad personalities that compose it have, and are aware that they have, an object in living." A cultural revolution would have to precede any political revolution, not only because it would ensure a qualitative change in power relations but also because cultural renewal would safeguard personality from illegitimate political authority. In effect, Brooks and Bourne recovered the conflict between the sacred and secular that had disappeared in their early visions of a new church and gave it a new form. Politics and culture were, of course, deeply intertwined, but they were not identical. The realization of spirit and consciousness in a revived democracy depended on intellectuals' maintaining that distinction and attending to the enrichment of American cultural life before they joined their countrymen in political action.[65]

Bourne's "Trans-national America" and a subsequent address, "The Jew and Trans-national America," clarified this new position on culture and politics. Bourne blasted the wartime advocates of the melting pot for longing for "an integrated and disciplined America" that reached synthesis through coercion. By contrast, his transnationalist community would centralize American culture into a new cosmopolitanism by first releasing the potential of the nation's ethnic and racial subcultures. This decentralist pluralism was the only democratic route to a "genuine integrity, a wholeness and soundness of enthusiasm and purpose," that would free American life from the polarity of Highbrow and Lowbrow. This opposition of a democratic cultural unity to coercive uniformity was also the theme of Bourne's lecture before the Harvard Menorah Society on Jewish-American culture, in which he endorsed the Zionist movement as the embodiment of his own dream of transnationality. Zionism allowed American Jews to weigh the claims of "cultural allegiance and political allegiance," with their Jewish national identity transcending the political boundaries of the American state. Loyalty to a cultural community ultimately superseded allegiance to any nation-state, and it became clear in Bourne's mind that intellectuals would have to clarify their own cultural loyalties before they committed themselves to the policies of statecraft. By acting as interpreters between ethnic folk cultures and the high culture of the modern university, intellectuals could play a pivotal role in the federation of national cultures in a new American community. This "enterprise of integration into which we can all pour ourselves" was the "work for a younger *intelligentsia* of America." The creation of a democratic culture would both shore up personality against the present demands of the militarist state and nourish a new politics of community for the future.[66]

Surprisingly, neither Brooks nor Bourne ever mentioned religion as a middle ground for American experience, despite the religiously charged language of their criticism. After all, religion had traditionally mediated between everyday life and transcendent meaning, and it continued to do so in the ethnic communities these critics admired. In their work, words like *culture*, *experience*, and *personality* became secular equivalents of religious experience. Experience was culture incarnate in society, a form of practical activity that resonated with some larger spiritual purpose. These critics' socialism derived from their spiritual longings, which found no response in an industrial capitalist society. Brooks condemned capitalism because it provided few opportunities for self-fulfillment in a cooperative enterprise that had meaning beyond the self. Capitalism had reduced all goals to self-interest, stifling the human drive for self-transcendence that alone gave meaning to life. "One cannot have personality, one cannot have the expressions of personality so long as the end of society is an impersonal end like the accumulation of money." Culture—now much more than high art and letters—would restore to life the transcendent goals that capitalism denied.[67]

These essays had another particularly religious dimension. They were secular jeremiads that owed much in rhetorical style to the Puritan culture their authors attacked. In these first expressions of their mature criticism, Bourne and Brooks surveyed a degenerate present, recalled the faded glories of a preindustrial past, and looked forward to a future regeneration of their society. Caught in the crossfire of a criticism that drew on history and a visionary imagination, the present moment appeared exhausted and yet rich with potential for renewal. As prophets of a new democratic culture, Brooks and Bourne judged the present from the perspective of a future they called the Beloved Community. "It must be a future America, on which all can unite, which pulls us irresistibly toward it, as we understand each other more warmly," Bourne predicted. A future "in which all can participate" would redeem the present, and a culture of shared experience would regenerate practice and ultimately politics. *America's Coming-of-Age* and "Trans-national

America" drew their power from a style that recalled a prophetic tradition with deep roots in American history and inspired readers with a transcendent vision of democratic community.[68]

These essays were also a significant landmark in Brooks's and Bourne's intellectual development, a sign that their own critical faculties had fully "come of age." After many false steps, they had formulated a project of cultural renewal and socialist politics that combined the critical reason of modern thought with the traditional loyalties of folk communities. That project gave Brooks and Bourne a way out of the paralyzing opposition of spirit and society that plagued their earliest work. It envisioned a way of overcoming the industrial division of theory and practice without succumbing to the progressivist temptation to remake theory in the image of scientific technique. It also gave these critics a method for bringing the virtues of English and French civilization to bear on a new American cosmopolitanism. A culture of lived experience was the only possible source for genuine self-realization: the individual would reach full potential as part of a collective enterprise of social transformation. Conscious experience would serve as the meeting ground for tradition and modernity, Brooks and Bourne argued, embracing both the customary bonds of settled communities and the consensual culture of scientific reason. It would provide a field of tension between the claims of culture and society, refining both for a new community life. An American spiritual and cultural renaissance, grounded in a full understanding of human experience, would lay the basis for a radically democratic politics.

4

Spiritual Pioneers

*Ours is the first generation of Americans consciously
engaged in spiritual pioneering.*
—WALDO FRANK,
Our America

The story of the *Seven Arts*, the journal that served as the organ for
the Young Americans' criticism from November 1916 to October
1917, has become a familiar staple of American intellectual history
in this century. The journal's close identification with an emerging generation of modern artists and writers, its declaration "that we are living
in the first days of a renascent period," and its publication of Bourne's
searing attacks on John Dewey and other prowar Progressives have
made it, in retrospect, an icon of the promise of American culture in the
1910s. The magazine was the most prominent expression of the hopes
for a democratic indigenous culture that inspired the entire Greenwich
Village "Little Renaissance"—from the Armory Show and the circle of
modernist artists around Alfred Stieglitz to the socialist writers and
artists associated with the Paterson Pageant and the *Masses*.[1]

The reputation of the *Seven Arts* is also connected to the circumstances surrounding the magazine's demise, when its wealthy patron,
Annette Rankine, aghast at antiwar articles by Bourne, John Reed, and
others, withdrew her financial subsidy and soon after took her own
life. The events following the journal's collapse added to the legend:
Bourne's tragic death in the winter of 1918, a victim of the influenza
epidemic that killed millions in Europe and the United States; the publication of Brooks's *Letters and Leadership* and Frank's *Our America*,
two books that summed up the *Seven Arts* project in cultural criticism;
the subsequent scattering of the journal's writers to such publications as
the *Dial* and the *Freeman*, which attempted but ultimately failed to
carry on the *Seven Arts*'s intellectual agenda; and the rise to prominence
of Harold Stearns and Paul Rosenfeld, secondary figures at the journal,
as major critics of the 1920s, and of Lewis Mumford, who followed the

Seven Arts religiously as a young man and who became its principal intellectual heir. When the magazine folded in October 1917, its farewell editorial explained its goal as "understanding, interpreting and expressing that *latent America,* that *potential America* which we believed lay hidden under our commercial-industrial national organization: that America of youth and aspiration: that America which desires a richer life, a finer fellowship, a flowering of mature and seasoned personalities." The posthumous idealization of the *Seven Arts* reflects a widespread sentiment, on the part of its survivors and historians, that the journal was itself part of a *"potential America"* crushed in the stampede to total war, antiradical hysteria, and "normalcy."[2]

It would be a mistake to view the *Seven Arts* simply as a forum for cultural nationalism, however. The magazine's promise of an American cultural renaissance was not an aesthetic counterpart to the ideal of a homogeneous political nationalism that infused the pages of the *New Republic* in its early years and inspired a generation of Progressive intellectuals and activists. To begin with, the editors of the *Seven Arts* were deeply committed to a cosmopolitan vision that admitted far greater variations in American cultural life than did Herbert Croly and other mainstream American Progressives. As Thomas Bender has noted, the magazine was "the first example of an ethnic collaboration, Christian and Jew, that sought to speak for an American national culture embracing 'different national strains.'" Of the five major writers for the journal, three—James Oppenheim, Paul Rosenfeld, and Frank—were Jewish, and the other two—Brooks and Bourne—were Protestants in flight from Protestantism. All drew on a variety of sources, both domestic and foreign, for a critical perspective on their country's culture. They looked as much to Marx, Morris, Nietzsche, and Freud for support for their project as they did to Emerson, Thoreau, Whitman, and James. David A. Hollinger has argued that their interest in an American artistic revival was part of a broader "transnational" cosmopolitanism that sought "to transcend the limitations of any and all particularisms in order to achieve a more complete human experience and a more complete understanding of that experience."[3]

If it is incorrect to describe these writers strictly as cultural nationalists, it is also not enough to argue that their cultural criticism focused exclusively on literary and artistic matters at the expense of political and social matters, or that their socialist rhetoric was nothing more than the wistful musings of a naive "lyrical left." The Young Americans' hopes for a democratic American culture rested squarely on Bourne's and

Brooks's early attack on the industrial division of labor. Their indictment of the genteel tradition in art and letters and their insistence on a
culture grounded in experience grew out of their analysis of the fatal
division between theory and practice in American society. Many years
later, Frank recalled the ethos that lay behind the radicalism of the
Seven Arts: "We were all sworn foes of capitalism, not because we knew
it would not work, but because we judged it, even in success, to be lethal
to the human spirit." The *Seven Arts* critics were undeniably interested
in fostering an indigenous American culture, but an exclusive focus on
their cultural nationalism misses their unique insights into modern society and the subtle relationship between their cultural criticism and
their political radicalism. Their calls for a democratic culture of "self-
expression" were intimately connected to the critique of the factory
system they had learned from Ruskin and Morris. An indigenous cultural renaissance was in their view impossible without the democratization of work and practical life.[4]

Above all else, the *Seven Arts* writers championed the ideals of personality and self-fulfillment that had preoccupied Bourne and Brooks
in their youth, putting them at the center of their vision of political
cultural renewal. They contrasted personality to both the autonomous,
self-reliant individual, whose passing was part of the shift to an industrial corporate society, and the "human herd" organized in hierarchical
bureaucracies and business institutions. Individuals would find self-fulfillment in democratic groups, not in privatistic withdrawal or in the
prescribed functions of the factory or the wartime state. Bourne's goal of
a "good life of personality lived in the environment of the Beloved
Community" rejected atomistic individualism and the coercive cohesion of industrial capitalism because both stifled the possibility of conscious construction of a humane social order. Bourne elaborated on this
position in a 1918 polemic against the cultural conservatism of Stuart
Sherman:

> There are not only the two orders—the jungle anarchy of impulse
> and the organized rationality of conventional institutions and ta-
> boos. It is exactly the discovery of this younger generation that
> convention is no more rational than the jungle, that the human
> herd, capitalized into an institution, is no less cruel than the preda-
> tory individual. The intelligent, veritably humanistic, personal plane
> can only be reached by transcending both the animal and the insti-
> tutional. In other words, personality is a struggle against both raw

"Nature" and that organized society in which Mr. Sherman so bravely takes his stand.

Bourne's statement is representative of the entire project of the Young Americans in this period. Harold Stearns, an occasional member of the *Seven Arts* circle, made the same point when he wrote that "it is delightfully ironical that no nation is so constantly talking about personality as we are," yet "respect for individual human personality has with us reached about its lowest point." The realization of personality would require neither "schools for 'self-expression,' and 'self-development,'" nor "futile rebellion by the younger generation," but what Stearns called "a complete transvaluation of values." Like Bourne, he saw personality as the outcome of a politics stressing "decentralisation and wide and deep variations" and of "the vivid and direct reminder of real values by the creative artist." True self-fulfillment grew out of artistic experience and participation in a democratic civic culture.[5]

The Young Americans' emphasis on the primacy of personality took on a distinctly political character in the middle and late 1910s, as the industrial centralization first evident in the factory culminated in the creation of Wilson's wartime state. In the specific context of World War I, the assertion of the need for attention to cultural and psychological issues in the pages of the *Seven Arts* had important political implications. Frank made this point explicitly in 1919, in his book *Our America*, in which he repeatedly opposed the demands of spiritual knowledge and cultural creation to those of an industrial civilization that drained human beings of their capacity for democratic self-fulfillment. "Ours is the first generation of Americans consciously engaged in spiritual pioneering," he wrote, contrasting his group's cultural explorations with the past exploitation of the American natural frontier. Political radicalism would have to advance into spiritual and intellectual frontiers to gather the moral and cultural materials for a democratic community life. As Brooks wrote in the *Seven Arts*, a new politics and culture first required "a program for the conservation of our spiritual resources."[6]

In the social and political landscape of wartime America, the reassertion of spirit and culture was a precondition of political action, a protest against the convergence of forces "lethal to the human spirit." The decision by the chief contributors to the *Seven Arts* to stress "self-expression" during the war was neither a flight from politics into romantic fantasy nor a nostalgic reassertion of individualism, but rather an argument that a new radicalism required deep cultural and psychological roots if it were to challenge the centralization of power in American society in the twentieth century. It was this historical terrain that made the concluding sentence of Frank's *Our America*—"And in a dying world, creation is revolution"—something more than therapy for intellectuals or empty boasting. The hardening of politics and social life into an objective environment, as unconscious as the frontier once conquered by Puritans and their successors, meant that a truly radical politics would begin with "spiritual pioneering."[7]

Forty years after the *Seven Arts* folded, Van Wyck Brooks recalled that its "real creator" was Waldo Frank. Brooks attributed the magazine's opening manifesto—with its confident announcement of an American cultural renaissance—to Frank, and there is evidence of Frank's voice and vision in virtually every issue of its brief existence. *America's Coming-of-Age* may have provided the journal with a foundation for its broad critique of culture and politics, but it was Frank who gave that critique its particular form of expression. James Oppenheim was the titular editor; in retrospect, though, even he had to admit that he "wasn't 'culturally' there with my colleagues." As associate editor, Frank provided the magazine with a prophetic stance that owed as much to Nietzsche and Tolstoy as it did to Whitman and with an enthusiasm about new currents in modern art and literature that escaped Brooks's notice. In large part, the *Seven Arts* was Frank's personal creation and a vehicle for his unique synthesis of religious prophecy, neoromantic aesthetics, and political radicalism.[8]

Frank arrived at his ambitious intellectual stance at an astonishingly young age. As an adolescent he kept notebooks full of aphorisms, observations, and precocious statements of his personal philosophy. "All the books that I shall write shall be proofs of God," he resolved, a credo that he repeated in his notebooks again and again during his lifetime. This pledge reflected Frank's belief that he had made a special compact with God to reveal His Word in his own writing. Frank's sense of calling drew him toward speculative philosophy and theology at the same time that he studied literature and tried his hand at writing fiction. As a student at Yale, he wrote the philosopher William Ernest Hocking for a reading list, describing his interests as "philosophy of religion and history and general spiritual development," which prompted Hocking to ask, "heavens, man,—what have you left out?" Frank read widely during his four years at Yale and managed to hold down a position as a drama critic for a local paper and complete a manuscript titled "The Spirit of Modern French Letters" before graduating with both a bachelor's and a master's degree in 1911.[9]

Frank's work on nineteenth-century literature reveals the direction of his thinking in his early years. In its introductory chapter, he adopted the romantic view that great writers embody the spirit of their age and argued for an examination of the "soul" or "spiritual ground" implicit in the works of Balzac, Baudelaire, and other French authors. Yale University Press accepted "The Spirit of Modern French Letters" for publication in 1912, but Frank withdrew the manuscript at the last moment. Frank remained committed to the writer's role as cultural oracle, but he reworked this romantic ideal in terms of his understanding of his own writing as "proofs of God." In his memoirs, he recalled that he was trying to move beyond the debate between Enlightenment reason and its romantic critics to a philosophy that embraced both rational thought and "the living core of knowledge which preceded thought and transcended thought." In aesthetic terms, this stance demanded a literature that pointed beyond itself to that mystical "living core of knowledge" without severing its ties to mimetic representation. As Frank wrote in a diary entry in the early 1920s, "The Goal in the Art of Fiction" was "to make stones sing—without their ceasing to be stones." Frank's philosophical and artistic positions were intimately related. In both cases, he refused to countenance a separation of spirit and the temporal world, despite his recognition that the eruptions of spirit into art and thought strained the limits of human culture to the breaking point. It was that strain on culture, that wearing away of its familiar contours, that gave art, literature, and philosophy their redemptive quality. As "proofs of God" in the phenomenal world, Frank's works were to be sparks illuminating the capacity for mystic knowledge that lay beyond human reason. Such sparks had to be held close to the stuff of everyday life, even as they threatened to set it aflame.[10]

As Frank explored the tensions in this dialectic of culture and spirit, he found similar oppositions at work in his choice of a career after college. Upon graduating from Yale, he returned to New York, where he spent a year and a half working as a journalist, first for the *New York Evening Post* and then for the *New York Times*. Frank plunged into the worldly milieu of big-city journalism, interviewing such political figures as Emma Goldman, Samuel Gompers, and Theodore Roosevelt. Meanwhile, his "serious" writing—his plays and stories—found no audience.

On one level, Frank felt drawn to a journalistic world in which he might comfortably "belong," but at the cost of ignoring his artistic and spiritual aspirations. Yet he simultaneously recognized the allure of withdrawing to a tiny "communion of saints" banded together by their contempt for worldly affairs. "In me, already," Frank recalled in his memoirs, "there was a tension of opposites to make me what I became." Rather than try to reconcile those "opposites" in New York, Frank found the decision partly made for him when he lost his job at the *Times*; a trip to Paris postponed the problem of how to live a saintly life in this world until his return.[11]

As it had for Bourne and Brooks, Europe beckoned with a ready-made solution to the problem of finding a home as a writer. Like Bourne, Frank found in Paris exactly what he missed in New York. He later remembered that New York had "seemed wholly body" to him when he left. It was "a vast town" in size but a "baby" in spirit "since it was concerned only with the mechanics of sheer physical growth." During his time abroad in 1913–14, he did not associate with other writers and intellectuals but instead spent his time studying Spinoza and observing the folkways of Paris. For Frank, it was a perfect combination. Spinoza remained a lifelong influence as a philosopher who united rationalism and a religious metaphysics in a new monistic system, and French organicism became the ideal for what Frank—like Bourne—yearned for in his own culture. Frank was impressed by the ease with which French society nurtured and welcomed artistic creation so that writers lived as "true priests," whose work "was considered a sacrament and a service: not because of what it brought, not for what it did—for itself." As with Bourne and Brooks, Frank's idealization of a foreign organic culture had obvious religious overtones. French literature flourished as a secular church, its value residing in its ability to weave spirit into the fabric of everyday life and thereby give it meaning.[12]

By early 1914, Frank had had his fill of life as an expatriate. He later confessed his uneasiness about feeling like a "parasite," living off the remains of France's organic civilization. Anticipating by fifteen years the experience of a later generation of American expatriates, Frank's growing admiration for European culture led him back to the United States to take up the work of regenerating the cultural and spiritual life of his own nation. The real task was not to live in a "communion of saints" abroad but to make American society habitable for saintly practices and in the process release the sanctified into the urban maelstrom of New

York. Frank's entries in his notebook from 1913 to 1914 indicate how much this project depended on working through the tensions that he identified in his personality and in his early speculations about art and literature.[13]

"Happiness is the union of sense and soul," Frank noted in one entry. "Sense cannot soar to soul, but soul can sweep down to sense. And alone when this degradation exists, is happiness." On the following page, he added: *"Earth is God's Heaven."* Frank's thinking throughout these years returned again and again to the theme of dragging "soul" into the sensual world so as to redeem that world as "God's Heaven." Like Bourne and Brooks, Frank was a thoroughly dialectical thinker who insisted on uniting opposites in order to sharpen the critical, adversarial function of culture in a complacent society. He confided to his notebook his belief in moral struggle as the source of all good in the world, as against the liberal notion of goodness as a "natural or instinctive virtue." "The human impulse to *change, combat* is at the foundation of Virtue," he countered. It followed, then, that art was most potent as a force for good when it induced an element of moral combat in human consciousness, confronting familiar truths as a militant gospel of cultural opposition.

An entry entitled *"Creed"* described Frank's view of culture's role in art's struggle to free itself from its social conditions: "Here is a motif for modern art—how man's Heaven is dragged to Hell by the tiny, tough sordidness of earth. Man's fairest spirit is fastened to a numbing death by the banale reaches of our economic state, much as the King of the Beasts was held prostrate by innumerable meshes. There is the crux of modern art." But Frank refused to absolve art of its responsibility to the "tough sordidness of earth." His decision to return to New York reflected his determination to fight the battle on that terrain. Although Frank always used an ideal of art as a means to transcendent knowledge as the standard by which he judged the value of social life, he resisted the temptation to view art itself as a refuge from all that ate away at individual spirit. Art had to mediate between society and spirit. It had to strain beyond itself as symbol to capture that which resisted representation in material form, but in so doing it had to come to terms with the familiar rhythms of a settled culture. "Art is the serving of Truth as an integral decoration of Life," Frank concluded, in his best early formulation of this idea. The word *decoration* may suggest a settled and untroubled view of art and its relation to social reality, but this was never

Frank's intention. The predicament of modern art, held captive by "our economic state," demanded a far-reaching process of cultural renewal that went beyond "mere" decoration to a transformation of "Life" itself. Frank deliberately gave art a dual role—as servant of transcendent "Truth" and "integral decoration" of everyday life—to preserve its potential as a critical force in modern society. At the center of the dialectic of spirit and society, art allowed individuals to tap a larger vision of spiritual meaning and draw upon that knowledge in refashioning the human community. This ethos of redemption through aesthetic experience informed all of Frank's later work. It inspired his vision of an American cultural renaissance as a project of spiritual regeneration and social reconstruction, and it gave substance to his own personal calling as author of "proofs of God."[14]

By the time he met James Oppenheim in the winter of 1915–16 and plunged into the work of editing the *Seven Arts*, Frank's thinking neatly complemented the intellectual enterprise that Brooks and Bourne had outlined in their early essays. That project is best described as *cultural criticism*, as distinct from political polemic or literary criticism. It was their wide-ranging inquiry into culture that separated their writing from either literary or social criticism, no matter how much their essays touched upon strictly literary or sociological issues. And it was an emphasis on criticism, or critique, that underscored their commitment to an oppositional content for art and literature as the basis for democratic community.

Integral to the enterprise of cultural criticism that all three men shared was a certain ambiguity in their use of the word *culture*. At various times, they employed the term as an alternative to *society*, as had the nineteenth-century tradition of English critics—from Blake and Burke to Ruskin and Morris—who invoked *culture* as an organic court of moral appeal far removed from the hierarchical, utilitarian standards of industrial capitalism. On other occasions, the Young Americans clearly understood culture in its genteel, Arnoldian sense, as a synonym for "high" art and letters. Yet when they spoke of culture as a middle ground between spirit and society, they often sounded much closer to a twentieth-century social-scientific equation of culture with an entire way of life. As a commonly shared system of values, symbols, and processes of social interaction, culture in this last sense included but was not limited to the masterworks of a civilization. In their cultural criticism, Brooks, Bourne, and Frank often slipped easily from treating one such type of culture to another, making broad connections between

developments in elite culture and the popular arts and between both of
these and changes in social and political organization.[15]

Although this approach to culture offered important insights into
the often obscure relationships between literature, society, politics, and
psychology, it had the obvious drawbacks of blurring the distinctions
between these realms and of often confusing readers about exactly
what problem these writers were addressing. A typical complaint about
Brooks's *America's Coming-of-Age* and his subsequent work in the
1910s and 1920s was his apparent uncertainty as to the causes—and
therefore the remedies—for the dissociation of Highbrow and Lowbrow
in industrial society. Was Brooks suggesting that writers were to blame
for their alienation from practical life? Or was his point that there had
to be a democratization of social conditions before Americans could
enjoy a rich cultural life? In other words, was the problem in culture one
to be engaged in its Arnoldian or its anthropological dimensions—in the
realm of individual writers or in that of American culture as a communal way of life? The difficulty, critics charged, derived from Brooks's
fudging the line between literature and society so that his harsh judgments of modern American life often took the form of an overly severe
dismissal of particular authors. Whatever the value of his appraisals of
American society, the argument went, Brooks was an unreliable guide to
the details of his country's literary history.[16]

The confusion that Brooks's work generated had much to do with the
often conflicting meanings that he, along with Bourne and Frank, attributed to culture. If pressed as to whether they sought to transform
"high" culture or an entire way of life, all three men probably would
have answered that the question was posed incorrectly, that it was impossible to imagine a renovation in culture in its Arnoldian sense without a corresponding change in social relations. The answer, in other
words, was both. By moving back and forth from a notion of high
culture as a secularized version of religious spirit to an equation of
culture and everyday life, the Young Americans kept in tight dialectical
opposition the two poles of their project in culture criticism. Culture as
ideal set off against culture as a communal way of life was the volatile
field in which the Young Americans judged particular works of art,
literature, and philosophy, as well as social and political institutions, for
their capacity for nurturing creative personalities. Lingering beneath
this conception was the quasi-religious spirituality that all three critics
shared. Like faith made manifest in the sacraments, liturgy, and ministry
of the institutional church, culture contained both an end beyond hu-

man history and a presence in that history that gave form and meaning to the strivings of common existence.

The *Seven Arts* was the product of this particular understanding of cultural criticism. In their essays for the journal, the Young Americans ranged freely over the fields of politics, psychology, aesthetics, and social thought in their search for a culture embedded in their country's practical life yet worthy of the highest claims of spirit. Although many of the articles it published were narrower in scope, the best contributions to the *Seven Arts* championed a radical politics of democratic community alongside a call for an American literary and artistic renaissance. The two elements of the journal's position were inseparable, as Frank well understood. The warring impulses in his own personality that pulled him toward saintly withdrawal and a superficial sense of belonging in worldly affairs were also at work in American culture. Both tendencies had to be overcome if art were ever to serve truth as life's decoration. But first, both tendencies had to be invoked, one against the other, to maintain the critical spirit he and his colleagues sought to impart to their countrymen.

From its inception, the *Seven Arts* dedicated itself to exploring the connections between self, culture, and society in a period of nascent "national self-consciousness." As Frank put it in the manifesto that served as the journal's prospectus, "In all such epochs the arts cease to be private matters; they become not only the expression of the national life but a means to its enhancement." Frank called upon American writers to contribute work that grew out of their own "joyous necessity"—out of their own personalities, as it were—"without regard to current magazine standards." Only an art born from such a process of "self-expression" could fully tap the intuitive and creative resources that a commercial civilization had denied. By championing an art of emancipated personality, the *Seven Arts* could claim to be "not a magazine for artists, but an expression of artists for the community."[17]

The journal's first editorial repeated the prospectus's linking of culture and personality in a project of communal reconstruction. "In an age that has lost the supreme emotional growth through religion," art had to create personalities capable of resisting the pressures of their immediate environment and of offering their own alternatives to it. The acquiescence of so many European thinkers in the demands of the war effort reflected the estrangement of the modern mind from the depths of

emotional experience. Lacking "outstanding personalities," modern artists oscillated between scientistic fantasies of technical mastery and a
contrived primitivism. Modern art had failed to plumb "the emotional
development of the race." It had neglected the "hidden desires" that
demanded expression. As a result, its creators fell victim to "the terrific
sweep of war" while its presumed audience rushed to the slaughter
without a clear sense of purpose or a consciousness of the meaning
behind its sacrifice.[18]

The key terms in the *Seven Arts* program for cultural renewal were
personality and *experience*. It was the lack of both of these that consigned culture to its fate as highbrow artifice or ethereal abstraction and
that gave politics and practical activity a narrow, utilitarian quality as
the efficient adjustment of means to ends. Just as a culture unrelated to
experience gave way to the premises of its social environment, so too
did individuals lacking in personality find their consciousness subordinated to the tasks of physical survival. Personality actively mediated
between the human mind and its surroundings, much as experience—in
Brooks's and Bourne's subjectivist reading of pragmatism—imbued social practice with the aesthetic resources of culture. Until the issue of the
war began to monopolize their attention, the journal's major writers
sought to reinvigorate a democratic community life by grounding personality in the experience of cultural creation and appreciation.

Brooks's essays for the *Seven Arts*, later revised and republished as
Letters and Leadership, best outlined the historical causes for the current crisis of culture and set the groundwork for the other contributors'
proposals for an American cultural renaissance. Fresh from his immersion in Morrisite radicalism, Brooks returned to the themes that had
occupied him in *The Wine of the Puritans* and *America's Coming-of-
Age*, but his latest diagnosis of his country's cultural plight had a social
and political dimension that was absent in the first of these early essays
and only implied in the second. It was the expansive appetite of American capitalist enterprise, Brooks now argued, that was to blame for the
degradation of high culture and folk culture alike in the United States;
and the industrial capitalism of the late nineteenth century was especially responsible for the sapping of Americans' capacities for cultural
and political self-government. Capitalism drew Brooks's fire less as a
system of economic exploitation than as an assault against "inner" and
"outer nature." For Brooks, the inner nature of personality was as much
the victim of commerce as was the ravaged outer nature of the American
countryside. With "only one human tradition" to draw on—the com-

petitive individualism that had conquered the New World—Americans languished "cold and dumb in spirit, incoherent and uncohesive as between man and man, given to many devices, without community in aim or in purpose."[19]

For Brooks, the frontier experience had resulted not in the democratic openness of American folkways—as popular mythology had it—but in a rootless, anomic existence that withheld from ordinary people the knowledge necessary to their own self-mastery. Viewing the frontier as an empty, lifeless terrain ready for exploitation, the pioneers never endowed their settlements with "that subtle fusion of natural and human elements which everywhere the European landscape suggests." Instead, they nailed together ramshackle boomtowns and abandoned them as soon as the lure of greater profits called them elsewhere. Brooks saw the results in the lack of a settled, traditional culture in American villages, in the absence of a native architectural style, and in the "morbid, bloodless death-in-life" that afflicted old colonial villages and western boom towns alike. These old towns were "old as nothing else anywhere in the world is old, old without majesty, old without mellowness, old without pathos, just shabby and bloodless and worn out." Failing to cultivate and thereby humanize their natural environment, Americans now watched their decaying communities give way to an unregenerate wilderness. The weeds that cropped up in their streets were nature's revenge "on a race that has been too impatient and self-seeking to master its inner secrets."[20]

Brooks's indictment of the pioneer phase of American history derived its force from his insights into its legacy for modern personality and culture. Like Frederick Jackson Turner and many other commentators, Brooks agreed that the experience of settling the American continent had played a definitive role in the formation of the American character. But for him, the effects were almost totally negative. The process of expansion and material accumulation had stunted full personal development by subordinating all extraneous impulses and aspirations to the habits of acquisition and brute survival. "Puritanism," Brooks argued, "was a complete philosophy for the pioneer" in his early stages; Emersonian self-reliance was its heir. Such philosophies aided Americans in their conquest of the frontier and in their repudiation of European feudal traditions, but they did so at the expense of any sense of collective experience that might shape a common culture. Taking for granted the abundance of material resources on the frontier, Americans had never had to face the trials of scarcity and the testing of character that resulted from adversity. The "chronic result of contact with a prodigal nature too easily borne under by a too great excess of will" was a superficial optimism, which was the result of a deeper character flaw—an ignorance about the inner emotional reaches of the self. The sturdy, self-reliant yeoman of the pioneer myth was, in reality, incapable of standing up to the natural world and claiming it for human habitation because he had no knowledge of what a genuinely human way of life might be: "Full of the old Puritan contempt for human nature and the sensuous and imaginative experience that seasons it and gives it meaning, the American mind was gradually subdued to what it worked in. For possessing as it did a minimum of emotional equipment, it had no barriers to throw up against the overwhelming material forces that beleaguered it, and it gradually went out of itself as it were and assumed the values of its environment." Brooks found a clear relationship between the character type and jerry-built towns of the pioneer era. In denying the full range of emotional experience necessary to a whole personality, the culture of pioneering had cut short the emergence of a native American culture.[21]

The absence of such a culture reflected not simply the strangling of individual artistic personalities by the demands of frontier survival and commercial expansion; it revealed also the more fundamental problem of America's rootless modernity, which Brooks had been condemning since *The Wine of the Puritans*. What the settling of the frontier had begun in stripping away the layers of accumulated traditions and values connecting Americans with Europe's organic cultures, industrialism now completed with a vengeance. Sounding very much like Morris, Brooks denounced the industrial division of labor, which everywhere had "devitalized men and produced a poor quality of human nature." The industrial separation of intellectual and manual labor divided "the orthodox culture of the world" between "the prig and the aesthete, those two sick blossoms of the same sapless stalk." European cultures could draw on a wealth of premodern traditions—from romanticism to artisanal craftsmanship—in resisting the devastating effects of industrial capitalism, but the pioneering experience had depleted this fund of cultural resources for most Americans. As he had in *Wine*, Brooks saw the modern individual as denuded of the collective culture of the past, but now he located this argument, however sketchily, in the context of the capitalist development that had won the American continent and built the country's industrial economy. By first dividing human personality against itself and then dividing work into separate and unintelligible procedures, American capitalism deprived ordinary people of the inner strength necessary to a real self-reliance and of the common cultural heritage required for a vibrant community life.[22]

The consequences of this long history for arts and letters remained as dire as they had seemed to Brooks in *Wine* and *America's Coming-of-Age*. The separation of Highbrow pieties of genteel culture from the Lowbrow practices of commercial acquisition remained Brooks's dominant motif. Matthew Arnold's injunction to know and preserve "the best that has been thought and said in the world" now struck Brooks as the apotheosis of Lowbrow consumption as Highbrow pretension. For those nineteenth-century Americans whose real concerns were pecuniary, Arnold's stricture became a guide to decorating their homes with half-understood artifacts and unread classics. "It upholstered their lives with everything that is best in history, with all mankind's most sumptuous effects quite sanitarily purged of their ugly and awkward organic relationships." The great writers of that century furthered this ideal of culture as a commodity by their remoteness from the mainstream of Americans' experience. "Our old writers," Brooks charged, "established as a common ground between themselves and their readers either the non-human world of external nature (Thoreau), the world of the will (Emerson), the world of memory and association (Longfellow), the emotion of special causes like abolition or the Civil War (Whittier, Lowell) or of special occasions (Holmes), but never the congruous world of human life in general." The fault was not entirely theirs, if one read Brooks correctly, for the social history of the United States—as he described it—contributed to the division of that "congruous world of human life" into incompatible realms: of suppressed emotions and an abstract, overintellectualized will; of genteel moralism and commercial realities; of a natural environment untouched by the loving care of human cultivation and an overweening confidence in the human mastery of nature; and of mindless drudgery and industrial planning. In such a polarized world, philistinism took the form not of cultural vulgarity but of an affectation of Arnoldian correctness in literary tastes.[23]

The lack of a true cultural or spiritual center to American life had its most immediate consequences, though, in the absence of either a true folk culture "existing on a common level and capable of responding to a common watchword" or of "a student class united in the discipline of common ideals." Without a settled popular culture or a self-conscious intelligentsia, ideas could neither take root in common experience nor challenge it. Instead, all new developments in art and ideas drifted off into faddism, idiosyncratic crankiness, or upbeat apologies for the status quo. Culture as an assumed common ground between intellectuals and their compatriots, as a medium of resistance to the demands of an unchecked capitalism, and as a settled haven for the testing and maturation of personalities—this was what Brooks yearned for and found so lacking in the United States.[24]

Increasingly, Brooks turned to Morris as a model for intellectual life in an organic culture, as well as a source for a romantic critique of industrial culture. Brooks's American hero, Walt Whitman, now paled in comparison to Morris. Whitman had saturated himself in the experience of nineteenth-century American democracy and had presented in his poetry a portrait of its inchoate longings for a civilization that transcended the culture of acquisition. But Brooks believed that Whitman failed to take the next step. He never reworked Americans' experience within his own self—never merged it with the experiences of his own personality—to give it back as a personal vision for social transformation. "As he grew older," Brooks complained, "the sensuality of his nature led him astray in a vast satisfaction with material facts, before which he purred like a cat by the warm fire." Morris, by contrast, developed his utopian program of "joy in labor" by delving into the English craft tradition and refining it in response to his personal meditations on the artisanal past and his dream of a socialist future. According to Brooks, it was this sense of a cultural-political position steeped in *experience*—in conscious interaction with his environment—and in *personality*—a true expression of the whole self—that gave Morris the authority to claim to speak from "my own feelings and desires" about the needs of English workers. Morris had personalized the English working-class resistance to the factory system by fusing it with his own experience as a romantic critic of commercial art. His literature and criticism escaped the limitations of both English labor radicalism and romantic aestheticism even as it drew heavily on these sources in popular and elite culture.[25]

Morris was Brooks's symbol of the creative interaction of ideas, experience, and personality that alone produced a collective cultural life. As he later put it in *Letters and Leadership*, "In happier countries literature is the vehicle of ideals and attitudes that have sprung from experience, ideals and attitudes that release the creative impulses of the individual and stimulate a reaction in the individual against his environment. This our literature has failed to do; it has necessarily remained an exercise rather than an expression." Brooks's subsequent diagnoses of the quandary of American culture were never as penetrating as this formulation in the pages of the *Seven Arts* and *Letters and Leadership*. His depiction of the interrelated crises of personality, experience, culture, and community life posed the problem that virtually all other contributors to the journal tried to address. Like Brooks, they believed that the ideal of the self-reliant individual was giving way to a "new individualism, which finds its gospel in self-expression." Art and literature had to deepen that process so that personality became the common ground for conscious interaction with the public world. They also agreed with his call for a culture of experience to mediate between the intelligentsia and popular ideas and, more broadly, between Highbrow ideals of art's spiritual mission and Lowbrow social practice.[26]

The contributors divided, however, on the appropriate way to reinvigorate personality and experience as the foundations for a collective culture of democratic community. On one side of the issue were Brooks and Frank, who, each in his own way, sought to shore up the critical content of these terms by setting off culture against the social conditions of industrial capitalism. On the other side, James Oppenheim and Paul Rosenfeld made the argument that a culture of experience and personality should, in fact, reflect such conditions. This latter position often took a very different course, as Rosenfeld and other writers departed from their usual view of an organic culture as adjusted to its social environment to portray art and selfhood as sanctuaries from practical life. Strangely, the participants in this discussion seem to have been unaware of the differences between them, at least during the time of the magazine's publication. All agreed on the need to articulate a response to the division of culture and society and to the feeble condition of experience and personality that Brooks had outlined in *America's Coming-of-Age* and his essays for the journal. But while Brooks and Frank sought to forge an American equivalent to the European cultural opposition symbolized by Morris, Oppenheim and Rosenfeld drew on similar language for arguments that ironically confirmed Brooks's critique of American culture. In searching for an easy resolution of the oppositions Brooks had located in American life, these latter contributors swung between an eager embrace of urban-industrial society and a retreat into culture and personality as disembodied realms of spiritual purity. Oppenheim and Rosenfeld were in many respects closer to the very early Brooks of *The Soul* and *The World of H. G. Wells* than they were to the Morrisite radical who joined Frank in attacking industrial capitalism and its culture of rootless individualism.

Brooks's proposals for a new culture followed logically from his analysis of the old. He called for "a program for the conservation of our spiritual resources" to safeguard moral and artistic traditions from the ravages of capitalist industrialization, a position that might best be described as a form of radical traditionalism. American writers and artists were to resist the temptation to represent urban-industrial society in an acritical way. A culture that simply affirmed that society would only contribute to the estrangement that Americans felt from their creations and from each other. Brooks's alternative was to reestablish contact with older traditions of moral discourse and aesthetic experience and, in the process, find a vantage point from which to assess contemporary American civilization. It was this, Brooks believed, that characterized the work of European thinkers such as Nietzsche, Morris, and Marx, who drew heavily on preindustrial and even frankly aristocratic sources so as to "build a bridge between the greatness of the few in the past and the greatness of the many, perhaps, in the future." Brooks encouraged American writers to do the same, while simultaneously reaching out to the popular culture of their contemporaries. Both radical and traditional, populist and conservative, this position held out the best hope, in Brooks's mind, of recovering that "buoyant fund of instinct and experience" lost to the ascendancy of the pioneering-industrialist way of life.[27]

Brooks carefully distinguished his argument for spiritual conservation from two apparently similar positions in contemporary American criticism, which he rejected as throwbacks to the Highbrow-Lowbrow antitheses of the past. Although he wrote as a humanist outraged by the consequences of the industrial division of labor, he had no patience for sentimental appeals to moral uplift and cultural education. The notion of raising public tastes "by a process of injection from the outside, by means of indiscriminate lecturing and the like," entirely missed the point that what had to be addressed in modern cultural life were issues of power and social organization and not just the ignorance of the public. Brooks's advice was "to begin *low*," on the level of the "lowest common denominator," by which he meant exploring the conscious interaction of emotions, intellect, and social environment that characterized the cultural experience of all people. It was this commitment to a public realm for culture that distinguished Brooks from conservatives such as Paul Elmer More, whose hectoring about humanism ignored social realities, and from aggressive popularizers such as William Lyon ("Billy") Phelps, who adopted a posture of virile anti-intellectualism in his literary criticism. Phelps identified with a caricature of popular taste,

Brooks charged, missing "the greenest and the fairest shoots of aspiration and desire" that the Lowbrow imagination was sending forth into the American earth. The real task was to make of culture what had once been the role of religion—a force that united believers in a common experience while providing them with a transcendent perspective from which to view and even criticize that experience. "Then, and only then," he wrote, "shall we cease to be a blind, selfish disorderly people; we shall become a luminous people, dwelling in the light and sharing our light."[28]

Brooks was often maddeningly vague about his solutions to the crises of culture, personality, and experience, offering no precise "program for the conservation of our spiritual resources." Still, a fairly consistent critical stance does emerge from his *Seven Arts* essays. Like Morris, Brooks held what might be called a "craft model" of culture. Brooks's hostility to the industrial division of labor led him to appreciate craftsmanship as an endeavor that welded tradition and innovation, work and creative play, into an ongoing reevaluation of an artistic legacy. This view of culture as craft placed Brooks in an anomalous position in early twentieth-century criticism, at home neither in the academic classicism of the New Humanists nor in the modernist "revolt against gentility" that characterized many Greenwich Village critics. In his craft vision of culture, Brooks sought something very close to what Alasdair MacIntyre has described as the essence of tradition. MacIntyre defines a "living tradition" as "an historically extended, socially embodied argument," which often turns on the very question of what it is that is appropriate to that tradition. Brooks saw craftsmanship as a "socially embodied" interaction between individual personalities and collective experience. An art that repudiated industrial standards for craft need not be nostalgic, nor need it take the dogmatic form of adherence to former modes of artistic representation. Rather, it would return to tradition for what MacIntyre has called "a grasp of those future possibilities which the past has made available to the present." The artist as craftsman would avoid the sterile opposites of fidelity to approved standards and a restless search for innovation that divided Brooks's contemporaries. An artist with a conscious sense of belonging to a craft would find a medium by which to deepen his or her self-understanding and a language in which to express a personal reaction to the social environment. The abolition of the industrial division of labor was a necessary step to the recovery of a common cultural ground, in which tradition provided a context for experimentation and critique.[29]

Brooks also held a craft model of the self. In calling for a more constructive attitude toward nature in his discussion of the frontier, Brooks implied that Americans needed a more thorough understanding of human nature and particularly of the unconscious, emotional elements of the psyche that the pioneer had shunted aside in the drive for expansion. Although this argument often had Rousseauean overtones, Brooks's ideal of free personality was not a plea for a "true" self buried beneath the encrustations of civilized behavior. Nor was his complaint with the American character based on a Transcendentalist premise that mind and nature were to commune on the plain of pure spirit. Despite their apparent differences, a naturalistic view of the self as nonrational impulse and an idealist joining of mind and nature as transcendent spirit had a great deal in common; in both cases, consciousness became a simple reflection of nature, rather than something that emerged out of a difficult process of interaction and struggle with the environment. Brooks often tapped the romantic defense of intuition and emotive being as a counterweight to the culture of industrialism, as when he exalted the "feeling-relation" over the "seeing-relation" in his quarrel with pragmatic sociology. But in general, he looked to self-expression for a crafted self, in much the same way as he looked to a culture of experience for an art of craftsmanship. Brooks's ideal self was consciously crafted in response to its experience. The crafted self grew by rubbing up against the rough grain of something beyond itself, assimilating that experience into its emotional depths and reflecting upon that experience so as to return to the world with a clearer sense of its strengths and limitations.[30]

Presented with the options of self-reliant individualism and the boundless sense of self he had analyzed in *The Malady of the Ideal*, Brooks chose his own ideal of the crafted or interactive self, which found its autonomy by participating in a public world of culture and experience. If the idea of culture as craftsmanship involved an ongoing conversation with the past, present, and future about the nature of craft traditions, then the crafted self—what Brooks meant by personality—was a kind of conversation as well, one that engaged the emotions and intellect of the individual in a dialogue with the social and natural environments. The crafted self and the crafted culture grew together, according to Brooks, as personality returned to culture for a language of its own expression and as artists delved back into the private self as a source for their own contributions to the renewal and reworking of cultural traditions.

The difficulty with this position was that Brooks's radical traditionalism lacked a foundation in any concrete American tradition. Other than Morris, Brooks's model for cultural regeneration was Goethe, whose *Faust*, Brooks believed, gave birth to Germans' consciousness of their own national identity. "By projecting in *Faust* a personification of spiritual energy anchored by a long chain of specific incidents in the concrete experience of the German people and thereby infusing into that experience the leaven of development," Goethe "not only electrified the German people but obliged it to create an environment worthy of itself." Unfortunately, virtually all of Brooks's historical analysis had pointed to the unlikelihood of such a cultural prophet emerging in the United States. Brooks's work implied that the roots of tradition had long since died out. Americans were aggressive moderns from their earliest origins and therefore lacked the preindustrial legacy that had fueled Goethe's romanticism and German cultural nationalism. In retrospect, what is so ironic about Brooks's position is that he himself was a very modern critic of American modernity. His sweeping attacks on the country's frontier experience, his misreading of Puritanism, and his rejection of literary Transcendentalism and its epigones left him no American vantage point for his attack on industrial life. Brooks was too much a modern to appreciate the persistence of republican and biblical traditions of politics and culture up through the late nineteenth and early twentieth centuries. When all was said and done, it was hard to see in Brooks's version of American history any "spiritual resources" worth conserving.[31]

Although the United States had no Morris to unite artisanal republicanism and literary romanticism in a potent critique of industrial capitalism, it had other figures to whom Brooks might have turned as examples of an oppositional tradition in American thought. The lives of Wendell Phillips, Henry George, and Eugene Debs could have instructed Brooks in the potential for self-criticism within mainstream American political culture, but there is no evidence that he gave these exponents of radical republicanism serious attention. Whitman and even William Dean Howells might have provided Brooks with a literary equivalent to radical republicanism. One could argue from a Brooksian perspective that both writers developed strains of nineteenth-century morality and popular sensibility to reach positions that challenged the industrial separation of culture and practical affairs. Brooks was too quick in dismissing such nineteenth-century figures as members of the "vast army of American cranks" whose voices grew shrill and unintelligible in the absence of any cohesive body of critical thought. And as Bernard De-

Voto and Constance Rourke would later point out, Brooks was insensitive to the rich folkloric and humorist traditions that mediated between high and popular culture in American literature and found a synthesis in Mark Twain's novels. For all his talk of tradition, Brooks was painfully ignorant of the elements of an adversary tradition in the politics and culture of his immediate predecessors. Too often, his stirring calls to ground culture and personality in a common tradition gave way to empty appeals for a new Goethe to create an American identity out of the thin air of modernity. In its treatment of its own historical antecedents, Brooks's criticism was as much an example as an indictment of his country's cultural rootlessness.[32]

    Waldo Frank largely avoided the issue of historical antecedents for his own critical project by recasting the terms of Brooks's analysis of America's cultural calamity. The factory system was less significant in Frank's view than in Brooks's; to Frank, the key problem of an industrial culture was the estrangement of the individual from the social world and of human beings generally from their own artifacts. Underlying this state of alienation was a more fundamental separation of spirit from the material world. Industrialism fostered a concern for mechanical processes that sapped people's capacity for self-reflection and conscious intervention in the world around them. By thus reworking Brooks's indictment, Frank set the problem of tradition in the context of recovering older forms of spiritual discipline through an art that served as the secular equivalent of religion. Frank opted for an Emersonian solution to the problem of tradition, despite his Brooksian distaste for Emerson's withdrawal from practical affairs. Frank's appeal to transcendent spirit as a surrogate tradition for American culture meant that his critical essays for the *Seven Arts* lacked the social dimension that Brooks had inherited from Ruskin and Morris. But it give Frank a greater appreciation for recent trends in American art and literature that Brooks ignored. Frank recognized that the divorce of spirit and the objective world had proceeded too far to hope for an American Goethe to create an organic literature of cultural wholeness. The industrial divide separating individuals from one another and from the public world they had created together could not be overcome so easily. A new culture would crop up in tentative, half-realized forms, as modern artists wrought new modes of aesthetic expression out of the interstices of personal revelation and everyday life.

Where Brooks pointed to the village as the symbol of his country's cultural rootlessness, Frank found life in the modern city the appropriate image of the predicament of spirit and the individual in industrial society. "Our centers of civilization differ from those of Europe in this," he claimed, "that they are cities not so much of men and women as of buildings." The skyscrapers looming over the ground level of human experience, casting shadows over the populace of the city, epitomized the apparent rule of society as an external abstraction over the lived experience of the individual. "There is a chasm between the created thing and the creator," Frank wrote, echoing romantic and socialist theorists of alienation; "and everywhere we are the underling and the unformed." Neglecting their spiritual capacities for the erection of an urban network of commerce and industry, Americans had lost control of their environment, which now stood before them as a hostile world unfit for human habitation.[33]

According to Frank, the ascendancy of efficient technique over a cultivation of art and spirit had eroded cultural traditions that once served to unify these two realms in an integrated way of life. Older manifestations of spirit in the art and religion of Western cultures had virtually disappeared from the new industrial landscape. In his portrayal of industrial society, Frank's reference point for a lost organic culture often varied. At times, he lamented the demise of a Homeric epic tradition that located collective spirit in the life of a heroic individual; at others, he looked to Dante and the Gothic cathedral as the culmination of the medieval synthesis of the individual and society and of the sacred and the profane; and yet on other occasions, he made references to the whole course of religious history—with special emphasis on the prophetic strains of Judaism and Christianity—to suggest how a transcendent sense of spiritual knowledge might be made immanent in daily life. In effect, Frank was unknowingly affirming Georg Lukács's contemporary arguments in *The Theory of the Novel* about how modernity had dissolved the communal spirituality that found its first literary expression in the consciousness of the epic hero. Industrial modernization, which had taken its most extreme form in the United States, had torn asunder the traditional relationship between individual spirit and any larger cultural context, Frank argued. By the nineteenth century, the transcendent found refuge only in the psychological interiority of the protagonist of the novel, while the social world became the object of sociological inquiry that overlooked its collective "soul" for scientistic laws of social development. American literature, in Frank's mind, found itself torn between these two poles of knowledge, incapable of merging them in a compelling portrait of a common life of spiritual integrity. "Our artists have been of two extremes," he wrote in a passage that recalls his own personal dilemma about an appropriate calling: "Those who gained an almost unbelievable purity of expression by the very violence of their self-isolation, and those who, plunging into the American maelstrom, were submerged in it, lost their vision altogether, and gave forth a gross chronicle and a blind cult of the American Fact."[34]

Frank's insistence on the need for a "sensitive reaction between ourselves and the whole" led him to give his own theory of "experience" a much greater religious dimension than it had, at least explicitly, in Brooks's criticism. Frank's quest was "for more consciousness—and always more"—to infuse individual experience with a revelatory knowledge of the relationship between self, society, and the cosmos. It was the role of "vision" to enable individuals to experience their surroundings instead of passively surrendering to them, "to make the boundaries of existence the boundaries of spirit." Unlike Emerson, Frank refused to counsel a mystical absorption in transcendent spirit as a refuge from a materialistic civilization. Frank looked to an art of vision to restore Americans' understanding of their relation to a world that they themselves had made by showing them what was human about that world and how it might yet be reassimilated into their experience. This did not mean that art and literature were to reflect the industrial conditions and thereby lend them a spiritual aura. Rather, such works were to restore individuals' consciousness of their existence as both spiritual and earthly beings and remind them of the capacity for memory and prophecy that lifted their imagination beyond their present condition. For Frank, a redemptive art gave the individual "that sense of unity and *at-homeness* with an exterior world which saves him from becoming a mere pathetic feature of it." Only then might Americans replace a civilization that denied their most exalted aspirations with a true community of vision and experience.[35]

In his *Seven Arts* essays and in *Our America*, Frank searched for examples of an aesthetic that engaged the novel experiences of industrial life while simultaneously tapping a religious sensibility that hinted at their transcendence. As always, France provided the model, in the form of the *unanimisme* of novelist Jules Romains. Romains impressed Frank as the novelist most successful in healing the breach between the literary and sociological insights of nineteenth-century European culture. Romains's protagonists were "collective groups," which Frank labeled the "new creatures of the new age." Romains's novel *The Death of a Nobody* had not flinched from portraying the jarring rhythms and frenzied texture of modern urban life, but it also depicted the persistent strains of older religious harmonies that united the French people in a collective culture. Its author remembered that "the bases of our life are still traditional and personal," still rooted in modes of vision and experience that long preceded the industrial age, even as he strove to capture what was new about life in a modern city. Romains had an advantage over American writers in that he could combine the deep psychological insights into individual personality of French novelists with the lingering organicism that still bound Frenchmen together. Frank warned against a literal importation of *unanimiste* techniques into a very different American environment. Americans could not assume, as Romains could, that they were bound to one another by an inherited language of culture and morality. Starting from such a premise, American writers would end up as apologists of the existing industrial order. Nonetheless, Romains remained a model for Frank of a prophet of a new culture, "one in which the newly organized individual would create the transfigured group."[36]

For Frank, the most promising American exponents of an aesthetics of redemptive experience were the novelist Sherwood Anderson and the photographer Alfred Stieglitz. Frank's choice of these two artists reveals how much he differed from Brooks, despite their common critique of industrial culture and their hopes for a new organic community. Compared to Brooks's heroes, Goethe and Morris, Frank's new men of culture were decidedly nonepic and certainly nontraditional. Neither one produced work that attempted, in a romantic vein, to capture the full sweep of American experience. Anderson's fiction and Stieglitz's photographs had a self-consciously fragmentary quality that called attention to the gap between their creators' desire to give form to their vision and the shortcomings of a conventional mimesis. Anderson's awkward, halting prose and Stieglitz's photographs of the urban landscape provided haunting glimpses of a spiritual or psychological presence that slipped through the cracks of American civilization, but that was all. Theirs was an art of miniatures, a magical aesthetics of momentary revelation that had more in common with the later work of a surrealist artist such as Joseph Cornell than with the romantic traditions that inspired Frank and Brooks in their search for an organic culture. They depicted the disjuncture of spirit and its realization in modern terms in vignettes of words and images that were shards of some obscure memory of wholeness. Frank turned to Anderson and Stieglitz as artists and as friends who were struggling, as he was, with the task of wresting spirit out of the "American Fact."

Frank was an early champion of Anderson's work. The *Seven Arts* published the stories that later became *Winesburg, Ohio*, and Frank acclaimed Anderson's first novel, *Windy McPherson's Son*, in the premier issue of the magazine as a sign of the "emerging greatness" of American culture. What Frank admired in Anderson was his personification of a generation's disaffection from commercial enterprise. Ever concerned with the connections between personality and culture, Frank saw in Anderson's life as an advertising man turned novelist the first glimmerings of a larger movement from business to self-expression in the United States. Anderson, he explained in *Our America*, was "a man imprisoned," who sought "release" from the "industrial disorder" in his fiction. He had escaped the chaos of life in Chicago for the rural Midwest of his childhood, where he uncovered the yearnings for love and some larger spiritual purpose in the lives of his mother and her neighbors. Anderson wrote Frank that "I am old enough to remember tales that strengthen my belief in a deep semi-religious influence that was formerly at work among our people." His work searched the midwestern landscape for lingering traces of such spirituality. The painful narratives of sexual repression, of loneliness and private despair that Anderson wove together in *Winesburg* were an American equivalent to Romains's method, Frank believed, linking the individuals of his town together in a still unconscious desire for compassionate fellowship. In Anderson's stories, Frank found in miniature version "the conflict of American life against its own rigid forms, the new upward-stirring, the fierce passion of renewal" that constituted the great spiritual drama of his generation. His ability to convey that drama derived from the struggle that Anderson had undergone within his own soul in becoming an artist. Anderson was no American Goethe, "simply a man who has felt the moving passions of his people, yet sustained himself against them just enough in a crude way to set them forth."[37]

Frank's relationship to Stieglitz was more complex and far more deferential than his friendship with Anderson. Stieglitz was Frank's senior by twenty-five years, and through the sheer force of his personality and the example of his artistic dedication he became both a father figure and a mentor to the young Frank. Stieglitz was more important to Frank as prophet of a new church of modern art than he was as a maker of specific photographs. As a cultural critic, Frank was captivated by the devotional community of artists and photographers grouped around

Stieglitz's gallery at 291 Fifth Avenue, which Frank described as a "religious fact." Visitors to "291" found themselves in "a church consecrate to them who had lost old gods, and whose need was sore for new ones"—a "refuge . . . from the tearing grip of industrial disorder." Here was the "communion of saints" Frank had dreamed of as a resting place for his own spiritual wanderings. The organic haven of 291 was the source of the flashes of spiritual illumination that shone through Stieglitz's photographs. What made Stieglitz so important, in Frank's mind, was his refusal to linger in his artistic sanctuary; 291 was a base for his expeditions into the "industrial disorder" of New York, from which emerged his photographic syntheses of urban experience and his own personal vision. As Frank later wrote in his memoirs, "His work revealed—in a cloud, in a face, in a hand, in the testicles of an old horse harnessed to a horsecar—the being of depth beyond the surfaces of space and time, whose experience by a people is their culture." Stieglitz was the embodiment of Frank's method for overcoming the industrial assault on spiritual community. His religious sense of mission enabled him to master technology—in this case, the camera—and put it to use to convey the latent potential for human renewal in an urban civilization. New York was still not 291, but through Stieglitz's lens it might come to see its capacity for the kind of communion that united the modernist saints at Stieglitz's gallery. Stieglitz's camera was able to do more than reflect urban-industrial realities because his aesthetics drew their strength from a secure sense of place in a community of friendship and shared purpose.[38]

Like Brooks's craft vision, Frank's aesthetics insisted on an art in but not of the modern world. What Brooks had sought to achieve by grounding art in a social-historical tradition uniting art and labor Frank articulated as a fragmentary art of revelation that would redeem the American spirit from its absorption in industrial life. Art had to grow out of some deep fund of experience if it were to play a part in social transformation. For Brooks, this meant a craftsmanlike devotion to art as part of a living tradition connected to work and play. For Frank, it meant the ability to imbue the artifact with the potent energy of the realized self, as in Anderson, or of community, as in Stieglitz. Both critics pleaded for a culture grounded in experience, but their understanding of that word as a dialectic of consciousness and practice—as a highly subjective realm of revelatory vision and personality—gave their proposals for a new culture of experience a critical content lacking in many of the other contributions to the *Seven Arts*. The care with which their criticism maintained a tension between culture and society becomes evident when it is read in conjunction with this other body of work. Where Brooks and Frank looked to culture as a dissenting presence in society and as a means to a new fellowship, writers like James Oppenheim and Paul Rosenfeld hoped that American artists would give voice to their society and seal a compact between culture and industrial life.

As editor of the *Seven Arts*, James Oppenheim expressed in his own work the journal's contradictory approaches to cultural criticism. The same person who could agree with Brooks and Frank on the need for a common culture in opposition to the industrial division of labor could also view the country's lack of tradition and its urban bigness and vitality as assets to be exploited by modern artists. In an early editorial for the magazine's second issue, he took the first course, attacking the overspecialization of art as a symptom of the failures of a culture of industrialism. Oppenheim began by questioning the assumption that because of "the increase of democracy one would naturally expect art to contact more and more of the majority." The proliferation of cheap magazines, phonographs, and popular theaters appeared to promote a true cultural democracy, but, in fact, just the opposite was the case. Artists of the Homeric and Elizabethan ages, and even the antebellum New England writers, were able to "express a people and become part of the consciousness of that people," yet contemporary art "seems to be largely the work of specialists in expression for specialists in appreciation." The triumph of expertise and elaborate technique in industry had invaded the cultural realm. "Never was the *machinery* of art more widely and thoroughly distributed," Oppenheim wrote in a passage that might have come directly from Brooks or Morris. "And never, among a great people, was there less of art." Commercial art prospered alongside a rarefied high culture that kept its distance from the masses. Oppenheim told his fellow artists and intellectuals to forgo genteel pretensions of refinement for an art of the "whole man." Only a culture that refused to separate "soul from body, the aesthetic from the emotional, the intellectual from the intuitive," could speak for and broaden American democracy.[39]

Unlike Brooks and Frank, Oppenheim failed to see any need to rely on earlier traditions of cultural or spiritual expression as counterweights to the industrial civilization he deplored. In this regard, Oppenheim was closer to the French writer Romain Rolland—who sent the journal a jubilant greeting that Frank translated for the first issue—than he was to his fellow editors. Rolland's message had certain ideas in common with the Young Americans' project; in particular, his call for American artists to "make of your culture a symphony" of its many races and ethnic groups echoed Bourne's transnationalism. But writing from a Europe engulfed in war, Rolland saw Americans as blessedly free of the traditions that were then devouring the Continent: "You are free of that vast load of thought, of sentiment, of secular obsession under which the Old World groans." American writers could best serve Europe and their countrymen, he believed, by making their country a sanctuary for liberalism and following Whitman in delving into the stuff of American life.[40]

Rolland may have shared Brooks's and Frank's excitement about America's coming-of-age, but he was miles apart from their understanding of their country's needs. They lamented the traditionlessness Rolland admired in American culture. And though they shared his respect for Whitman, they were skeptical of the poet's naive identification with the full sweep of American life. Oppenheim, however, became ever more Whitmanesque with each new issue of the journal, drifting into free verse that—as Frank recalled—"revealed the superiority of Whitman's" and rhapsodizing about the nation's resources for writers. For Oppenheim, the "American Zarathustra" would find "in the land of Bigness," the land of "the vastest crops, the tallest skyscrapers, the largest railroad trackage, the heaviest tonnage, the most complete personal comfort" on earth, a subject matter unparalleled by anything in European literature. Gone were Frank's critique of the city as a symbol of modern alienation and Oppenheim's own early reservations about equating American technological advances with cultural greatness. Now he reveled in this "land of sensations and facts" and called on his comrades to do the same. "This embracing of social experience, this grapple and struggle with the facts of life, this willingness to be as others at least for a segment of the human arc" had characterized the writing of Shakespeare, Goethe, and Milton, Oppenheim argued, and should furnish American artists with a model of how to approach their own environment.[41]

Oppenheim never grasped the subtle notions of experience and personality that gave Brooks's and Frank's theories of cultural renewal their critical edge. Instead, he articulated a positivist view of consciousness as the reflection of external social forces that was precisely the target of his fellow editors' criticism. In an essay titled "Art, Religion and Science,"

Oppenheim revealed the scientistic assumptions that supported his criticism. Complaining that "our artists are conservative, if not reactionary," in their hostility to science, he made a plea for scientific inquiry as the appropriate successor to religious belief. Both viewpoints encouraged an attitude of self-renunciation in the pursuit of some higher knowledge, Oppenheim claimed, but he made no effort to expand on this argument to show how religion and the scientific frame of mind promoted a skeptical attitude toward the charms of the temporal world. On these grounds, Oppenheim could have made a convincing case for a scientific culture as a source of critical reflection. Instead, he told artists "to bring man up to the level to which power has been brought; to do with man ... what has been done with nature," as if art could be applied to human consciousness in the same way that science had been employed in the exploitation of natural resources. Oppenheim ended the piece by urging readers to "look to the present, face reality as it is," and "know the new dynamic energies released" by modern science and industrial technology. The critic who had begun condemning the "machinery of art" of industrial civilization ended up by endorsing art as an expression of machines.[42]

Although his criticism became more "scientific," Oppenheim's editorials grew ever more fuzzy and impressionistic as the magazine's editor tried to make sense of American involvement in World War I. In March 1917, Oppenheim seemed to welcome intervention as an antidote to the "ennui" and "purposelessness" of "an unrelieved industrialism." The war would be the culmination of the tendency toward bigness and vitality that Oppenheim admired in American life; it would force the United States finally to "grow up and take its place in the world." Three months later, in an editorial in the same issue as Bourne's essay "The War and the Intellectuals," Oppenheim argued the futility of resisting the war. Though he saw American involvement as a consequence of the failure "to create great peace and great persons," he was resigned to the world-historical forces that swept his country into the conflict. "We could not expect to be the calm island in this raging sea," he concluded. "We too are sucked into the storm: we too must fill the void of a century of shallow living." The war apparently broke Oppenheim's will to respond to events with either decisiveness or independence. Just as he counseled artists to submit to their social environment, his own contributions dissolved into rambling, free-form poems about the inexorable necessity of the war. In the end, the poet-editor produced only obscure missives addressed to the ghosts of Whitman and Abraham Lincoln, which hinted that the carnage would end in some apocalyptic moment of global revolution. But the key point was that he saw no role for art in such a transformation, which now loomed on the horizon as a product of forces beyond human control. In the meantime, Oppenheim slipped into the part of the world-weary writer, muttering, as if to himself: "We wait the Voice . . . we wait the Storm."[43]

Oppenheim's essays confirmed Brooks's powerful insight that the rush to identify culture with practical life and the detached lyricism of a moralistic culture were two sides of the same coin. Both positions had given up on art and literature as means of apprehending and thereby transforming the social world. Whether as vitalistic prophet of an "American Zarathustra" or as mystical seer of revolutionary intuition, Oppenheim resigned himself to the impotence of culture and consciousness before modern social conditions. The same might be said of Paul Rosenfeld, although Rosenfeld wisely avoided following Oppenheim's path into political commentary. Two essays by Rosenfeld for the first issue of the *Seven Arts*—an article "The American Composer" and a pseudonymous piece on Stieglitz's 291—revealed how the language that Brooks and Frank developed might be drained of its critical content and put to use in a reaffirmation of the industrial divorce of culture and society.

"The American Composer" echoed themes familiar to readers of Brooks's *America's Coming-of-Age*: the need for an American art strong enough to be measured by European standards, the separation of artists from their community, and the failure of a purely intellectual culture to come to terms with the conditions of modern experience. But Rosenfeld was far less willing to blame industrial social relations for such problems than Brooks was. It was the American composer's fault that he failed to answer the public's craving for a native music; his inability "to draw the substance of his art from out the life that surges about him" condemned his work to irrelevance. Dropping Brooks's and Frank's dialectical relationship between personal vision and experience, Rosenfeld expounded a far simpler ideal of music as the mirror image of its society. Great art required "that openness by means of which the spirit of a whole community, of a nation, of whole continents and ages, comes into a man, and transforms him in its own image." Like Frank, Rosenfeld described this process of self-renewal in religious terms, as if artists were overcome by a blinding flash of revelatory insight into their relationship to the world. But Rosenfeld saw this as a one-sided transformation: artists were in no way empowered to remake the world. American music, in Rosenfeld's mind, suffered from its composers' "lack of faith in the American destiny." The essay's ending suggests just how deeply this particular idea of "faith" differed from Frank's aesthetics of spirit as a redemptive force. Almost chanting, Rosenfeld called for a new relationship between the artist and America: "From the cowardice of withholding ourselves we must now part. It is something more than an interest, half-hearted or full, that is demanded of us if we cherish our salvation, personal and common. From us there is now asked the surrender of ourselves to her life, the gift of ourselves to her future. There is asked of us supreme faith in her, love of her, belief that her highest good is the highest good of all the world. . . . It is faith alone that can let her come in on us and make us new." Rosenfeld was right to describe this union of culture and community as a "surrender of ourselves." In his view, culture was superfluous as a source of critical insight into its social environment. Artists had to undergo a mystical cycle of death and rebirth in submission to a new god—America—that would remake their souls in its image.[44]

In the same issue in which Rosenfeld exhorted musicians to surrender to American society, he also encouraged readers—this time under the pseudonym "Peter Minuit"—to leave that society for the artistic cloister of Stieglitz's 291. Like Frank, Rosenfeld wrote of the gallery as a modernist chapel, with Stieglitz as the suffering servant of artistic rebellion. "One grieves to think how often there must come to him the bitterness that reaches all men who offer themselves to the world," Rosenfeld wrote in one particularly sticky passage, "at moments when they realize how little the world knows how to use their gift." What made Rosenfeld's piece so different from Frank's remarks was not its sycophancy—like other members of Stieglitz's inner circle, Frank was prone to such excesses—but its remarkably one-dimensional portrait of 291 as a sanctuary for spiritual withdrawal and psychic health. Frank, after all, had seen 291 as a home which Stieglitz left for the streets of New York, inspired with a vision of refashioning urban life in a new artistic form. Stieglitz was Frank's philosopher-king venturing back into the cave after finally seeing the light. Rosenfeld's narrator, "Peter Minuit," acted as the reader's tour guide of the gallery. It was "a place where art should serve as a means to self-consciousness," he explained before leading his reader into the sacred spot, "as a challenge to the time, as a revelation, as a stimulus to new creative activity." But these preparatory remarks, so much in keeping with the Frank-Brooks theory of an art of experience, had little to do with the scene "Minuit" presented as he led his readers in. There they found a warm, quiet place away from the noise and pressures of urban life. "Minuit" recommended a visit to 291 "to those who seek the gallery at a moment when the individual staying power is near collapse, when energy subsides and faith crumbles and vanishes." Only in such a "traitor moment" did the gallery's true significance "reveal itself." Rosenfeld insisted that Stieglitz's "lofty conception of art" did not value culture as "a refuge from the world, but as a bridge to consciousness of self, to life, and through that, to new life and new creation again." But his essay suggested otherwise. Its lasting impression was of a visit to a shelter for the shell-shocked, a place where weary sophisticates might go to recharge their spirits and soothe their nerves before returning to the street. "Life, life, a thousand times, is the important thing for Stieglitz," Rosenfeld explained. "It is his religion." In Rosenfeld's portrait, 291 became less a base for a critical assault on American industrial society than a complement to it—a center for aesthetic vitality as compensation for the loss of creativity and personal control in other areas of life. Frank's Stieglitz carried a sword as he went forth into the world; Rosenfeld's Stieglitz offered consolation and rest for the pilgrims who stopped at his sanctuary.[45]

Rosenfeld's description of 291 as a therapeutic retreat found its counterpart in "Following Freedom," a piece published in September 1917 with the byline "By an American Immigrant" that was largely an undistinguished attack on the jingoism of the American mob. The author spent most of the piece lamenting the threat posed to American liberties by the "dark, irrational instincts" of wartime hysteria. The essay is such a startling contribution to the *Seven Arts* because of its privatistic notion of personality as a refuge from the ravages of war and vulgar nationalism. "The highest virtue that a man can exercise at such a time is the austere preservation of his self-hood," "Immigrant" told readers; "the best gift he can make to his fellowmen is the gift of his unbending soul." But the writer urged no stance of principled opposition, along the lines of Bourne's outspoken criticism of the war. Rather, he comforted readers with the thought that "at least in the quietude of his own mind he can live as though war were but a disastrous accident and the achievement of permanent and serene values our real goal." In this conception, "the liberty of personalities to be themselves" meant little more than the freedom to withdraw into the hard shell of the self and wait for better days.[46]

The *Seven Arts* program of fostering personal growth and grounding art and literature in lived experience fractured into two opposing projects. Rosenfeld's vision of 291 as a clinic for the cultured and "Immigrant"'s call for a retreat into personality, represented a genuine betrayal of Brooks's and Frank's vision of a democratic culture of experience. Genteel culture now reemerged in a modernist guise as a leisure-time distraction suitable for enjoyment after work. Meanwhile, personality devolved into the worst parody of self-reliance: the isolated, atomistic individual cringing in fear of contact with a hostile world. The courses that Rosenfeld and Oppenheim had taken revealed, by contrast, the complexities of the choice that Brooks and Frank had made in favor of personality and experience as sources of a critical culture. They also showed how easily a search for a union of the artist and community could become a quest for a resting place for the intellectual, where he might shake off the tensions that Brooks and Frank deliberately maintained in their criticism and feel at peace with world. The Rosenfeld-Oppenheim position in the *Seven Arts* demonstrated how culture could default on its mission of placing personality in conscious dialectic with its surroundings. "The tragic thing," as Frank put it, "is that art . . . can lose itself in the surface complexities of a civilization; can end by becoming a mere expression of the materials from whose tyranny it rightfully should free us."[47]

The strength of Brooks's and Frank's criticism for the *Seven Arts* was its resistance to any easy resolution of the conflicts in modern life between self and society and between work and the artistic imagination. Their criticism strove to heal the divisions in their culture, but it did so with the understanding that such a process required steadfast opposition to any simple idealization of existing social realities and to any aestheticist withdrawal into the uncontaminated realm of the self. "We looked upon art as a sharing of life, a communism of experience and vision, a spiritual root of nationalism and internationalism," the journal's farewell editorial explained. Starting from the premises of "a communism of experience and vision" meant—at least in Brooks's and Frank's work—ruling out Transcendentalist idealism and acquiescence in the given world as equally threatening to the flourishing of personality in the Beloved Community.[48]

It was a similar fear of easy resolutions in the interplay of self, culture, and society that lay behind the journal's other major project as the war eclipsed immediate hopes of an American artistic renaissance. In their critiques of pragmatism and of prowar Progressives, Bourne, Brooks, and Frank drew on their theories of culture, personality, and experience to defend a political role for intellectuals as creators of values. This argument followed naturally from their cultural criticism, but it was the experience of honing familiar ideas in wartime that finally engendered the Young Americans' clearest statements of how their work might inform a new politics of democratic community.

5

The War and the Intellectuals

Idealism should be kept for what is ideal.
—RANDOLPH BOURNE,
"The War and the Intellectuals"

n his antiwar essays for the *Seven Arts*, Randolph Bourne confessed that the support John Dewey and other Progressives gave to the war effort had taken him by surprise. His own belief in progress and in the ability of intelligent people to find peaceful alternatives to military conflict had run aground in the spring of 1917. It was not just that he disagreed with Dewey and his followers over intervention in the war as a means to social democracy at home and arbitrated settlements abroad. The real casualty of the war was Bourne's faith in pragmatism, which had informed most of his thinking since his college days. "What I have come to is a sense of suddenly being left in the lurch," he admitted, "of suddenly finding that a philosophy upon which I had relied to carry us through no longer works. I find the contrast between the idea that creative intelligence has free functioning in wartime, and the facts of the inexorable situation, too glaring. The contrast between what liberals ought to be doing and saying if democratic values are to be conserved, and what the real forces are imposing upon them, strikes too sternly on my intellectual senses."[1]

The Young Americans' analysis of pragmatism transcended the specific issues of support for the war and Wilsonian foreign policy. In trying to understand the causes for the rush of Deweyan pragmatists and other liberals to the war effort, they specified exactly what it was they disputed and what in Dewey's philosophy they still retained. Their argument in the late 1910s proceeded along two lines. In large part, it attempted to recall pragmatism to its original promise of directing events through a theory of socially informed practice. Bourne declared that the alienated young people who remained suspicious of the claims made by Dewey and his disciples for the war were "genuine pragmatists," who "fear any kind of an absolute, even when bearing gifts. They know that the longer a war lasts the harder it is to make peace." In this sense, Robert Westbrook is correct to emphasize "the in-house, Deweyan nature of much of Bourne's critique" of Dewey's position. Bourne and his colleagues accused Dewey of not approaching the war pragmatically, of failing to use intelligence to guide or even reverse processes at work in American society instead of succumbing to them. Yet there was another element of the Young Americans' discussion of pragmatism that, at the very least, significantly expanded Dewey's philosophy of experience and, on occasion, pushed beyond its categories altogether. [2]

In addition to charging Dewey with a failure to adhere to pragmatic method, the Young Americans began to question that method itself. Drawing freely on the nineteenth-century romantic critique of utilitarianism, Bourne, Brooks, and Frank argued that Dewey's definition of *experience* was too narrow, that it failed to encompass the imagination as well as the intellect. It was the inability of pragmatism to envision a role for aesthetic and spiritual *values* in shaping social experience that explained Dewey's acquiescence in the war effort, they charged. Their alternative was a highly subjectivist pragmatism that gave as much— and, on occasion, more—weight to the claims of love, intuition, art, and spirit in a critical philosophy of experience as it did to the deliberative reason and open communications that Dewey stressed. As critical intellectuals of the Left, they would combat the equation of a philosophy of social experience with one of social adjustment by resurrecting the romantic ideal of unfettered subjectivity. At the same time, they would berate moral idealists and advocates of art for art's sake for abstracting ethics and culture from the conditions of everyday life. This synthesis of romanticism and pragmatism was replete with its own share of tensions and contradictions, especially in its union of political and cultural radicalism, but it provided the Young Americans with the philosophical underpinnings for their own position as dissenters within the progressive intelligentsia.[3]

Bourne accused Dewey and his followers of forsaking the creative tension between ideals and existing conditions that he saw as the critical dynamic in pragmatism. Without that tension, the injunction to ground ideals in practice meant "a mere surrender to the actual, an abdication of the ideal through a sheer fatigue from intellectual suspense." In his essays for the *New Republic*, Dewey had counseled liberals to give up their pacifist absolutism and recognize "the immense impetus to reorganization afforded by this war." Dewey insisted that intellectuals take hold of the "social possibilities of war" and shape them in accordance with social-democratic values: "I have little patience with those who are so anxious to save their influence for some important crisis that they never risk its use in any present emergency. But I can but feel that the pacifists wasted rather than invested their potentialities when they turned so vigorously to opposing entrance into a war which was already all but universal, instead of using their energies to form, at a plastic juncture, the conditions and objects of our entrance." Bourne's complaint was that Dewey had overemphasized the "plasticity" of that historical juncture, in which "the least democratic forces in American life" were clamoring for war. By throwing in his lot with reactionary nationalists and militarists, Dewey was deluding himself about his ability to subject such forces to rational control. The pressures of "war-technique"—as Bourne constantly termed the war effort—would override Deweyan principles. "War determines its own end—victory, and government crushes out automatically all forces that deflect, or threaten to deflect, energy from the path of organization to that end." Moreover, Dewey's polemics against the absolutism of his pacifist and socialist critics left those principles obscure at best. There was no such ambiguity among conservatives, Harold Stearns pointed out in *Liberalism in America*, which restated much of Bourne's critique. "*They* had no doubt what things were worth doing. *They* had no doubt that the destruction of German cities, the devastation of Europe, the embittering of the world, were the happy objects for which they so cheerfully sent out young men to die."[4]

Dewey and the prowar liberals at the *New Republic* had mangled both sides of the pragmatic imperative to ground ideals in social experience, according to Bourne. They had failed to articulate a clear set of alternative ideals distinguishing the progressive position on the war from that of the American Right, and they had mistaken the ravages of "war-technique" for the consciously informed practice Dewey understood as experience. The result was a hollow idealization of horror: "The American intellectual class, having failed to make the higher syntheses, regresses to ideas that can issue in quick, simplified action. Thought becomes an easy rationalization of what is actually going on or what is to happen inevitably tomorrow." "Idealism," Bourne snapped, "should be kept for what is ideal."[5]

In effect, Bourne charged Deweyan pragmatism with repeating the empty opposition of Highbrow ideals to Lowbrow realities that Brooks had denounced in *America's Coming-of-Age*. In complete disregard of the pragmatic imperative to test ideas in practice, Dewey and the other Progressives at the *New Republic* had tried desperately to put the best face on things by claiming that the war was serving liberal principles. "Croly and Lippmann," Bourne wrote a friend, "were obsessed with the idea of themselves controlling the war-technique in a democratic manner, preventing excesses, protecting women and children in labor, raising a democratic army of conscripts, everything polite, well-bred, humane, enlightened. They are now slightly aghast at the terrible forces they have unloosed, and we may now see futile walrus tears about the 'mistakes' of the Government, the 'unwise' censorship, etc., all of which was completely implicit in the whole affair and was foreseen by every pacifist from the beginning." The *New Republic*'s war aims were mere wishful thinking, Bourne claimed, no different from the sentimental pieties of genteel culture in their inability to affect social reality. Meanwhile, Dewey and his allies had reduced their understanding of social experience to an unconscious set of processes that compelled the allegiance of intellectuals. The result was to reaffirm the tendency in industrial life to uphold utilitarian standards as the sole measure of value. Frank made explicit this connection between Brooks's critique of the culture of industrialism and Bourne's polemic against Dewey in *Our America*, his 1919 epilogue to the *Seven Arts*. He condemned pragmatists for subordinating experience to an "abstract conception of Progress, in which the world is really posited as a sort of locomotive." A philosophy of experience, in this view, had made human practice the reflex of mechanical laws of "Progress," while substituting optimistic rhetoric for serious thought.[6]

What Bourne and the other *Seven Arts* critics objected to in Dewey's thought was its apparent equation of science as critical inquiry with a technical ideal of applied science. Dewey's conflation of these two understandings of science in his critique of idealism had produced serious contradictions in Bourne's early educational theory, insofar as it led Bourne to blur the distinction between the revival of community life through critical thinking and the application of administrative techniques by a new professional elite. If the former course promised to overcome the industrial division of labor by giving citizens the intellectual tools for self-governance, the latter reinforced the distinction between knowledge as a property of the privileged few and unthinking work for the many. The reduction of thought to an efficient means to an end, as opposed to a source of speculative self-reflection, represented the worst tendencies in industrial culture. When Deweyan intellectuals embraced "war-technique" as a means to progressive ends, Bourne argued, they had abdicated the responsibility of the pragmatist to stimulate critical thinking for positions of power within the existing division of labor. Rather than creating new values with other citizens, they had identified intelligent social practice with the technical exploitation of nature.

"To those of us who have taken Dewey's philosophy almost as our American religion," Bourne had to confess, "it never occurred that values could be subordinated to technique." Dewey's default before the premises of industrial life forced Bourne to confront the "unhappy ambiguity in his doctrine as to just how values were created," which had plagued pragmatists in their attempt to ground thought in experience as a way of transforming that experience. It was at this point that he turned to romanticism to bolster the critical content of pragmatism. "Vision must constantly outshoot technique," he wrote in "Twilight of Idols." "It is now becoming plain that unless you start with the vividest kind of poetic vision, your instrumentalism is likely to land you just where it has landed this younger intelligentsia which is so happily and busily engaged in the national enterprise of war."[7]

In turning to a romantic conception of "poetic vision" for an antidote to a debased pragmatism, Bourne echoed Brooks's critique of pragmatism as a modern surrogate for literary culture. Brooks attacked James and Dewey for allowing scientific method to usurp "the place which poetry alone can fill adequately." "That is to say, it has assumed the right to formulate the aims of life and the values by which those aims are tested, aims and values which, we are led by history to believe, can be effectively formulated only by individual minds not in harmony with the existing fact but in revolt against it." What Bourne interpreted as a betrayal of pragmatism Brooks saw as its essence—namely, the "harmony" of thought with "the existing fact"—and, in response, he upheld a romantic conception of the artist as prophetic outsider. Art would resist the colonization of vision by technique. Since artists were able to draw on their imagination to create values for a new order, Brooks asked, "does not pragmatism turn the natural order of things inside out when it accepts the intelligence instead of the imagination as the value-creating entity?" The real need was for prophets of the imagination to "repudiate the social organism altogether and, rising themselves to a fresh level, drag mankind after them."[8]

Of all the Young Americans, Brooks was the most extreme in opting for a romantic alternative to pragmatism. Bourne used similar language when he complained that "men cannot live by politics alone" and urged Nietzschean "malcontents" to "seek the vital and the sincere every-where," rather than submit to Dewey's precepts for responsible action in wartime. Such romantic flights of fantasy especially appealed to Bourne in moments of great despair, when he yearned for peace and security in a pure utopia of the spirit. "I crave some pagan monastery some 'great, good place,'" he confessed to a friend in the fall of 1917, "where I can go and stay till the war is all over." He and Brooks even entertained the idea of establishing a communal colony in Westchester, complete with "an expensive cook and perhaps a community auto." "My imagination takes wing," he told a correspondent after describing their plans, "and am recovered from my depression." But these dreams passed quickly, and Bourne joined his friends in using romanticism to flesh out the abstract body of pragmatic thought.[9]

Bourne believed that a reassertion of romantic values would revive pragmatism by forcing it to take into account the full range of human aspirations and emotions. This meant understanding experience as "a subjective matter"—as Frank put it—shot through with aesthetic and spiritual vision. Frank explained that "to experience takes time and meditation and an inner sense of values: demands the stoppage of head-long muscular activity." A philosophy of experience had to encompass "man's capacity to feel life as a whole," as embodied in artistic and religious practices, as well as the capacity for critical reason that charac-terized Dewey's scientific method. In essence, this position was less a repudiation of pragmatism than a reassertion of its original principles, one that recalled William James's respect for the ways in which the nonrational elements of the human imagination shaped the workings of reason.[10]

Central to this revised version of pragmatism was the Young Ameri-cans' emphasis on *values*—a term equal in significance to *personality* and *experience* in their essays of this period—as the appropriate object of intellectuals' attention. Bourne, Brooks, and Frank did not appeal to romantic notions of spirit and intuition to resurrect Highbrow detach-ment in a new form. In flight from an instrumental culture, intellectuals could not hark back to genteel moralism. Attention to values provided a way out of this predicament. Mediating between abstract ideas and social practice, values took root in the emotional reaches of human personality. They played a role in the workings of civic culture in a way that more specialized intellectual disciplines could not. Values were not the property of experts but a kind of second nature that individuals drew on in their day-to-day activity. By definition, they were a common cultural legacy, articulated more precisely perhaps by some, disputed more forcefully by others, but still a public language of social experience. As critics and creators of values, intellectuals had the responsibility for grounding ideas in the rich sediment of myth, folklore, and morality that nourished values informing customary behavior. Values, in short, were the crossroads on which the romantic and the pragmatic critiques of industrial culture met to submit practice to conscious control.

Bourne's opposition of values to technique can be understood only in relation to his continued commitment to Dewey's goal of renewing American democracy through a public philosophy of experience. This continuity in Bourne's criticism reveals how much he shared with Brooks's and Frank's vision of an American cultural renaissance, as well as how little sympathy all three men had for an aestheticist retreat from politics. The Young Americans saw the recovery of insights into culture and personality as the necessary first step toward a genuine philosophy of experience and a revived democratic community. By recognizing the convergence of romantic and pragmatic elements in their thought, it becomes possible to see how they sought to unite cultural renewal and political change. "The conservation of American promise," Bourne explained, required a period of intense cultural and theoretical preparation before it could inform new forms of democratic experience. "We can be skeptical constructively, if, thrown back on our inner resources from the world of war which is taken as the overmastering reality, we search much more actively to clarify our attitudes and express a richer significance in the American scene." Intellectuals had to dig down deep into the recesses of culture and formulate values that could, in later times, redeem social practice as fully human experience. "We must go through a period of static suffering, of inner cultivation," Frank told readers in the closing pages of *Our America*. "We must break our impotent habit of constant issuance into petty deed." This was by no means a counsel of apathetic withdrawal. In training the weapons of romanticism on Deweyan liberalism, the Young Americans hoped to revitalize a radical-democratic politics by giving it a deeper appreciation of the problems of culture and psychology that plagued industrial civilization and had undermined earlier efforts at social reform.[11]

Bourne best expressed the implications of this revision of pragmatism for radicals in a passage describing the mission of American culture in an age of world war:

> If America has lost its political isolation, it is all the more obligated to retain its spiritual integrity. This does not mean any smug retreat from the world, with a belief that the truth is in us and can only be contaminated by contact. It means that the promise of American life is not yet achieved, perhaps not even seen, and that, until it is, there is nothing for us but stern and intensive cultivation of our garden. Our insulation will not be against any great creative ideas or forms that Europe brings. It will be a turning within in order that we may have something to give without. . . . It is absurd for us to think of ourselves as blessing the world with anything unless we hold it more self-consciously and significantly than we hold anything now.

The Young Americans' synthesis of romantic and pragmatic thought centered on the "intensive cultivation" of values as part of a prolonged strategy for radical change. Far from advocating political quietism, they summoned intellectuals to "turn within" to the conscious formulation of values in order "to give without" to a project of democratic renewal.[12]

Upholding romantic notions of spirit, intuition, and the artistic imagination against Dewey's emphasis on scientific method and technique, the Young Americans hoped to revive pragmatism as a dialectical theory of human experience. Leaning to their pragmatic right in their critique of the rootlessness of nineteenth-century gentility, they then shifted their balance to their romantic left in disputing the drift of Dewey's thought during the war. Such shifts in priorities were not expedient measures taken in the heat of intellectual battle. Rather, they developed out of a coherent core of assumptions about the importance of cultural change and personal renewal to a new politics of community. Bourne, Brooks, and Frank had spent the better part of the decade working through the implications of such ideas before they issued their polemics against Dewey and his disciples. An ongoing reassessment of pragmatic and Fabian progressivism was the hallmark of Bourne's and Brooks's earliest work, and it would continue to be a central concern for Brooks, Frank, and Mumford in the 1920s and after.

Still, serious problems persisted for the Young Americans in their conception of their own role as radical intellectuals in an increasingly conservative age. The prewar American Left looked feeble in comparison to its counterparts in western Europe, but it still provided a political backdrop to the critical discussions carried out in the pages of the *Seven Arts*. These writers' program for an American cultural renaissance always assumed the existence of a growing popular movement of dissent, whose cultural expressions might parallel their own efforts toward an indigenous art of American experience. The synthesis of theory and practice that the Young Americans had jealously guarded as the goal of pragmatic theory had as its counterpart a belief in the future convergence of a popular "transnationalism" with the cultural project of radical intellectuals. With the coming of the war and its attendant hysteria and government-sponsored vigilantism, intellectuals of the Left were even more removed from any possible popular audience. In this context, the call for a period of cultural and theoretical preparation made practical sense—since imminent political change was out of the question—but it also bordered dangerously on an appeal to sectarianism or even irrelevance. The nationalist hysteria sparked by the entry of the United States into the war in April 1917 had severed any connection between popular practice and intellectual criticism. It left the Young Americans with the unenviable prospect of succeeding their genteel forefathers as the high priests of disembodied ideals.

Compounding this difficulty was the very synthesis of pragmatic and romantic ideas that these critics had knit together over the course of the decade. Their pragmatism pushed them toward a position as intellectual agitators in the public realm, where they would promote open discussions about culture, values, and politics. But the hostile climate of public opinion during and immediately after the war made that role increasingly difficult. A more attractive option was to adopt the posture of romantic prophet, which enabled intellectuals to sidestep the issue of the waning public sphere and intuitively express the latent will of the people. If the first role rehabilitated the intellectual's vocation as a civic moralist, the latter tempted him with the illusion of becoming the nation's seer. [13]

These two currents ran through Bourne's understanding of his role as a critical intellectual. Determined to resist the "premature crystallization" that had led the Deweyans to a reckless identification of "war-technique" with experience, Bourne sought out a position in which he would hold taut the tension between his own ideals and the realities of American life. He told Brooks that it was better to foster a " 'vital myth,' " whose impact could never be "weighted tangibly," than to "be found pointing complacently to tangible results," as the prowar liberals had done. Intellectuals should act as "a ferment or a goad," instead of rushing to realize their vision through the existing structures of political action. They should resist the pressure to assimilate thought to its environment that was the central feature of industrial culture. [14]

This position separated Bourne from the prowar pragmatists at the *New Republic*, but it also made him an uneasy ally of the socialist Left, which shared his opposition to the war. Just a year before he launched his attack on Dewey, he had raised objections about the atmosphere of populist sentimentality that inhibited serious theoretical debates on the Left. In a 1916 essay "The Price of Radicalism," he lashed out against the Left's habitual suspicion of intellect as an effeminate affectation. Intellectuals active in labor or socialist movements found themselves constantly admonished to "put aside their university knowledge" and "touch the great heart of the people." "His intellectualism he must disguise," Bourne complained. "The epithet 'intellectual' must make him turn pale and run." The Left, in Bourne's analysis, was as guilty as the Progressive intelligentsia of subordinating critical thought to the dictates of some unconscious motive force to history—in this case, the class struggle, as interpreted in the most narrowly economic terms. It is to Bourne's credit that such left-wing anti-intellectualism did not drive him from politics or provoke in him an exaggerated fear of popular ignorance, as it would a later generation of skeptical radicals. Bourne's response was to call on radical intellectuals to serve a traditional function as servants of truth, a position that placed him on the Left but also kept him loyal to an older project of humanistic inquiry. "The only way by which middle-class radicalism can serve," he wrote, "is by being fiercely and concentratedly intellectual." Bourne was quick to point out that this did not mean posturing as proletarians or "repeating stale dogmas of Marxism." "It had better mean a restless, controversial criticism of current ideas, and a hammering out of some clear-sighted philosophy that shall be this pillar of fire. The young radical today is not asked to be a martyr, but he is asked to be a thinker, an intellectual leader." [15]

In reasserting the intellectual's traditional role as skeptical thinker, Bourne was arguing from the standpoint of Brooks's indictment of America's rootless modernity in *America's Coming-of-Age* and the *Seven Arts*. It was the lack of an intellectual group embodying older forms of moral and humanistic authority, Brooks had argued, which left Americans helpless before the onslaught of industrialization. Bourne's antagonism to the Progressive and socialist intellectual roles available in his own time derived from the commitment he shared with Brooks and Frank to the role of the critic as a seeker of public controversy. The idea of the intellectual's obligation to provoke ever wider debates about the good life harked back to Socrates and to the biblical prophets. In an industrial society that reduced culture to adornment or made it a reflection of thoughtless practice, the reassertion of that traditional vocation was itself potentially subversive.

Bourne spoke for this radical-traditionalist conception of the intellectual life in the final sentence of "The War and the Intellectuals": "If the American intellectual class rivets itself to a 'liberal' philosophy that perpetuates the old errors, there will then be need for 'democrats' whose task will be to divide, confuse, disturb, keep the intellectual waters constantly in motion to prevent any such ice from ever forming." Though phrased as a counterexhortation to Dewey's advice for effective action, this remains Bourne's best statement of his view of the intellectual's public role. It is also a fine example of his lingering debt to Dewey's idea of a democratic public. The best hope for the renewal of the public sphere, Bourne argued, lay in the presence of intellectual gadflies who constantly recalled their countrymen to an understanding of their role as democratic citizens. Bourne's ideal polis—his Beloved Community—was alive with a plurality of discussions. Intellectuals stood watch at their center, not as elite guardians of morality but as representatives of the public's conscience, attentive to each citizen's capacity for self-reflection and excellence.[16]

This generous conception of the democratic intellectual was increasingly at odds with the elitist implications of Bourne's other stance in his final years, namely that of Nietzschean "malcontent." In part, Bourne's democratic vision of the intellectual's role fell victim to the war, which narrowed the options for gadflies in the public realm. As Michael Walzer correctly notes, "the tone of Bourne's writing changed in 1918," as he became "increasingly skeptical about the 'possibilities' of American life—and increasingly bitter in his skepticism." There had already existed within Bourne's thought a tendency toward a prophetic posture that undermined the most promising aspects of his position, but that tendency became more pronounced in the last year of his life. Thus Bourne slipped into an easy literary snobbery in a 1918 essay when he asserted that "all good writing is produced in serene unconsciousness of what Demos desires or demands." "The artist must write for that imagined audience of perfect comprehenders. The critic must judge for that audience too." Such a remark followed logically from Bourne's desire to keep in sharp dialectical tension the critic's loyalty to the ideal and the demands of social practice. But it also transposed into the realm of the imagination the possibility of any reconciliation between ideas and practical activity. The Beloved Community, in this view, became the dream of preaching to an "audience of perfect comprehenders," not the public discussions of the democratic polity.[17]

The war had driven Bourne to despair about the immediate possibilities for public action, but this approach seemed to close off forever the role of civic conscience that he had outlined in 1917 in "The War and the Intellectuals." The posthumously published "History of a Literary Radical" confirmed this trend in Bourne's thinking. There his mind turned to "little pools of workers and appreciators of similar temperaments and tastes" as an alternative to "fighting the Philistine in the name of freedom, or fighting the vulgar iconoclast in the name of wholesome human notions." This strategy of recovering alternative values in "intensively self-conscious groups" had much in common with Bourne's revision of pragmatic politics, but he now made no mention of how—or even if—intellectuals were to reach out of their own "temperamental community of sentiment" to the public at large. Bourne's "democrats" came only to disturb the waters of their own Bohemian eddies, instead of stirring up the mainstream of public experience.[18]

The gradual eclipse of Bourne's understanding of the intellectual as civic conscience is evident in a remarkable letter he wrote to Brooks in March 1918. Using Brooks's *Letters and Leadership* as a launching point for his own speculations about intellectual leadership, Bourne summed up the major elements of his critique of the Progressive intelligentsia. The liberals at the *New Republic* had lost the respect of "malcontents" like Brooks and himself by virtue of their "callousness" toward "creative values." "The political liberal somehow seems to assume civilization," Bourne wrote, and then plunges immediately into institutional reforms. "He does not ask himself whether these schemes will, conformably to our national tradition and temperament, make the individual and the group life richer." Nor was there any clearer understanding of what he and the other Young Americans meant by a Beloved Community of free personalities in the ideas emanating from the universities, the labor movement, or the socialist Left. "The result is that the mind that would speculate about what is going on in American life, or what might be done with it, or what one's relation is to it, is left without any one to think its thought for it."[19]

Bourne's awkward phrasing revealed everything that was disturbing about this new direction of his thinking about the role of intellectuals, who were now to lead the growing class of "malcontents" and "think its thought." He congratulated Brooks on the "certain superb youthful arrogance" in his book "that it is we and our friends who are to be the masters," noting that Brooks's demolition of his adversaries left "by mere process of elimination" those in his own circle as the only ones capable of assuming leadership of a new American culture. Perhaps Bourne had written too soon after reading Brooks's passages on Goethe as a model for American cultural renewal. In any case, he now embraced a fully romantic solution to the problem of transcending the division between his "community of sentiment" and the public at large. The Young Americans were to provide the disaffected members of the "malcontented class" with its "new gospel." "I have dim notions of how that leadership could be created," he confided; "people must be appealed to desire certain things mightily. Then the 'leaders' will be simply those articulate souls who can express most convincingly those desired values. In any such enterprise, leadership loses all its snobbery. It becomes a true co-operation with the attentive ones in a clearing up of our spiritual mist."[20]

On one level, this view of leadership was fully in keeping with Bourne's democratic alternative to Deweyan liberalism. He still abhorred the social-scientific pose of technical expertise that remained the dominant model for Progressive intellectuals. Moreover, his emphasis on a "true co-operation" with other "malcontents" in the formation of "desired values" grew directly from the subjectivist pragmatism he developed in opposition to Dewey in 1917. But in moving toward Brooks's defense of the artistic imagination over technical reason, Bourne cut the ties to Dewey's notion of the public that had given his earlier statement of the intellectual's role its power as a model for democrats loyal to truth and the public sphere. To be sure, the actual constricting of the American public sphere in 1917–18 played a role in driving Bourne to a romantic position as intuitive prophet of values. But the danger of such a move was always present in his thought as he tried to combine a quasi-religious prophecy with the searching criticism of pragmatic method. Whatever the advantages of Bourne's prophetic stance over the technocratic pretensions of his progressive contemporaries, there was nothing very democratic about intellectuals "thinking thoughts" for other people. Bourne's romanticism showed no understanding of such objections, however; he merely asserted that the "snobbery" of leadership would disappear with the mists that he and his friends would sweep out of the American mind. In the months before his death from influenza in December 1918, Bourne had traded in the contentious debate of the Beloved Community for the warm unanimity of communion with like-minded souls.

In Bourne's case, the choice of the prophetic vocation came at the expense of his faith in the public realm. By contrast, Waldo Frank made a conscious appeal to the public as a romantic seer. Much of Frank's later career—especially in the 1930s, when he tried to join his own brand of romantic anticapitalism to the orthodox Marxism of the Communist party—can best be understood as a series of repeatedly frustrated efforts to act as a spiritual leader in the world of politics. The war years and their immediate aftermath were Frank's first experience in this endeavor, and they set the pattern of disappointments that would mark his subsequent forays into the public sphere. Of all the Young Americans, Frank was especially prone to an overblown oracular rhetoric that claimed for artists and intellectuals a position as visionary leaders of a new American community. Edmund Wilson later complained that Frank "writes in a style—to me, never quite satisfactory—that combines James Joyce with the Hebrew prophets." Frank's aspirations as an intellectual were of a piece with his stylistic pretensions: he was to be not only the prophet of a new art and literature but the catalyst of a religious awakening that would bind Americans together in a new community. This sense of his own mission led him to try to combine the two roles of civic moralist and romantic outsider that had warred with each other in Bourne's mind in 1917–18. At the same time as he was registering as a conscientious objector to World War I—"to this war" only, he stressed—Frank also felt a strong identity between his own work as a critic and the course of American destiny. "I was no longer alone!" he later remembered when describing the *Seven Arts* period. "I belonged to America and America belonged to me. There was no demarkation between my contacts as an editor and as a man."[21]

That sense of belonging faltered with the folding of the *Seven Arts* in late 1917. The journal collapsed not only because its financial supporter cut off funding over the publication of antiwar essays—other funding

might have been obtained from Scofield Thayer of the *Dial*—but because Frank and James Oppenheim could no longer work together. Personal battles between the editors over control of the magazine belied its
rhetoric of artistic community. Still, Frank sought other opportunities to
act as a dissident prophet of American promise. His *Our America*, published late in 1919, summed up the *Seven Arts* project and staked out a
position for Frank as a likely successor to Bourne as the critic who most
successfully united radical politics and cultural analysis. Brooks wrote
with ecstatic praise after reading the book. "You have blazed trails that I
am going to follow joyously," he told Frank. "To me this book is the first
clear, sure note of our new day." Soon after finishing *Our America*,
Frank went to the Midwest to join the populist Non-Partisan League as
a journalist and an activist. "Sure, I wished to be famous," he admitted
in his memoirs; "but deeper I wanted to be accepted, wanted my dream
of America to be accepted." The plunge into politics proved abortive,
and Frank soured on the league and politics generally within a few
weeks.[22]

Frank's experiences in 1919 provide a jarring coda to the Young
Americans' hopes for an American renaissance in the 1910s. With his
writing and his activism, Frank was honestly trying to live the life of
spirit in the public realm. The experiment was not entirely a failure. *Our
America* was a fine piece of work, perhaps the best book Frank ever
wrote, and his brush with populism left a legacy of political sympathies
that bore fruit years later. Frank's generous vision of American potential
is evident in both projects. But his work also revealed the limitations
of the Young Americans' attempt to act the part of seer while appealing
to the public conscience. The tensions in their thought—between romanticism and pragmatism, spirit and society, culture and politics—had
sharpened their critical insights into American industrial culture, but
they offered little advice on how to live as intellectuals in anticipation of
the Beloved Community.

Our America exemplified the paradox of the position Frank sought
for himself and his colleagues. The book's stunning last line—"And in a
dying world, creation is revolution"—was a bold declaration of Frank's
intention to forge a new politics out of the cultural climate that gave
birth to the *Seven Arts*. At the decade's end, the spirit of cultural radicalism still remained estranged from that of political revolution, Frank
complained. "The men who listen to Stieglitz have not yet quite joined
him in their mind with the example of Bill Haywood." Meanwhile,
radicals had not learned to tap the spirit of creative revolt that animated

the new movements in art and literature. The task ahead was to exploit the subversive power of art as a way of unlocking the latent potential of the American public, which lay submerged in the lockstep routines of an industrial civilization. "The material of the creative act is there," Frank wrote. "What waits is the creative impulse."[23]

Frank's call to cultural revolution reflected his own understanding of American culture as a product of unequal power relations. He borrowed liberally from Charles Beard's history of the ascendancy of capitalist interests in the United States, giving that story a cultural dimension absent in Beard's work. Like Brooks, he condemned the toll of the country's commercial expansion on the American imagination and saw industrialization as a further assault on individual subjectivity. To Brooks's history of spiritual declension Frank added the emergence of an urban mass culture "designed to catch the dulled attention of the molecular units" of a bureaucratic society. The political cleavages of that society were not entirely those of class or of "interest," though Frank made references to the economic exploitation of workers and other groups. More significant was the division between the forces of the imagination and those elite groups who benefited from the "herd"-like complacency of the American public: "Every nerve of the American controlling organism strains against the life of liberal thought and revolutionary faith: against the cult of any beauty that is not slavish and minor. Whitman and his sons cry for their multitudes to be born anew: and the American powers take every step to preserve them in a state of ignorance, flatulence, complacency which shall approximate the Herd." Frank's equation of cultural creation and revolution derived from his conviction that political domination penetrated deep into culture and the individual psyche. The triumph of large-scale business enterprise had brought with it the massification of everyday life—the reduction of community to a herd existence. Reversing that process meant rekindling the fire of the imagination in a people whom work had made docile and whose leisure was given over to commercial spectacle. Frank's cry of power to the imagination was a political response to the cultural relations of power in his day.[24]

With that end in mind, Frank searched through American history for examples of individuals and groups who personified the alternative values he hoped to foster in a new culture. Abraham Lincoln stood alone in Frank's book as the only American political figure gifted with a "mystical sense of life." In looking to Lincoln as a model of prophetic leadership, Frank seemed to go out of his way to refute Herbert Croly's attempt to enlist Lincoln in the Progressive cause in *The Promise of American Life*. Croly worshiped Lincoln as a man who stood above his people and disdained their petty localism; he was a prototype for Croly's disinterested politics of expertise. By contrast, Frank's Lincoln "was not intellectually aloof from his fellows and his time. He was no intellectual virtuoso. He believed in American institutions." Once again, Frank refused to join his Progressive peers in seeking a public position for intellectuals as experts in command of specialized knowledge. Lincoln was an exemplary character in Frank's cultural history because, in good romantic fashion, he intuitively understood and gave voice to the will of the people: "Abraham Lincoln prophesies the break from the materialistic culture of pioneer America: personifies the emergence from it of a poetic and religious experience based on the reality of American life—and in terms so simple that they have become the experience of all. This is our true wealth in Lincoln." This was Frank's most democratic statement of his ideal of creative leadership. The romantic-democratic intellectual was a mystic of the common good, a leader who drew together the diverse elements of the public realm in a vision of republican union.[25]

Unfortunately, the rest of *Our America* belied the democratic implications of this model of intellectual life. Frank's discussion of Lincoln ducked the more troublesome aspects of this vision—he never asked, for example, whether the mystical prophet was necessarily a democratic or responsible leader—but it at least suggested a common public realm in which Lincoln appealed to his fellow citizens. This was not the case of the other oracular figures Frank held up as examples of intellectual leadership such as Thoreau, Whitman, and Stieglitz. The only apparent connection between these men and their compatriots was a collective spirit that they alone seemed capable of articulating. Comparing Whitman to Moses, Frank wrote that "a deep unconscious impulse made the transfer from his own election, to his people. Since he was chosen, his was a chosen people." Rightfully opposed to the Progressives' tendency to exalt the intellectual's distance from the popular mind, Frank still found it difficult to formulate a democratic role for the intellectual in public life. His romantic ideal of an intuitive bond uniting the prophet and his people merely asserted such a role without explaining how it might work in practice.[26]

In fact, the romantic model of intellectual leadership often bordered on being reactionary in its implicit disdain for the inarticulate, slumbering masses. That such disdain need not be implicit was well known to

Frank, who had come across a conservative variant of such rhetoric in his correspondence with D. H. Lawrence during the *Seven Arts* period. Lawrence wrote Frank in 1917, "I disbelieve *utterly* in the public, in humanity, in the mass. There should be a body of esoteric doctrine, defended from the herd. The herd will destroy everything. Pure thought, pure understanding, this alone matters." Frank never went this far himself, but his own use of romantic language often came close to Lawrence's arrogant elitism. His mystical sense of "the whole" bordered on Lawrence's idea of an "esoteric doctrine" inaccessible to the masses. Frank's criticism tended to reserve such divinatory knowledge for a select group of prophets capable of expressing the spiritual longings of a people.[27]

When Frank turned from discussing artists and intellectuals to describing the "buried cultures" that preserved alternative values in an industrial age, he tended to idealize countercultures that—by his description—lacked any conception of a democratic public. In good romantic form, Frank rhapsodized over the cultures of blacks, Hispanics, Indians, and other outsiders as bastions of *Gemeinschaft*. In the midst of a bureaucratic civilization, there still existed peoples who organized their lives in face-to-face communities, according to values of mutuality, spirit, art, and respect for nature. After visiting Native American settlements in New Mexico in 1918, Frank wrote Anderson that "here, of a sudden, all of a deep great gentle culture swam into my vision—a culture whose spiritual superiority to ours no intelligent man would question." He returned to the same theme in *Our America*: "The uncorrupted Indian knows no individual poverty or wealth. All of his tribe is either rich or poor. He has no politics. He has no dynastic or industrial intrigue—although of course personal and fraternal intrigue does exist. His physical world is fixed. And in consequence all his energies beyond the measure of his daily toil rise ineluctably to spiritual consciousness: flow to consideration of his place and part in Nature, into the business of beauty." Frank's treatment of Native American culture tells more about his need to claim some "buried culture" for his own than it does about the multiplicity of tribal cultures he lumped together as a single Indian civilization. Most important, it speaks volumes of the dangers in Frank's attempt to create a romantic-democratic role for intellectuals as prophets of a new American culture. For what seems to have most appealed to Frank in his portrait of Indian culture was its lack of a politics, of any realm in which deliberative reason and contentious debate might shape a collective way of life. Presiding over Frank's "buried culture" was the figure of the cacique—"the interpreter between Nature and his people"—whose use of magic enabled the tribe to live in harmony with the cosmos. The cacique was Frank's intuitive prophet at his least democratic. Frank placed Lincoln in the context of some broader public dialogue with other Americans about their shared religious and political traditions. However fuzzy this formulation was, it at least acknowledged an ongoing discussion in which the political-cultural prophet took a leading role. The intellectual-as-cacique, on the other hand, recalled Lawrence's rantings about an elite removed from "the herd" by its possession of "esoteric doctrine." In the end, Frank's romantic-democratic stance for intellectuals threatened to strip the public of any real role except as an echo to the prophet's call.[28]

The ambiguities in Frank's understanding of the radical intellectual's public role are all the more evident in the series of letters he wrote Sherwood Anderson about his experiences in the Midwest in November and December 1919 working for the Non-Partisan League. Frank took a job as a writer for a paper for the league in Ellsworth, Kansas, but he admitted to Anderson that he was "the rottenest propagandist you ever did see." "I cant [sic] stay on the surface of political creed," he explained; he was constantly searching for the kernel of spirit in the farmers and miners he met, for the religious impulse that Anderson had taught him lived on in the rural heartland. "I found it easy to just visit around with the men and women, and talk human with them. and [sic] perhaps tell them a few of the things that had occurred to me, and how I felt toward them." How these rural populists responded to the things that occurred to the author of *Our America* is a mystery, but it is clear that Frank viewed his new associates in much the same way he had seen the "buried cultures" he had described in that book. They were decent people who lived close to the soil and held on to a vision of America as a moral commonwealth. But they were also simple people, who lacked the words to express that vision or their experiences. "There is so earnest and innocent a willingness in them to be good and to be right," he told Anderson, "and they have no measures, they have no eyes for the measure of the Kansas sky which should be measure enough."[29]

During his brief stay in Kansas, Frank felt torn between his longings to identify with the people he met as their prophet and his revulsion at the political machinations at work in the Non-Partisan League. Frank wrote Anderson that the "poor sweet dull brothers" he was coming to know were bound to him by the loving embrace of his heart. "I do know that in a way infinitely easy and compelling, I am at one with these men and women and these children." But this identification consisted largely of an intuitive union with his acquaintances as parts of a wider cosmic whole. Describing that sense of union, Frank could erase the very particularities of the people he met. As prophet of the prairies, Frank poured his emotional and psychological state into his letters, to the exclusion of any real description of life in the Midwest. His letters were more evocative of the huge "Kansas sky" than of the people who lived beneath it. "I feel that their dullness and their ugliness are mine," Frank wrote of miners he met in Osage, Kansas. "They are Me. I can look into their eyes, as I can look into the eyes of a horse, and into the eyes of myself, and say You are Me. I am You." Frank's political work, by contrast, allowed for no such easy merging of himself with the folk. "I cannot feel clean, after I have written a political paragraph," he confided to Anderson. "I am really happy only in my own world, which is your world also, dear Sherwood, where there is no yesterday and no tomorrow—no judging and no deciding—only infinite beauty and infinite motion into the fixity of truth." Frank had tried to convince himself that Kansas populists also inhabited that world, but exposure to their political organization revealed that it failed to live up to the "fixity of truth" that now subsumed Frank's image of rural community. Having first depicted these farmers as living in intuitive harmony with their new visitor, Frank now retreated to a purer vision of a spiritual world he and Anderson shared alone.[30]

Frank's final break with the Non-Partisan League came in December 1919, when he attended the movement's national convention in St. Paul. The convention's internecine politics disgusted him as a betrayal of the spirit of goodness and community that he had found in the grass roots of the movement. That experience put an end to any illusions that he "could ever function *politically*," he wrote Anderson.

As I went up in the scale of authority, there gradually faded out all that was sweet and gentle and lovable in the farmers' world—: the farmers' world—its life—faded away. In its place, doctrine, dogma, figures, political manipulation, words. In place of the farmers' world, the usual carpentry of lives. I am telling you nothing new. You know all this. So did I. But it was, nevertheless, a rich experience. For here, projected, was the Socialist State that is coming next. And, Beloved Man, it will be quite as far from thee & me, quite as ignorant & quite as hostile to our gods, as Tammany Hall. Let it come. O yes. Bless it—give blood to it—for it will at least, perhaps, more decently apportion food and sunlight. But let us know it for what it is. Let us be brave and admit that political representation will *always*, *must* always be a game for the tricky, the brutal . . . the shallow.

The episode was a sad ending to Frank's activities throughout the latter half of the decade. In his personal life, he had tried to overcome the warring desires to plunge thoughtlessly into public life and to withdraw to a private "communion of saints." In his cultural criticism, he had sought to establish art as a mediating point between spirit and social experience. As part of his contribution to the Young Americans' debate with Dewey, he had tried to synthesize romanticism and pragmatism so as to give the crucial concept of experience its fullest possible meaning. And as a public intellectual, he hoped to be both a Lincoln and a Whitman, giving voice to the political and spiritual potential of his people.[31]

Yet his encounter with the Non-Partisan League showed how difficult these various syntheses actually were. Frank's romantic vision of intellectual prophecy overburdened the intellectual's public role with an ideal of intuitive union with his audience that he could never achieve in any real political context. When presented with the conflicts endemic to any political endeavor, Frank floundered and eventually retreated to his friendship with Anderson, whose fictional characters were perhaps easier to identify with than the organizers at the Non-Partisan League. In his despair, he gave vent to an elitist rage against the populace that recalled the worst aspects of Lawrence's position. The same day he wrote Anderson of his political disillusionment, he fired off a similar letter to Brooks, announcing that "politics is a lie." "Representative government under any plan will bring into the places of power men who are shallow, plausible, insensitive." Frank's delicate synthesis of politics and culture in the *Seven Arts* and *Our America* had come apart in his own experience. Unable to remake the public sphere as a mirror image of the intellectual's private vision, Frank followed Bourne in looking for shelter among friends.[32]

From one perspective, Bourne's and Frank's experiences suggest the futility of trying to preserve premodern values in a disenchanted world. Their withdrawal into an enclave of spirit, in the face of an inhospitable climate of opinion, recalls their youthful explorations of the feminine ideal as a dream of mystical union with their environment. Such aspirations found no welcome response in the postwar American polity, and thus the Young Americans turned inward—into the self or the loving acceptance of friends—for protection. Writing in 1918, Max Weber saw an equally hopeless fate for the spiritual life in the modern age. "Precisely the ultimate and most sublime values have retreated from public life," he observed in "Science as a Vocation," only to take refuge in "the transcendental realm of mystic life or . . . the brotherliness of direct and personal human relations." All attempts to resurrect such "ultimate" values were doomed to failure, Weber concluded, pointing to the "miserable monstrosities" of monumentalism in art and the "worse effects" created in the attempts to "construe new religions without a new and genuine prophecy." Such "academic prophecy" might create "fanatical sects but never a genuine community." Arguing from Weber's premises, one might interpret the Young Americans' work in the late 1910s as a rear-guard struggle against the rationalizing forces of modernity. The odds were stacked against Bourne, Brooks, and Frank from the start: it is not surprising that they produced a "fanatical sect" among themselves instead of a "genuine community."[33]

The difficulty with this argument is that it cedes in advance the battle that the Young Americans believed might yet be won against positivist modes of thought and a bureaucratized social existence. It is not at all clear, in retrospect, that the forces of an instrumental modernity were as monolithic or as all-powerful in 1918 as Weber thought. The Young Americans certainly believed that many elements of modern culture and social thought promoted a new respect for human consciousness that might be turned against the dehumanizing legacy of nineteenth-century industrialization. Their interest in personality as a means to self-expression within a Beloved Community reflects their anticipation of new, liberating forms of individuality and social action created by modern conditions. Although much of their historical analysis led to conclusions consistent with a Weberian pessimism, the Young Americans also believed that it was still possible to reverse the nineteenth century's relegation of spirit to a private realm. There was no reason, as they saw it, to assume that industrial patterns of behavior were inalterable or that individual subjectivity had to give way to a bureaucratic ethos of social adjustment.

Instead of viewing Bourne's and Frank's experiences in 1918–19 as evidence of the hopelessness of the Young Americans' entire cause, it is more fruitful to see them as a significant departure from the effort to make culture and spirit transformative forces in American life. In this regard, these two critics' turn to a romantic intellectual model was as much a "premature crystallization" of their work as Dewey's prowar stance was of the pragmatic program of social reform. By resorting to such a posture, Bourne and Frank tried to patch over the divide separating their criticism from the realities of industrial society by positing an intuitive union between the critic and his audience. The identity of thought and its object—a mainstay of romantic philosophy—was a useful counterweight to the positivist prescription that theory take hold of society in the same way that science transformed the natural world because it preserved consciousness as the medium uniting both theories of human activity and that activity itself. A neoromantic cultural criticism granted to the objects of its inquiry the capacity for reason and aesthetic experience denied them in technocratic theories of social change. But in defending such a view, Bourne and Frank undermined the tensions between culture and society and between spirit and practice that gave their work its force as a stimulus to critical thought. Their romantic intellectual role upheld the cultural prophet as the meeting ground for these different realms, as if his capacities for intuitive understanding could easily heal the wounds that industrialization had inflicted upon a common culture. Bourne and Frank had set themselves the improbable task of living their own lives as the embodiment of a new cultural synthesis. In the process, they had ignored their own warnings that such a synthesis could arise only out of a thorough transformation of social relations. It proved impossible to resolve the conflicts they had identified in American culture within their own private experience. "It is no fun being a free man in a slave-world," Bourne confessed to a friend. The intellectual-as-prophet was no substitute for a democratic community life.[34]

The Young Americans' critical theory was strongest when it remained resolute in its criticism: when it opposed "the good life of personality lived in the environment of the Beloved Community" to both aimless subjectivism and unmediated, objective experience. They joined the debate with Dewey at the juncture of those two realms—in his conception of consciously informed practice or "experience"—and urged pragmatists to maintain the critical imagination as the central element of a democratic culture. Bourne, Brooks, and Frank understood that the war liberals' fascination with administrative technique threatened the pragmatic goal of reviving democracy as a common enterprise of critical inquiry. Their emphasis on the need for a sustained meditation on values as an integral part of such an enterprise was a healthy corrective to the positivist undercurrent in pragmatic liberalism and an essential contribution to any democratic theory of cultural renewal. Nonetheless, their reaction against the technocratic elements of wartime liberalism also led them at times to reject the best features of pragmatism. Recoiling against Dewey's subordination of values to "war-technique," they often embraced a romantic position that dissolved the conflict between theory and practice in the intuitive vision of the prophetic artist. By implying that personal intuition and mysticism could mediate between the constituent elements of experience, Bourne and Frank betrayed the promise of their own subjectivist revision of pragmatism—just as Oppenheim and Rosenfeld had done in their cultural criticism for the *Seven Arts.* The ideal of an interactive self reshaping its own consciousness as it humanized the environment, of the craftsman uniting knowledge and action through a collective practice, remained the Young Americans' most powerful alternative to the culture of industrialism. Withdrawing into the spiritual preserve of the romantic self—or, conversely, seizing the public world as an arena of emotional union—left no room for the critical dialectic of consciousness and social activity that was the basis of these writers' finest work. It left no room, in other words, for culture itself.

To return to the theoretical and spiritual preparation they had argued for during the war, the Young Americans had to put aside the "premature crystallization" of prophecy for a more thorough attention to culture as a medium of collective experience. That was the challenge facing Lewis Mumford in the 1920s as he took up the work that Bourne, Brooks, and Frank had begun in the *Seven Arts.* The analysis of cultural forms that engaged social realities in a dialogue with future possibilities held out the greatest promise for a deeper understanding of the democratic potential of modern American life. Such a project might well return the Young Americans' criticism to the impasse that Weber had described in "Science as a Vocation." But it might also provide a way out, once the collective language of cultural representation became the model for a new politics and a new ethos of community.

Randolph Bourne, early 1910s. Randolph S. Bourne Papers,
Rare Book and Manuscript Library, Columbia University.

Van Wyck Brooks, January 5, 1921, sketch by Lewis Mumford.
Lewis Mumford Collection, Art Department, Monmouth College.

Van Wyck Brooks, 1931. E. P. Dutton Records, George Arents Research Library for Special Collections, Syracuse University.

Waldo Frank, 1920, photograph by Alfred Stieglitz.
D-501 Waldo Frank, 1920, Alfred Stieglitz, 1864–1946,
National Gallery of Art, Washington, D.C., Alfred Stieglitz Collection.

Lewis Mumford, January 26, 1920, self-portrait.
Lewis Mumford Collection, Art Department, Monmouth College.

Lewis Mumford, 1926. Lewis Mumford Collection,
Art Department, Monmouth College.

6

Culture against the State

*We may perhaps approach our social institutions a little more
courageously when we realize how completely we ourselves
have created them; and how, without our perpetual "will to
believe" they would vanish like smoke in the wind.*

—LEWIS MUMFORD,
The Story of Utopias

Creative thought had proved no match against "war-technique," but
the Young Americans remained committed to cultural renewal as
the precondition of political change. The success of war mobilization confirmed their belief that industrialization had eroded the cultural
resources of a democratic community. Without a secure sense of place,
tradition, and cultural identity, all elements of American group life
crumbled before the onslaught of the wartime state. "The State is a
jealous God and will brook no rivals," Bourne wrote. By colonizing
once-autonomous areas of social life and subjecting them to its direction, the state undermined the local associations that supported a vital
culture. A politics that aimed at the capture of the state was misguided
from the start, the Young Americans argued. Under current conditions,
the state was more likely to capture its assailants than succumb to them.
If political change were to mean more than a shift in personnel, radicals
would have to regenerate cultural life as an alternative to the institutions of the militarized state.[1]

For the Young Americans, World War I represented not only a diplo-
matic and human disaster but an unprecedented moment of rupture in
the history of culture and politics, one that demanded a complete rethinking of the premises of liberal and socialist theory. "The whole era
has been spiritually wasted," Bourne had despaired, as the logic of prewar Progressivism came to fruition in military mobilization, not in his
Beloved Community. The belief that the war was a turning point in
Western history, upsetting all progressive dogmas, lay behind Lewis
Mumford's draft of an essay on the crisis of international socialism,
which he wrote in 1915 but never published. In it he condemned the
orthodox Marxism of the socialist Left for seeing the demise of capital-

ism as an evolutionary process "independent of human guidance." The Left had come to treat capitalism as "a stage that had to be accepted, with its limitations," since it bore within itself the embryo of a new order. Even more damaging was the Left's belief in inevitable progress, which meant in practice that socialists were "more fervent than their bourgeois contemporaries in embracing the capitalist regime." The war had discredited such assumptions forever. "The idea of waiting patiently for the divine far off event which was to usher in the Socialist State" had run aground: "the event ushered in was the Great War." Any new radical movement would have to acknowledge that the war invalidated all notions of progress and automatic social advance. It would have to retrieve the utopian radical legacy that "the resultant society is dependent upon the deliberate choice of the human beings within it." If the war brought to a head those social trends that deprived men and women of their subjective potential for self-fulfillment, a new radicalism would reassert rational agency and conscious choice as the sources of political action.[2]

This strategy of mobilizing the resources of culture against the state had been an important strain of the arguments for cultural renewal in Bourne's "Trans-national America," Brooks's *America's Coming-of-Age*, and many of the essays in the *Seven Arts*. The war forced the Young Americans to clarify their argument and make explicit its divergence from mainstream Progressivism. Even in their least overtly political writings, they operated under the assumption that their explorations in cultural criticism served to assemble the rudiments of an alternative politics of community. During the decade after the war, the task of formulating a political defense of culture largely fell to Mumford, who inherited Bourne's dream of a Beloved Community and took his place after the war as the most politically minded of the Young American critics. For Mumford, such a community would be founded "on a basis of divided loyalties and dispersed interests." The war had "brought the individual face to face with the state and divested him of all associative interests." Now, the time had come to embed individualism in the social relations of a civic culture: "Civil life means association, with the family, the trade union, the grange, the chamber of commerce, the professional institute, the church, the theater, and the forum intermediating between the life of the individual and his life as the member of a political (military) state." Mumford looked to a new radicalism to restore the cultural conditions for a democratic politics. His strategy was not to avoid politics but to avoid the state, to reestablish in local community life a set of values and loyalties that might bind Americans together in nonstatist forms of association.[3]

In keeping with the Young Americans' revision of pragmatism, Mumford tried to cultivate a culture grounded in the fullest possible human experience. At the heart of his criticism in the 1920s was a plea for "organic" experience. Mumford searched for Frank's mystical "knowledge of the whole" in more prosaic quarters: Patrick Geddes's holistic sociology, regional planning, and the human capacity for symbolic interaction. The anchor of Mumford's critical stance was the ideal of a "whole" life: the individual intensely engaged with his or her surroundings. As Mumford later described it, the concept of cultural organicism "implied a whole complex of ideas and allusions ... partaking of the nature of an organism, as distinct from a lifeless object, a system, a machine, or an abstraction. Among these ideas were those of vitality, rootedness, indigenousness; being part of a larger whole; adhesion to a place, a period, a culture; and finally—not least—travelling freely back and forth between the inner and the outer world, but being exclusively concerned with neither alone."[4]

If the state fostered "mechanical" traits of docile obedience, a culture of organicism promoted an active interchange between the conscious individual and the social environment. It recovered the aesthetic and historical dimensions of personal experience, which had been sacrificed with the demise of a collective culture. Art and history would free subjectivity from the tyranny of actual conditions, enabling the individual mind to reflect upon itself and its surroundings with an aim to their mutual reformation. Moreover, an organic community would encourage collective practices that engaged citizens as makers of their own destinies. Through scientific experiment, social research, ritual, and civic participation, individuals would realize themselves as part of a larger collectivity. As the decade progressed, Mumford recognized that the source of such activities lay in the language of aesthetic forms and symbols that men and women used to humanize their surroundings and in turn give concrete expression to their own desires and intuitions. The increasing prominence of questions of architectural and literary form in Mumford's writings from the 1920s reflected his belief that a new politics of community had to grow out of shared modes of cultural expression. Symbolic interaction was the basis of all organic experience, in Mumford's view, and the best model for a democratic community of free association.

Living a full life—the goal of an organic culture—required a particu-

lar viewpoint on life, one that gave equal weight to the different elements of experience and saw the subject as inextricably linked to the
objective world. The problem with industrial culture, Mumford argued,
was its one-sided elevation of one or another fragment of experience as
a determining force to which all other forms of belief and activity were
subject. The prophets of an organic community would have to maintain
in their criticism the holistic vision that mainstream culture had lost. By
drawing connections between art and social life and between science
and culture, they would begin to restore an understanding of how a
human life might be lived by whole men and women. Their critical
method would prefigure the Beloved Community. "We cannot be satisfied with a segment of existence, no matter how safely we may be
adjusted to it," Mumford wrote in *The Story of Utopias*, "when with a
little effort we can trace the complete circle."[5]

The lesson of the war years, then, was the need for culture as a
defense against the encroachment of the industrial state and for a particular kind of cultural experience as the seedbed for political renewal.
Throughout the 1920s, Mumford propounded what Alan Trachtenberg
has called a "social aesthetics—a grounding of social criticism upon an
aesthetic premise," in which the creative imagination recovered older
bonds of tradition and community in preparation for a new politics. As
Trachtenberg has pointed out, Mumford followed Brooks's call for a
"usable past" to give his aesthetic project a strong historical component. He searched the American past for embers of creative desire that
could reignite a longing for a new organic community in his contemporaries. History, in his mind, was a form of moral archaeology, which
excavated the communal structures and languages that predated the
modern state as foundations for new strategies of cultural resistance. At
the same time, Mumford sought to make history an aesthetic project,
thereby introducing the past into the symbolic language of the present
generation. As he wrote his cultural histories of the "usable past,"
Mumford's larger goal of communitarian democracy was never far from
his mind. The ascendancy of the rootless state made clear the need for
roots.[6]

Bourne, Brooks, and Frank had arrived at their unique synthesis
of romantic and pragmatic criticism in the course of their debates
with Dewey and prowar liberals in the late 1910s. The Progressives'
disastrous attempt at translating pragmatism into a statist politics of

social reform reinforced the Young Americans' commitment to cultural renewal. Mumford's route to a romantic pragmatism was in some ways easier. Like Bourne, he deeply admired Dewey as a philosopher of experience and an educational reformer. And he followed Brooks in piecing together a radical critique of industrialism from the various Fabian, romantic, and distributist currents of the turn-of-the-century English Left. But whereas his friends saw no immediate predecessor for their position, Mumford had the example of Patrick Geddes, the Scottish regionalist, as a figure who united social science and romanticism in a holistic theory of social reform. In 1914, Mumford came across a copy of the text on evolution Geddes wrote with J. Arthur Thomson in the biology library at City College. Within a year, he had read Geddes's *City Development* and *Cities in Evolution* and had begun a correspondence with Geddes's associates in Britain that eventually put him in contact with Geddes himself. Although the two men did not meet until 1923, Mumford immediately grasped the importance of Geddes's work and began to elaborate its implications for American thought in his own writing.

An eclectic thinker whose propensity for systematic theorizing was always at odds with his own disorganization and eccentricities, Geddes passed on to Mumford a way of thinking about culture and society that was remarkably consistent with the approaches of the other Young Americans. Geddes's biological theory of social development set the groundwork for Mumford's organicism, as did his vitalistic rejection of a static materialism. For Geddes, the goal of social reform was "civic regeneration," by which he meant the reconciliation of antagonistic elements of industrial life: ideals and practice, the country and the city, art and industry, and religion and science. Geddes's chief legacy to Mumford's theory of cultural renewal was his belief that the task awaiting modern societies was one of reworking an entire way of life—creating, in effect, a new civilization—so as to enrich individual personality and recover local bonds of association. This meant looking beyond the politics of statecraft to a semireligious movement of civic renewal as a remedy for industrial ills.[7]

Beneath such a theory of cultural rebirth, underlying virtually everything Geddes (and later Mumford) wrote, there was a faith in the creative response of living organisms to their environment: what Mumford called Geddes's philosophy of "life insurgent." As Mumford would explain in *Technics and Civilization*, Geddes held that "every form of life ... is marked not merely by adjustment to the environment, but by insurgence against the environment." It followed that an organism was "both the victim of fate and the master of destiny: it lives no less by domination than by acceptance." In human life, "this insurgence reaches its apex" because historical understanding and aesthetic experience enable men and women, on occasion, to transcend their given surroundings. Faith in life itself, in the potential of the living to remake and revivify the material world, was the guiding principle behind Geddes's and Mumford's hopes for cultural renewal.[8]

In this regard, Geddes was part of a vitalist current in Western thought that included such figures as Nietzsche, Bergson, and James. For all these thinkers, the goal of philosophy was the enrichment of life: without such a vitalist first premise, social relations grew mechanical and creative thought gave way to the sterile categories of nineteenth-century positivism. As Geddes put it in his final book, *Life: Outlines of Biology*, which he coauthored with J. A. Thomson in 1931: "Life is the unity; its full study is synthetic; its analyses are but temporary divisions of labour, of which the results have ever to be incorporated into our understanding of Life." "Life insurgent," for Geddes, was the river that nourished all human endeavor, the source to which intellectuals must return, in a baptism of renewal, to maintain the vitality of their civilization.[9]

Such a vitalistic program also shaped Geddes's conception of his own role as an intellectual leader who combined the functions of the Old Testament prophet and the natural scientist. This example of Geddes as the committed intellectual—in fact, as the model of the insurgent self—may have been his greatest personal legacy to the young Mumford. "For what distinguishes Geddes's thought," he would write in 1929, "what sets it apart from the special researches he has drawn on or swiftly anticipated, is the total personality behind it." He was a generalist in ideas, whose interests spanned biology, sociology, religion, and art, and a pragmatist in action, who gave practical expression to his thought in urban planning, education, and civic life. Geddes left Mumford with a concrete example of a modern, scientific moralist who urged his fellow citizens toward a dialogue about the common good.[10]

Mumford's eclectic education and wide-ranging interests as a young man made him particularly receptive to Geddes's ideas. Throughout his youth, Mumford alternated between different career choices. His walks with his grandfather left him with a love of city life, the details of which he recorded in sketches, paintings, and copious notes. The romance of New York's neighborhoods and architecture was matched only by the romance of science. In high school, Mumford entertained the possibility of becoming an electrical engineer. Once enrolled as a night student at New York's City College, however, he planned a career as a philosopher, inspired by the idealized version of classical Athenian culture he discovered in his philosophy courses. "The Greek idea of balance (harmony, proportion) as essential for the full development of all the powers of a human being made a deep impression on me," Mumford later recalled, and it left him ready for the theories of biological and social holism he found in Geddes's work.[11]

Between 1912 and 1919, Mumford's education proceeded in fits and starts. Though he took courses at Columbia, New York University, and the New School, as well as City College, he never completed a bachelor's degree. Reading Geddes's work in 1914–15 convinced him to give up an academic career in philosophy, a conviction deepened by his impatience with the curricular requirements of regular college work. Excited by Geddes's work in sociology and urbanism, Mumford worked briefly in 1916 as an investigator for the Joint Arbitration Board of the Dress and Waist Industry, gathering data on working conditions as part of Sidney Hillman's experiment in a "new unionism" of industrial arbitration. The following year saw him at work in Pittsburgh at a cement testing laboratory operated by the U.S. Bureau of Standards. Illness and then the Great War further complicated Mumford's education. Though he shared Bourne's reservations about American war aims—he read the *Seven Arts* avidly while in Pittsburgh—Mumford did not openly oppose the war. He registered for the draft in 1917 and then enrolled in the navy in April 1918. For almost a year he trained to be a navy radio operator, reviving his youthful fascination with electronics, while stationed in Cambridge, Massachusetts. "From the beginning," however, Mumford "was in the Navy but not of it: my mind remained elsewhere." Unsuited for the regimentation of military life, he found solace in the editions of Plato and Emerson he carried in his midshipman's blouse. By the time he returned to New York in 1919 to take a position as associate editor at the *Dial*, Mumford's experiences as student, sociologist, and sailor had left him with interests too diverse for a specialized profession. To the young Mumford, Geddes's sprawling theoretical scope was a vindication of his own educational wanderings. Geddes's work showed Mumford that it was possible to unite the study of science, sociology, and aesthetics in a new philosophical synthesis. Geddes himself proved that it was still possible to live the Greeks' balanced way of life in the twentieth century and that a young man whose intellectual ambitions spilled over from one discipline to the next might yet find his appropriate calling.[12]

Geddes was unique as a social theorist who joined the discoveries of nineteenth-century science to a romantic critique of industrial capitalism. Geddes had begun his career as a biologist, and his subsequent work in social theory always bore the imprint of nineteenth-century evolutionary thought. A student of Thomas Huxley, Geddes later turned against Huxley's theory of nature as a "mingling of militaristic, mechanical and venal elements." He had similar complaints about Charles Darwin, whose theory of evolution as a competitive struggle for survival had such enormous repercussions in late nineteenth-century Anglo-American social science. Geddes retained Darwin's view of evolution as the result of an organism's functional interaction with its environment, but he found Petr Kropotkin's emphasis on the role of mutual aid in biological development more to his liking than the Darwinist idea of survival of the fittest. Geddes's evolutionism gave his sociology a historical dimension, casting society as a product of the interaction of remnants of the past, present conditions, and ideals of the future. At the same time, he was an early proponent of an ecological worldview: his social theory always located the individual in an interlocking web of biological and social relationships.[13]

This biological background made Geddes a cultural determinist and a critic of capitalism. Culture, for Geddes, was an organic unity that nurtured the well-being of the individual and the evolution of society as a whole. His view of human culture as an ecology of reciprocal relationships drew him to Ruskin's polemic against classical political economy. Like Ruskin, Geddes had no patience for an atomistic society of Economic Men: the "whole man" participating in communal life was his goal. He believed that "the so-called 'aesthetic revival,' " of which Ruskin was the foremost representative, indicated the first glimmerings of "the Industrial Reformation, of that re-organisation of production—of products and processes, of environment and function, which is the nearest task of the united art and science of the immediate future." The only problem, in Geddes's mind, was that romantic critics of industrialism were too utopian in their dismissal of modern society. They had failed to grapple with the actual conditions of life in the new commercial cities and factory towns and offered as alternatives only escapist fantasies of withdrawal. Geddes's response was to ground Ruskin's moral-aesthetic indictment of industrial capitalism in the insights of science.

The romantics have too often been as blind in their righteous anger as were the mechanical utilitarians in their strenuous labour, their dull contentment with it. Both have failed to see, beyond the rude present, the better future now dawning—in which the applied physical sciences are advancing beyond their clumsy and noisy first apprenticeship, with its wasteful and dirty beginnings, towards a finer skill, a more subtle and more economic mastery of natural energies; and in which these, moreover, are increasingly supplemented by a corresponding advance of the organic sciences, with their new valuations of life, organic as well as human.

Geddes stood in much the same relation to the romantic critics of capitalism as Brooks did to the Transcendentalists. He welcomed their attack on the soulless individualism of the marketplace but wished to ground their ideals in the social practice of modern life.[14]

Geddes believed that French social scientists provided a methodology for exactly the kind of moral-scientific synthesis he was looking for. Auguste Comte's positivism and Frédéric Le Play's sociology gave Geddes the empirical tools lacking in the English romantic tradition and reinforced his hostility to the anarchic individualism of the nineteenth century. Comte and Le Play were both deeply conservative, even reactionary thinkers, whose appeals to scientific synthesis and social harmony derived from their opposition to Enlightenment skepticism and the corrosive effects of liberalism on traditional values and social relationships. Both men sought to wean their fellow conservatives from their sentimental attachment to the *ancien régime* by arguing that social science provided the keys to a new order free of the class conflicts and ideological struggles that raged throughout postrevolutionary Europe.

In turning to Comte and Le Play to bolster Ruskin's brand of romantic radicalism, Geddes was playing a difficult intellectual game. Though both traditions were hostile to competitive individualism, they clearly diverged on questions of social justice and political democracy. It is unclear whether Geddes worked through such contradictions in his own mind. His study of Comte and Le Play centered on methodological issues and their belief in empirical social inquiry. Le Play's social surveys were the immediate forerunner of Geddes's regional surveys, which he used to collect information necessary to regional planning and social reform. Geddes borrowed Le Play's categories of Place, Work, and Family as the foundation for his inquiries into social organization. As Mumford later noted, Geddes demonstrated that "Le Play's formula is the exact equivalent in sociology for the biologist's organism, function, and environment." Such primary social relationships, Geddes believed, rooted individual behavior in biological processes—the rhythms of nature and reproduction—that resisted the modernizing forces of industrialization. A social science grounded in such categories would recognize humans' dependence on nature and their ability to shape natural patterns in accordance with their own powers of reason: "[Le Play's] line of reasoning begins with the soil and its natural products; it continues with man, the creature of work and place; it culminates in man the builder of cities and creator of arts and sciences; and it returns through all the vicissitudes of war and peace to end again in the soil with its fertility renewed and increased by the hand of man, or ruined and destroyed by the same hand. The tale of that cycle, in its full complexity, is the history of civilization."[15]

Le Play's cycle of human alienation from and return to nature dovetailed with Geddes's biological conception of society as evolving toward a new organic unity. Both Comte and Le Play had prophesied the emergence of a unified, planned society out of the chaos and waste of industrial capitalism. Borrowing the terminology used to distinguish the paleolithic age from the neolithic era, Geddes argued that the "paleotechnic" period of early industrialization was giving way to a "neotechnic" industrialism. Just as neolithic civilization had substituted a gentler agricultural way of life for the warlike civilization of the paleolithic era, neotechnic innovations in city planning, conservation, sanitary conditions, and social cooperation were humanizing the forces unleashed by a primitive paleotechnic society. Underlying this momentous transformation were the new discoveries of biology and the other natural sciences and the technological innovations of the second industrial revolution— particularly in electricity and chemistry—which promised a clean, decentralized industrialism free of the pollution and human degradation that attended the factory system. In effect, Geddes used the progressivism inherent in Comte's and Le Play's thought to rework Ruskinian romanticism on an evolutionary basis. The neotechnic community of the future was Ruskin's neomedieval organic society in modern form.[16]

Geddes saw the process of building a neotechnic society in both scientific and moral terms. One element of his work suggested that the neotechnic future was destined by forces of social evolution which the social scientist could uncover and then help bring to fruition. But Geddes was unusual as a follower of Comtean positivism in his tendency to use analogies from the natural sciences to refute mechanistic notions of automatic social progress. Technological innovations might make an ecological society of small-scale industry possible, but ultimately citizens would have to revive a classical notion of politics as civic participation if such a society were ever to come into existence. Geddes hoped that the regional survey would put scientific method to use in the moral mission of "civic regeneration." He encouraged surveyors to think of themselves as members of the social organism they were studying. Society was not, for Geddes, an inert mass or a bundle of forces subject to immutable laws; rather, it was a living organism that the social scientist studied from within. The regional survey was to reawaken civic consciousness by making the active citizen both the subject and the object of its inquiry. In Edinburgh, Geddes displayed the findings of one such regional survey in a museum and educational center he called the Outlook Tower. By thus returning his findings to the public sphere, Geddes sought to make social science a "nucleus of spiritual influence" for a new polity.[17]

Like Dewey's progressive school, the Outlook Tower would function as a countercultural laboratory within paleotechnic society, promoting the "increasing substitution of man in the role of creator for man as a creature of circumstance and habit." Through knowledge of the geographical and historical factors that shaped their lives, citizens would free themselves from the assumptions of an industrial civilization and recognize their own resources for a humane community life. The regional survey, the Outlook Tower, and eventually the university were to play the role that the cathedral had played in the Middle Ages as the focus of a regionally based moral community. Geddes's network of civic associations would succeed the cathedral as "the living and throbbing organ of social life which gathered into itself, and re-expressed as corporate individuality, the finer aspirations of citizen and rustic alike." Mumford later described Geddes's ideal of a revitalized university as the center of civic life. "Such a university, Geddes believed, would leave the liberating imprint of science and historic thinking on all the activities of a community, as the Church had once imprinted its theological and esthetic visions on the medieval town."[18]

In his memoirs, Mumford recalled that "from the beginning it was in biology that [Geddes] had made his most lasting contribution to my education—and even more profoundly to my life." Mumford absorbed Geddes's holistic view of civilization as a dynamic organism, his ecological interpretation of cultural and biological processes as reciprocal relationships, and his evolutionistic cast of mind. For Geddes and Mumford, society was neither rent by class conflict nor the inadvertent by-product of a multitude of individuals in pursuit of self-interest. At its best, it was a healthy organism in functional interaction with the historical and natural forces that shaped it; at its worst, it was a diseased cell, invaded by a virus that upset the delicate balance of its internal components and set it at odds with its environment. Geddes's hope of using a synthesis of environmental and social science to reintegrate the urban and rural worlds cured Mumford of the "contempt for country ways and rural personalities" that he imbibed from Marxist and Fabian socialism. Mumford's tutelage in Geddes's work left him with a vitalistic vocabulary—of *growth*, *cultivation*, and *renewal*—that infused all his work. The title of Mumford's series of masterworks in the 1930s, 1940s, and 1950s, "The Renewal of Life," reveals Geddes's imprint on his thought. What Mumford wrote of William Cobbett in 1921 he might also have said of Geddes: that he "had the peasant's wit to understand that the most profound, the most radical revolution would be, not a red, but a green one." [19]

Geddes's "green" politics were of a piece with the radical position Mumford also found in such thinkers as Ebenezer Howard, Pëtr Kropotkin, and Thorstein Veblen. In Howard's program for garden cities and Kropotkin's *Fields, Farms, and Factories*, Mumford encountered a decentralist vision of a mixed economy of small producers and cooperative enterprises located in communities that balanced urban culture with the benefits of a rural environment. Like Geddes, Howard and Kropotkin hoped to break the hold of the nation-state over an atomized population by encouraging the development of local centers of community life. All three men had in common with Veblen a neorepublican radicalism that upheld the virtues of craft and local citizenship against the parasitic forces of finance capitalism. Their indictment of industrial capitalism was neither Marxist, since it saw no internal dynamic of class conflict at work in production, nor traditionally liberal, since it paid little attention to natural or civil rights. Instead, it shared with the late nineteenth-century republicanism of Henry George a defense of an organic community of producers against the disruptive forces of speculation, statism, and monopoly, which they believed had invaded the harmonious commonwealth of an earlier era. [20]

Mumford derived his political perspective from thinkers who sought to revise George's brand of defensive republicanism, with its nostalgia for agrarian culture, into a program for rebuilding community on a modern basis. Howard's tract *Garden Cities of To-morrow* echoed George's attacks on the inflation of land rents by real estate speculators. Following George, Howard held financiers responsible for the squalor of the modern metropolis. But he felt that George's single tax was a simplistic panacea and argued instead for magnet garden cities to draw people out of overcrowded, polluted cities. As Geddes had modernized Ruskin's romantic critique of capitalism, Howard would update George's vision of a moral commonwealth by equipping it with the tools of modern social science and urban planning. Similarly, Veblen and Kropotkin expected new developments in engineering and technology to revitalize the republican tradition and make it a viable basis for social reconstruction in the industrial age. Geddes's call for a moral-scientific movement of "civic regeneration" had much in common with these efforts. Though such an enterprise neglected the social relations of production that Marx had identified as the source of industrial degradation, it had the merits of maintaining an emphasis on culture and community absent in mainstream socialism. Moreover, this "adversary tradition" of republican radicalism remained far more skeptical of the benefits of the industrial division of labor than were most Marxists and therefore more inclined to seek small-scale cooperative alternatives to the factory system. Its advocates argued that the problem facing industrial societies was not one of economic redistribution but of rehumanizing social life—a theme that became a constant refrain of Mumford's work in the 1920s. Mumford inherited this idiosyncratic blend of anarchist, republican, and progressive politics and sought to make it the basis for his own project in cultural criticism.[21]

Yet the very qualities that made this green radicalism so attractive as an alternative to conventional socialist and liberal politics were the causes for its most glaring weaknesses. A neorepublican ideal of organic community worked well as a counterexample to the bureaucratization of industrial social life, but it offered little as a tool of political analysis. As Helen E. Meller has observed, Geddes's organicism assigned equal weight in social organization to wealth, power, social structure, culture, religion, geography, and a host of other factors, thereby obscuring exactly how one or another of these factors might shape or even determine other institutions and practices. This holistic perspective had the advantages of avoiding the rigid economic determinism that plagued turn-of-the-century socialist thought and of placing a high priority on those practices that engaged individual subjectivity in remaking the objective world. But Geddes's theory made it difficult to imagine how fundamental social change might come about at all because it imagined no underlying division or conflicts in its ecology of reciprocal social relations.[22]

This vagueness about social causation complemented an elitist political streak in Geddes's work that cut against the grain of his producerist republicanism. Geddes borrowed Le Play's notion of the need for "social authorities," drawn from those social classes least touched by industrialization, who would lead in the rebuilding of an organic social order. He also adopted Comte's distinction between "temporal" and "spiritual powers" in social leadership and suggested that the problems of industrial society stemmed partly from the ascendancy of the former over the latter. The "long-protracted subordination of the spiritual view" after the Middle Ages was to blame for the "externalism and individualism which, since the Renaissance, have been characteristic of art and industry." Because Geddes's organicist social thought had paid so little attention to political conflict and class relations within society, he found it difficult to sustain an ideal of a popular movement for democratic renewal. Too often, "civic regeneration" became indistinguishable from a bid by "spiritual powers" for the authority now claimed by the state. Under Comte's influence, Geddes moved from attacking the tyranny of the state to a denunciation of the tyranny of the majority over enlightened intellectuals. "Representative government fails to yield all that its inventors hoped of it," he wrote in a 1904 paper on civics as "applied sociology," "because it is so tolerably representative of its majorities." A neorepublican concern for local community and a shared culture could inspire both a defense of democracy and plans for the reign of a new clergy of regional planners.[23]

Mumford's reading of Geddes's green radicalism gave special significance to his insistence that cultural and moral reconstruction had to prefigure a new organic community. Geddes taught Mumford that the problems of industrial society required a transformation as sweeping as that which had undone the medieval civilization of the twelfth and thirteenth centuries. A new polity first required a new moral ethos, but one grounded in a thorough understanding of modern social conditions. Mumford shied away from the woolier aspects of Geddes's thought—such as the "thinking machine" that Geddes devised, by folding paper in tiny squares, to organize categories from different disciplines—and he had less use for Comte's positivist faith in "spiritual powers" than Geddes did. He also resisted Geddes's efforts to draw him into his immediate circle of followers. When Geddes's associate and collaborator Victor

Branford invited him to England in 1920 to become acting editor of the *Sociological Review*, Mumford made the trip but ultimately turned down the job; he returned to the United States under the influence of Brooks's essays in the *Freeman*. Three years later, when he finally met Geddes, he rebelled against his mentor's attempts to enlist him as his personal secretary, editor, and surrogate son. Still, the early Mumford was in almost every way a Geddesian. Like his master, he believed that social science, biology, and romantic cultural criticism aimed at a common goal of fashioning a neotechnic organic community out of the chaos of paleotechnic industrialism. He looked to humanist radicals and regional associations—not to the nation-state—to resurrect the classical polis on a newly scientific basis and to give individuals a richer fund of communal experience. Mumford took Geddes at his most democratic as his model for the activist intellectual. For both men, the ideal public thinker was neither a revolutionary ally of the oppressed nor a technician who engineered social reform from above. Instead, he resembled a patient gardener, bereft of all illusions about controlling nature or of giving way to its untamed wildness. Intelligent cultivation and renewal were the intellectual's goals. He tended a public culture as a devoted gardener would his garden, alert to the rhythms and patterns of forces he himself lived and might yet shape but could never master.[24]

With Geddes as his mentor, Mumford entered the intellectual debates of the postwar years with a cultural politics remarkably similar to that of the other Young Americans. Geddes played the same role in his education as Dewey had in Bourne's, giving his ideal of cultural renewal a materialist basis in social conditions that was often missing in Brooks's and Frank's literary exhortations. After Bourne's death, Mumford took his place as the leading social and political thinker of the Young America circle. Geddes prepared him well for such a position by giving his neotechnic prophecy a foundation in the same romantic, republican, and social-scientific currents that had coexisted—however uneasily—in Bourne's best work. Still, his legacy to Mumford was as mixed as Dewey's was for Bourne, and his synthesis of anticapitalist thought as potentially unstable as that of the Young Americans in the 1910s. Geddes provided only an intellectual orientation, not a precise blueprint for civic rebirth. The ambiguities of Geddesian radicalism would also plague Mumford's attempts to rebuild culture as a bulwark against the modern state.

The immediate forum for Mumford's Geddesian radicalism was the *Dial*, which hired him as an associate editor in 1919. The *Dial* had undergone a major overhaul under the direction of Martyn Johnson, who moved the journal from Chicago to New York and hired Thorstein Veblen and John Dewey as editors of a special section on problems of postwar reconstruction. Mumford joined Veblen and Dewey at a propitious moment, when both men were searching for a federalist guild socialism as a middle way between capitalism and Soviet communism. Although the magazine changed hands within the year, putting an end to the "reconstruction" project, in the early 1920s Mumford carried on his explorations in a nonstatist politics in the *Freeman*, the *Menorah Journal*, *Commonweal*, and a number of other publications. In many ways, Mumford's work in the immediate postwar period bridged the gap that had separated the *Seven Arts* and the *New Republic* in the late 1910s. Mumford was versed in the social-scientific language of Dewey and other pragmatic liberals, but his political and cultural sympathies were closest to Bourne's communitarian radicalism and Brooks's ideal of cultural renewal. At a time when Dewey, Veblen, and their followers were rethinking their own politics in the wake of Versailles, Mumford sought to build on Bourne's insights into the rise of the wartime state while reaching out to other progressive thinkers for concrete examples of civic renewal.

Bourne and Mumford were unusual among turn-of-the-century radicals in identifying the state and warfare as sources of political repression. Like Veblen—whose work influenced both men's thinking on this subject—Bourne and Mumford regarded the state as heir to primordial acts of violence that subjected the creative "instinct of workmanship" to the darker instincts of acquisition and plunder. In their view, war was not simply the reflex of economic imperialism or nationalist hysteria, as socialists and liberals had it. War, in Bourne's famous refrain, was "the health of the state." "It automatically sets in motion throughout society those irresistible forces for uniformity, for passionate cooperation with the Government in coercing into obedience the minority groups and individuals which lack the larger herd sense." War created the state in the first place, and it provided the crucial dynamic for the state's growth at the expense of other social institutions. The nation-state justified its strength by pointing to the need for military defense, while governments took up arms to protect interests of state. In an age of total war, the state gained an unprecedented autonomy because its needs required the mobilization and exploitation of a society's entire resources. As Bruce Clayton observes, Bourne came to see "that modern nations *need* war. Their economies depend on war, and the people depend on the economy. Once weapons are designed and built—in the name of peace, of course—they must be deployed." War, in short, had become its own justification.[25]

The autonomy of the modern state was nowhere clearer than in its success at waging war in the face of popular apathy. Bourne remarked on the absence of any real enthusiasm for the war effort, either among members of his generation or within the populace at large. Support for the war was a matter of acquiescence in the absence of genuine alternatives, he argued. The ability of the state to mobilize a listless, apathetic army of conscripts only testified to its success in rooting out alternative objects of popular loyalty. "The government of a modern organized plutocracy does not have to ask whether the people want to fight or understand what they are fighting for," Bourne wrote, "but only whether they will tolerate fighting." Such passivity also reflected the ease with which industrialism had undermined traditional forms of collective belief and action. Raw power had subverted cultural authority as the organizing principle of modern society. Mumford explained how the nineteenth-century ideal of liberal individualism had fostered the growth of the modern state. "Historically the state has not become weakened by the emphasis on the isolated individual," he wrote in 1919; "it actually has tended to take over functions which would otherwise be in the hands of vigorous voluntary associations."[26]

For Bourne and Mumford, the same qualities that made the modern state such a danger to peace and democracy also held out hope for its gradual supersession by voluntary forms of association. The freedom of the modern state from popular control had as its obverse its alienation from the popular will. If, as Mumford argued, the primitive state was "a foreign institution thrust upon the more or less peaceful inhabitants of a given territory by a group of hunter-warriors," it might still be possible to resurrect an autonomous social existence outside the domain of the state. Americans' dormant community life might yet be revived and made a pacific bulwark against the state's encroachment. This did not mean "pitting the individual personality against the crowd"—as Bruce Clayton mistakenly assumes in his discussion of Bourne's antiwar essays—but rather pitting the claims of a collective culture against the forced mobilization of the wartime state. Bourne and Mumford sought a renewed love of land, culture, and community—in short, a renewed patriotism—to sustain resistance to official appeals for national unity.[27]

Building on Bourne's insights in "Trans-national America," Mumford distinguished a freely held patriotism from the coercive nationalism of wartime. Whereas the first grew out of a shared language and respect for common religious and cultural traditions, the latter was the invention of the nation-state, which perverted the citizen's love of a way of life into a doctrine of military supremacy. To clarify his distinction, Mumford called the voluntary patriotism of community *culturism*— "the belief in a system of common values, and the effort on the part of the community to work these values out in its daily life"—as opposed to "its bastard offspring," *nationalism*. Writing for the Jewish *Menorah Journal*, Mumford pointed to the tenacious cultural identity of diaspora Judaism as an example of a thriving culturism with no connection to a nation-state. He warned American Jews against cultural assimilation and against opting for a nationalist Zionism as a means of maintaining their identity. Assimilation would lead only to "a dissolution of values," but Jewish nationalism threatened to subordinate a way of life to the usual requirements of national defense. Culturism, for Mumford, was a middle course between liberal individualism and nationalist belligerence. It was "rooted in the integrity of the local community"—"in its common *shul*"—which preserved group identity from the ravages of the marketplace and the bureaucratic state. After the war, Mumford thought he saw the resurrection of such local, voluntary associations in the shop steward and shop committee movements in British and American labor unions and in the soviets of revolutionary Russia and Hungary. Other promising signs were the myriad professional and trade associations that established international exchanges with little regard for their home governments' foreign policies. Their success proved that "the way to decrease the activities of the national State is to ignore it," as Thoreau and Gandhi had predicted. Culturists would best combat nationalism by "thinking creatively" in local groups, Mumford argued, thereby acting as "the germ of a new society."[28]

After Bourne's death in 1918, Mumford emerged as the member of the Young American circle who made the most explicit connection between culturism and an antistatist politics of democratic community. The progressive school, the movement for workers' education, and the revival of regional languages and literature all contributed, in Mumford's view, to the resurgence of local bonds in the face of the nation-state. Such bonds fostered a loyalty to culture that subverted the authority of the state. Harold Stearns made much the same point in his essay "The Claims of Loyalty." "How strong are men's affections to their church, their family, their immediate neighbourhood," Stearns wrote, "as compared with some intangible Federal entity at Washington." "To-day," he concluded, "the problem of loyalty is to find those objects which we can love, to break through the miasma of abstractions and concepts and imaginative entities to visible and sensuous objects to which our affections can spontaneously cling."[29]

As attractive as this culturism was as a means to the Beloved Community, it had its share of ambiguities for Mumford's work in the 1920s. As heir to republican notions of civic friendship and public virtue, the culturist ideal promised a revival of participatory democracy on a new cultural foundation. Culturists would outwit the guardians of the nation-state by fostering a pluralistic federalism of institutions and cultures. Once citizens established alternative loyalties to small-scale, local groups, the state would lose the passive assent that had been its only real mandate. Meanwhile, such groups would promote values of aesthetic experience and mutuality that strengthened both the individual personality and local community life. In this formulation, culturism was a strategy for the dismantling of the mobilized state and its replacement by a network of voluntary associations.

This decentralist ideal of culturism could coexist, however, with less democratic plans for subverting the state's supremacy. Ignoring the state in favor of cultural transformation often meant ignoring the public realm altogether and urging, instead, that a new cultural elite assume positions of power. In this case, culturism became a strategy for circumventing conventional politics and for claiming a place within an administrative state. Artists and intellectuals would bypass the stalemated politics of faction to join professionals and technicians as engineers of social reform. The confusion between these two currents of cultural politics runs throughout Mumford's early work. At stake in such confusion was the difference between democratic localism and a pluralism of professional planning agencies. In looking to culture for alternative sources of power to the state, culturism ran the risk of sacrificing the civic culture of democracy to the authority of a mobilized intelligentsia.

Even more dangerous was the possibility that, in ignoring the state, a culturist strategy might belittle issues of power and conflict. One strain of culturism promised a renewal of politics, but another made vague references to replacing the state with a community of love, with little understanding of the social strife and division such a transformation would entail. Despite his realistic assessment of the obstacles to capturing the wartime state and turning it to democratic purposes, Mumford

often assumed that the state would simply wither away after a pro-
tracted period of coexistence with an alternative culture. "We may perhaps approach our social institutions a little more courageously when
we realize how completely we ourselves have created them," he predicted in *The Story of Utopias*; "and how, without our perpetual 'will to
believe' they would vanish like smoke in the wind." Invoking James's
voluntarism against the state was an ambiguous political strategy. Directing his attack against the state's weakest point—its lack of popular
loyalty—Mumford ceded in advance the state's monopoly of power and
violence. By constructing alternative sources of local authority, culturism might tap unknown reservoirs of popular will and delegitimize the
nation-state, creating in its place a vital public democracy. But it might
end up only promoting the status of a cultured minority, leaving unchanged the political roots of a degraded public sphere.[30]

With his brief experience on the "reconstruction" *Dial* behind
him, Mumford found himself increasingly homeless in the postwar cultural and political climate. Born in 1895 and shaped by the
intellectual climate of the *Seven Arts*, Mumford was still too much a
product of the Progressive era to join in the atmosphere of disillusioned
hedonism that prevailed among young intellectuals after the war. "The
chief mark of the younger generation is a sort of spiritual amnesia," he
complained, "and their notion of the good life is that of the bourgeoisie,
minus the responsibility." A generation that had come to see liberal and
socialist pieties betrayed on the battlefield had no patience either for the
past or for visions of a better future. The war had severed any connection with the cultural life of the past—now abused as a cheap swindle—
while at the same time undermining the "promise of continuity" that
Mumford saw as the basis of a "measured, disciplined, purposeful life."
Mumford deplored the "collapse of tomorrow" engendered by total
war, but he knew that his own worldview derived from that very hemor-
rhage of the historical process. As he wrote Geddes in 1923, "There is a
real barrier to understanding between us in the fact that you grew to
manhood in a period of hope . . . whereas I spent my whole adolescence
in the shadows of war and disappointment, growing up with a generation which, in large part, had no future."[31]

Too modern to believe in Victorian notions of automatic moral progress, Mumford was still ill at ease in a postwar world that saw no
alternatives to a rootless present. His decision to write a history of

utopian thought in 1922 grew directly out of this uneasiness. *The Story of Utopias* would be a "usable past" for a generation that had no past, reminding them of the seeds for future renewal sown in the years before the war. By writing the book, Mumford would situate himself on either side of the bloody divide that separated the nineteenth and twentieth centuries, drawing on the utopian speculations of a more confident age to redress the skepticism and homelessness of his fellow moderns.[32]

Mumford took up the study of past utopias for political reasons, as well as for purposes of cultural morale. It was the emptiness of conventional views of a progressive future—whether in their liberal, pragmatic, or Marxist varieties—that drove youth in the 1920s to a cheerless reveling in the present, he argued. All such ideologies presented the future as the inevitable product of the forces that had created the horrors of war and industrial production. To many on the Left, the Russian Revolution represented a break with the evolutionistic socialism of the nineteenth century, but Mumford dismissed Soviet socialism as the culmination of earlier tendencies toward militarism and industrial concentration. As early promises of a federation of soviets gave way to the Leninist state, Mumford charged that "the change from Tsarism to the dictatorship of the proletariat involved merely a change in personnel . . . not in method."[33]

The failure of socialism resulted from its inability to imagine a way of life qualitatively different from industrial capitalism. By glorifying the factory system and the state as the harbingers of the cooperative commonwealth, socialists had cut themselves off from truly cooperative forms of association that sprang up on the margins of industrial civilization. It was no wonder, then, that the Soviet Union was turning to bourgeois society for examples of successful modernization. Without alternative values or an understanding of local cultures or communities, it reproduced the worst elements of capitalist industrialization. "Have not the Soviet technicians been as ready to deify the Taylor system as the American Society of Engineers?" Mumford asked. Even Veblen's work revealed the poverty of the radical imagination after the war, he admitted. Veblen's original distinction between an "instinct of workmanship" and the appetite for acquisition still appealed to Mumford as a way of restoring a producerist radicalism on a fresh basis, but his program for a revolution of engineers overlooked the question of values that Mumford insisted upon as the basis for a postindustrial civilization. "Because we lack any common humane standards," Mumford wrote in a review of Veblen's *Engineers and the Price System*, "the Utopia of

Engineers, even at its best, is likely to be little better than the Moham-
medan paradise of business." The rush to identify the good life with the
efficient life that characterized virtually all segments of the Western Left
after the war was evidence for Mumford of the collapse of socialism as
an animating ethos of cultural opposition. "Between the bleakness of
our mechanical achievements and the impoverishment of our social
dreams there is little enough to choose."[34]

Writing the history of the future was Mumford's response to the
bankruptcy of contemporary visions of the future. Utopianism captivated him with its promise of a clear and distinct break with the present,
a promise so often belied by the historical assumptions of its proponents. Even as utopians urged a new life, Mumford realized, they often
used their own geographical and historical surroundings as the backdrop to their images of the promised land. It was exactly that subtle
interplay between the futurist imagination and its own location in time
and space that Mumford explored as the basis for a usable future for
shell-shocked moderns. Like the utopian thinkers of the past, modern
radicals would have to set their visions of the future in close relation to
current realities without idealizing the present as itself utopian. By rethinking utopianism with an eye to its relation to history and social
conditions, as Geddes might have done, Mumford hoped to offer his
contemporaries a more full-blooded future than the genial optimism
of prewar liberalism. Any new radicalism, Mumford was convinced,
would again have to learn to think things "whole," instead of fastening
on one element of human endeavor—such as economic life—as the mo-
tor of historical change. "The conclusion I drew for myself," Mumford
later wrote of the postwar period, "was that the situation demanded,
not specific attacks on specific evils and specific points of danger, but a
wholesale rethinking of the basis of modern life and thought, for the
purpose of eventually giving a new orientation to all our institutions."[35]

The Story of Utopias was ostensibly a history of utopian literature
from Plato to the present, but toward the end of the book it became
clear that Mumford's real subject was the set of "social myths" that
operated in modern life as "the ideal content of the existing order of
things." Because he believed that "an idea is a solid fact" with social
consequences, and not simply a reflection of socioeconomic conditions,
Mumford was able to sort out the hegemonic "idola"—or ideas—of
industrial civilization and show how they worked to maintain an essentially repressive social order. His discussion of the myths of the Country House, Coketown, the National-State, and Megalopolis, though re-

served for the book's tenth chapter, actually set the agenda of the entire work. By revealing the powerful hold that the "idola" of industrialism had over the modern mind, Mumford made a case for the significance of culture as a force of oppression and as a resource for social reconstruction.[36]

Modern life, in Mumford's analysis, was brutally riven by the separation of work and culture that resulted from the victory of the factory system over the medieval guild tradition. The opposition of degraded industrial labor and a frivolous culture—of Coketown and the Country House—was as central to Mumford's criticism as it had been to Brooks's. The reorganization of the European city in the modern age was emblematic of the developments Mumford deplored. As the urban icons of a shared culture—the cathedral, the market, and the guildhall— gave way to the factory as the geographical center of the city and as planners imposed the gridiron on the city's natural contours and neighborhoods, the quantitative standards of machinery became the dominant idola of practical life. "The factory became the new social unity; in fact it became the only social unit," Mumford wrote, so that soon its design dominated the entire urban landscape. By the mid-nineteenth century, every public building in Coketown resembled the factory, a grim visual testament to the collapse of alternative visions of a public life. Coketown was the city stripped bare for production, the good life replaced by the "Goods Life."[37]

The myth of the Country House, by contrast, was one of a life of ease and bounty. Although the Country House had once existed as a self-sufficient economic unit, since the industrial revolution it survived as a parasitic center of leisure-class culture. Its residents lived "a completely functionless existence" dedicated to the pursuit of "limitless possession." The leisured inhabitants of the Country House surrounded themselves with the loot of the world's cultures, turning their environment into a museum of eclectic styles and artistic treasures. Mumford agreed with Veblen that such "gourmandism in the arts" reflected the disjuncture between culture and function, which now made possible the marketing of aristocratic tastes to the public as a whole. Wrenched from any communal function, art became just another commodity to be enjoyed at one's leisure, as much a product of alienated labor as the textiles and steel manufactured in Coketown. "Coketown for the workaday week, the Country House for the weekend, is the compromise that has been practically countenanced," Mumford concluded. Leisure-class tastes became the engine of industrial production, stimulating demands for new goods and subduing workers with visions of their own Country Houses as refuges from factory work. In place of a whole life lived in interaction with one's community, modern men and women lived a bifurcated existence, which compensated for a starkly utilitarian public sphere with the promise of private consumption.[38]

The National-State and Megalopolis served as the "connecting tissue" uniting Coketown and the Country House, in Mumford's mind. In keeping with the republican strains of his radicalism, Mumford denounced these capitals of state power and high finance as visible symptoms of the moral disease raging through a once healthy social organism. The National-State overrode the geographical regions of nature that had nourished local cultures for centuries and stimulated false loyalties to a political abstraction. Whatever its claims, the state's real function was to cement an alliance between the exploited workers of Coketown and the leisured inhabitants of the Country House in defense of a completely abstract notion of community.[39]

In Mumford's view, the collapse of a meaningful core to civic life symbolized by the demolition of the medieval city had led to a scramble to fabricate substitutes that obscured the real costs of industrialization. The myth of a weekend Country House, with its planned obsolescence in culture, was one such substitute; the mobilized National-State was another. But the command post of such myths, the center that broadcast the ideology of an artificial community, was Megalopolis. A frenzied, overcrowded capital of parliamentary politics and high finance, Megalopolis was a world in which face-to-face interaction had been banished for "intercourse through the medium of paper." In place of a regional culture rooted in traditional customs and language, Megalopolis advertised the benefits of a culture of conspicuous consumption to the fictional polity created by the National-State. A paper culture was the obvious complement to the paper community of the National-State, for Mumford. In both cases, the scale of social organization had grown so inhuman that only a retinue of social parasites—advertisers, financiers, and state officials—could identify with their creation and call it their own. Their sole function, as far as Mumford could tell, was to celebrate their way of life as a realized utopia and thus maintain social harmony. "So the chief aim of every other city in the National Utopia is to become like Megalopolis; its chief hope is to grow as big as Megalopolis; its boast is that it is another Megalopolis."[40]

The power of these four "social myths" in industrial society revealed the thinness of any alternative utopian tradition. Mumford's case against the reigning utopias of the modern Left was that they failed to address the central issue of industrial culture: the eclipse of a notion of the common good by the myths of Coketown and the Country House. Instead of addressing the need for practical expressions of the good life—for modern successors to the cathedral, university, and guild—utopian thinkers since Francis Bacon had only created their own versions of the National-State and Megalopolis. Such utopias "are all machinery," Mumford claimed: "The means has become the end, and the genuine problem of ends has been forgotten." The neglect of the end of a good life for the individual and the community was the common defect of virtually all programs on the Left, from "the hideous cog-and-wheel utopia of Edward Bellamy" to the "partisan" utopias of Marxists and the labor movement. Mumford attacked the Left for avoiding the scientific study of social conditions as the basis of utopian speculation and for promoting political divisiveness at the expense of any conception of what united individuals in functioning communities. Above all, he faulted "partisan" ideologies on the grounds that they had dismissed the inner life in their single-minded preoccupation with the state. They had abandoned the world of imagination to the purveyors of Megalopolitan myths. "The problem of realizing the potential powers of the community," he argued, "is not simply a matter of economics or eugenics or ethics as the various socialist thinkers and their political followers have emphasized." Rather, "the first step in reconstruction is to make over our inner world, and to give our knowledge and our projections a new foundation."[41]

Mumford sought a way out from the alternatives of romantic "utopias of escape" and the mechanical "utopias of reconstruction" that cropped up in pointless succession in modern culture. His goal was a true utopia of reconstruction that drew on idealist thought to reinvigorate social practice. This was a task for a humanized science directed to local community goals, along the lines of Geddes's regional survey and Outlook Tower. Utopianism had to be brought down to earth in institutions and processes rooted in a specific time and place. Social reconstruction needed to proceed on two fronts, Mumford argued. It had to retrieve an ideal of a good life that had been buried beneath the artificial utopias of the modern age. At the same time, it had to find ways of giving that ideal concrete expression in the functional relationships of everyday life.[42]

The content of Mumford's new utopianism was less clear than his prescriptions for how to begin imagining one. Aside from revitalizing local culture and authority on the basis of communally owned property and regional institutions, he had few specifics to offer his readers. Instead, *The Story of Utopias* suggested that utopia was less an end point of human endeavor than a continual process in which the good life consisted of a pursuit, not a specific goal. "What has been more conspicuously lacking," Mumford wrote of modern utopias, "has been people who are accessible to the existing knowledge, people whose minds have been trained to play freely with the facts, people who have learned the fine and exacting art of co-operating with their fellows; people who are as critical of their own mental processes and habits of behavior as they are of the institutions they wish to alter." Forty years after writing the book, Mumford observed that *The Story of Utopias* was "an antiutopian tract," but this was an overstatement made from the perspective of hindsight. The Mumford of 1962 was too much influenced by the antiutopian turn of his work in the 1940s and 1950s to remember fully the utopian dimensions of his first book. But his book had achieved a rethinking of the utopian project as an ongoing method for seeking out the good life, not the realization of a static paradise at the end of human history. The Beloved Community—a phrase Mumford employed at various points in the book—might best exist for moderns as an open-ended process of dialogue about the common good.[43]

Mumford's promising revision of utopianism was at odds, however, with the more disturbing elements of idealist and sociological thought that still informed much of his thinking. His use of Plato's *Republic* as a measure of how far modern utopians had strayed from the promise of their origins illustrated the strengths and weaknesses of his vision of an organic community. Mumford consistently downplayed the elitism of the Platonist tradition, emphasizing instead those aspects of *The Republic* that corresponded to the civic regionalism he had learned from Geddes. What Mumford found compelling in Plato's utopia was clear enough: its depiction of a small-scale community "within bounds"; its subordination of wealth to the pursuit of a just community; its golden mean between asceticism and luxury; its parallel perfection of the individual soul and the community; and its insistence on community service as a form of intellectual self-discipline.[44]

But equally evident were characteristics that betrayed the darker side of Mumford's thought and raised serious questions about his larger project of marshaling the culture of utopianism against the industrial state. The centrality of Plato's *Republic* in Mumford's book suggests two fundamental political difficulties in his theory of an organic culture:

first, an overvaluation of the role of social-scientific intellectuals as directive forces in community life, and second, an unwillingness to confront the significance of power as a category of social analysis. In both cases, Mumford was trapped by the worst features of the utopian tradition, even as he sought to make it accessible to a dialogue of civic renewal.

Despite his critique of the industrial division of labor, Mumford was surprisingly receptive to the rigid functionalism of Plato's division of labor, in which "justice is to perform one's own task and not to meddle with that of others." "The state is like the physical body," Mumford wrote of *The Republic*, with different organs interacting as harmoniously as the instruments of a symphony orchestra. It followed that the political body needed a "head," and Mumford was quick to defend Plato's rule by philosopher-kings as the reign of a "genuinely disinterested" aristocracy possessing the ancient equivalent of "what we should today call sociology," as opposed to "fake aristocracies that are perpetuated through hereditary wealth and position." Throughout his discussion, Mumford suggested that the functional equilibrium of parts in an organic community required intelligent direction by an intellectual elite. Thus he applauded Plato's eugenics and the Republic's abolition of private life for the warrior class as an astute recognition that "the little utopia of the family is the enemy—indeed the principal enemy—of the beloved community." And he distinguished philosopher-kings from conventional statesmen by pointing to the former's disdain for "petty laws, regulations, and reforms" when the "essential constitution of the state" required "breeding, vocational selection, and education." Mumford's only real complaint with this state of affairs was that Plato had banished poets and artists from the Republic, instead of inviting them to join the philosopher-kings in their exploration of the ideal. Nowhere in the chapter did he confront the possibility that Plato's functionalism was as undemocratic as the industrial division of labor, that it assumed the existence of a permanent slave labor force, or that it equated knowledge with power and thus granted to intellectuals an unprecedented control over every aspect of public and private life. In light of his praise for *The Republic*, Mumford's sociological "knowledge of the whole" sounded ominously like the power of the knowledgeable *over* the whole.[45]

For a critic of the powerful nation-state, Mumford could be woefully oblivious to the ways power actually functioned. In praising the functional organization of Plato's Republic, he was blind to the authoritarian implications of rule by an intellectual elite. Nor did he see the Platonic roots of the technocratic modern utopias he abhorred such as Edward Bellamy's *Looking Backward*. Mumford's complaint that Bellamy's utopia overemphasized "the part that wholesale mechanical organization, directed by a handful of people, would play in such a reconstruction" might be applied—with allowances for technological differences—to the functionalist regime of Plato's philosopher-kings. By the same token, Mumford had inherited from the idealist tradition a political naïveté that undercut his appeals for a practical utopianism. When he assumed that, "without our perpetual 'will to believe,' " social and political institutions would "vanish like smoke in the wind," he mistook the reigning "social myths" of industrialism for the power relations of modern society. To assume that new ideas alone would topple Coketown and its progeny was to reduce utopianism to wishful thinking. Mumford's Platonist idealism left him as optimistic as any Victorian liberal about the ability of intelligence to tame the forces of unreason.[46]

The Story of Utopias was strongest when it took Plato's method, the Socratic dialogue, and not his literal example as the model for a renewed utopianism. Whatever its flaws, though, the book remains an indispensable introduction to Mumford's thought. As Donald L. Miller observes, it is "perhaps the single most important book for understanding Lewis Mumford's career and achievement." For the rest of his career, Mumford would draw on his central idola of Coketown, the Country House, the National-State, and Megalopolis in his polemics against industrial civilization. His early protest against the mechanistic tendencies of modern culture became a constant theme of his work, as did his attack on the modern state as the enemy of community life. As a romantic critic of the industrial division of labor, he would hold fast to the medieval guild ideal as proof of the artificiality of the modern separation of work, culture, and leisure. As a republican moralist, he would insist on the centrality of a common understanding of the good life to any politics of social reconstruction. *The Story of Utopias* sketched out this agenda at the same time it laid bare its internal contradictions. Whether as culturist or utopian, Mumford confronted the same stark reality that the *Seven Arts* critics had run up against in the late 1910s. A politics aloof from a collective cultural heritage was doomed to reproduce the worst features of industrial civilization. Moral exhortation alone, however, was no substitute for a culture of experience or a popular movement for political change. In the absence of any basis in practical activity, culturism became a rallying cry for aspiring philosopher-kings or a Country House for the defeated.[47]

In a letter to Brooks in 1925, written as he was composing the lectures that became *The Golden Day*, Mumford noted, "I find, consolingly, that my standards in architecture and literature are one, so that the good life that hovers in the background has, at all events, a unity of interior and exterior." When read in light of his efforts to revive utopianism, Mumford's studies in American architecture and literature from the 1920s display a persistent attempt to pose alternative idola to the social myths of industrialism. *Sticks and Stones* (1924), *The Golden Day* (1926), and the host of essays and reviews that accompanied them are, of course, exercises in cultural history and criticism, but they are more than that. These works show Mumford working his way out of the dead end of idealist thought by reconceiving its goal of a fully conscious subject as an aesthetic project. His ideal of the good life did, indeed, "hover in the background" of these studies, much to the dismay of literary and architectural formalists; that ideal now took shape, however, as a set of symbolic forms that Mumford embraced as an alternative to Neoplatonist and positivist modes of thought. The interpretation and reconstruction of social reality as symbols became for Mumford the defining essence of human life. Since aesthetic experience mediated all of human existence, the creation of new social myths had to start in the medium of artistic form, rather than in the utopian milieu of abstract ideas. Mumford's cultural studies rescued culturism from the airy idealism of *The Story of Utopias*, while vindicating art as a liberating practice of personal and social renewal. The "will to create" now replaced the "will to believe" as the center of his cultural criticism.[48]

Mumford's architectural writings never strayed from the belief in civic regeneration he inherited from Geddes. "The only expression that really matters in architecture," he proclaimed in *Sticks and Stones*, "is that which contributes in a direct and positive way to the good life." The final chapter of that book ended with a restatement of Howard's and Geddes's garden city program and a reminder that "a city, properly speaking, does not exist by the accretion of houses, but by the association of human beings." Mumford's interest in architectural forms was hardly formalist: he insisted on locating the iconography and design of the city in their social and historical contexts.[49]

Throughout the 1920s, Mumford's critical judgments on architecture reflected his involvement with the Regional Planning Association of America, which he had founded in 1923 with Clarence Stein, Benton MacKaye, Charles Harris Whitaker, Stuart Chase, Henry Wright, Frederick Lee Ackerman, and other enthusiasts of the regionalist movement.

Like all these men, he believed that the products of the second industrial revolution—automobiles, radio, electricity, and the telephone—made possible the dispersion of industry in small-scale settlements that combined the best features of urban and rural culture. As Carl Sussman rightly notes, this program was not some Jeffersonian tirade against urban life. "To the contrary, the RPAA members actually responded to what they perceived as the disintegration of urban values" caused by the parallel development of the skyscraper city and the bedroom suburb. The garden city would recapture the civic unity of work, culture, and family life that had once existed in the medieval city—and then briefly in the New England colonial village—before its division into Coketown, Megalopolis, and the Country House. Mumford's explorations in architecture and design always had this goal in mind. In his critical writings, he searched new developments in form and structure for an architectural language uniting the disparate elements of modern life into a new cultural synthesis.[50]

In his architectural criticism from this period, Mumford hammered away at the mélange of fragmentary styles that characterized American architecture and interior design. The disintegration of the city center in the modern age had as its stylistic counterpart the dissolution of any coherent iconography fusing function and visual expression. Coketown's architecture reflected the mechanical functionalism of the factory and warehouse, which devalued all needs save those of production. In Megalopolis, the skyscraper symbolized the triumph of real estate speculators determined to gain the maximum profit from every inch of territory. With the design of the workplace subordinated to such narrow, utilitarian ends, the design of the Country House became a playground for a veneer architecture of eclecticism and imitative revivalism. Mumford took special pains to demolish the cult of the "picturesque"—still the reigning standard of the academy—which, in spreading from the Country House to the monumental architecture of Megalopolis, had given the modern city "the air of a ransacked museum." The perversion of the instinct of workmanship by the commercial demand for novelty resulted in machines and buildings covered with the scrawl of archaic designs. In obscuring what was vital in modern engineering and technology, Mumford argued, the picturesque architecture of the turn of the century mirrored genteel literature in its estrangement from lived experience.[51]

Mumford often sounded very much like Brooks in his scathing attacks on the legacy of nineteenth-century architecture. On one side stood the "barracks architecture" of the factory, the tenement house, and the office building, designed primarily by engineers, who adhered to strictly technical standards of building. On the other stood the counterfeit "picture-book architecture" of churches, schools, public buildings, and the homes of the wealthy. Between the extremes of Highbrow and Lowbrow architecture, there existed no true vernacular architecture uniting form and function, expression and use. Mumford saw the glimmerings of such an architecture in the most unexpected places. The anonymous designs of steamships, grain elevators, cafeterias, railroad stations, bridges, and the rear facades of buildings often displayed a greater unity of structural simplicity and grace than the elaborate academicism of "high" architecture. But these innovations were ignored amid the rash of stylistic fads that littered the American city with souvenirs of earlier eras. At bottom, the dissolution of a coherent style reflected the disappearance of the craft of mason-builder that had flourished in the Middle Ages and lived on in the United States through the early nineteenth century. The mason's replacement by engineers and academic architects, both beholden to powerful financial interests, was a major theme of *Sticks and Stones*. As in Brooks's literary criticism, Mumford upheld a craft model of architecture as the social foundation of a common cultural language.[52]

In his proposals for a new architectural iconography, Mumford welded the functionalist currents of Veblen's work and the new developments in European modernism to the holistic conception of culture he found in Geddes, Ruskin, and Morris. Like Ruskin and Morris, Mumford believed that "a 'style' is fundamentally the outcome of a way of living, that it ramifies through all the activities of a community, and that it is the reasoned expression, in some particular work, of the complex of social and technological experience that grows out of a community's life." The Gothic cathedral was a true expression of life in the medieval city because it shaped architectural form out of innovative building techniques and the spiritual demands of a Christian community. To achieve a comparable integration of utility and expression in modern architecture, he argued, meant finding some middle road between the utilitarian functionalism of "barracks" design and "picture-book" eclecticism. Thus Mumford propounded a humanized aesthetics of the machine, following Veblen in seeking to free technological development from commercial dictates, while at the same time trying to make decorative beauty an intrinsic element of structural technique.[53]

In the process, Mumford found himself in a unique position at the center of debates raging over the arts-and-crafts movement, industrial technology, and the emerging modernism of the International Style. To hold on to the literal styles of Morris's neomedieval architecture was to fall into the "picturesque" trap of stale revivalism. Mumford agreed with Morris on the need for an architecture and domestic design using regional traditions and indigenous materials but held that "one must accomplish these ends to-day not as William Morris accomplished them in the Red House but as Morris would have used them had he been born in our generation and had profited by our many advances." To realize the union of form and function in the industrial age, Mumford argued, meant adapting the clean, efficient style of modern machinery to Morris's purposes—in effect repeating Frank Lloyd Wright's famous prescription in his 1901 Hull House lecture, "The Art and Craft of the Machine." The problem was that in endorsing the crisp, dynamic aesthetics of the machine in his polemics against picturesque frivolity, Mumford often seemed to be advocating the same drab utilitarian style he railed against in Coketown. "Before we can have any tolerable modern ornament," he wrote, "we must first learn to erase every distracting vestige of earlier forms," a statement that bordered on a formula for an ascetic, streamlined architecture devoid of any contact with either history or the aesthetic imagination. Though commendable as an attempt to rework expression on an original basis, this strain of Mumford's functionalism was the architectural equivalent of cultural lag theory: architects needed to catch up with their more advanced colleagues in engineering and machine design. Nor was it entirely clear how a machine aesthetic addressed the divorce of art and construction that resulted from the loss of masonry as a craft. As it had for Dewey and his followers, Mumford's admiration for the achievements of applied science blunted his insights into the cultural consequences of the industrial division of labor.[54]

Mumford was saved from endorsing a purely utilitarian iconography by his use of Geddesian organicism to flesh out the doctrine of artistic functionalism. As he grew more familiar with new developments in American and European modernism in the course of the decade, Mumford became increasingly wary of the spare, geometrical design pioneered by figures such as Walter Gropius and Le Corbusier and more inclined to the humanist architecture of Louis Sullivan and Frank Lloyd Wright. Like Mumford, the European modernists had grasped the divergence of industrial building techniques from traditional modes of artistic expression. They "have faced this situation with inexorable logic:

they have modified or curbed their feelings so as to fit the construction!" "In the desire to plan and design on modern lines for the *modern man*," he wrote in 1928, "some of the continental designers have already caricatured the possibilities of our present mode of existence, and in providing for the modern, have forgotten the man." By taking technology as their model for an architectural vernacular, Mumford argued, European modernists reproduced prevailing standards of utility instead of posing more humane alternatives. Their fascination with the machine led them to take "novelty as a desirable quality in itself," again separating architectural form from social function.[55]

Just as the *Seven Arts* critics had sought to broaden the concept of "experience" by supplementing pragmatism with the romantic defense of the artistic imagination, Mumford argued for a functionalist architecture that would express the widest assortment of human needs. Artistic creativity, neighborly civility, and the attachments of friendship and family life were as functional to the community as industrial enterprise and demanded equal attention from modern architects. This "organic functionalism," as Mumford would later call it, had more in common with Wright's use of natural forms and local materials than with the hard-edged geometricism of the International Style. The best form, Mumford now argued, was one that embodied the full potential of human life. Form still had to follow function, in Horatio Greenough's famous dictum. But it had to follow a new ideal of function, one that existed neither in the factory nor the engineer's office but in the will to create a fully humane society.[56]

By the mid-1920s, the creation of symbolic form had assumed a central place in Mumford's culturist theory. Forms and symbols had an integral part in the renewal of community life by virtue of their ability to prefigure new modes of social relationships in terms of legible iconographic materials. The utopian promise of culture, Mumford was coming to believe, was its capacity for engaging social groups in an artistic language of self-reflection. A vital style was an open-ended conversation between members of a community through the medium of a shared public language. Citizens shared their understanding of themselves through that medium, and they were transformed in the process: a dialectic of self-representation and self-realization through form. Though this symbolic variation of Mumford's culturism still assigned a privileged position to artists and architects as prophets of a new community, it was far more democratic than the Platonic utopianism he espoused in *The Story of Utopias*. Mumford translated the most promising element of his first work—the redefinition of utopia as a public dialogue—into symbolic terms, hoping to stimulate a new awareness about basic human needs at the point at which ideals and practice, expression and function, converged in a public culture. The real story of utopias, his work now suggested, was to be found in the forms and symbols used in its telling.

The Golden Day provided the theoretical underpinnings for Mumford's turn to symbolic form as the medium of social reconstruction. Based on lectures on American civilization he delivered in Switzerland in the summer of 1925, *The Golden Day* was the most powerful statement of his critical position to date. Though many of its ideas were borrowed directly from Brooks, Bourne, Frank, and Geddes, the book had an original quality that derived from Mumford's confident authorial voice. In the past, his pronouncements on the good life had interrupted his prose as awkward moralistic intrusions. Now, he was successful in uniting his vision with the structure and language of his narrative. The book's organization—opening with a glimpse of Europe's crumbling medieval synthesis, then shifting to its final efflorescence in New England's literary renaissance, followed by a treatment of cultural decline after the Civil War, and closing with Mumford's hopes for modern renewal—expressed the cycle of growth, decay, and rebirth that was the heart of Mumford's organicism. Mumford filtered the literary history of the nineteenth century through that of the settlement of the American landscape, highlighting the interplay between culture and environment at work in his country's literature. His subject was "the spiritual fact of American experience," or as he later put it, the "forms and meanings," "relationships and values" of American culture. For this story, Mumford's vitalistic rhetoric of biological metaphors was appropriately functional. As *A Study in American Experience and Culture* (the book's original subtitle), *The Golden Day* was an example of Mumford's symbolic culturism.[57]

The guiding premise of *The Golden Day* was that the literature of antebellum New England furnished insights into American experience that challenged the "pragmatic acquiescence" of modern culture. "The Transcendentalists are just what I want to play off against the Pragmatists," he wrote Brooks; "my own instinctive Platonism vibrates to them, and since I was brought up, so to speak, on pragmatism my attitude to the first has some of the enthusiasm of the convert." Indeed, in his new-found enthusiasm for Transcendentalism, Mumford lashed out against his pragmatic elders in a one-sided polemic that had none of the nuances of Bourne's earlier attacks. Whereas Bourne—and, to some extent, Frank and Stearns—indicted Dewey for betraying the promise of pragmatic thought, Mumford echoed Brooks's sweeping dismissal of James and Dewey as enemies of the imagination. James's pragmatism was nothing more than the philosophical equivalent of Frank Norris's and Theodore Dreiser's wooden naturalism, Mumford charged: it betrayed the "attitude of compromise and acquiescence" that characterized the entire Gilded Age. His critique of James as "the reporter, rather than the creator" of social experience was fully in keeping with the revisionist pragmatism that Bourne had formulated during the war, but Mumford was too busy decrying the whole endeavor as "a blessed anesthetic" to consider his own debt to Jamesian categories. His treatment of Dewey was a good deal more appreciative, though he took pains to show how Dewey's instrumentalism neglected the importance of art— not as an instrument to other ends but "as a *mode of life*." The criticism was telling. In spite of his rhetorical excesses, Mumford was not simply opposing Transcendental "idealism" to pragmatic "objectivism." As he told Brooks, "I am dealing with ideas in the larger sense—that is, as the *forms* of the race." Mumford's encounter with Emerson, Thoreau, and Whitman led him from an abstract Platonic idealism to symbolic representation as the alternative to a debased pragmatism.[58]

As he traced the unfolding of the idea of American newness in the writings of these three authors, Mumford depicted the progressive materialization of Emerson's idealist dialectics in literary form. Mumford's turn to Emerson was in many ways a logical move, given the interests he had in common with the other Young Americans. The intuitive understanding of experience he shared with Bourne, Brooks, and Frank owed at least as much to Emerson as it did to James. Despite the young Brooks's disdain for Emerson's Highbrow detachment, his suspicion of political institutions and his ideal of the artist as prophet of the whole man immersed in an organic community echoed classic Emersonian themes. Mumford absorbed these elements of Transcendental thought, but he saw their development as part of a historical process culminating in Americans' cultural self-representation. Emerson's idealism was the starting point of a new symbolic language. The peculiar circumstances of life on the Atlantic seaboard in the antebellum period gave birth to a unique synthesis of New World optimism and a neo-Puritan spirituality that was the final flower of medieval culture. Emerson's Transcendentalism had to be understood in the specific context of the balanced communities of early nineteenth-century New England. It was the "thoroughly socialized existence of the New England town" that checked the individualism of his doctrine and made it a function of creative participation in public life. Emerson's theory of self-reliance may have been a "barbarism," Mumford admitted, but it had "the virtue of getting beyond the institution, the habit, the ritual, and finding out what it means afresh in one's own consciousness." By stripping away outmoded social arrangements in search of their animate core of vital ideas, Emerson was clearing the way for forms and symbols expressing the future potential of his country's experience.[59]

What Mumford valued in Emerson's philosophy was its recognition of "the formative role of ideas" in reconstituting the world in terms of a symbolic language. "He saw the importance of 'dialectic' in placing new patterns before the mind which did not exist, ready-made, in the order of Nature." Emerson's aesthetics transcended the boundaries of idealism by reconciling matter and spirit in cultural expression. Both "were phases of man's existence," Mumford wrote. "Matter passed into spirit and became a symbol: spirit passed into matter and gave it a form; and symbols and forms were the essences through which man lived and fulfilled his proper being." This dialectic of mind and its environment through the medium of art was Emerson's chief legacy to Thoreau and Whitman and the element of his work that Mumford thought most useful to a twentieth-century movement for cultural renewal: "The mission of creative thought is to gather into it all the living sources of its day, all that is vital in the practical life, all that is intelligible in science, all that is relevant in the social heritage and, recasting these things into new forms and symbols, to react upon the blind drift of convention and habit and routine. Life flourishes only in this alternating rhythm of dream and deed: when one appears without the other, we can look forward to a shrinkage, a lapse, a devitalization. Idealism is a bad name for this mission; it is just as correct to call it realism; since it is part of the natural history of the human mind."[60]

Mumford's interpretation of Emerson as a figure who escaped the pale abstractions of idealism neglected those elements of Transcendentalism that were an idealist protest against the tyranny of the material world. Nor did it appreciate the threat that Emerson's mystic spiritualism posed to the material embodiment of values in cultural artifacts. Mumford read Emerson selectively, with an eye to George Santayana's work, which he singled out as the most promising modern alternative to pragmatism. Santayana, he wrote, "restored idealism as a mode of thinking creatively, as the mode in which art and ritual take on an independent existence and create a new home for the spirit." Mumford's Santayanesque view of Emerson was a critical step in the development of his theory of cultural change. Reacting against the "pragmatic acquiescence" of modern American thought, Mumford took heart from the power of symbolic language to engage self and society in a dialogue of redefinition and reconstruction.[61]

Thoreau and Whitman were Emerson's heirs, according to Mumford, in that they used his dialectical method to create a literary vocabulary appropriate to American experience. Thoreau's naturalism was an artistic endeavor, attentive to the possibilities of an aesthetics patterned after the shapes and processes of nature. Thoreau "returned to Nature in order to become, in a sense, more cultivated and civilized," Mumford wrote, "not in order to return to crudities that men had already discarded." He studied the woods for an imagery consistent with living "a whole human life" in the settlements of the New World. Whitman took Thoreau's artistic expression of Emerson's dialectics to its final conclusion. In Mumford's view, Whitman had remade himself as a symbol, presenting his own life as a mythic expression of American promise.

> The imperturbable landscape, the satisfaction and aplomb of animals, the ecstasy of hearty lovers, the meditations of one who sits withdrawn in the crowd, or on a mountain top—Whitman extracted from these things a new shape, which was himself. Every poem of Whitman's is the man; every part of the man threw forth tendrils which clung to the objects of poems. One could not become a sympathetic reader of Whitman without re-forming oneself into an approximation of this new shape. . . . He created a new pattern of experience and character. The work he conceived still remains to be done: the America he evoked does not as yet exist.

Whitman's work was the apogee of symbolic representation as a utopian art form, the literary equivalent of the organic functionalism Mumford sought in architecture. His poetry was a testament to the ability of art to transform the world, first by transmuting lived experience into an aesthetic language and then by using that language to express an experience that still lay in the future. With Whitman, Mumford felt, American literary form fulfilled its ultimate function: "to crystallize our most precious experience and in turn to modify, by that act of crystallization, the daily routine."[62]

Mumford's greatest achievement in *The Golden Day* was to transform the past itself into an aesthetic artifact, to make the legacy of
Emerson, Thoreau, and Whitman accessible to a generation in search of
its own appropriate symbols. This was what he and Brooks had meant
by "a usable past," not the instrumental use of history to justify present concerns. Mumford followed the example of Emerson, for whom
the past "was neither a prescription nor a burden: it was rather an
esthetic experience. Being no longer inevitable in America, that is, no
longer something handed down with a living at Corpus Christi or a
place at court, the past could be entertained freely and experimentally. It
could be revalued," Mumford explained. Where Whitman's poetics anticipated a future community and introduced its forms into the discourse of the present, Mumford's work tried to make history a part of
the symbolic medium of his contemporaries. *The Story of Utopias* had
tried to free postwar culture from the grip of the present, but *The
Golden Day* offered a method for achieving that goal. Preaching the
virtues of past and present to a rootless generation was an artificial,
even futile gesture that only confirmed the break in historical continuity
occasioned by the war. To intervene in lived experience, historical understanding had to take part in the supple, ever-changing language of
culture.[63]

Mumford's theory of forms and symbols as the source of a new
community was largely lost on John Dewey, who criticized *The
Golden Day* for its remoteness from the scientific-industrial culture of
the twentieth century. Angered by Mumford's treatment of the "pragmatic acquiescence," Dewey charged in the *New Republic* in 1927 that
Mumford had mangled his theory of art and distorted James's work to
fit pragmatism into a preconceived model of American intellectual decline. Dewey, in fact, agreed with Mumford on the value of art as a
means to the "renewal of spirit"; "not, it would seem, a base end, and
certainly not a utilitarian one." Where he and Mumford were at odds,
he claimed, was on the relationship between ideals and social realities.
Ignoring Mumford's emphasis on forms and symbols, Dewey painted
The Golden Day as an idealist defense of pure thought against any taint
of involvement with experience. "All serious thinking combines in some
proportion and perspective the actual and the possible," he countered,
"where actuality supplies contact and solidity while possibility furnishes
the ideal upon which criticism rests and from which creative effort

springs." Mumford's sin was to disdain the actual—and, in particular, to omit any consideration of science and technology, without which modern criticism was "arbitrary," "'transcendent' and ultimately of one's own personal conceit." Dewey reminded Mumford that the values he desired of a richer human life were possible, for the majority of people, only through the use of industrial technology. This was what was at stake in instrumentalism, not some "acquiescence" in the values of a commercial society. "Not all who say Ideals, Ideals, shall enter the kingdom of the ideal," Dewey concluded, "but those who know and who respect the roads that conduct to the kingdom."[64]

If Dewey's criticism parodied Mumford's position as a nostalgic idealism, Mumford's response neglected those elements of pragmatism he had reiterated in his own thinking about the relation of culture to social experience. He identified his critique of pragmatism with that made by Bourne, Brooks, and Frank a decade earlier, noting that although "most of my generation began as pragmatists," they had since gone on to Spinoza, Santayana, Croce, Plato, and Geddes for "a hold on wider realms of thought and life than the pragmatists have been interested in." "We were, perhaps, the ungrateful heirs of William James's great liberation; but it was part of our sad experience to find that the philosophy which had rescued the academic world from an arid theological provincialism was in itself also a provincialism." Mumford essentially repeated the Young Americans' earlier case against Dewey's work: that it ignored the aesthetic dimensions of experience; that it posited a relationship between technological means and humane ends that ultimately sacrificed values to technique; and that it left no place for either historical understanding or the creative imagination as alternatives to prevailing modes of thought. "It is not that we reject Mr. Dewey," he wrote with more than a hint of condescension; "that would be ingratitude: but that we seek for a broader field and a less provincial interpretation of Life and Nature than he has given us."[65]

Perhaps Mumford refused to acknowledge how much he shared with Dewey because he had come to depend on Dewey as a foil in his cultural criticism. To a certain extent, *The Golden Day* needed the "pragmatic acquiescence" as a symbol of the mechanical utilitarianism that had supplanted the organic vitality of Emerson's "Golden Day." The entire architecture of Mumford's criticism followed the romantic pattern established by Brooks in *The Soul*. Mumford's cultural history charted a familiar course: a nurturing communal culture had been replaced by an inhuman industrialism, which he hoped was giving way to some new organic civilization. Dewey's support for the war apparently justified, in Mumford's mind, portraying pragmatism as the ideological expression of industrial capitalism. No matter how much Dewey adapted his pragmatic theory of experience to encompass questions of value or to account for artistic creativity, he had come to occupy a set place in Mumford's cyclical theory of the death and rebirth of America's organic culture.[66]

The *New Republic* exchange was neither man's finest hour. In the heat of intellectual battle, Dewey and Mumford paid no attention to what they had in common, choosing instead to refight the wars of 1917–19. Dewey's piece, for example, ignored Mumford's efforts to make symbolic language the medium for debates about the good life. His charge that Mumford's criticism of modern society was ultimately arbitrary, because it lacked a foundation in scientific technique missed Mumford's argument that cultural forms were the distinguishing feature of all human interaction—including science—and thus provided an appropriate anchor for social criticism. Dewey's crack about the empty call of "Ideals, Ideals" might have been an adequate response to *The Story of Utopias*, but it had little bearing on Mumford's later explorations of literary and architectural form. The Mumford of *The Golden Day* was no simple idealist.

Mumford was equally indifferent to potential points of contact with Dewey's work. Throughout the 1920s, Dewey gave increasing attention to the place of art and values in his philosophy of experience—a project that produced the 1925 lectures that became *Experience and Nature* and culminated in the publication of his *Art as Experience* in 1934. During this period, he insisted that the problem of creating a democratic community was essentially one of communication, an idea that had much in common with Mumford's emphasis on a common language of cultural forms. In *The Public and Its Problems*, published shortly after his exchange with Mumford, Dewey called for "the perfecting of the means and ways of communication of meanings so that genuinely shared interest in the consequences of interdependent activities may inform desire and effort and thereby direct action." "Communication can alone create a great community," Dewey wrote in a passage that Mumford himself might have written. "Our Babel is not one of tongues but of the signs and symbols without which shared experience is impossible."[67]

Admittedly, a great deal still separated the two thinkers and not just animosities left over from the war years. Mumford was receptive to industrial innovations in architecture and design, but he continued to fault Dewey for believing that modern science and technology could serve as instruments of a democratic culture. By the same token, Dewey's emphasis on politics and social institutions made him wary of Mumford's culturism, which by 1927 had lost most of the overtly political overtones of his *Dial* period. Mumford still held firm to his initial hopes for a nonstatist politics of local association, but he now saw that such a politics had to begin slowly with a change in the forms and symbols of modern civilization. Even as they taunted each other in the pages of the *New Republic*, Dewey and Mumford were exploring complementary themes in American politics, culture, and social thought. A genuine dialogue about the significance of symbolic interaction to a democratic polity and a philosophy of experience would have been of tremendous value to both men. It might have clarified the precise relationship between cultural communication and civic institutions and between participatory democracy and aesthetic form, which remained only vaguely defined in their work. It is no exaggeration to say that the absence of such a dialogue was one of the real tragedies of the decade.

For a thinker as thoroughly political as John Dewey, the relationship between Mumford's postwar critique of the state and *The Golden Day* must have been hard to discern. By the mid-1920s, Mumford was less willing to assert that institutional remedies to the fragmentation of a civic culture already existed. The cathedral, market, and guildhall of the medieval city remained his standard for regional associations that united citizens as spiritual and political participants in their own history. But his concern for new artistic forms and symbols suggested that it was still too early to consider what modern organizations should take their place. *The Golden Day* ended with a call to cultural renewal, not the utopian blueprints for new communities that dominated his conclusions to *The Story of Utopias* and *Sticks and Stones*. Now his main purpose was to defend art as a social practice that united "imaginative desire, desire sublimated and socialized, with actuality: without this union," he held, "desires become idiotic, and actualities perhaps even a little more so." Mumford still believed in regional planning, of course, but his emphasis on aesthetic experience opened up civic reconstruction to the "socialized desire" of a public culture, rather than viewing it as the application of social science by a handful of philosopher-kings. By establishing a consensual community in the language of art, literature, and everyday life, he argued, new forms and symbols prefigured a society that had done away with the coercive authority of the factory and the wartime state. If it was not yet possible to live Thoreau's "whole human life," one might glimpse such a life in the supple signs and conventions that humans used to order and give meaning to their experience.[68]

By the mid-1920s, Mumford was convinced that a politics of culturism had to take root in the language of symbolic interaction if it were ever to engage citizens in the task of civic regeneration. In this respect, Mumford was restating the premises of the *Seven Arts* on the priority of cultural renewal over immediate political change. The similarities between his position and that of Bourne, Brooks, and Frank a decade earlier were certainly evident; what was less clear was the extent to which Mumford had revised fundamental elements of the Young Americans' argument. By calling attention to the processes of symbolic interpretation that mediated all human experience, Mumford had freed that argument from its reliance on romantic and transcendent definitions of culture. Although he reiterated Brooks's defense of the aesthetic imagination in his critique of pragmatism, his treatment of cultural forms derived less from a romantic notion of artistic genius than from an understanding of human nature. For Mumford, the human capacity for symbolic representation was the central premise of any movement for cultural renewal. He certainly valued the work of creative artists in fashioning new forms and symbols, but he placed such contributions in the context of the ongoing redefinition of culture that characterized all social life. Thus Mumford's criticism had less need for visionary seers of wholeness than either Frank's or Brooks's work and gave little attention to the transcendent, otherworldly bases of cultural expression. It defined a role for intellectuals that avoided the twin dangers of utopian elitism and romantic prophecy. Intellectuals had a part to play in the rebuilding of civic life as creators and interpreters of forms, not as political leaders or mystical oracles. Their place was in the midst of the dialogue of symbolic meaning that constituted human experience. The political prospects for culturism, Mumford had come to recognize, rested on its ability to become truly cultural.

7
In Search of a Usable Self

"I embrace ALL," says Whitman. "I weave all things into myself."
Do you really! There can't be much left of you when you've done.
When you've cooked the awful pudding of One Identity.
—D. H. LAWRENCE,
Studies in Classic American Literature

Throughout the 1910s, Bourne, Brooks, and Frank had portrayed American life as a terrain of unresolved conflicts. The antagonism between masculine and feminine qualities they had explored in their own personalities found echoes in the tensions between culture and society, Highbrow and Lowbrow, theory and practice, and spirit and the material world that provided the central themes of their work. Their attention to personality, experience, values, and culture itself grew out of their determination to overcome the divisions in American industrial society by recovering modes of thought and being that engaged the self and its environment in a mutual process of renewal and reconstruction. The notion of creative personality embedded in a culture of experience upheld an ideal of the interactive self remaking its consciousness—its values—as it humanized the world around it. Culture was the perfect medium for such a process, the Young Americans argued, because it combined subjective and objective experience in an organic whole. As Mumford's work demonstrated, culture was at the core of human nature. The symbolic language of interpretation that constituted the human world was the basis of an interactive ideal of selfhood. Forms and symbols created a familiar environment out of alien surroundings; they provided a setting for the dialogue between inner and outer experience that nourished free personalities.

The Young Americans' view of culture as a medium of communication between different elements of American life had tremendous value for their criticism. It enabled them to play Highbrow ideals off against Lowbrow practice, to recall literature to its roots in social experience while rejecting a mimetic culture that merely reflected its environment, and to challenge both the self-reliant individual and the well-adjusted self as failed experiments in self-realization. Most of all, it fueled their opposition to commercial expansion and the industrial division of labor, which, in destroying craft, had separated practical activity from the creative imagination. Their radical view of the interaction of the self with its environment placed a premium on reflection and critique as the sources of any vital culture. Thus the Young Americans' work was at its best when it served a critical function and when its vision of a Beloved Community looked to self-reflection and self-criticism as the constituents of the good life. When their writing turned from such concerns to utopian prophecy, it suffered all the problems of "premature crystallization" that Bourne had criticized in pragmatism. Steering a difficult course between the self and society, culture remained a force for community only when it maintained the critical edge inherent in Mumford's dialectic of symbolic communication. If their prophetic tendency often led them to overly simple syntheses of the polarities they identified in American society, their critical method suggested an ideal of civic renewal modeled after the dynamic at work in the imaginative apprehension of the world. In this view, the promise of an organic culture was not a final resolution of cultural conflicts but a common language for interpreting and uniting in aesthetic form the divided realms of modern experience.

The Young Americans' theory of cultural renewal also provided an answer to the problem of personal identity that had plagued them in their early years. Bourne, Brooks, Frank, and Mumford had each rejected the alternatives of feminine gentility and soulless masculine practice that seemed the only options available to them as young men. Repelled by the sentimentalism of genteel culture, they had indulged in fantasies of mystical union—of merging with the feminine ideal—that preserved the moral idealism of literary gentility in a disembodied realm of pure spirit. Despite the lingering appeal of such fantasies for these writers, their criticism ultimately rejected an escapist solution to the degradation of practical life. By choosing to act as men of letters and critics of culture, the Young Americans sought a vocation that combined their quasi-religious aestheticism with involvement in society.

In the atmosphere of the 1920s, however, the critic's relationship to society—and the relationship of self-renewal to public regeneration—became increasingly attenuated. Bereft of any immediate hope for political change and distanced by temperament and conviction from the self-referential culture of literary modernism, the Young Americans were hard put to define a space for culture and criticism as a language mediating between the antitheses of American life. "It was not so easy, this living between two world," Brooks wrote of Henry James's position as an American in Europe: "One got nothing for one's pains but neglect, insults, derision. One received no recognition anywhere: what was worse, one lost touch all round, one ceased to understand, one found oneself gradually encompassed by an atmosphere that was somehow non-conducive." In describing James's predicament, Brooks had hit upon his own dilemma, and that of Frank and Mumford, during the 1920s. Mumford largely resolved the problem by grounding his critical method in the dialectics of symbolic communication. The existence of culture was itself a sign, for Mumford, of its potential for personality, new values, and a fully humanized social experience. Brooks and Frank found the widening gap between their personal vision and their cultural and political environment a more difficult challenge. Faced with the obstacles to creating a common cultural medium, they turned from the broader issues of cultural renewal that had concerned them in the 1910s to a critical literature of the self. That course presented two options: either fortifying the self against a hostile environment or seeking an immediate union of the self and its surroundings through various forms of mysticism. In either case, their original enterprise of healing the breach between self and society—of embodying in culture Bourne's "good life of personality lived in the environment of the Beloved Community"—began to come apart. The isolated self could not support the hopes Brooks and Frank had previously invested in the Beloved Community. A purely spiritual mysticism overrode the need for a democratic culture and, perhaps, the need for any culture at all.[1]

"Literature needs a 'frame,' " Mumford wrote in his notes for a 1927 lecture on American criticism, by which he meant a philosophy rooted in a particular time and place and a set of social practices. It was exactly such a "frame" that seemed to be missing in American culture and in the criticism of the Young Americans themselves by the late 1920s. Without a clear sense of how culture might mediate between subjective desire and social reality, criticism lost its intellectual foundation and threatened to become empty exhortation. Mumford recovered such a frame by turning to the moral issues raised by his study of Herman Melville. His interest in the psychological dimensions of Melville's work led him to explore the ethical and philosophical premises of a new culture. For Brooks and Frank, the loss of culture as a mediating language had more tragic consequences. It was not just their criticism that lacked a frame, in tradition, morality, or collective experience, but, increasingly, their very selves. Their calls to bring aesthetic consciousness to bear on social conditions gave way to a preoccupation with shedding all boundaries between individual spirit and the objective world. In the process, they desperately tried to stave off the marginality they had decried in genteel culture and the specter of self-disintegration that had terrified them in their youthful encounters with the feminine ideal. "The rarest consummation in America," Frank wrote in 1924, "is achieved personality." As an isolated enterprise, removed from any practical experience of building the Beloved Community, the search for personality was doomed to failure. Brooks's breakdown in the mid-1920s and Frank's anguished quest for mystical "wholeness" during the same period are testimony to the psychic costs of the crisis in the Young Americans' critical project.[2]

Paradoxically, Brooks's movement from cultural criticism to questions of selfhood began after the war with his decision to forgo the broadly social and political issues of his early work for a focus on literary matters. Brooks left the *Seven Arts* convinced that the journal's antiwar stance had been a mistake, and after the magazine's demise he cut his ties with its political agenda. His move to Carmel, California, in 1918, to write his book on Mark Twain, was one indication of the distance he was putting between himself and New York's politicized intelligentsia. When he returned to the East in 1920, he chose to settle, not in New York, but in Westport, Connecticut. The essay he wrote on Bourne's career, as an introduction to a collection of Bourne's literary writings, was another such sign. As editor of the 1920 volume *The History of a Literary Radical*, Brooks left out the bulk of Bourne's political essays and claimed in his introduction that Bourne was giving up politics for literary criticism at the time of his death. "As regards Randolph's own writings I am perfectly clear," he wrote Frank. "I'm afraid many of his friends won't be pleased because I have found most of his political and anti-war writing incredibly below the level of his best and quite ephemeral." After the war, Brooks gave up the wide-ranging intellectual project he had shared with Bourne in the mid-1910s. Brooks entered the 1920s convinced of the need to shore up cultural life as an enterprise separate from politics. Although he earlier had claimed that such activity was a first step to a new democratic community, Brooks now held that cultural renewal was primarily the work of dedicated artists and writers, not the stuff of social reform. The war had led

Bourne and Mumford to view culture as a resource for a nonstatist politics. For Brooks, the task at hand was a collective act of will among members of an emerging artistic aristocracy. The absence of any larger movement for cultural and political change demanded that the nation's creative artists assert themselves as a self-organized group, heroically adhering to the standards of the creative life in the face of popular hostility. "As for ourselves," Brooks wrote in "The Literary Life in America," "we still have this advantage, that an age of reaction is an age that stirs the few into a consciousness of themselves." A newly confident literary class had become Brooks's surrogate for a middle ground of cultural experience.[3]

"The Literary Life in America," Brooks's contribution to the famous symposium on "Civilization in the United States," edited by Harold Stearns, was the major statement of his shift in emphasis after the war. The 1921 essay repeated many of his standard themes about the plight of culture in a commercial society, but Brooks departed from the political implications of his previous work by faulting American writers for yielding to the premises of their society. "What constitutes a literature is the spiritual force of the individuals who compose it," he wrote. "If our literature is to grow, it can only be through the development of a sense of 'free will' on the part of our writers themselves." The issue of creative will became a central preoccupation of Brooks's work after the war. He argued that great literature required a "certain courage" on the part of its authors and a "successful pursuit of the ego." Though still critical of the social conditions that stifled creativity in industrial America, Brooks now appeared to hold writers primarily responsible for their predicament. They suffered from a failure of nerve, from a lack of courage to resist the blandishments of an acquisitive society. Brooks's interest in creating an institutional center to the "literary life" followed from this diagnosis. The absence of an aristocratic tradition or an ethos of voluntary poverty left creative people vulnerable to the enervating atmosphere of commercialism that had sapped the resistance of generations of authors. A corporate body of writers became Brooks's solution to the crisis of morale in American literature. "Great men form a sort of windshield behind which the rest of their profession are able to build up their own defences," he explained. They were exemplars of cultural heroism, who inspired the lesser ranks of the artistic army while fortifying the will of those who might otherwise give in to the enemy.[4]

As literary editor of the *Freeman* from 1920 to 1924, Brooks continued to hold the fort of culture against the assault of commerce and the

inner rot of disillusion and despair. In his weekly essays, Brooks returned time and time again to the need for a self-conscious "remnant
insulated against the common life and its common values." Neither
patronage by the wealthy nor popular support could create a healthy
American culture, Brooks argued; rather, artists and writers would have
to organize themselves as a group to protect themselves and their standards. Whereas Brooks's radical traditionalism had led him in the 1910s
to draw on preindustrial traditions of craft and aristocratic culture in a
critique of the industrial division of labor, his *Freeman* essays suggested
that the creation of a literary caste was an end in itself. At times arguing
for a literary aristocracy, at others for a Morrisite guild of artistic craftsmen, Brooks was primarily concerned with sustaining morale among
America's isolated artists and writers.[5]

Brooks's program for a literary guild harked back to his *Seven Arts*
essays in its use of a craft model for cultural life. Claiming that Veblen's
"instinct of workmanship" united writers and workers alike, he held
that authors could best contribute to the development of a vital labor
movement by opposing their own standards for craftsmanship to the
shoddy commercialism of capitalist production. The American working
class lacked "a sustained corporate vision of some better order of
things," Brooks wrote, and it was this "corporate desire, enlightened
desire," that an artistic guild was uniquely equipped to provide. "The
only writers who can possibly aid in the liberation of humanity are those
whose sole responsibility is to themselves as artists," he concluded. This
argument had a great deal in common with Bourne's call for a self-
consciously intellectual radicalism in the 1910s, but its suggestion that
artistic thinkers provide the labor movement with its "corporate vision"
was a step back from Brooks's Morrisite radicalism from the same period. Brooks's response to the industrial division of labor was increasingly one of literary inspiration, which had only the most tenuous relation to a larger effort at transcending the divorce of work and culture.[6]

Thus Brooks could also endorse a far more restrictive model of literary organization, as when he devoted his *Freeman* columns to appeals
for a cultural aristocracy. "For what does this aristocracy accomplish?"
he asked his readers.

It creates, in the first place, by its rightful prestige, such a sense of
the splendour of the vocation that sensitive men, perceiving it, are
eager to put up with an army of devils, eager indeed to pass
through purgatory, in order to have even a chance of serving a cult

that is so divine. It preserves the secrets of the vocation so that men of good will can come to it and learn the discipline by which the human spirit gains possession of itself and finds its direction. It creates standards by which men can measure themselves; it sets up signposts that prevent men from wandering off the highway and getting their feet entangled in quicksands. It infuses literature and the literary life with grace, magnanimity, knowledge, passion, disinterestedness and all the other conquests of which great men alone are fully capable but which all of us can share in a measure. These are some of the services an aristocracy of the spirit renders to literature. Without them, indeed, literature in the proper sense cannot exist at all.

Brooks's aristocratic and guild ideals upheld the goal of preserving non-utilitarian artistic values from the onslaught of purely commercial standards. In this regard, he still wrote as an American heir to the English tradition of nineteenth-century cultural criticism, which opposed the moral ideals of gentility to industrial capitalism. Yet in the *Freeman*, Brooks sounded a good deal more like Arnold defending high culture from the philistines than he did like Ruskin or Morris. Moreover, the very terms of his defense of an "aristocracy of the spirit" betrayed his increasing obsession with strengthening the psychological resolve of the nation's creative artists. Brooks's aristocracy might claim from capitalist society a free space for noncommercial values, but its more immediate function was to keep writers from "wandering off the highway" into the "quicksands" of discouragement and loneliness.[7]

Brooks's judgments on contemporary literature reflected the new importance he gave to psychic health as the goal and precondition of a thriving culture. As the 1920s progressed, Brooks's differences with the modernists at the "new" *Dial* and with socialist writers and critics became ever more apparent. In his polemics against naturalist fiction and modernist aesthetics, Brooks defended the heroic self of nineteenth-century realism and romanticism as a model of creative mastery. His idols were novelists such as Goethe, Tolstoy, Dickens, Hugo, and Dostoevsky, whose protagonists were "whole men" capable of rising above the limits of their environment by uniting action and spiritual vision. Brooks read their work as a didactic literature of moral heroism; its characters were studies in self-formation, a counterweight to the centrifugal forces at work in an atomistic society. Modern American literature, by contrast, seemed to Brooks devoid of any sense of "greatness" and of the "hierarchy in human activities" that sustained heroic individuals. "Unless men are inspired in their youth with a sense of these things, they cannot truly develop a creative will." The survival of American culture required not only a guild consciousness among writers but a confident, unified sense of selfhood capable of protecting the individual aspiring to artistic greatness.[8]

Brooks's disputes with his contemporaries revolved around these psychological issues. He attacked writers on the Left for not giving their characters a vigorous sense of their own identities. Upton Sinclair's naturalism undermined his socialist ambitions, Brooks charged, by portraying workers as helpless masses and appealing to readers to pity them as passive victims of oppression. Sinclair's characters lacked the emotional depth and capacity for human agency that Brooks valued in the heroic protagonists of the nineteenth-century novel. The Left's tendency to deny the potential for moral heroism was compounded by its scientistic disdain for a literature of emotional, spiritual, or even aesthetic values. Brooks attacked Max Eastman's criticism for "trying to give literature the *coup de grace*" by ridding poetry of all vestiges of a prescientific mentality. "He wishes to humiliate literature," Brooks wrote; "he wishes to think that literature has nothing to teach us. He has a deep contempt for his own vocation that constantly leads us to ask why he pursues it." For Brooks, the "scientific" socialists' emphasis on lawlike social forces and on the oppression of a collective mass of humanity came at the expense of any insight into literature's role as a source of personal courage. The strong self had no place in either a politicized naturalism or a Marxist criticism.[9]

If the Left was guilty of ignoring the need for a heroic literature, modernists were even more to blame—in Brooks's eyes—for promoting a culture of self-referentiality, which revealed the self as internally divided and therefore incapable of the confident wholeness Brooks treasured in nineteenth-century fiction. American modernists had once seen the author of *America's Coming-of-Age* and *Letters and Leadership* as their champion. They had welcomed his attacks on literary gentility and his calls for an American renaissance as harbingers of an indigenous avant-garde. By the early 1920s, it was clear to both Brooks and the modernists that they were no longer allies. The *Dial* gave Brooks its annual literary award in 1924 out of respect for his position as herald of the young generation of writers but devoted most of its announcement to congratulating William Butler Yeats for winning the Nobel Prize for literature. In a backhanded compliment to Brooks, the editorial acknowledged that "one can recognize the supreme importance of such a figure even if one fails to accept the whole body of his doctrine." Brooks, in turn, had no patience for the formalist aestheticism that reigned at the *Dial*. "A strange, brittle, cerebral aristocratism has succeeded the robust faith of the last age," he wrote in the *Freeman*. "Today the 'triumph of abstract thought' and of an art divorced from humanity is very evident in the literary world."[10]

Brooks attributed the appeal of formal experimentation in literature to the shock of the war, which had "made reality hateful and seared and withered the life of the emotions." Disillusioned with the struggle for selfhood, modernist writers delighted in "a sort of learned spoofing" that was the pastime of a "parvenu intellectuality." Brooks was not defending literary conventions for their own sake. He feared that an innovation in style without any corresponding engagement of moral or social values would end up in a shallow cult of novelty unhinged from any larger cultural endeavor. Modernism, for Brooks, was the Highbrow culture of the twentieth century: a rootless aestheticism that had dispensed with the lingering moralism of its genteel predecessors. The collapse of humane values during the war, he argued, had deprived modern literature of anything solid to protest or affirm. "It is unable either to uphold or to react against anything either socially or morally important, and consequently has no fulcrum." The heroic protagonists of romantic literature had been rebels as well, but their rebellion took for granted the existence of social values that, however violated in practice, might still be revived in the future. Brooks condemned modernism for applauding the dissolution of any common fund of values, which reduced literature to a "sterile aestheticism" and abandoned the artist to a self-destructive nihilism. As always, the problem was one of sustaining the individual writer's creative will. "Left to himself, separated from these general currents of a living society, the individual can accomplish very little. He becomes an 'infinitely repellent particle,' feeding on his own states of mind."[11]

Brooks's preoccupation with the need for a didactic literature of artistic heroism reflected his worries about his own faltering will. As early as 1919, he was writing Frank of "a strange and disturbing experience" he had in Carmel. "I am too susceptible to atmospheres, shockingly susceptible. And I begin to think that a battery which has lost its charge never gets recharged in California! I am full of unreasoning disgust with this lovely village of Carmel and this crooning Pacific for seducing me into a void of somnolence I cannot seem to shake off." The problem was more than lazy days at the ocean and irritation at the superficiality of conversation in Carmel. As James Hoopes notes, during the period he was writing *The Ordeal of Mark Twain* in Carmel, Brooks "was entering the cycle of depression and alternating mania which would characterize his life for the next decade." As an adolescent and young man, Brooks had been prone to fantasies of mystical union, which turned quickly into nightmares of self-disintegration, but he had managed to hold such impulses at bay for most of his early career. Now, after the war, they returned with a vengeance, and Brooks found himself in utter terror of losing self-control.[12]

These fears were exacerbated by his sense of intellectual isolation in the first half of the decade. In search of an organic community where free personalities realized themselves in interaction with others, Brooks had come up against the hard realities of postwar America. His criticism after the war became increasingly defensive; he had given up the interactive self and the Beloved Community for the security of the artistic guild and then for the self-reliant individualism of the romantic hero. Brooks's antagonism to modernism revealed a deep fear of self-consciousness in literature, as if the self-referential nature of literary form posed a threat to his own embattled self. Ironically, what Brooks objected to in modernist literature was its very emphasis on the author's inner state of mind, as refracted through the stylistic medium of literary work. This literature of the self was not what Brooks was looking for, however; it portrayed a psyche at war with itself, incapable of the confident unity of vision and action that Brooks admired in heroic characters. It deliberately undermined the authority of the narrator, peeling away the layers of language and artifice that made up the writer's voice like the skin of an onion. Even Brooks's analysis of the past indicated a wariness of the analytical intellect when applied to the problems of selfhood. He attributed Melville's desperate career to his "excessive subjectivity," a point he made in the *Freeman* and repeated in an essay on Melville in 1927. Artistic subjectivity, once the very trait that Brooks had invoked as necessary to self-realization and a vital culture of experience, now threatened the conditions for literary creation.[13]

Brooks's financial problems in the years after the war added to his fears of self-disintegration. Up to that time, he had supported himself and his family with a series of odd jobs in publishing and editorial circles, supplementing that income with the money he and Eleanor earned from translating. By the 1920s, such a regimen had clearly taken its toll on Brooks. He resented insinuations from Eleanor's family that his writing was insignificant and that he had failed to support his family properly. Editorial positions at the *Seven Arts* and the *Freeman* provided some stability, but when the latter magazine folded in 1924, Brooks found himself once again scrambling for employment. "The future is a bit vague," he wrote Mumford soon after the *Freeman*'s demise. "What isolated particles we all are!" Casting about for work, Brooks saw himself as a "particle"—the same word he had used to describe modern writers uprooted from any communal values. Brooks's opposition to modernism obviously derived from positions laid out in his writings of the 1910s, but his strenuous assertions of artistic courage took place against a backdrop of doubt about his own capacity for heroic action.[14]

It was in this atmosphere of suspicion about the brooding self-consciousness he shared with many modernists that Brooks wrote his trilogy of literary biographies, *The Ordeal of Mark Twain* (1920), *The Pilgrimage of Henry James* (1925), and *The Life of Emerson* (largely completed by 1926, though not published until 1932). The books were to form a Hegelian dialectic, with the Highbrow James set off against the Lowbrow Twain, ending with Emerson as the embodiment of an American intellectual synthesis. Brooks's search for synthesis was interrupted, however, by the prolonged breakdown that set in with full force in 1925–26 and brought him to the brink of madness and beyond until his recovery five years later. As he explored the lives of Twain, James, and Emerson, Brooks sought examples of personal strength and creative will. He scrutinized their work for lessons in heroism to sustain writers against a debilitating doubt and the corrosive competition of the marketplace. His subjects were less important to him for what they wrote, ultimately, than for how they had survived in a hostile environment. Brooks's sights had narrowed from the Beloved Community of an organic culture to the safety of a literary class and, finally, to the pursuit of an exemplary life. His quest for a usable past had become a search for a usable self.

Brooks's venture into biography afforded him little protection from his inner torments. Amid the bouts of giddy optimism and despair that accompanied his writing, Brooks found it impossible to escape the parallels between the psychological problems he traced in Twain and James and his own sense of self-disintegration. Taking James's side in his critique of Twain's cult of celebrity, he then resembled Twain in condemning James's mature work as the daydreams of a would-be

European aristocrat. In the end, he found no solid ground of his own. Brooks was as unsure as Twain or James about whether to opt for success as an apostle of American virtues or to confront Americans with the tools of a critical intellect sharpened in contact with European high culture. By the time he finished the James book, Brooks was emotionally and intellectually exhausted. "It is finished as a *tract*," he wrote Mumford in 1924, "but I haven't the heart to write tracts any longer. I mean to do the real thing, and can, with time." He admitted, though, that "the *analytical work*" of writing "wore me down most fearfully and convinced me that analysis is for me no longer." After recovering from the first of many breakdowns that followed the book on James, Brooks longed to do "the *positive* thing" in criticism, as he felt Mumford had done in *The Golden Day*. He proclaimed "the necessity of re-asserting the idealistic point of view" in his biography of Emerson. "Everything I have done so far has been a kind of exploration of the *dark* side of our moon, and this blessed Emerson has led me right out into the midst of the sunny side." But by the time *The Life of Emerson* finally appeared in 1932, six years after its completion, Brooks's affirmation of antebellum culture rang hollow. Analysis had, indeed, proved too much for him. With the Emerson book, Brooks traded in the spirited, critical voice of his early work for a forced air of misty lyricism that became the dominant note of the rest of his career. Even worse, Emerson had personally failed him as a guide to literary heroism. In confronting the polarities of his own mind in the lives of Twain and James, Brooks uncovered a psychic wound that could not be healed simply by doting on the "sunny side" of life. Retreating to the self in the 1920s, Brooks had freighted his personality with a burden it could not possibly bear in a vain effort at resolving the tensions of American culture through sheer will.[15]

The Twain and James books each provided glimpses of the psychological unity Brooks was searching for in this period. Brooks's most favorable depiction of Twain's life appeared in his brief discussion of Twain's work as a pilot on the Mississippi in his early twenties. That period became a kind of golden age for Twain in later life; he recalled that "a pilot in those days was the only unfettered and entirely independent human being that lived in the earth." The Mississippi pilot was the most positive of the many nautical metaphors that, as William Wasserstrom has observed, pervade Brooks's work. In *America's Coming-of-Age*, he described his country as an uncharted Sargasso Sea; before that, he had written in *The Soul* of his desire to submerge himself in the "vast ocean" of humanity. He found a more balanced alternative in Twain's career as a pilot, one that steered a middle course between the destructive assault on nature of Twain's pioneer era and his own mystical impulses to watery dissolution. The pilot's life allowed Twain to combine practical achievement with creative artistry, Brooks claimed. "Piloting was, in the first place, a preeminently respectable and lucrative occupation; besides this, of all the pioneer types of the Mississippi region, the pilot alone embodied in any large measure the characteristics of the artist." The pilot was to Twain what the craftsman was for Brooks, a figure who integrated the aesthetic imagination into social experience. Twain's pilot days must have had another appeal to Brooks as he searched the literary past for lessons of personal courage. Riverboat pilots were pillars of self-mastery. They put the river's currents to work for their own purposes and, in so doing, combined the advantages of civilization with the allure of escaping its limits.[16]

What appealed to Brooks in James's career was a similar moment of poise between two worlds. Brooks found much to admire in the novels and criticism James wrote in the 1870s and early 1880s, which drew on the insights of European culture to expose the bland innocence of American life. He quoted at length from the famous passage in James's biography of Hawthorne declaiming the absence of a traditional basis for American literature, an argument that Brooks had often reiterated in the 1910s. James's early writings, Brooks believed, had succeeded in "presenting the struggle for the rights of personality"—now "the central theme of all modern American fiction"—because he had been able to "conceive personalities of transcendent value." Brooks's enemies were also James's early foes: "the representatives and advocates of mass-opinion and of movements that mechanize the individual. He was the first novelist in the distinctly American line of our day: the first to challenge the herd-instinct, to reveal the inadequacy of our social life, to present the plight of the highly personalized human being in the primitive community." This James sounded like the young Brooks, hoping to sustain a culture of transcendent personalities through a dialogue between American practicality and European intellect. At his best, James was Brooks's pilot of the Atlantic, seeking a steady course between Europe and the United States.[17]

These positive images of mastery and balance paled before the evidence Brooks compiled of both authors' failure to overcome their internal divisions. Brooks transformed Veblen's instincts of workmanship and acquisition into psychological categories, encouraged, in part, by Bernard Hart's psychoanalytical handbook, *The Psychology of Insanity*,

which made the "creative instinct" the motivating impulse of the unconscious life. Thus Twain was a man divided from within by the conflicts
that Brooks had diagnosed in American culture at large. His "balked
personality" resulted from his repression of his "creative instinct" and
the subsequent explosion of a "gregarious acquisitive instinct." Similarly, James was torn between his desire to regenerate American culture
and the dreamy exoticism of Europe, the product of a youth spent looking at art and picture books that filled him with "nostalgia for that far-
away paradise." Both men, in Brooks's view, had failed to grow to
maturity. James's later novels were as much fantasies of childhood as the
adolescent rebellion of Huck Finn.[18]

The qualities that kept Twain and James from their full potential as
heroic artists were precisely those elements of Brooks's life that caused
him increasing despair throughout the 1920s. Brooks's friends were
quick to tell each other of the parallels between his portrait of Twain's
domestic life, with its empty facade of genteel comfort, and the pressures that Brooks himself faced at home and from his in-laws to make a
success of his career. Encouraged by his wife and by William Dean
Howells to tone down the darker, satiric elements of his work, Twain
embraced the genial role of national humorist who confirmed tough-
minded Americans in their contempt for artistic beauty, humanistic values, and all things European. Even Twain's masterpiece, *Huckleberry
Finn*, was an innocuous jab at the American conscience that threatened
no one, Brooks claimed, since its message was that of an "irresponsible
boy" tolerated by his elders. Brooks's exploration of Twain's "ordeal"
of psychic division returned him to the threat that life in a commercial
society posed to his own critical abilities.[19]

It was the James book, however, that brought Brooks face to face
with his own internal conflicts. "I was to realize, looking back," he
wrote in his autobiography, "that I had been quarrelling with myself
when I appeared to be quarrelling with Henry James." The new style
that Brooks adopted lent itself to self-analysis. Whereas the book on
Twain preserved Brooks's dominant role as a narrative voice, *The Pilgrimage of Henry James* blurred the lines between critic and subject,
enabling Brooks to mingle autobiography with biography. He modeled
his approach on that of Léon Bazalgette in *Henry Thoreau, Savage*,
which he had translated into English. Bazalgette had tried to banish
himself from his work on Thoreau, employing a pastiche of unmarked
quotations, paraphrases, and commentary so as to enter as fully as
possible into Thoreau's interior life. Brooks later called this technique,

which he also used for *The Life of Emerson*, "a sort of imputed autobiography." It gave him the freedom to delve much further into the
psychology of subjects, as if living within the mind of a James or an
Emerson would protect him from his own. In the case of Henry James,
the method backfired. Instead of shielding him from despair, it plunged
him into the thick of his doubts about his capacity for the qualities of
literary heroism he had advocated in his criticism.[20]

Brooks's critique of the later James as a deracinated Highbrow obsessed with "esoteric things, personal mysteries, methods and secrets"
proved as dissatisfying, ultimately, to Brooks as it did to James's many
admirers. He felt guilty about the book as soon as he finished it, convinced that he had wronged James in some terrible way. In the depths of
his madness in the late 1920s, Brooks was plagued by "nightmares in
which Henry James turned great luminous menacing eyes upon me. I
was half aware, in connection with him, of the division within myself,
and with all the bad conscience of a criminal I felt I had viewed him
with something of Plato's 'hard little eye of detraction.' " James's brutal
stare was Brooks's deluded image of the guilt he felt at betraying himself
by attacking James's work. James's homelessness was his own predicament: he too had felt torn between American and European culture. He
now felt guilty for turning his back on his youthful Europophile aestheticism and for giving up the critical stance toward American culture
he now associated with James's penetrating gaze. James had raised
problems about the role of the critic in the United States and the place
of high art in a commercial civilization that Brooks could not resolve
and now lacked the will to confront. The life of the pilot navigating
between two worlds was too exhausting, and Brooks's retreat into par-
ables of personal courage had only made things worse. At the point
of the individual self, the tensions within American culture became
unbearable.[21]

Brooks craved a final release from the travails of selfhood. Having
sought safety in the self, he now turned on James for keeping him there.
James's problem was the same as Melville's: an "excessive subjectivity"
that deprived readers of their need to enter into the minds of confident,
heroic characters. "The great writers are transparent mediums," Brooks
wrote, "mirrors . . . through which life freely passes back and forth
between the mind and the world. The later James stands between ourselves and life and creates his illusion by benumbing our sense of human
values." James's keen analytical mind was an obstacle to Brooks's desire
to flee the self and its insoluble conflicts and merge with the outer

world. "The watcher is too apparent in these novels," he complained; "we are always more conscious of him than of what he knows." In dismissing James's later work, Brooks succumbed to his weariness with personality as a source of critical engagement with the environment. The prospects for a middle ground of cultural experience were too bleak, and the personal costs of sustaining the dualities of American life too great, to continue down that path any longer.[22]

The Life of Emerson was the work of a man in flight from self and culture. In identifying himself with Emerson, Brooks ignored the moral lessons of Melville's "excessive subjectivity": that unity with the world is finite and provisional, that it grows out of a recognition of human limits and is always a field of inner conflict and struggle. "The discovery of human limitation merely opens the way to one's brothers," writes Wilson Carey McWilliams of Melville's work, "making dependence on men seem mild in a universe still more alien, and causing responsibility for them to appear as an affirmation of the worth of the self that was lacking elsewhere." It was exactly this sense of the tensions inherent in the individual's desire for communion with others—which the Young Americans had once sought to capture in their ideal of personality and which Mumford discovered in the mediating language of symbolic form —that Brooks could not tolerate by the mid-1920s. With Emerson, he alternated between fantasies of self-destruction in mystic union with nature and in megalomaniacal dreams of a boundless, expansive self that swallowed up the physical world. These delusions were two sides of the same coin. In both cases, Brooks sought escape from the limits of self and the contingencies of culture.[23]

Even Brooks's style in *The Life of Emerson* was a repudiation of Melvillean subjectivity and a desperate effort to stave off his deepening depression. The pastiche technique of the James book had given him full reign to explore his own conflicts as they expressed themselves in James's mind, but it now allowed him to efface his personality from the written page. Amid the unacknowledged quotations and "imputed" accounts of Emerson's moods, Brooks could lose his own identity in the stuff of the past. The technique had become a literary equivalent of mysticism, with biography as a means to self-transcendence. Brooks's breakdown in 1926 was provoked, in part, by his inability to finish the Emerson book. He felt that the biography needed an analytical conclusion, summing up his views of Emerson's career, but could not bring himself to write it. Eventually, Mumford convinced him to publish the manuscript as it stood. "Emerson's philosophy is embodied in every word and embedded in every page," he assured Brooks in 1929. Mumford hoped that publication of the book would draw Brooks out of his psychic collapse. His assessment of the book's saturation in Emersonian themes was correct, but he missed its significance. Brooks was incapable of writing a final chapter in his own voice. As an independent narrator and critic, he had virtually disappeared from his work.[24]

The critical position of Brooks's early essays was equally missing in *The Life of Emerson*. Mumford had turned to Emerson for his dialectics, which he put to use in a theory of culture as a dialogue between the individual and the environment. Brooks, by contrast, embraced those aspects of Emerson's thought that did away with the need for culture. In the process, he stood on its head the critique of Emersonian Transcendentalism he had made in *The Wine of the Puritans* and *America's Coming-of-Age*. No longer the prophet of an airy Highbrow idealism, Emerson was now "open at every pore to the common life" of "congenial Concord." This portrait of Emerson as a prophet rooted in Concord's organic community was only a vestigial reminder of Brooks's earlier position; he spent most of his book celebrating Emerson's affirmative vision of modernity, which upheld the superiority of the New World's "naked man" to Europe's encrustations of custom, prejudice, and traditions. Brooks even took Emerson's side against Ruskin, rebuking "this bird of night" for his "lamentations on the state of modern society." Brooks had once condemned the Enlightenment tradition for stripping the individual bare of the social relationships and cultural heritage that promoted self-expression. Now he endorsed Emerson's progressive view of history. Traditions of culture and community were obstacles to be overcome in the mystical pursuit of Emerson's "deified self."[25]

The most powerful passages in *The Life of Emerson* were those in which Brooks recreated Emerson's moods of mystical reverie when surrounded by nature. Entering into such moments, when Emerson "would suddenly lose the sense of his personality," relieved Brooks of his own exhausting struggle for selfhood. "This was the feeling that Emerson had shared so often. You listened, you obeyed, and then you acted with all the force of the unconscious. It was not your petty will that directed you then, your limited intelligence, your personal self with its prejudices, but a deep inward necessity. You surrendered to the spontaneous life within you, and your nature flowed with the river of the universe." In such a state of ecstatic surrender, Emerson remade the world in the image of his own "nakedness," leveling the distinctions that gave men, women, and nature their uniqueness. "He had left his human relations behind him, wife, child, friends, and returned to matter, to the rocks, to the ground," Brooks wrote, "and he seemed of one substance with air, light, carbon, lime and granite." Emerson's mysticism was an imperialism of the self, claiming territory that was not its own. In Brooks's narrative, Emerson literally became the New England countryside, his mind and body indistinguishable from the foliage of the woods: "It was like returning to some ancestral home to rejoin these vegetable demons: his heart seemed to pump through his body the sap of this forest of verdure. He ceased to be a person; he was conscious of the blood of thousands coursing through him. As he opened with his fingers the buds of the birch and the oak, as his eyes followed the thistle-balls drifting in space, covered with their bright races, each particle a counterpart and contemplator of the whole, he felt himself dilating and conspiring with the summer breeze." Passages like these proved that Brooks had lost none of his talents as a writer. But the absence of his former narrative voice and of any hesitancy about Emerson's intuitive equation of self and nature marked a genuine crisis in Brooks's critical theory. He had dissolved the tensions between culture and society, spirit and practice, and the self and its surroundings, that had given his earlier work its critical force. All such conflicts disappeared in the lyric mysticism that now informed his criticism and his narrative style.[26]

Throwing off the burdens of culture and the limits of selfhood proved no help to Brooks, however; his condition deteriorated drastically in 1925 and 1926. The author in search of nakedness and freedom from all constraints was ultimately obsessed with death. For the five years of his "season in hell," Brooks fed on his own morbid preoccupations. No longer the confident pilot of cultural renewal, Brooks imagined himself "a capsized ship at night with the passengers drowned underneath and the keel in the air." The darker side of Brooks's Emersonian solution to the problems of personality revealed itself in delusions of persecution that alternated with fantasies of bringing the entire world to an end with his own death. He imagined at one point that his caretakers were plotting to bury him alive, at another that the British Parliament had passed a bill to the same effect. "There was even a day," he recorded in his autobiography, "when I had a sudden vision of the end of the world, a catastrophe caused solely by my fate. For this had occasioned a breakdown of all who were attached to me and who were also, in consequence, buried alive, while those who were attached to them came to the same end, and so on, and on, *ad infinitum*. As in some monstrous cosmic general strike, all mankind was engulfed, all movement ceased. I could see the steamships stopping in the middle of the ocean, while invisible waves of horror encircled the world."[27]

Brooks eventually recovered from such delusions, but his attempt to shed culture and personal finitude for self-liberation had taken a permanent toll. Brooks lived the rest of his life with "a hard ball of panic" in his stomach "that was never entirely to disappear." He was driven by his desire to keep that terror at bay, to stay as removed as possible from the psychic and intellectual complexities that had nearly destroyed him in the 1920s. The relentlessness with which he later pursued, volume after volume, the Makers and Finders series in American literary history was one sign of his determination to check his own tendency to "excessive subjectivity." The new turn in his criticism initiated with *The Life of Emerson* was another. His goal of an organic culture of democratic community gave way in the 1930s to an idealized vision of his country's literary past. Brooks's new-found traditionalism was no longer the open-ended critical conversation he had envisioned in his *Seven Arts* essays but, rather, a reified abstraction composed equally of antiquarianism and affirmations of American progress. In *The Wine of the Puritans*, he knew better than to "deliberately *establish* an American tradition" on the Enlightenment foundations of American culture, but after his breakdown, Brooks spent thirty years doing exactly that. The point is not that Brooks gave up entirely on his earlier ambitions. *The Flowering of New England* and *The World of Washington Irving*—the greatest of the Makers and Finders volumes—did make a major contribution in recovering the democratic aspirations of antebellum literary culture. But in comparison to his earlier work, these acts of recovery appeared a rear-guard action, more an attempt at literary restoration than a project linking cultural history to political renewal. Nor did the later volumes delve as deeply into the tragic limitations of modern experience as had Brooks's first essays. Despite his intentions, Brooks never mastered Melville or James—or, for that matter, Nathaniel Hawthorne and Edgar Allan Poe, two other dissenters from Emerson's optimistic creed. In the 1940s, his appeals for a positive literature of liberal goodness would distance him from Frank and Mumford and alienate a younger generation of critics that had cut its teeth on his early writings. Brooks's chronicle of tradition freed him, at last, from the struggle for personality and a culture of lived experience.[28]

Brooks embraced Emerson's mysticism as a relief from the travails of selfhood. By contrast, Waldo Frank had argued from the start of his career that the pursuit of mystical "wholeness" was fully compatible with—and, indeed, indispensable to—the development of free personalities in an organic community. With the shrinking of political options after the war, Frank's work gave ever more attention to problems of the self and to the need for cultural leaders who had achieved a full understanding of their relation to "the Whole." "There can be no integration of America without the group whose sense of the Whole will make it whole," he wrote in 1929 in *The Re-discovery of America*; "there can be no group without the person whose sense of the Whole is his life." Throughout the 1920s, Frank expounded on the necessity of grounding politics and culture in a "naturalistic mysticism" that viewed the self in terms of its place in society and the cosmos. "Selfhood is falsehood," he argued, "unless it is experienced as a relative focus in the unity of all men and all being." As the fulcrum between culture and the cosmos, the self had a capacity for transcending given social arrangements and subjecting them to critical analysis. A self awakened by mystical experience to its full dimensions was a vital source of cultural reflection and critique in a period when political opposition had seemingly evaporated. Nonetheless, Frank's criticism and his own experiences with mysticism indicate the difficulties of maintaining a critical dialectic of self and society when both are viewed as fragments of a cosmic whole. Incantations to wholeness could not patch up the divide that separated Frank's personal vision from that of his countrymen; nor could a mystical embrace of transcendent unity overcome the fissures that ran through modern industrial culture. In a society that had no use for mystic prophets, the search for a method of self-transformation became indistinguishable from a quest for personal identity.[29]

The transfiguring mystical visions Frank experienced in 1920 and 1921 reinforced his belief in mysticism as a resource for cultural criticism. These mystical encounters were pivotal moments in his life, confirming his belief in his childhood covenant with God and spurring him to an astonishing period of literary productivity for the rest of the decade. His notebook entries from February 1920 describe "three direct visitations of God," which followed on a tormented period of soul-searching during a trip to Richmond, Virginia. Like all mystics, Frank struggled with the challenge of conveying his sense of divine illumination through language: "What I saw I can never describe. It was pure space—Nothingness—Everything. A marvelous pale, light—silent infinitude it was, it did nothing. I did nothing. I saw it. And below, somehow, in a dim corner, was, uprising, touching—just touching, just piercing this infinitude—a gnarled branch of a tree. Black, bent like the anguished arms of the hurt men and women of the world."[30]

A year later, Frank had a similar moment of mystical rapture, which he described in a passage of his notebooks that he later reprinted in the avant-garde journal *S4N*. He followed a long line of mystics in describing this experience in sexual terms. Lying on his bed, Frank imagined "a grey vaguely light-shot Fog that thickened as the Dart of my consciousness . . . bright gold . . . thrust deeper in it." "My state," he noted, "was like the tunneling by a train through a vast and swelling mountain: train and mountain were equally myself, but throughout I knew that the train, the Dart, was more closely plotted with my mundane life than the Fog-mountain." The culmination of this vision—the union of Frank's conscious "Dart" with the "Fog"—recalled his intuition of "oneness" in Richmond the year before.

> All was a sort of sphere, a form created by the curving and thrusting beyond themselves and beyond the dimensions and realms of themselves of many spheres, until they joined in one as in a globe curves and flatnesses thrust and join and mount. This Sphere moved unevenly from the measure of myself lying, with various but invariable adverse motions. Upon the part nearest the Dart its path was a short straight plotting of the time-space of myself lying in bed asleep. But in its beyonder volumes it swung vastly, swelled in searching steadfast motion so that one instant up there covered far more . . . was of a different measure altogether . . . than the whole time-space of the going-on below where I lay naked in bed. . . . And yet the All was one form and I of it. . . . I was in touch ecstatically with the plunging and immobile All.

Frank claimed to be conscious of what was happening to him during this experience. He was simultaneously aware of his own limited self and of his identity with "the All." "This little path . . . was clear in my mind like a Dart: but also the moving in the Fog-form which was stroked with light."[31]

Both of these passages display characteristic elements of Frank's "naturalistic mysticism." In each experience, Frank retained some understanding of finitude—whether his own or that of the "hurt men and women" whose suffering he imagined as "a gnarled branch of a tree"—

even as he plunged into a sense of union with the divine. Yet such understanding was obviously secondary to the overwhelming experience of the All: the tree was relegated to a "dim corner" of Frank's vision; "the Dart" disappeared at the climax of mystical ecstasy. A tension always existed in Frank's mind between his need to affirm "the Whole" and his desire to embrace the particularities of human life. That tension was as evident in his mystical experiments as it was in his work. Moreover, these experiences indicate the lingering hold of an idealized notion of feminine values on his imagination. In his second venture into mystical knowledge, Frank was simultaneously male and female—both "train" and "mountain," "Dart" and "Fog"—until the final act of self-transcendence freed him from gender into a realm of blissful being. In considering the significance of the experience for his work, Frank believed that "the Hand of God had moved me . . . through the Domain of Himself: and had placed me again in that Part of Himself which is man." This interpretation was certainly in keeping with Frank's sense of personal mission since childhood, but it smoothed over the contradictory elements of his mysticism. Denying any dualistic separation of the transcendent and earthly worlds, Frank also stripped his own identity of gender. The crude sexual metaphors he employed to describe his vision depicted a union with himself, as both man and woman, that erased all sexual distinctions and culminated in a cerebral experience far removed from any physical sexuality. This was sexual union without eroticism, a communion with the All without a recognition of the other. To make such a vision relevant to the human world of culture and diversity would prove to be a nearly impossible task.[32]

In the wake of these experiences, Frank stood at a crucial juncture in the pursuit of spiritual oneness. For Western mystics, the period after such moments of illumination has traditionally been a time of spiritual agony, in which the mystic struggles to reconcile the memory of the divine with the reality of earthly existence. The great majority of mystics never move beyond such experiences to the higher stages of the "mystic way." For those who do, however, a final reconciliation with the spiritual life follows on a long period of self-purification, as the mystic seeks to strip away the egoistic impulses of the will and shed the burdens of self-consciousness. "This, I know this: that this is the climax of my life," Frank wrote after his visitations from God in 1920. "I face disaster: I go down, ruined, broken, into death—or I go up into life." The challenge of the "mystic way" was both intellectual and deeply personal for Frank; the goal of living in harmony with the transcendent whole he had glimpsed, however briefly, set the course of his career as a critic and every other aspect of his life. "Are Truth and God even relatively accessible to man?" he asked himself four years later. "I dedicate my life to this answer. Even if it shall be negative—in my case—I care to live to no other end."[33]

Frank denied that mysticism involved a purely contemplative approach to life, and he faulted George I. Gurdjieff, A. R. Orage, and their followers for viewing the pursuit of spiritual knowledge as a quietistic withdrawal from practical endeavors. "I aspire to express the Divine *within* the human sphere," he wrote in his notebook in 1925: "I resist the temptations of any golden way or short-cut to cosmic knowledge or cosmic participation, beyond what as a man I may normally exploit." As a self-styled "naturalistic mystic," Frank hoped to "generate cosmic knowledge & divine vision within the human domain—not, as in so many religious activities employ this impulse to know as an incentive to escape." Frank was still enough of a pragmatist to believe that experience was the proving ground of all knowledge, even the "knowledge of the Whole." Eastern mysticism was too otherworldly to play a part in his project of cultural renewal. He turned instead to the example of Spanish mystics, whom he discussed at length in *Virgin Spain*, his 1926 study of Spanish culture and history. Writing of Salamon B. Judah Ibn Gabirol, a Spanish Jewish mystic of the eleventh century, Frank described an early variant of his own "naturalistic mysticism":

> Life is the form of God in matter: the willful imprint of divinity on earth. This concept gives to the rapt activity of the mystics who embrace it an earthward, a practical direction. If the world is pattern of God's will, the highest human spirit cannot in the highest vision transcend the earth or grow detached from it: he must work in the earth and through earthly deed enact God's revelation.
>
> Gabirol, first of Spain's literary mystics, founds this tradition which at the end is to produce in Spain a lineage of mystics who are men of action: a lineage far removed indeed from the commoner progeny of mystics who, as they approach God, leave the terrestrial life.

Following Gabirol, Frank held that the spiritual life was a discipline of practical activity. Mystics would draw on their experience of union to fashion a way of life that recognized the self's location at the intersection of culture and the cosmos. Their method of living would raise human endeavor to a consciousness of the Whole at the same time it brought that consciousness to bear on the necessities of the individual and the social group. "The true mystic," he wrote in *The Re-discovery of America*, "is he who, *with his life*, expresses the cosmic self, in a way comparable with personal self-expression."[34]

As it had in the 1910s, aesthetic experience had a central place in Frank's work in the 1920s as an activity that mediated between the individual's subjective and practical faculties by bringing together the material world and the absolute. "The process of art is the endowment of a particular experience with the full measure of life. The work of art is a fragment of word or substance informed with the wholeness of spiritual vision." Artistic creation was a form of practice that was not mere technique, in Frank's view. Means and ends were indistinguishable in great art; the All was inherently bound up with the beauty of the particular artifact. For the "naturalistic mystic," art was a bridge between divine illumination and the phenomenal world, a means of forging a "unity between the self and what is not the self." Hence Frank's criticism consistently defended a literature of spiritual values against socialist naturalism, Dada and the avant-garde, and the debunking tradition represented by H. L. Mencken. In a world that had lost traditional forms of religious discipline, aesthetic experience was the last hope for a practical ethos of personal revelation.[35]

For the prophetic artist, however, the problem still remained of how to sustain a sense of the Whole in one's life and work. Frank looked to the history of earlier cultures for examples of a pragmatic mysticism that wove spiritual knowledge into the fabric of lived experience. His mystical experiences revived his interest in Judaism, particularly the prophetic strain of Old Testament Judaism, which recalled the Jewish people to their mission of embodying God's will in ritual and daily routine. The Mosaic code had once enabled Jews to live religious ideals in practice, he argued, and any contemporary movement for spiritual renewal would have to adopt a similar methodology for integrating the claims of the spirit with everyday life. The difficulty was that the tenets of Mosaic law bore no relation to modern conditions, a problem he also confronted in his treatment of Spain's spiritual legacy in *Virgin Spain*. Like the Spanish philosopher Miguel de Unamuno, Frank believed Spain's economic backwardness had preserved Spaniards' innate religiosity from the encroachment of modern industry and the narrow pursuit of technical ends. The Spanish people retained Unamuno's "tragic sense of life" in the face of a militant creed of liberal progress. At the same time, Frank recognized that the Jewish and Catholic mysticism that had thrived in medieval Spain and lingered still in that country's folk traditions was dying out and that Unamuno's defense of Catholic Spain against liberal Europe was in reality an admission of defeat. "Like Don Quixote, Unamuno fails to realize that the modern world can only be defeated with modern weapons." The Old Testament and medieval Spain provided examples of lives organized around an awareness of "the Whole," but they offered no immediate lessons for the modern self in search of fulfillment.[36]

By ruling out quietistic withdrawal and a return to past religious practices, Frank's naturalistic mysticism was left with the task of envisioning a modern life of wholeness. But if modern industrial culture was inimical to "knowledge of the Whole," and if Jewish law and medieval Catholicism proved unsuited to contemporary conditions, there appeared to be no way to give mystical knowledge a permanent foundation in everyday life. Frank's theory of mystic self-consciousness as the source of cultural renewal gave special attention to those practices that mediated between spirit and society and enhanced the individual's potential for self-transcendence and self-criticism. Yet his own analysis of modern civilization left little reason to believe that such practices could be restored as a collective discipline of spiritual reflection. The best that could be hoped for were momentary flashes of divine illumination, which the prophetic artist might seize upon and use in his or her work and which others might then draw upon in their efforts to master modern society. Even this process was fraught with ambiguities. How was the artist to integrate the knowledge gained from such experiences with the materials of industrial society? How would modern culture furnish the individual with the capacity to resist its assault on wholeness and accomplished selfhood? If Frank rejected a revival of religious traditions, he could not explain how mystical experience alone would generate alternative values to those of an industrial society.

Frank's mysticism made it difficult for him to imagine an adequate method for living a whole human life. Mysticism proved an unsatisfactory source of critical insight into modern social conditions because its ultimate goal—regardless of Frank's insistence on "naturalism"—was the obliteration of any separation between self and society and between consciousness and the cosmos. By contrast, the prophetic tradition Frank admired in Judaism heightened the tension between the Jews' destiny as a chosen people and their degraded state in order to hold them responsible to the authority of an angry God. The Old Testament prophets used their position as representatives of the transcendent within Jewish history to reinvigorate the religious practices of their people. Frank's mystical union of the self with the Whole eliminated the tension between temporal and spiritual realms that had given prophetic Judaism its force as a recurrent movement for Jewish renewal. The mystic affirmation of the All offered no comparable method for introducing a hierarchy of values and spiritual loyalties into everyday life. Frank's ideal of the critical self as structured by society and the absolute ran aground in his mystic search for oneness, which dissolved psychic conflicts in an ideal union of self, culture, and cosmos. Without a means of holding the self and society accountable to the claims of a higher authority, Frank risked identifying the Whole with the real and sacrificing the self's capacity for reflection and critique along with its egoistic will.

The contradictions of Frank's naturalistic mysticism came under careful scrutiny in the late 1930s from the theologian and social theorist Reinhold Niebuhr, who had struck up a friendship with Frank on the basis of their common interest in giving politics a new basis in organic experience and religious ethics. Niebuhr understood that Frank sought to revive self-consciousness as part of the "knowledge of the Whole," but he doubted that the two goals were compatible. "Can you really do all you want to do in terms of your mysticism?" he wrote Frank. Niebuhr shared Frank's respect for the prophetic strain in Judaism, which maintained "the ethical tension in life without relaxing it either in the direction of dualism or monism." But a critical ethics of selfhood, he argued, would have to recognize such a tension as inherent in human nature; it would have to accept the inevitable conflicts that arose within the psyche between man's bodily state, his position in a society not entirely of his own making, and his ability to transcend those conditions and "conceive a world of justice." Niebuhr knew that Frank's mysticism differed from Eastern transcendentalism and other dualistic philosophies of spiritual withdrawal. Nevertheless, he denied that any mysticism could provide a proper foundation for selfhood because it failed "to come to terms with the problem of depth in human life. It must either find God in the soul or in the mind or it must indiscriminately affirm the whole body and the whole world of nature." Despite Frank's emphasis on the self as the pivot of a new culture, his mysticism offered no way of reconciling the self's aspirations to transcendence with its divided existence. In the end, Frank had to surrender what was most valuable in the Judaeo-Christian ideal of selfhood—its internal divisions and capacity for reflection—to achieve a full apprehension of the cosmic Whole. The Christian Niebuhr was closer to the Old Testament prophets than Frank was: to deny that conflicts between the self, society, and the cosmos were inescapable elements of the human condition was to fall victim to self-dissolution or to idle dreams of bending the world to one's personal will.[37]

Had Niebuhr known of Frank's struggles to achieve self-awareness through mystical union during the 1920s, he might have felt even more justified in dismissing mysticism as a guide to critical consciousness. In the years following his visions at the start of the decade, Frank grew increasingly impatient with the obstacles in culture and in his own personality that prevented the consummation of his journey along the mystic way. His notebooks record "voluptuous visions of Death," which beckoned him with the promise of release from his anguished state as a seeker of the Whole in a finite world. "I have been weary much, desperate much," he confessed in 1924; "my mind, giving way to the ease & need of respite, leads me into Death. As once, I day-dreamed of Fame, Riches, Power, Fabulous Fair women—now, my inclination draws me to visions of a death-bed that is the one sweetness in which I seem now able to believe: the sweetness of giving-up and of immediate dissolution." He concluded that giving in to such fantasies of self-destruction would be the "supreme disloyalty" to his life's work and tried to put them out of his mind, but his notebooks indicate that this flirtation with death became nearly obsessive in later years. Despite his claims that a naturalistic mysticism would reinforce the self's awareness of its identity, Frank's battle to resist the impulse to self-disintegration proved nearly as difficult for him as it did for Brooks.[38]

Frank could also resemble Brooks in swinging wildly from moods of despair to grandiose delusions of omnipotence. In these latter moments, he gave in to the ambitious claims of his ego, demanding that friends and family alike acknowledge his position as prophet of a new civilization. His mystic vision of cosmic union made him intolerant of the differences that separated him from his dearest associates. Not only did his first marriage, to progressive educator Margaret Naumburg, break apart, so did many of his friendships. Virtually all his friends within the American intelligentsia—including Brooks, Rosenfeld, Anderson, Stieglitz, Gorham Munson, Jean Toomer, and Hart Crane—came to see that Frank's appeals to community and spiritual fellowship were belied by his overbearing ego. In a penetrating essay on Frank's first novels, Rosenfeld noted the lack of individuation in Frank's fictional characters. They were all elements of a single Whole: the author's personality. Frank's inability to brook even the most minor disagreements among friends was of a piece with his failure to create convincing characters. Fears of self-disintegration alternated with an aggressive self-assertiveness that prevented understanding of others on a basis of equality and mutual respect for differences.[39]

Only in the privacy of his notebook writings was Frank willing to concede that his search for wholeness had failed to endow him with a secure sense of self. In two remarkable journal entries from December 1928, Frank confronted the consequences of this failure. The first, entitled "The Public Position of Waldo Frank in 1928 (notes for a future historian)," described Frank's reputation in the third person. The reception of Frank's work was "widespread and vague," he explained. "He had fame of a kind, but no definite audience. There were of course thousands of individuals who had read some of his work, & been even deeply impressed. But there was almost no one who had read him entire & to whom his literary personality appeared as more than a mere fragment of what he had really given." Frank's "literary personality" suffered from the same crisis that afflicted his inner life. It lacked any connection with the Whole—defined as an accepting, unanimous audience—and thus existed only as a "fragment" of its full potential. Frank described himself as a "nebula" in the public's mind, whose work had attracted a handful of separate groups that failed to congeal in a unified following. *Our America* had won over one circle of literary radicals, and the *unanimiste* fiction he wrote in the 1920s appealed to another. Neither of these groups found much to admire in *Virgin Spain*, which "had committed the sin of taking a Catholic country seriously," nor did the liberals who read his criticism in the *New Republic* see anything of value in Frank's mysticism. "The publics so won were separate: neither he nor an integrating power in any appreciable group of readers had organised his image & influence into a whole." Frank's "notes for a future historian" betrayed the fragility of his sense of personal identity. If the mystic self was indistinguishable from society as an element of the Whole, then the uneven responses to Frank's work posed a real threat to the integrity of his personality. As a mystic prophet without a people, Frank was indeed a "nebula."[40]

In the second notebook entry from this period, Frank acknowledged that his "nebulous" public personality was the result of his shortcomings as a mystic seeker of the All. "The Inner State of Waldo Frank at the Close of 1928 (notes for himself)" portrayed Frank "at a profound Crisis." His work, "as a man & as an artist," was a failure precisely because he had never learned to give concrete expression to his "knowledge of the Whole." "He realised that, whereas the intuition of his spirit had always been true, his power to embody that spirit, realise that intuition, had been far feebler than he supposed." Far from surrendering the will to live in harmony with the absolute, he had succumbed to "the adoration of his own inflated ego—the impulse to prove not only *God*, but no less how 'godlike' *he* was." There was "an electric connexion" between "his cult of wholeness philosophically," he admitted, and "his own failure to achieve such wholeness in any personal form."[41]

Desperate to find a way of sustaining wholeness beyond fleeting visions of illumination, Frank settled on a technique for spiritual health that sacrificed whatever critical dimension remained in his theory of the mystical self. Frank adopted a series of breathing exercises he called "the method," which he had learned from F. Matthias Alexander, the Australian-born apostle of physical therapy and correct posture. Part charlatan and part health reformer, Alexander raised his genuine insights into the effects of industrial work and leisure on human physiology into a quasi-religious therapy of psychic salvation that won the acclaim of John Dewey, George Bernard Shaw, and Aldous Huxley, as well as Frank. In three introductions to American editions of Alexander's books, Dewey praised his work as a psychological complement to pragmatism. Alexander offered classes in London and New York on the correct approach to walking, standing, and sitting so as to free the neck, head, and torso from constricted positions. In addition, he exhorted students to learn to control their breathing and to direct the habitual and involuntary movements of their bodies. Dewey, who confessed to being "an inept, awkward and slow pupil," wrote that the classes were "the most humiliating experience of my life, intellectually speaking," but he lauded Alexander's method for enabling him to submit his bodily movements to conscious control. Such minor gains in posture and physical agility were only the first step in Alexander's ambitious program of human renovation. As the title of his first book, *Man's Supreme Inheritance*, suggested, he believed that the fate of civilization rested on such exercises, an idea that earned Bourne's ridicule in a review for the *New Republic*. "He has a physiological technique which is apparently a kind of reversed psycho-analysis," Bourne wrote in 1918, "unwinding the psychic knots by getting control of the physical end-organs." Bourne believed that expecting exercise to resolve psychological and cultural problems was a major misreading of human nature, especially when human beings were proving themselves capable of a deep, relentless irrationality. "Is an era of world-war," he asked, "quite the most convincing time for so far-flung a philosophy of conscious control?"[42]

Frank evidently thought that it was. In a 1919 review of *Man's Supreme Inheritance*, he praised Alexander's method for controlling the reflexes and other physiological functions. Alexander's technique was the anatomical counterpart to modernization, he argued; it enabled men and women to take charge of their bodies with the "deliberate, organized" methods that had rationalized the social environment. The "dangerous gulf between the demands made by society and by our minds upon our organism" revealed itself in the breakdowns and "soul sickness" that afflicted Frank's contemporaries. Alexander's teachings, in Frank's account, provided a way of adjusting the body—and, by extension, the self—to the demands of modern life. Alexander couched his theory in evolutionistic terms, insisting that his regimen of exercises "will enable us to move slowly but with gradual speed towards those higher psychophysical spheres which will separate the animal and human kingdoms by a deep gulf, and mankind will then enjoy the blessings which will be the natural result of capacities fully developed." Bourne's description of this technique as a "reversed psycho-analysis" was more apt than he may have realized. Alexander traced the roots of psychic disorders to biology but refused to acknowledge the intractability of such distress within the unconscious mind. His psychology deliberately ignored Freud's work on the unconscious processes of psychic development for a theory of the mind as a product of reflexes and habitual movements. Whereas Freud had come to see the psyche as structured by an underlying conflict between culture and biology, Alexander's goal was a fully acculturated self that had transcended biology through proper exercise.[43]

Frank enthusiastically took up Alexander's cause, claiming that his technique for physiological self-control was the methodology needed to sustain the "knowledge of the Whole" in modern life. Frank took courses from Alexander in the 1920s, as did his second wife, Alma Magoon, and he practiced "the method" with great regularity, refining his breath control so as to approximate the state of self-awareness he had previously achieved in moments of mystical oneness. *The Rediscovery of America* concluded with a prescription of Frank's version of the Alexander technique as a modern equivalent of Mosaic law and other earlier forms of spiritual discipline. "Our need . . . since we would create the Whole, is for a method whereby our values can be naturalised into terms of actual living." Alexander's exercises fulfilled Frank's need. After his trenchant diagnosis of the maladies of modern civilization—its loss of a practical metaphysics, its elevation of industrial technology and a positivist cult of science over religion and ethics, and its cultural impoverishment amid a proliferation of mass-produced sounds and images—Frank could only offer his readers a formula for studying their breathing and other reflexive actions. "What I need is to establish within me *the image*, to sustain and nurture within me *the image*, of myself as part of the Whole," he wrote in the book's final chapter. Frank argued that a successor to Jewish law would restore the capacity for self-criticism to modern culture and thereby lay the basis for a vital community life. But now the quest for wholeness ended with a program of exercises that sacrificed reflection and critique to improved posture and rhythmic breathing.[44]

Frank's conversion to Alexander's method was not a momentary detour from the mystic way, but its culmination. The outline of a technique for self-observation at the conclusion of *The Re-discovery of America* reappeared thirty years later in *The Rediscovery of Man*, Frank's final statement of his naturalistic mysticism, as a "Method for Inducing Revelation." Given Frank's private struggle with self and the debilitating impulses to self-destruction that beckoned him with promises of release, one can only conclude that Alexander's regimen served a therapeutic function. Instead of sustaining the experience of revelation, it sustained Frank's own identity against the tendency to self-dissolution that was the darker side of his mystical cult of oneness. Yet, on another level, these two elements of Frank's mystic way were in no way opposed. In its denial of any conflict between human consciousness and its environment, Alexander's psychology was the logical counterpart to Frank's mystic ideal of self-effacement. From either side of Frank's mysticism came the impetus to make over everything beyond the conscious will, to cast off the limits of nature, tradition, and finally selfhood in a desperate hunt for the All. Frank's hopes for critical self-awakening gave way to a technology of the self that mirrored industrial society in its drive to master nature by technical means. Alexander's method may have rescued Frank from the torments that drove Brooks to his breakdown, but it exacted a tremendous toll. Frank's critical theory foundered on its resort to shallow therapies, and Frank himself never succeeded in joining his prodigious spiritual vision to a recognition of his own limitations. "How is a man to go on living," he asked himself in 1929, "in a world whose fundamental *premises* he refuses?" Whatever relief "the method" may have offered him, it could not deliver him from that predicament or give him a satisfying reason to endure it.[45]

"The road on which we enter is a royal road which leads to heaven," wrote Santa Teresa, the greatest of the Spanish mystics. "Is it strange that the conquest of such a treasure should cost us rather dear?" The tragedy of Frank's life was not the cost he paid to pursue the mystic way, but the shabbiness of the treasure he found there.[46]

"Happiness," according to Spinoza, "consists in a man's being able to maintain his own being." The passage was a favorite of Herman Melville's, and Lewis Mumford believed it described Melville's endeavor to find a way out of the debilitating pessimism that nearly destroyed him after *Moby Dick*. "In a more fruitful age," Mumford wrote of Melville, "his being would have been maintained in harmony with, not in opposition to, the community: but at all events his vital duty was to maintain it." Melville's public work and private struggle for self-preservation presented Mumford with a model of moral realism and personal courage in the face of a hostile or indifferent public. To read Mumford's 1929 biography, *Herman Melville*, in light of Brooks's and Frank's turmoils in the 1920s is to realize how much separated Mumford from these men, despite his allegiance to the intellectual project they had mapped out in the 1910s. Whereas Brooks had opted for an Emersonian solution to the difficult tasks of realizing personality and a culture of experience, and Frank had followed Whitman in pursuit of a oneness indistinguishable from a boundless self-consciousness, Mumford discovered in Melville a figure who had learned to temper the impulse to transcendence with a loving acceptance of human finitude and whose literary creations embodied in form the wholeness he could never attain within himself. The Melville book may be unreliable as biography (F. O. Matthiessen, for one, went out of his way to note its errors of fact and interpretation), but its significance lies in its relation to Mumford's thought and to the Young Americans' search for an organic culture of personality and experience. Previously, Mumford had concentrated on the political implications of his aesthetic theory, arguing that the symbolic dialogue of culture embodied the human capacity for democratic community. With *Herman Melville*, he·went a step further, taking his ideal of cultural interaction as the foundation for a moral philosophy of life. From Melville Mumford learned that maintaining one's own being meant overcoming the self's impulse to obliterate the other in a frenzied struggle against its own limitations. Like William Morris, Melville served Mumford as a figure who had pursued the romantic quest for self-transcendence to its logical conclusion and, in so doing, had redefined that quest in contingent, cultural terms. Although the self could never escape the confines of nature, "the effort of culture, the effort to make Life significant and durable," survived beyond a single lifetime to order the raw materials of a brute existence. If the self in culture was Melville's answer to the fate that overtook Ahab and Pierre, it was also Mumford's solution to the search for selfhood that drove Brooks mad and deprived Frank of his identity and inner peace. Self-transcendence was cultural or it was nothing at all: it required a love that transfigured the world into forms and language and thus compensated for the tragedy of human limitation.[47]

In the figures of Ahab and Pierre, Mumford recognized, Melville had exposed the fatal weakness of Emerson's doctrine of "cultural nakedness." The refusal of a universe that resisted the claims of human certainty lay behind both characters' journey to self-destruction. "The white whale stands for the brute energies of existence," Mumford wrote of *Moby Dick*; it was a "meaningless force," like the arbitrary destruction of a volcano or tornado, that obsessed Ahab and led him to his death. For Ahab, the white whale was the metaphysical "Whole" that eluded human comprehension. It was not the whale itself he wanted to destroy, he confessed, but the "inscrutable thing" (as Ahab called it) that lay behind its white "wall." Ahab's quest was indeed noble; in Mumford's mind, it epitomized the human aspiration to knowledge of the self and the universe. But it was futile in its means, which tore aside the tissues of human fellowship and culture in a final assault on the mysteries of existence. Dismissing his crew's practical whaling lore and ridiculing their desire to return home safely to family and friends, Ahab joined the whale as a blind, ravaging force of the elements. "Cultural nakedness" stripped him of his humanity, along with the cares and concerns of a settled culture. Pierre's fate was the same as Ahab's: the naked self, driven only by its desire for a dream of union with the unknowable, was a living corpse. "By vast pains we mine into the pyramid," Melville wrote in *Pierre, or the Ambiguities*; "by horrible graspings we come to the central room; with joy we espy the sarcophagus; but we lift the lid—and nobody is there!—appallingly vacant, as vast as the soul of man."[48]

Mumford read *Pierre* as an autobiographical portrait of Melville's psychological distress after the apathetic response to *Moby Dick*. In the late 1850s and 1860s, Melville followed Ahab and Pierre in divesting himself of emotional attachments and withdrawing to a private world of bitterness and resentment. The challenge of Melville's middle years, according to Mumford, was his struggle to reconcile the imaginative powers that separated him from his contemporaries with an acceptance of life itself, as reconstituted in customs, institutions, and culture. In the end, it was a struggle to recognize that the form of the great white whale he had captured in *Moby Dick* was a more appropriate goal for human striving than the destructive effort to conquer, and finally eliminate, the otherness of the universe. The whale as "the Whole" would always remain a mystery, given the finite conditions of human life. The most Melville, or anyone else, could hope to accomplish was to shape a cultural whole out of images and language. Melville vindicated human knowledge, Mumford argued, by offering his readers the mythology of the whale as an alternative to Ahab's insane chase after the whale. That was his greatest literary achievement. His personal triumph came in the 1870s and 1880s, when he recognized that such knowledge redeemed his own tragedy as an artist with the promise of a world made meaningful by love and artistic creation. With *Clarel* and "Billy Budd," Melville realized that "the white unrefracted truth" of existence—the empty void he had captured in the monster of Moby Dick—was not the sum of a full human life. The closing stanzas of *Clarel*, with their invocation of natural cycles of rebirth and regeneration, and Billy Budd's tragic affirmation of the pairing of necessity and freedom, were proof for Mumford of a resolution to Melville's years of despair. "Whatever be the ultimate nature of things," Mumford wrote, "the universe man conceives is still held together at his own center: its significance is part and parcel of his own."[49]

Melville's accomplishment in later life was even greater, Mumford argued, for having occurred at the very moment when industrialization was enshrining Ahab's lust for raw, unmediated experience as the goal of modern civilization. Industrial society was the realization of Ahab's mad dream, according to Mumford; it viewed sheer mechanical power and quantitative growth as ends in themselves, the pursuit of which overrode the fragile victories of form and faith. In *Clarel*, Melville himself drew the connection between an industrial culture and Ahab's boundless will to power:

> Arts are tools;
> But tools, they say, are to the strong:

Is Satan weak? Weak is the wrong?
No blessed augury overrules:
Your arts advance in faith's decay:
You are but drilling the new Hun
Whose growl even now can some dismay;
Vindictive in his heart of hearts,
He schools him in your mines and marts—
A skilled destroyer.

Melville realized that Emerson's cultural nakedness, as embodied in an Ahab or a Pierre, was the unacknowledged goal of a technological cult of power. By subordinating all ends to increased production, industrialism reduced the individual to a primitive state of helplessness before the white whale's aimless terror.[50]

In *Moby Dick*, Mumford found Melville's crucial lesson for the twentieth century: the lesson that the modern world could be tamed and made human through a new aesthetic form. If industry subjected science and practical knowledge to the demands of power, Melville's novel married a scientific respect for fact to the aesthetic imagination. He offered his lengthy descriptions of whaling technique, whale anatomy, and the whale's place in Western art and literature as examples in literary style of a cultural synthesis that rejected cultural nakedness for an affectionate apprehension of the world. "Moby-Dick thus brings together the two dissevered halves of the modern world and the modern self," Mumford wrote, "its positive, practical, scientific, externalized self, bent on conquest and knowledge, and its imaginative, ideal half, bent on the transposition of conflict into art, and power into humanity." *Moby Dick*'s legacy was the symbolic language for a new society, one that responded to the industrial fascination with power by reviving the love of nature and community inherent in artistic expression and that created whole men and women out of the fragmented selves of Ahab and Pierre.[51]

If *Moby Dick* was a usable past for those in search of a new civilization, Melville's life was a usable self that Mumford and his contemporaries might learn from in their anxious expectation of that civilization. Melville's importance for Mumford's generation was his understanding of the "tragic sense of life" as a middle way between acquiescence and a self-destructive struggle for the All. For citizens of an advanced industrial society, the latter seemed the only available alternatives: one chose between "accepting outward conditions as inward necessities" and devolving into a precultural ego in search of transcendent truth. In either case, "the White Whale of brute energy reigns supreme," Mumford wrote, degrading life as mere living or uprooting the self from the cultural sources of sustenance and support. Melville's tragic recognition of limits was essential to modern culture—not because it lifted the burden of an imperfect world from one's shoulders, but because it alone sustained the self in the "heroic effort" to reclaim that world for human endeavor.

> Death, which biologically is merely the terminus of a natural process, acquires significance for man because he anticipates it and modifies his activities so as to circumvent it: by memory and foresight, by choosing his ends, dreaming of immortality, erecting monuments and statues and museums, and above all, by transmitting the written word, man creates a destiny beyond his life's physical span. It is just because the worms lie in wait that man defies the gods, cherishes the images he has created and the relations he has solidified in custom and thought, and centres his efforts on those things which are least given to meaningless change. Though the sensible world is not derived, as Plato thought, from the heaven of ideas, the opposite of this is what every culture must strive for: to derive from the sensible world that which may be translated to a more durable world of forms.

Only the tragic sense of life could secure the self against the fury that consumed Ahab and Pierre and against the numbing despair of Melville's middle years.[52]

Like Brooks and Frank, Mumford had retreated into the self in the face of a hostile environment, but what he found there was the ability to accept the self's limitations as the condition for their transcendence. "Man's defence lies within himself," he had come to understand, "not within the narrow, isolated ego, which may be overwhelmed, but in that self which we share with our fellows and which assures us that, whatever happens to our own carcasses and hides, good men will remain, to carry on the work, to foster and protect the things we have recognized as excellent." More than any other of the Young Americans, Mumford recognized that "the good life of personality lived in the environment of the Beloved Community" was a goal that could be approached only in a single life, and then only through the collective enterprise of human culture. There would always be a tension between personality and community, as Ahab's passion to know the inscrutable made men and women restless and uneasy in their given state. But it was precisely that tension that held the greatest promise for a genuine Beloved Community, by adding to the dialogue of symbols and meanings that gave shape to those aspirations in approximate form. Entering that dialogue required that one accept the limits of the "knowledge of the Whole" accessible to human consciousness, not seek their elimination through mystical oneness. By decade's end, Mumford had grasped a truth that eluded Brooks and Frank and that might have spared them the full force of their anguish: that cultural expression, however incomplete, was the medium of the moral life and the self's noblest reward.[53]

8

Organic Community

I believe in a rounded, symmetrical development of
both the human personality and the community itself.
—LEWIS MUMFORD,
"What I Believe"

In the thirties, I wanted to be ravished by a community.
—WALDO FRANK,
Memoirs of Waldo Frank

s early as 1922, in *The Story of Utopias*, Lewis Mumford identified the central dilemma of his communitarian project in culture
and politics. The mutualistic language of the various religious,
romantic, and republican traditions that informed his criticism served
well as a counterweight to industrial conditions and as a corrective
to the utilitarian strains in liberal and socialist thought, but it proved
less useful as a guide to practical action to transform actual conditions. Visions of organic community returned time and again to the unsatisfying alternatives of transcendentalist withdrawal or a barracks socialism. The rhetoric of culture as an alternative to society invariably
led, it seemed, to the choices sketched out by Emerson and Bellamy—
to what Mumford called "the utopias of escape and the utopias of
reconstruction."[1]

In their cultural criticism of the 1920s, 1930s, and after, Mumford
and Waldo Frank constantly sought a way out of this dilemma, yet in
retrospect their work often appears as trapped in the dualities of culture
and society, of ideals and practice, as the society they criticized. Despite
the virtues of communitarianism as a critique of culture and personality
in an industrial age, its value as a guide to political and social transformation was limited. Frank's efforts to outline a metaphysical politics
grounded in an activist mysticism relied ultimately on the imperial will
of the creative prophet. Meanwhile, Mumford's analysis of an emerging
neotechnic utopia in the 1930s so closely identified the promise of community with the achievements of the second industrial revolution and
with the ascendancy of a professional-administrative class as to blunt
the critical, oppositional character of his intellectual position. In both
men's work, the elusive hope for a strong, tightly knit community based

on shared values displaced the more promising idea of renewing the public realm as a center of collective dialogue and debate. As a result, the open-ended pragmatic utopianism they shared at times with John Dewey gave way to dreams of cultural synthesis premised entirely on artistic leadership or to technocratic programs of cultural and social planning.

The limitations of Frank's and Mumford's communitarianism are most evident in their attempts to make sense of the emerging mass or consumer culture of the early twentieth century. Confronted by the technological, economic, and cultural innovations of the "New Era" of the 1920s—radio, film, the news industry, automobiles, spectator sports, and mass consumer spending—both Frank and Mumford searched for some Archimedean point "beyond culture" from which they could judge and evaluate the relationship between such developments and the genuine spiritual and cultural needs of their fellow citizens. Mysticism provided Frank with such a vantage point; Mumford found a similar perspective in the intellectual and social position of social scientists and engineers. Both choices could have profoundly antipolitical implications. From the illusory heights of the mystic way or of social science, ordinary people appeared little more than a directed "herd" in a mechanistic "jungle." Instead of recognizing that they were as much a part of the culture they criticized as their fellow citizens, Frank and Mumford chose a perspective on mass culture analogous to the view of city dwellers from a skyscraper: in both cases, anonymous antlike individuals appear overwhelmed by impersonal structures that dominate the landscape. The view is instructive insofar as it reveals our institutional and environmental surroundings, but it distorts the lived experience of those who view their reality from the ground up by exaggerating the uniformity and predictability of their existence.

Frank and Mumford were horrified by the megalopolitan culture of mass consumption they described in this period but found it difficult to offer alternatives that envisioned their contemporaries as a polity, as opposed to a herd or a mass. In most of their work from the 1920s and 1930s, they saw their goal primarily as providing a unifying moral or cultural ideal to people who were already united through bureaucratic and technological organization. But in seeking to transform such organization into organic community, they too often neglected the political conflicts that would be required to realize their vision. Whatever the virtues of communitarianism as an alternative to conventional progressivism, there was no escaping the contested public sphere that had always been at the center of liberal and socialist politics. In ignoring the centrality of the public realm in their cultural criticism, Frank and Mumford risked returning to the empty alternatives of Emersonian "escape" and Bellamyite "reconstruction."

Nonetheless, Frank's and Mumford's critical perspective on modern culture implicitly suggested a way out of this dilemma in communitarianism. As a result of their own youthful mysticism and concerns for spirituality, the Young Americans emphasized an ideal of organic experience uniting inner and outer life that remained at the core of their mature conceptions of personality, culture, and community. By the late 1920s and early 1930s, this ideal had taken a somewhat more concrete form as a vision of cultural citizenship in which individuals derived satisfaction and meaning as participants in and products of a democratic culture. Although Frank and Mumford found it difficult to develop this idea fully in their criticism, beyond a few tentative references, their attempts to imagine people as citizens of culture provided their most compelling alternative to Emerson and Bellamy and their most promising synthesis of romantic and pragmatic cultural criticism.

As in all his cultural criticism, Frank approached the culture of "the machine" not in terms of technology, or even of social organization, but as a problem of values and personality. "To believe that society can be transfigured," he wrote the Marxist editor V. F. Calverton, "without transfiguring the deep psychic patterns which have evolved the social structure which makes revolution necessary, is naive utopianism." The origins of mass culture lay in the dissolution of the Catholic metaphysics of medieval Europe, in Frank's view, and in the subsequent substitution of a technological and commercial *Gemeinschaft* for a shared culture of spiritual wholeness. The failure of modern civilization to create a holistic successor to the religious culture of the Mediterranean—"the womb of Europe," as Frank called it, in a telling evocation of his own youthful longings of maternal union—had left the individual an isolated atom "moving alone in a herd through a bewilderment of motions." Without an adequate conception of the self's relation to society and the cosmos, such "atoms" were easy prey for a commercial culture that deformed the longing for community into conformist, spectatorial pastimes.[2]

Throughout the 1920s and 1930s, Frank was quick to head off suggestions that he was opposed to industrial technology. "I am no enemy of the machine, no harker-back in dialectical disguise to an impossible romantic or Tolstoyan Nature," he explained in *The Re-discovery of America*. Technology appeared to threaten humanistic values because the machine had become a symbol of the unchecked will to power, now freed from the restraints of a religious ethic. "We flounder before the machine, we are features more or less groveling of its external life, because we lack an instinctive metaphysical consciousness to make us master and absorb it—to fuse the machine with all its elements of will and act into our expression." Criticisms of the machine missed the point that the apparent domination of society by technological values was the result of much deeper cultural problems, Frank argued. The resolve to control technology and set it to work for human purpose was dependent on the creation of an alternative set of values that gave priority to mutual aid and love over self-aggrandizement and the worship of power.[3]

At its best, this argument demonstrated that Frank's critique of modern mass culture was no inverted technological determinism, blaming all social evils on the machine, since it took aim at the ideology that promoted a cult of technological novelty and the acceptance of automatism as the standard of social behavior. But at its worst, the argument appeared to sidestep the need for any political or social reconstruction as a challenge to the reign of a commercial mass culture. The very values that were to master the new technological and institutional arrangements of modern society had to "rise organically from the facts of our hideous present," according to Frank. From this perspective, the limitations of modernity were purely spiritual: the herd had to be transformed into a community by giving purpose and meaning to social groupings already in existence. By refusing to take his critique of industrial civilization to its logical, Morrisite conclusion—as a thorough repudiation of bureaucratic centralization and the factory system—Frank left himself in a peculiar bind. He held up the premodern organic community as an ideal against which to measure the purposelessness of mass culture, but he also looked to "the facts of our hideous present" for spiritual resources for the reconstruction of that earlier community.[4]

Frank was in an especially awkward position because so much of his criticism in the 1910s had echoed Brooks's revolt against literary gentility and had called on artists and writers to make lived experience the basis of an indigenous American culture. In the early 1920s, however, Frank found himself under attack from avant-garde writers who, under the influence of European Dada and surrealism, celebrated the vitality of American urban mass culture as an alternative to the genteel tradition. Such American writers as Harold Loeb, Matthew Josephson, and Malcolm Cowley turned on the author of *Our America* for betraying his Whitmanesque heritage by disdaining the vibrant new popular culture of the American city. Josephson wrote for many of his fellow Dadaists when he exalted an American culture "where the Bill posters enunciate their wisdom, the Cinema transports us, the newspapers intone their gaudy jargon; where athletes play upon the frenetic passions of baseball crowds, and skyscrapers rise lyrically to the exotic rhythms of jazz bands which upon waking up we find to be nothing but the drilling of pneumatic hammers on steel girders." For avant-garde writers like Josephson, who had fled New York for Paris, mass culture promised liberation from genteel sentiment and from the propagandistic moralism that pervaded the official rhetoric of World War I. But what seemed like liberation in a European context, Frank responded, looked in the United States like another typically American concession to practicality and unassimilated activity. The Dadaists' fascination with urban mass culture was in Frank's view simply a more sophisticated version of the pioneer's homilies about Yankee know-how and rugged individualism as antidotes to European refinement. Dada made sense in a Europe steeped in religious and artistic traditions, he argued; its protest against seriousness could have a healthy, regenerative effect in a culture that still placed some compelling moral restraints on personal behavior. In a young, wholly modern country like the United States, however, Dada's idealization of energy and random action was likely to have a corrosive effect on all values. By glorifying the machine age, American Dadaists were actually celebrating the will to power. "Europe called for Dada by antithesis: America for analogous reasons calls for the antithesis of Dada. For America *is* Dada. . . . What we need, by way of rounding our lives into livableness, is a bit of seriousness for ourselves."[5]

Frank's dismissal of urban mass culture in his exchanges with the Dadaists fit uneasily with his argument that "the facts of our hideous present" provided the resources for a new organic community. Moreover, in his critical writings on spectator sports, the cinema, jazz, and other cultural manifestations of the Machine Age, Frank seemed uncertain as to where he should situate himself as a critic. Was he the antimodern defender of traditional religious metaphysics appalled by a centerless modernity? Or was he at home with the machine and its cultural progeny, searching only for an animating vision to give meaning to a way of life that was irreversible? The first position risked the familiar charge of being a hopeless romantic, of wanting to turn back the clock on modernity. The second skirted dangerously with the very acquiescence in modern commercial culture that Frank had rejected in his polemics with the Dadaists. At various times, Frank adopted both of these perspectives in an attempt to shake his fellow Americans out of the "complacent stupor" he abhorred in a consumer culture.[6]

In those essays in which he opted for the first position on the culture of the machine, Frank upheld premodern *Gemeinschaft* in opposition to what he considered the artificial cohesion of the modern herd. When writing of the Catholic organicism of Spanish and Latin American cultures, or recalling the Scholastic metaphysics of medieval Europe, Frank portrayed himself as a spokesperson for values and priorities increasingly alien to his compatriots in baseball parks and jazz halls. Frank's tendency to use traditional, "primitive" cultures as a foil for American mass culture had a great deal in common with the anthropological writings of Margaret Mead, Ruth Benedict, Edward Sapir, and Elsie Clews Parsons in the 1920s and 1930s, all of whom used ethnographic accounts of non-Western peoples to make implicit and explicit criticisms of Western industrial civilization. Like these anthropological writers, Frank employed examples of traditional culture to relativize contemporary society, hoping to make readers aware of communal and ecological alternatives to their own social and cultural practices. Thus in an account of a steamship voyage home from a Florida vacation, Frank juxtaposed the Babbitt-like babble of his fellow tourists about real estate and boom towns with the imagined voices of the Spanish conquistadors in search of the Holy Grail in the New World. In a contest between boosters and believers, there was no question where Frank's sympathies lay.[7]

The contrast with such supposedly primitive cultures revealed the essentially primitive nature of what appeared most progressive about American industrial culture. It was North Americans, not Latin Americans or Samoans, who lived in a jungle, according to Frank: "A jungle is simply a luxuriant external nature, uncontrolled and unregenerate by man. And savages are men, possibly bright and enterprising, who by no concepts transcending the immediate needs of sense have made this nature theirs; men who have not learned to assimilate their world together with their personal desires into some kind of Whole." Americans lived as true "savages" in the "jungle" of mass culture insofar as they responded passively and unthinkingly to the raw exercise of power and the tedium of industrial life. The overwhelming message of Frank's descriptions of 1920s mass culture was that its blandishments enticed men and women into a thoughtless stupor that constituted a new form of savage tribalism. The grid plans of American cities, the traffic of roads choked with automobiles, the bored faces of spectators at baseball games and prizefights, and the insatiable hunger for news all testified to a growing depersonalization of human experience and the closing of opportunities for individual introspection and reflection on social practice. Dissatisfaction with such an existence rarely transcended a craving for some novelty—a news headline, a new model car—which fueled advances by the market into every sector of social life. "*America as a whole*," he wrote in 1929, "is saturated with the vision and with the values of Wall Street."[8]

This totalistic view of modern mass culture led Frank, as it later would Theodor W. Adorno, to dismiss jazz as the musical accompaniment of capitalist industry. The appeal of jazz, Frank recognized, lay in "our reaction from the dull throb of the machine," a cry of protest against the industrial organization of human culture. But jazz channeled that protest into a reaffirmation of the productive ethic of capitalism. "Jazz is a moment's gaiety, after which the spirit droops, cheated and unnurtured. This song is not an escape from the Machine to limpid depths of the soul. It is the Machine itself! It is the music of a revolt that fails. Its voice is the mimicry of our industrial havoc." Jazz was the music of conformity disguised as personal improvisation. Unlike critics who emphasized the popular roots of jazz, Frank could hear only "a mass response to our world of piston rods, cylinders and mechanized laws." Jazz's popularity was evidence of the totalitarian nature of mass culture, which managed to deflect all protests into harmless channels, drown out all opposing voices, and subdue the agonized conscience with promises of unimagined comfort and illicit pleasures. Long before Herbert Marcuse coined the phrase *repressive desublimation*, Frank pointed to jazz as an example of the way consumer culture promised momentary release from puritanical restraints to defuse popular dissatisfaction with industrial life.[9]

Frank's one-sided portrait of mass stupefaction, passivity, and complacency in consumer culture anticipated subsequent accounts by Robert and Helen Lynd, the Frankfurt School critics, David Riesman, Dwight Macdonald, and C. Wright Mills, which portrayed mass culture as simultaneously atomized and overly organized in artificial structures. Like these later critics, Frank attacked consumer culture for being both self-obsessed and overly extroverted; its excessive concern for personal comfort went hand in hand with a profound suspicion of introspection and self-criticism. Likewise, his treatment of the "herd mentality" of mass culture indicted modern society as lacking in genuine solidarity even as it promoted increasingly homogeneous forms of social identity. The apparent cohesion of modern culture rested on the masses' apathetic acquiescence in their own manipulation and organization by technical and commercial elites, not on popular expressions of mutual aid.

Despite the overwhelming tendency of Frank's criticism to emphasize the massification of popular consciousness in a consumer culture, he did occasionally glimpse the ways in which mass culture gave expression to popular demands for new forms of personal identity and community. His condemnation of jazz, for example, did acknowledge that the music's popularity rested on its apparent ability to provide release from industrial tedium. There was in mass culture, Frank admitted, signs of a "misplaced will to unity" among Americans that might yet give way to more spontaneous and democratic forms of social organization. In particular, Frank singled out Charlie Chaplin's success as an indication that film could serve a subversive function by expressing broad popular dissatisfaction with a bureaucratized world. Frank's admiration for Chaplin provided him with an alternative to his traditionalist perspective on mass culture. Instead of dismissing all of modern popular culture as a declension from the medieval synthesis, Frank could locate his own critique of consumer culture in the context of a counterculture emerging from within the heart of Hollywood.[10]

The evolution of Frank's thinking about Chaplin reveals his desire to trace in "the facts of our hideous present" an immanent critique of modernity. An initial assessment of Chaplin's work, first published in the *Seven Arts* in 1917, was brief and dismissive: "Charlie Chaplin is an extremely brilliant clown, but he is an unhealthy one." Chaplin's slapstick violence, largely directed against women, reflected the morbidity of a puritanical society. But by the time he published *Our America* in 1919, Frank's judgment of Chaplin had mellowed. There was "social criticism in his antics" that was especially effective because it rose "naturally, organically" from the "low social base" of his audience. During the early 1920s, Frank and Chaplin met and became friends. Frank's writings on Chaplin subsequently grew even more appreciative, and Chaplin joined Stieglitz in Frank's pantheon of twentieth-century revolutionary leaders. Chaplin's solitary struggles with the representatives of authority, repeated in film after film, vindicated for Frank the romantic tradition's defense of aesthetic and spiritual values against the abstract calculus of a commercial society. Though his audience knew nothing of the romantic critique of the cash nexus, it identified with the tramp's desperate efforts to preserve his dignity and grace in a hostile, spiritless world. "In the dark theater hall, they dare, before this sharp assertion of a soul unfleshed by custom, to know their soul." As defender of the sacred core of "grace and loveliness and wistful dream" within every individual, Chaplin legitimated deep, often unacknowledged longings for self-expression and for a loving, accepting community that otherwise found no echo in mass culture. Whereas in 1919 Frank had hoped to bring together the aesthetics of a Stieglitz and the politics of Big Bill Haywood, he now advocated a political and cultural revolution uniting Chaplin's vision of self-liberation with Lenin's collectivist "technique." Chaplin's films portrayed "myths of refuge within the self," but they were an essential part of the "preparatory process" required for a more "creative union" in the future.[11]

Frank's appreciation for Chaplin carried his critique of mass culture beyond the antimodernist disdain for the herd that characterized most of his commentaries from the 1920s. Chaplin's protest was hardly that of a traditional defender of a medieval metaphysics. His antinomian romanticism was as much a product of the dissolution of premodern culture as the expression of the will to power in technology. By arguing that Chaplin's struggle for personal grace prefigured some new Beloved Community, Frank suggested that the reconstruction of cultural wholeness required the liberation of aspirations and intuitions that industrial production had banished to the realm of private life. Organic community would involve, then, not so much a return to the medieval synthesis but a new kind of solidarity born from the unfulfilled private desires of the modern self.

Frank's proposal for a distinctly modern successor to the medieval synthesis had a great deal in common with similar arguments made by Progressive intellectuals in the late nineteenth and early twentieth centuries, who sought modern equivalents to small-town democracy and provincialism, but it also differed from them in significant ways. Whereas social theorists such as Jane Addams, Charles Horton Cooley, John Dewey, Robert and Helen Lynd, and other Progressive communitarians sought to reconstruct solidarity on the basis of an Enlightenment conception of rational deliberation and scientific inquiry, Frank opted for a modern version of folk culture knit together by the creative will of the prophetic artist. Such a position essentially squared the circle of his precarious position as critic of mass culture—he could speak both for premodern values and as an architect of an emerging modern communal culture—but it also revealed the political limitations of his programs for organic reconstruction. For in the end, despite his best intentions, Frank's approach remained distinctly transcendentalist, relying on the visionary imagination of the artist to embody community through his or her own expression. Other members of such an organic community, those presently massed together as a thoughtless herd, remained as passive as ever: only now, they would give their approval to the vision of their prophetic leaders.[12]

The evolution from traditional folk culture to mass culture and finally to an organic culture was, in Frank's view, always a process of elite leadership. "The leader," he wrote in *The Re-discovery of America*, "is related organically to the group as is the consciously acting mind to the instinctive." Artists such as Stieglitz and Chaplin—and presumably Frank himself—were at the center of Frank's theory of organic transformation because they alone could infuse existing social reality with animating purpose; they alone could give the herd a consciousness of itself as a modern community. The movement such prophets were to lead would not make traditional liberal or socialist appeals because these missed the need for spiritual wholeness as the source of any social action. "There will be no time in consequence to clamour for 'rights,'" Frank explained, "no breath to bewail 'injustice.' Only eyes turned outward see life in these false terms; there are no rights, and there is no injustice."[13]

By denying the traditional language of liberal, republican, and socialist protest—the rhetoric of natural rights and justice—Frank came dangerously close to a denial of any need for popular participation in a democratic project of reconstructing community. His openly elitist conception of the relationship of groups and their leaders gave ordinary people no role in formulating their own visions of community. Rather, Frank held that the leader's status derived from his prophetic articulation of the semiconscious needs of others. The leader "is one whom others follow because his action illumes the consciousness and will of what lives integrally in them and because to act with him articulates or fulfills their life." Such a formulation of political and cultural change cast Frank's appreciation for Chaplin in a sinister light. Even as he admired Chaplin's subversive commentary on modern culture, Frank held on to the idea of popular passivity in the face of mass culture. The herd in the audience still acquiesced in the image flickering on the screen before it; only now, Frank approved of that response because he agreed with Chaplin's message. Very much like Robert Lynd and Herbert Mar-

cuse after him, Frank imagined liberation from mass culture along manipulative, undemocratic lines that mirrored the political arrangements
of a consumer society. He would join Chaplin, Stieglitz, and other artists
in giving collective purpose to a bureaucratized populace through the
sheer exercise of his creative genius. Frank had not so much given up the
search for a community of free personalities that had inspired the *Seven
Arts* as he had reserved the liberation of personality for a select group,
who would literally personify the aspirations of the entire community.
Frank was right: this project had nothing at all to do with the language
of rights or the language of justice.[14]

If such a vision had any practical consequences, these involved the
creation of exemplary works of art and the living of exemplary lives that
would embody for the masses the possibilities for spiritual cohesion and
meaning within "the facts of our hideous present." As Alan Trachtenberg and Robert L. Perry have argued, Hart Crane's epic poem of
American technology, *The Bridge*, was probably the most successful
literary achievement to emerge from Frank's ideal of modern organic
synthesis. But here too the political limitations of Frank's organicism are
immediately evident, for as Trachtenberg notes, Crane's poem expresses
"hope for a purely aesthetic transformation of a world already remade,
reconstituted by industrial and corporate capitalism into mechanized
space and time." Like Frank's personal quests for wholeness, this attempt to aestheticize industrial technology rested on an imperial conception of the mystical self, which sought to extend its domain to all
realms of existence, imbuing them with the force of the artist's own
character. Oblivious to the material realities of an external world, this
project overlooked the undemocratic nature of the industrial order it
sought to endow with new meaning.[15]

A similar blindness to the need to challenge American social and
political arrangements marked Frank's calls in *America Hispana*, his
1931 study of Latin American cultures, for "an *integral* socialism which
would transfigure the present industrial body on the basis of the true
concept of the person." Frank's seven-month tour of Latin America in
1929 reinforced his belief that the Catholic peasant culture of the Hispanic world retained an organic mutualism and a mystical sensibility
largely lost in industrial North America. Arguing for a New World
socialism that would blend the best of both cultures, Frank veered
erratically from penetrating criticisms of the progressivist vision of
most American socialists to endorsements of North American industrial
progress as the only means available for the implementation of Latin

Americans' organic ideals. At various points, Frank was alert to the authoritarian tendencies within industrial concentration and to the dangers of basing socialist hopes on mechanical notions of progress: these hopes "might readily be transmuted into a socialism retaining capitalist values. This would be a socialism in which the true person—real human consciousness—had no place; in which man functioned only as part of the pack in the activity of production and consumption." But elsewhere in the book, Frank suggested that the "feminine," mutualistic values of Latin America could find concrete realization only through the "masculine" industrial organization of the United States. North American means would achieve South American ends.[16]

Frank's attempt to find a third way between Emersonian "utopias of escape" and Bellamyite "utopias of reconstruction" had merged the least attractive features of both visions, collapsing the organic rhetoric of wholeness and interconnectedness with the very processes of bureaucratic organization he had hoped to overcome. The result was a transcendentalist gloss on Bellamy's militarized utopia of industrial regimentation. In an entry in his notebook from 1932, Frank wrote:

> *The one hope* is: to propagate in our people the sense of the Person as the individualized Focus of the Cosmic. This sense, if it becomes a cultural experience, will produce individuals who—as persons— will be varied and diverse: and who—as conscious integers of the whole—will be able to commune & to cross-fertilize each other. Thus, *within* the economic uniformity of a collectivist-machine world, which might evolve a new order of harmonious diversity: a new polarity, a new counterpoint. A new *Culture* to replace the Christian one, which grew by the conjunction of inner vision & outer variety.

During the first half of the 1930s, Frank believed that the Soviet Union had achieved such a cultural revolution "within the economic uniformity of a collectivist-machine world." Despite his active involvement in leftist politics during this period as a fellow traveler of the Communist party, what is striking about Frank's writings on Soviet communism and Marxism is the consistency of his vision of cosmic oneness and his lack of interest in politics as an arena of conflict and contention. Soviet society appealed to him as an initial synthesis of industrial order with an organic understanding of the self's relation to society and the cosmos.[17]

Dawn in Russia, Frank's record of his visit to the Soviet Union in the fall of 1931, praised Stalin's regime for wedding the religious mutuality of Russian folk culture to industrial efficiency. Soviet Marxism struck Frank as the logical continuation of the Russians' "mystical feeling" of "life as an interrelated whole." Even factory workers laboring under the exhortations of a loudspeaker were "happy workers" in Russia because they were "whole men and women. Although the individual job be endlessly repeated," Frank wrote, "although they stand enslaved for hours to the turn of a wheel which they must feed and feed—yet in these dismal halls there is a whole humanity" because "the least of them knows that he is making a Worker's Union, that he is creating a world." In Stalin's Russia, the factory had become a Beloved Community.[18]

"In the thirties, I wanted to be ravished by a community," Frank later admitted in his memoirs. "Most of all Communism, although I could not accept it, tempted me, I believe and—when I saw the Communist youth—moved me—because it seemed to offer a *community*; and to belong to a community was what I needed." It is not Frank's apology for Stalinism that is so troubling in his writings from this period, however, but the indifference to politics that had characterized his entire conception of an organic community since the end of World War I. Frank found in the Soviet Union in 1931 much of what he had been looking for in a future organic American community. Although Frank would speak less generously about the Soviet Union by the late 1930s, he never broke clearly with the antipolitical and antidemocratic features of his mystical communitarianism. He would continue to search for aesthetic and spiritual alternatives to modern mass culture for the rest of his life, still maintaining the idea of herdlike passivity that was at the core of his portraits of the consumer culture of the 1920s. The goal of a social or cosmic self—a self merged spiritually with the rest of the universe—led Frank to smother the *Seven Arts* critique of the industrial division of labor in a fuzzy rhetoric of wholeness that celebrated mass organization as a means to organic solidarity. From the 1920s on, Frank remained committed to a mystical doctrine devoid of conflict, debate, or disagreement: a utopia of leaders and followers joined organically in silent, timeless assent.[19]

When the liberal journal the *Forum* invited Lewis Mumford in 1930 to contribute a statement to its series "What I Believe," he used the occasion to sum up the cultural ethics he had formulated in his biography of Herman Melville. The creation of a human environment rich in symbols and shared values was the only way to give meaning to a life in which achievement always fell short of ultimate aspiration and evil betrayed hopeful ideals. Mumford recognized that such an ethos placed him outside conventional political categories on the Left because both liberals and Marxists exalted increased productivity and the conquest of power over sustained inquiry into the good life. "Instead of the one-sided practical activity fostered by the ideals of the utilitarians and the working out of modern technology, with its intense specialization," Mumford explained, "I believe in a rounded, symmetrical development of both the human personality and the community itself."[20]

At the same time that he summed up his cultural and moral creed from the 1920s for the *Forum*, Mumford's thinking about how to achieve a mutual project of personal and community reconstruction was undergoing drastic changes. Mumford's perspective in *Herman Melville* was in many ways tragic, acknowledging human finitude as a way of sustaining hope in an imperfect world. The culturalist ethics outlined there appeared to caution against hasty resolutions of the conflicts between the self and society or of the conflicts within the self. Mumford's reading of the characters of Ahab and Pierre led him to an ethics of limits, of containment, as a check against the will to power that fueled a technological society. Moral deliberation, commitment to craftsmanship, and participation in the fashioning of a shared civic culture were the slow but inescapable means to personality and community, not technocratic utopianism or mysticism.

Yet by the early 1930s, Mumford seemed restless with the uncertain prospects offered by such an ethics when applied to political and social change. Critics pressed him to clarify the concrete institutional implications of his position, and Mumford himself believed the time had come to flesh out his cultural criticism into a full-blown theory of the potential for a new organic synthesis within modern civilization. The first two books of his Renewal of Life series, *Technics and Civilization*, published in 1934, and *The Culture of Cities*, published in 1938, offered history and prophecy on a grand scale according to the evolutionary categories he inherited from Geddes. Mumford traced the decline of the medieval synthesis of eotechnic civilization, the emergence of a destructive paleotechnic industrialism, and the first glimmerings of an organic neotechnic culture in the early twentieth century. In outlining the "development of value within the machine complex itself," as he described his portrait of a neotechnic order, Mumford looked to modern social science and technology for forms and values capable of restoring community on a modern, scientific basis.[21]

Although the increasingly political mood of American intellectuals after the 1929 Crash probably explains much of Mumford's new urgency about sociological and political matters, it is clear that by the end of the 1920s Mumford was already considering how to expand the theory of postindustrial regional planning he had developed with the Regional Planning Association of America into a coherent program of social transformation. His work with the association in the 1920s focused on regional development of garden communities that would unite the best elements of rural and urban life by using new technologies and new inventions such as the automobile, radio, and steel-and-glass construction. This attempt to update Ebenezer Howard's garden city ideal through the products of the second industrial revolution was in many ways at odds with the Morrisite condemnation of industrial life in his books of cultural criticism. Even a critic as close to Mumford's perspective as Waldo Frank noted the "wistful and vague" tone of the conclusion to *The Golden Day* and the difficulty Mumford encountered when he tried to move from his historical portrait of preindustrial mutuality to the forces for organic renewal in the twentieth century. Mumford was "in love with the gesture, the dream, the childhood faery of our past," Frank complained in a 1926 review of the book, "yet he rejects the *body*—our present interim of the Machine and of the romanticisms of the Machine—whereby alone this promise from our past may be organized into a living future." Less sympathetic critics pounced on precisely this same problem in Mumford's approach to modern culture. Writing in the socialist *New Masses* in 1927, Genevieve Taggard accused Mumford and other "Ruskinian Boys" of being "false and literary" in their critique of industrialism. "The Machine Age has one meaning," she argued, "it need neither be rejected nor aestheticized—it can be accepted as a very interesting and enormously clever way of trying to do some of the work that has to be done."[22]

Mumford could dismiss Taggard's charges as another example of Marxists' devotion to technology, but Frank's critique was more difficult to counter because it overlapped with his own interest in locating organic tendencies at work within industry and applied science. He assured Frank in correspondence that "the matter-of-fact acceptance of the machine is the point from which I begin." In architecture, he had "already arrived . . . at an appreciation of the Machine" by way of the work of such European modernists as Gropius and Le Corbusier. "I've accepted all the positive gains that have come with this movement, and am looking towards the next stage—instead of assuming that the machine is a standard and criterion of all effort." This next stage involved the introduction of organic forms into modern design and the infusion of organic values into industrial planning and organization. By 1933, as he was writing *Technics and Civilization*, this "return to the organic" was even more appealing to Mumford. As he explained to Alfred Stieglitz, the synthesis of organic and industrial culture prefigured in Stieglitz's photography had come to fruition in technology, "and back of that is the promise of a mighty revolution" in modern civilization.[23]

The political implications of Mumford's hopes for a "return to the organic" within industrial society were deeply ambiguous. His belief in making lived experience, not abstract utopias, the basis for cultural criticism could lead both to the theory of symbolic interaction he had articulated in the 1920s and to projects that idealized the existing social order as an incipient organic community. In an unpublished manifesto, "Preface to Action," written in 1931, Mumford wrestled with the political means at hand for the creation of a neotechnic culture, alternating between a generous program of democratic radicalism and a frankly elitist confidence in social engineering from above. Starting from the premise that "a revolution, like an election, is always a contest between minorities"—indeed, that "it is futile to wait for" majorities to make revolution—he surveyed the alignment of political forces at hand in the United States and found virtually all wanting. Liberals and social democrats lacked the vision and principles necessary to creative action, while fascists sought to accelerate the concentration of state power that had begun under industrial, paleotechnic society. The southern critics of industrial culture who wrote *I'll Take My Stand* in 1930 had made significant contributions to a new politics, with their appreciation of rural culture and their consistent attack on state capitalism. But their program of agrarian restoration was "haunted by the wistful phantoms of the past—the gentry, episcopalianism, feudalism, a narrow nativism." Among the political forces at hand, only the Communist party possessed an inspiring "myth" capable of guiding a revolution. "The communists are the only ones, up to now, who mean business."[24]

Mumford was no more enamored of the ideology and strategy of Bolshevism than he had been after the Russian Revolution. He still rejected the Soviet model of Marxist revolution for its devotion to the centralized state and the factory system as emblems of socialist progress. Moreover, communist tactics in the United States and Europe repelled Mumford as opportunistic and dangerous; in their disdain for legal procedure and their fascination with violence and military discipline, they were likely to provoke fascist reaction, not socialist revolution. The "war-psychology" of communist strategy came from mimicking Lenin's conspiratorial party in the Soviet Union instead of "assimilating fresh experiences and reacting against our own special background." Like Edmund Wilson, who urged American radicals in January 1931 to "take Communism away from the Communists," Mumford sought an American Left that would grow out of local conditions and use the language of a native radicalism. "Communism in America cannot be a[n] imitation of the Russian variety," Mumford wrote in his would-be manifesto; "it must appeal to the pride and self-confidence of the American, connect with his own traditions of revolution and equality, give play to his residual individualism, recognize his experimentalism and his capacity for self-help, summon to itself the spiritual energies from such relevant sources as Thoreau and Whitman."[25]

This promising agenda for a nondogmatic American socialism led Mumford in two very different directions in his "Preface." His critique of conventional Marxist and liberal politics and his calls for an indigenous radicalism recalled the heady blend of Morrisite and anarcho-syndicalist ideas in his writings immediately after World War I. Once again, he rejected socialist optimism about the steady proletarianization of the work force. Factory workers had become "exiles from life" as a result of the destruction of craft organizations and traditions; they experienced "a poorer sense of their manliness and womanliness" and "a diminished sense of vitality." A new politics would begin by challenging the industrial division of labor in the name of a "cooperative intelligence." "Industrial workers must learn to think, plan, direct," Mumford wrote, and "professional workers must learn to perform bread labor and take over their share of the remaining drudgery." "The society of the future" would not be divided between "slaves and specialized castes," between unskilled workers and managers, but "an intelligent society of amateurs." Above all else, a new politics had to start with everyday practice, not abstract future promises: it had to create "a discipline for the daily life" that prefigured a community of creative personalities.[26]

Such arguments directly contradicted the second strain of reasoning in Mumford's paper, which looked to skilled professionals, managers, artists, and humanist intellectuals to lead this organicist radical movement. "No program for transforming our economic society can hope for success in America if it does not call forth the active sympathy and cooperation of a strong nucleus of economists, engineers, production managers, administrators, architects, community planners, foresters, doctors." Calling such professional experts "Scipian" revolutionaries— in contrast to the slower, more cautious Fabians—Mumford urged the use of social science and regional planning to demonstrate the desirability of collectivism through concrete example. Although Mumford broadened his category of experts beyond those usually mentioned by advocates of social engineering to include artists, poets, and humanists like himself, this element of his new politics was fully in line with the undemocratic progressivism of such 1930s liberal technocrats as Stuart Chase, Alfred M. Bingham, and George Soule. Mumford's goal was a society of amateurs, but his politics relied on expert leaders who would demonstrate to the public the best route to organic community, as revealed by social science, biology, and other specialized disciplines. "The Scipians will gather strength by means of that ultimate demonstration," he asserted. "With plans, with concrete ideals, they will appeal to the groping intelligence and the underlying desires of the majority: demonstrating their clarity of purpose and their technical skill, they will win assent." Mumford's values were at war with his technique. As in Frank's mystical formulations of prophetic inspiration, leaders were to transform the "groping intelligence" and "underlying desires" of a devitalized, inarticulate majority into didactic images that won public assent. Such a politics rested on demonstration, not argument, on expert guidance, not popular participation, and on assent, not consensus. By choosing such means, Mumford hopelessly compromised his program for an indigenous democratic radicalism. "I and mine," he quoted Whitman, "do not convince by argument: we convince by our presence."[27]

Technics and Civilization and *The Culture of Cities* capture nicely the conflicts within Mumford's organicist vision in the 1930s. Their most significant contribution to a critical understanding of technology and urbanism lies primarily in their historical analysis, not in their prognosis for organic renewal. Mumford's determination to counter the tendency to view technological innovation and urbanization as autonomous forces led him to emphasize the historical origins of myths that ceded individual agency and initiative to the very products of human creativity. It was the ideology of technical automatism and the cult of megalopolitan bigness—not any deterministic dynamic centered in technology or cities themselves—that most threatened human community, he insisted. Mumford's historical methodology was a political critique of the culture of industrialism insofar as it set processes that had come to appear as autonomous in the broader historical context of cultural change. His intention was to show how "men had become mechanical before they perfected complicated machines to express their new bent and interest." The collapse of the symbolic universe of medieval Christianity had left a spiritual absence in Western culture which the cult of technology had come to occupy. In an "empty, denuded world," bereft of familiar cultural landmarks, "the invention of machines became a duty. By renouncing a large part of his humanity, a man could achieve godhood: he dawned on this second chaos and created the machine in his image: the image of power, but power ripped loose from his flesh and isolated from his humanity." Similarly, the modern city had substituted the factory and the office building for the medieval city's "civic nucleus" of church, public market, and university, an architectural rendering of the intellectual displacement of spirit by productive power. Mumford's historical analysis suggested that the crisis of personality in modern civilization required the reconquest of technology and city development by culture, which would constrain technical knowledge within the boundaries of ethical and aesthetic disciplines.[28]

Yet when Mumford turned to an explicit discussion of the prospects for political and cultural alternatives to paleotechnic industrialism, his argument became increasingly murky, if not downright contradictory. *Technics and Civilization* and *The Culture of Cities* contain some of the most penetrating criticisms of the cultural consequences of the industrial division of labor in American social thought, but they both end in celebrations of the emerging power of professionals and managers within industry and government. Mumford's historical investigations traced the ascendancy of such groups back to the acquisitive and predatory impulses of a militaristic early capitalism, which had crushed popular craft traditions and local cultures. But his neotechnic prophecy looked to the very same cultural forces to create a more humane industrialism. Repeating Thorstein Veblen's theory of the incompatibility of "leisure class" values and humans' efficient "instinct of workmanship," Mumford argued that the "financial acquisitiveness which had originally speeded invention now furthers technical inertia." "The machine is a communist," Mumford claimed in an assertion of technological determinism that ran directly counter to his historical methodology; a technics created for warfare and profit making would now shrug off its archaic roots and usher in organic community.[29]

Mumford believed that innovations in the natural and social sciences, industrial and architectural design, and the social relations of factory production heralded a modern successor to the medieval cosmology. Together with the new technology available through electrical power and chemical inventions, these new intellectual disciplines made possible an organic synthesis that would foster an appreciation for the fully developed human personality. But by extending his enthusiasm for such neotechnic novelties to include the new systems of work discipline pioneered by Frederick Winslow Taylor and Elton Mayo, Mumford revealed his shallow understanding of the political implications of the second industrial revolution. Mumford believed that Taylor's scientific management displayed a healthy interest in "the worker himself as an element of production," a concern marred only by Taylor's acceptance of capitalist profit motives—as if these two elements of Taylorism could be neatly severed in a neotechnic society. Elton Mayo's science of human relations foreshadowed "socialized industry, in which the worker himself is fully respected" and "rational organization, social control, physiological and psychological understanding" are the new standards of civilization. If Frank and Crane aestheticized industrial capitalism to achieve organic community—investing machinery with an aesthetic and spiritual authority derived from the poet's own creative powers—Mumford gave humanistic legitimacy to the aspirations of modern management, which now claimed the right to order and plan the entire range of human experience. Mumford's neotechnic prophecy confused organicism with organization and the socialist community of the future with a more sophisticated system of managerial controls under advanced industrial capitalism.[30]

Mumford's enthusiasm for new forms of industrial planning and human relations organization reflected the profound hostility to politics that pervaded long sections of *Technics* and *The Culture of Cities*. Given his loving treatment of medieval solidarity, it is not surprising that Mumford viewed liberal politics with suspicion or that he endorsed William Morris's suggestion in *News from Nowhere* that the best use for Parliament in the socialist future would be as a dung heap. Modern liberalism had fragmented the social organism into a scramble of irrelevant issues, he complained. The "old civic unity" of the medieval city had given way to parliamentary debates over "abstract issues" and to attempts to "solve by purely legal formulae matters that demanded concrete experiment and the co-operation of engineers, architects, administrators, [and] artists." The failure of liberalism revealed the need for a new elite of "temporal and spiritual powers"—the Scipians of his unpublished manifesto—to use progressive education, regional planning, and industrial design to educate the populace in scientific method. "We will create a whole generation," Mumford predicted, "that will look upon every aspect of the region, the community, and their personal lives as subject to the same processes." Once again, organic community culminated in unanimity, with all members joined in agreement on the new metaphysics revealed by the prophets of modern organicism.[31]

This static portrait of a depoliticized planned community found its cultural equivalent in the machine aesthetic Mumford sought to make the basis for an artistic synthesis of technology and symbolic form. The same critic who decried the destruction of the symbol-laden cosmos of the medieval mind now praised modern technology for promoting a functionalist aesthetics of "precision, calculation, flawlessness, simplicity, economy." "The concept of a neutral world," Mumford explained in an astonishing reversal, "untouched by man's efforts, indifferent to his activities, obdurate to his wish and supplication, is one of the great triumphs of man's imagination, and in itself represents a fresh human value." Even the concept of the interactive self that had been at the center of Mumford's criticism in the 1920s took on the characteristics of its stripped-down cultural environment in the neotechnic future. In the fiction of Ernest Hemingway, and in the representation of the external human facade in film and still photography, Mumford detected the emergence of an impassive, objective personality type at one with its surroundings. "The change is significant: not self-examination but self-exposure: not tortured confession but easy open candor: not the proud soul wrapped in his cloak, pacing the lonely beach at midnight, but the matter-of-fact soul, naked, exposed to the sun on the beach at noonday, one of a crowd of naked people." What had begun as an enterprise to rescue the creative capacity of human personality from the confines of urban-industrial automatism had become its opposite once Mumford turned from history to prophecy. With culture redefined as the absence of symbolic texture, and personality recreated as an externalized self open to photographic inspection, Mumford's organic community had created an aesthetic and personal discipline that was the perfect match for its politics of scientific management.[32]

Fortunately, the mechanistic utopia sketched out in the concluding chapters of *Technics and Civilization* and *The Culture of Cities* did not remain for long the guiding force in Mumford's cultural criticism. The events of the late 1930s and 1940s—from the rise of totalitarianism to the use of atomic weapons to end World War II—profoundly shook

Mumford's confident appraisal of the prospects for a humanistic organicism arising from "within the machine complex itself." In *Faith for Living*, *The Condition of Man*, *The Conduct of Life*, and other publications from the 1940s and 1950s, Mumford returned to the ethical speculations of his Melville biography and to the Morrisite critique of industrialism of his work in the 1920s. By the time he wrote again on historical sociology in the 1960s and 1970s, with *The City in History* and the two-volume study *The Myth of the Machine*, Mumford had developed a more consistent and devastating perspective on modern civilization, counterposing political localism, respect for handicrafts and decentralized technical systems, and an ethos of personal restraint to the religion of bigness, technological innovation, and state power he saw everywhere at work in postwar America.

But even as Mumford soured on the promise of a neotechnic resolution of the division between personality and modern culture, he held on to a communitarian vision of political change that obscured conflicts over power in modern society. After 1940, Mumford returned again and again to the example of the early Christians' withdrawal from Roman civilization as a model for twentieth-century communitarians in a decadent industrial culture. At times, Mumford's new Christian rebels resembled his earlier ideal of Scipian experts, whose mere presence and powers of demonstration would transform the popular imagination. Mumford's friend and fellow regional planner Frederic J. Osborn made Mumford's tendency to valorize prophetic intellectuals explicit when he wrote a letter in 1942 suggesting the founding of a new "church," with its own "organisation and personnel ... specialised on personal conduct and with practical wisdom derived from both a liberal education ... and from close and intimate contact with all sorts of men and women in every kind of personal crisis from childhood to old age (in other words a 'priesthood')." That theme of cultural withdrawal by the few, self-conscious members of a spiritual elect remained a dominant motif in Mumford's later writings. In 1970, in the second volume of *The Myth of the Machine*, Mumford placed his hopes for change in a politics of retreat that sought "not to capture the citadel of power, but to withdraw from it and quietly paralyze it." Only such acts of spiritual disengagement could "restore power and confident authority to its proper source: the human personality and the small face-to-face community." This new position at least avoided the naive optimism of Mumford's organicism of the 1930s, but it too lacked any careful attention to political issues. Whether as neotechnic organicism or as a decentralist radicalism of moral witness, Mumford's communitarianism rarely envisioned a popular movement of sustained conflict or engagement with the dominant institutions of modern politics. Community could take shape on the margins of power among members of a new priesthood, or come to full bloom under the expert care of Scipian planners, but not in a prolonged contest for power.[33]

Mumford's theory of organic renewal foundered precisely on the mutualistic language that gave his work such power as a source of cultural criticism. The words that Mumford returned to in all his writing—*culture, community, organicism*, and the like—were a significant advance from the tendency of positivist social theory to reify the industrial division of human experience into artificial categories. Such concepts served as repositories of alternative values of solidarity, mutual aid, and love that Mumford invoked in opposition to the dual processes of institutional bureaucracy and individual rootlessness he detested in modern life. Transposed to the realm of politics—where it often took the place of a rhetoric of rights, justice, debate, and deliberation— Mumford's vocabulary blunted understanding of the necessity of a conflicted public sphere to a democratic theory of social transformation. Mumford's recognition that the political crisis of modernity was at its root cultural, reflecting the broader myths and ideologies of an entire way of life, was a profoundly important insight, but it led him too often to assume that cultural leadership would in and of itself produce new communities. Even worse, a language that stressed communal identity and understanding risked becoming deeply authoritarian, especially when joined to a theory of elite leadership and mass passivity. Organic community proved more useful as a critique of politics than as its substitute.

These shortcomings in Frank's and Mumford's organicist critique of industrial culture tempt one to dismiss the entire enterprise as an enormous mistake, an example of what is bound to go wrong with any critique of modernity premised on a positive evaluation of traditional practices. From the vantage points of conventional liberal or Marxist politics, a radicalism that speaks the language of community and self-realization seems doomed to failure from the start because it overvalues culture and consciousness at the expense of power and blurs the distinction between public life and private virtue in its quest for the common good. Most of Frank's and Mumford's critics, particularly those on the Marxist Left, invoked such themes in the 1930s and 1940s. James T. Farrell, probably the harshest of the Young Americans' critics, labeled Mumford "one of the leading spokesmen of the new cult of the irrational" (among whose numbers he included Brooks, Frank, Archibald MacLeish, Reinhold Niebuhr, and Jacques Maritain). Mumford's organic synthesis of aesthetic, religious, and ethical values was only "a fog, a mist, a camouflage" for Farrell, "concealing the naked and brutal facts of societies past and present." V. F. Calverton, Sidney Hook, Meyer Schapiro and other like-minded critics on the Left agreed in dismissing the Young Americans' talk of culture, values, and community as either empty-headed mysticism or outright mystification that served to preempt more radical political solutions. Liberal critics such as Alfred M. Bingham and Richard H. Rovere joined the chorus, warning of the fascist tendencies of any discussion of organic community and branding Frank and Mumford as objectively reactionary.[34]

Such writers were largely justified in their critique of the apolitical nature of much of the Young Americans' work; moreover, they were correct to note the centrality of mystical or prophetic conceptions of cultural leadership in their programs for civic and artistic renewal. Still, the terms of this critique reveal the thinness of American progressive thought on questions of art, ethics, and culture. For the vast majority of liberals and leftists in the 1930s and 1940s, such matters were indeed nothing more than "fog . . . mist . . . camouflage," as Farrell put it. They were, in the eyes of most Marxists, superstructural matters that disguised the objective social relations of production; or they were, in the liberal view, the residue of industrial progress—a cultural lag that would be eliminated once consciousness caught up with behavior. To dwell on such issues was the worst kind of sentimentalism, from this tough-minded progressive perspective: the real issues were political and economic, and these had nothing to do with culture.

The intellectual Left's anemic conception of the relationship between culture and politics during the 1930s and 1940s makes Frank's and Mumford's insistence on the aesthetic and moral foundations of public life a far more attractive approach. At the very least, these critics took questions of form and value seriously; they responded sympathetically to the public's desires for small-scale communal structures instead of branding such longings as an atavistic brake on progress. "Change in America is laborious and secret," Frank wrote; "it persists against the obdurate will of those very institutions which constantly mouth 'progress.' " Most important, by making the realization of personality the

goal of cultural renewal, the Young Americans gave legitimacy to longings for moral meaning and personal identity that liberals and Marxists
alike would have banished to private life or dismissed as false consciousness. Frank and Mumford placed at the center of their cultural criticism
the emotional, symbolic, and value-laden aspects of social experience in
which most people understand themselves and their surroundings. The
charge that such an emphasis obscured political issues is important, but
it may also be reversed and turned against the Young Americans' critics,
whose vision of politics lacked an understanding of the self as anything
other than a political actor. In their concern for a narrowly defined
politics, devoid of moral evaluation and symbolic language, American
progressives have generally uprooted the public sphere from its location
in a particular place and particular set of traditions. They have ignored,
in short, the cultural components of citizenship.[35]

The idea of cultural citizenship, though never clearly articulated as
such, still remains the most compelling aspect of Frank's and Mumford's
theory of organic community. The belief that organic community could
consist of a "society of intelligent amateurs" that lays buried under the
elitist currents of much of Frank's and Mumford's work in the 1930s
found its best expression in Mumford's regionalism. At those moments
when he addressed the need for popular participation in the recovery
and reconstruction of regional identity, Mumford spoke for an ideal of
men and women as citizens of their own culture, as participants in
public life who drew deeply on the resources of their community to
make their surroundings a home for human aspirations. That ideal of
cultural citizenship deserves to be salvaged from the rest of the Young
Americans' organicist theory—with its antidemocratic cult of prophetic
leaders, its denigration of popular politics, and its mystical conception
of cultural unanimity—and reasserted as a third alternative to the utopias of escape and reconstruction in the communitarian tradition.

The Young Americans' organicism proved least useful as a guide to
social change when it remained caught in the alternatives of escape and
mechanistic reconstruction. The first route relied ultimately on the prophetic critic's apprehension of a metaphysical unity located somewhere
outside his own culture, which he in turn sought to embody as a didactic
lesson for others—either in the form of an exemplary spiritual community in exile or as a work of artistic vision that revealed timeless truths.
The second route tended to idealize already existing institutional structures as immanent forms of organic solidarity, trusting only to the wisdom of specialists and administrators to complete a process already in

motion. In both cases, community rested on a conception of total una-nimity on one single vision of the good, as revealed to the public through its prophetic vanguard. In both cases, knowledge of that good —of "the Whole," as Frank would say—required the transcendence of the given world by a select few who would reinvigorate culture with their newly acquired awareness of spiritual or scientific truths.

By contrast, the incipient ideal of cultural citizenship in the Young Americans' work looked to practical wisdom and symbolic language rooted in the plurality of human experiences as the main resources for a challenge to industrial civilization. In this more modest utopianism, the task of the critic was not so much to transcend the instrumental logic of a technological culture by recourse to intuition or holistic science but to put it in its place as just one of many cultural tools and languages that human beings might draw on in constructing a more humane commu-nity. By returning technical culture to a broader "human ecology" of skills, values, and symbols, men and women would have the opportunity to pick and choose among a diversity of traditions and practices. More-over, they would give up the hope of one central truth—be it the myth of technological progress or mystical wholeness—as the guiding force of human experience for a web of contingent, provisional truths capable of sustaining personal growth through participation in public life. Cultural citizenship takes shape, in this view, as both means and end because full, democratic access to the cultural traditions of a community is necessary to a process that must inevitably result in the refashioning of those traditions and the creation of a new relationship between the self and its culture. As Jeffrey Stout writes, "The creation of new vocabularies al-ways begins with existing linguistic patterns, making something new out of something found."[36]

Mumford most clearly described this idea of cultural citizenship as a process of "making something new out of something found" when he discussed how symbolic form and small-scale community structures em-powered people to act in ways that blurred the boundaries between artifact, mass spectacle, and public participation. The religious proces-sions of the Middle Ages were models for Mumford's own visions of an organic experience uniting practice and belief and of the possibilities for self-discovery and self-creation in the collective appropriation of shared cultural resources. "As in the church itself," he wrote of such proces-sions in *The Culture of Cities*, "the spectators were also communicants and participants: they engaged in the spectacle, watching it from within, not from without: or rather, feeling it from within, acting in unison, not dismembered beings, reduced to a single specialized role. Prayer, mass, pageant, life-ceremony, baptism, marriage, or funeral—the city itself was a stage for these separate scenes of the drama, and the citizen himself was actor."[37]

In this passage, Mumford described a process of locating the self in a participatory culture that is quite different from the timeless, mystical assent that dominated much of Frank's thinking. Here, unity derived from the experience of representing one's self to oneself and to others as symbolic form, of achieving an understanding of one's cultural loyalties and possessions through shared rituals in public space. Art, architecture, and ritual converged in a place to express human aspirations to transcendence through culture, in a public setting that was enriched and remade by individuals acting as participants in civic life.

Mumford's objection to the metropolitan mass culture of the twentieth century was that it failed to provide such forums for the diversity of human roles and practices and thus closed off opportunities for individuals to refashion themselves and their environment. Public life fragmented human experience into narrowly defined occupations and spaces designed for specialized functions. Meanwhile, fantasy and the creative imagination found outlets only in leisure activity that was as rigidly organized as the workplace. The location of the public world of work into the skyscraper office building, "a sort of human filing case," had as its flip side a suburban culture that "encouraged a complete segregation of consumption from production." Uniting the extremes of a public sphere given over to technical rationality and a privatized leisure centered in the suburbs was the commercial culture broadcast from the metropolis, which drowned out the accents and rhythms of regional and local cultures and subsumed the exercise of "substantial rationality" in a steady stream of new fashions and novelties. "What happens in the economic world happens also in the play-world: the listener to the radio, the spectator at the motion picture, tends to be passive and machine-conditioned."[38]

Regionalism appealed to Mumford because he believed that it was only in the context of a small-scale, comprehensible environment that the individual could join with others in the rituals and practices that had once formed the basis of civic culture. "Small groups: small classes: small communities: institutions framed to the human scale, are essential to purposive behavior in modern society." Mumford's goal was to detach the participatory municipal culture of medieval processions from its connections to authoritarian religious and political institutions and to make experimental process and the dynamics of symbolic language, not feudal metaphysics, the core of a new set of community values. Following Dewey, he saw the progressive school as the institution best suited for such a project. The school would replace the rigid dogmatism of the church with an open-ended gospel of personal growth and public renewal that could interact fruitfully with the rules and daily practices of other institutions. An education rooted in the lived experience of one particular region would of course be conditioned by that region's culture, history, and geography, but the practical knowledge and experimental cast of mind gained through such an education would allow for a communal redefinition of the individual and his or her culture analogous to that achieved through medieval ritual.

> The cultivation of the senses, by visual and tactile explorations of the environment, the intensification and communal refinement of feelings in the group activities of sport, in the theater, where the spectator and actor may interchange parts, in the civic festival and religious ritual, above all in the relations of friends, lovers, mates— this is the essential *business* of life, and all other business is trivial except as a preparation and an underpinning to these experiences. The active routine and the orderly duties of workshop, farm, and office are likewise essential contributions to this education: but so far from education's being ordered merely to prepare the pupil for assuming the economic responsibilities of maturity, it is no less important to order industry so that it will contribute to the maturing educational needs of its members.

Full citizenship in one's culture—by way of an education steeped in local experience—evoked loyalty to a process of civic reinvention through symbolic form, not passivity and conformity.[39]

As in his program of neotechnic organic transformation, the responsibility for creating regional places for the exercise of cultural citizenship rested largely in the hands of the Scipian intellectuals and planners Mumford identified in his 1931 "Preface to Action." But when Mumford speculated most freely about the regional utopias he advocated, he found room for a participatory politics that cut sharply against the grain of his Scipian program of elitist reconstruction. Once the Scipians had finished their job of organic planning, grass-roots politics would take over, and ordinary people would have a central role in the civic life of the community. Here Mumford returned to his own roots in the populism of Morris and Henry George and to Dewey's pragmatic conception of the public sphere and advocated local-level participatory democracy as the best alternative to an abstract liberalism. However vitiated by its reliance on a strategy of initial planning from above, this vision of regionalism in action retains intact the democratic impulse that originally motivated Mumford and the other Young Americans.

The real alternative to the empty political patterns of the nineteenth century lies, not in totalitarianism, but in just the opposite of this: the restoration of the human scale in government, the multiplication of the units of autonomous service, the widening of the cooperative processes of government, the general reduction of the area of arbitrary compulsion, the restoration of the processes of persuasion and rational agreement. Political life, instead of being the monopoly of remote specialists, must become as constant a process in daily living as the housewife's visit to the grocer or the butcher, and more frequent than the man's visit to the barber. If the leisure that man has been promised by the machine counts for anything, it must count for the extension of the privilege of being an active political animal. For every phase of group activity, industrial, professional, educational, has its political aspect: each activity raises special problems of power, organization, control, and discipline—problems that cry for intelligent and orderly solutions.

Regional citizenship rested on what Clifford Geertz would later call "local knowledge"—the diversity of practices and modes of reasoning common to a specific place—which Mumford contrasted to the abstract legalism of parliamentary liberalism. This is Mumford's organic community at its most attractive. Public life in an organic regional community would be the ongoing creation of citizens who drew on their diverse cultural perspectives to articulate a range of understandings of the good life, which might then converge in symbolic expressions of a collective civic identity. Citizenship mediated through symbolic form would strengthen the public sphere by defining the common good of a region's people as the use and reinterpretation of its aesthetic practices and ethical norms. What unites a people as citizens, in this view, is not their mute allegiance to the holistic science of Scipian intellectuals but their loyalty to culture: to the process of symbolic interaction that leads often to conflict and disagreement but may also cohere in provisional artistic forms and other manifestations of consensus that give meaning to local community life.[40]

Too often, in the criticism of Mumford and the other Young Americans, this generous vision of a democratic culture gave way to a rhetoric of mystical wholeness, prophetic leadership, and organic mutuality that dissolved politics in silent communion and emptied their ideal of community of the voices and aspirations of real people in real communities. But by insisting that the fully realized self needs a sense of place—a distinct cultural location—and that a democratic polity can flourish only when embedded in a rich "human ecology" of symbolic form, the Young American critics made a precious contribution to our understanding of the relationship between politics and culture.

They made that contribution as much by their example as by their prescriptions for organic renewal. Even at their most mystical and otherworldly, even when most disdainful of the "herd mentality" of their peers, the Young Americans wrote books and articles in the vernacular of their country's literary, moral, and political traditions, posing radical questions in terms familiar to their fellow citizens. The public example of these critics' "antagonistic connection" to their country's values and traditions of discourse may in the end be their greatest political legacy to contemporary radicals, proof that loyalty to one's culture has nothing to do with quietism and complacency. Their critical writings are saturated with images, ideas, and rhetorical devices drawn from Transcendentalism, republicanism, prophetic religion, and pragmatism, a record of how one group of Americans discovered materials close at hand for criticizing their own culture. They also record the ways such local materials answered, however tentatively, the longings for union and transcendence that had preoccupied these men since childhood. In refashioning their culture's public languages, they refashioned themselves as individuals, finding personality at last as citizens of culture.[41]

Epilogue

We are more fortunate than Brooks and Bourne,
because they are a part of our radical tradition.
—RICHARD CHASE,
The Democratic Vista

The Young Americans' theory of a "usable past" places a special burden on any historian attempting to evaluate the significance of their work. The confusion of the historian's task of creatively reinterpreting the past with the revision of history for propagandistic purposes has discredited, for many, the very idea of a usable past. But the Young Americans did not reduce historical knowledge to ideological imperatives. When they spoke of a usable past, they meant to stress that history was indispensable to any understanding of modern culture—and indeed to full citizenship in a democratic community. "We Americans," Mumford complained in 1925, "have always had an infirm sense of history: to us, the past is simply the immediate precursor of the present; it is something we are outliving or sloughing off or getting beyond; that is, something almost disreputable, or at least indiscreet."[1]

For the Young Americans, history, like aesthetic experience, was a means of transcending the boundaries of one's own individual existence. It was a way to reflect on the conditions that placed one in relation to the past, to grasp the potential for change that lay within one's self and one's society. The past was usable in the same way that culture was: it made the relationship between individual consciousness and objective social forces accessible to the critical intelligence of the community as a whole. By returning historical processes to the language of public discourse, the study of a usable past reminded men and women of their talents and limitations as moral agents. "It has taken us a long time to assimilate the notion by which every real culture lives and flourishes," Mumford wrote, "that the past is a state to conserve, that it is a reservoir from which we can replenish our own emptiness, that, so far from being the ever-vanishing moment, it is the abiding heritage in a community's life. Establishing its own special relations with its past, each generation creates anew what lies behind it, as well as what looms in front; and instead of being victimized by those forces which are uppermost at the moment, it gains the ability to select the qualities which it values, and by exercising them it rectifies its own infirmities and weaknesses."[2]

The reception of the Young Americans' cultural criticism by later generations has largely confirmed Mumford's account of his country's historical amnesia. A few others did follow Bourne, Brooks, Frank, and Mumford as dissenters within the progressive intelligentsia. Reinhold Niebuhr, Dwight Macdonald, Dorothy Day, Richard Chase, C. Wright Mills, and Paul Goodman, to name only the most obvious examples, all drew on the Young Americans' thought in their critiques of modern liberalism or in their efforts to pose communitarian alternatives to the bureaucratic culture of advanced industrialism. Bourne's ideal of the Beloved Community became a slogan of the early New Left and the civil rights movement. Bourne himself briefly achieved the status of a cultural icon in the 1960s, when a later generation of antiwar radicals embraced him as a spiritual godfather. Mumford's critique of industrial technology and the megalopolis gained a new audience at the same time, and his writings continue to inspire those in search of a "green" politics and an ecologically sound way of life.

Yet the Young Americans' work has generated no coherent tradition of cultural and political theory. F. O. Matthiessen, Alfred Kazin, and Sherman Paul are the most outstanding heirs to the Young Americans' attempt to make literary history an expression of cultural criticism. Their writings form an intellectual program that links the Young Americans' project to the academic field of American Studies. But the commitment to cultural history as a political critique of self and society that these mid-twentieth-century writers learned from Bourne, Brooks, Frank, and Mumford remains at best a dissident current within contemporary American Studies scholarship. More overtly political intellectuals have, for their part, neglected the Young Americans' insistence on the cultural crisis underlying the impasse of participatory politics in advanced industrial society. Each generation of critical intellectuals has had to rediscover their original insights into the culture of modernity and the politics of the administrative state. Even the socialist Left, which ought to find something of interest in the work of an indigenous radical intelligentsia, has generally shunned their analysis for more familiar Marxist orthodoxies. In 1957, Joseph Starobin, then a former leader of the Communist party, wrote Frank of his surprise at reading

The Re-discovery of America, a book he had avoided during his years of militancy. "I found the book a revelation," he told Frank. Starobin was shocked to discover that Frank and Mumford "were the very men who had explored the crisis of capitalist civilization in depth. You explored it with perspective, and with a concept of the wholeness and fragmentation of Man which should have been part of the Marxist understanding, but in the hands of men who called themselves Marxists and weren't, this understanding became trivial and superficial. The loss was ours."[3]

Marxists have not been the only ones to suffer from inattention to the Young Americans' work. Another more sizable group—left-liberal critics of liberalism—has also been weakened by its ignorance of its predecessors. Its critique of the modern liberal tradition wallows in a state of perpetual intellectual underdevelopment, to the detriment of liberals of all persuasions. The important questions the Young Americans asked some seventy years ago—about the ethical shallowness of Progressivism, the cultural consequences of the industrial division of labor, the dangers posed by the centralized state to local communities, and the crisis of personal identity in a corporate society—have been raised for discussion only at rare intervals, often without any awareness that they had ever been asked before. A coherent intellectual tradition grounded in their criticism would give these questions a deeper resonance in public discourse. Such a tradition would allow contemporary critics of modern culture and politics to build on the Young Americans' work, instead of repeating its original observations. A vital usable past based on the Young Americans' cultural criticism would free present-day criticism from the endless rediscovery of past positions.

The need for such a living tradition of critical thought becomes especially evident in light of the current crisis of American liberalism, which in the 1980s received its most searching analysis in works by philosopher Alasdair MacIntyre and the group of social scientists working under the direction of Robert N. Bellah. MacIntyre's *After Virtue* and the Bellah group's *Habits of the Heart* reiterate themes that occupied thinkers like John Dewey and the Young Americans at the start of this century, although neither book acknowledges the existence of these precursors. Such an omission is not surprising, given the increasing specialization of intellectual disciplines since the first decades of the twentieth century. Bourne, Brooks, Frank, and Mumford deliberately crossed conventional boundaries between literary history, philosophy, and the social sciences. They practiced the vocation of what Russell Jacoby and Michael Walzer would call the "public" or "socially connected" intellectual, committed above all else to the revitalization of civic discussion, not to the creation of new esoteric disciplines. In their view, academic specialization mirrored the industrial organization of culture as an esoteric technique; the Babel of disciplinary languages was one more sign of the disintegration of a common culture and community life. From the vantage point of an overspecialized academy, the Young Americans' work necessarily seems eclectic and impressionistic. To reassert the force of their original insights into subjects treated by later commentators is not to engage in intellectual genealogy, however. At issue is the failure of contemporary cultural criticism to renew itself in dialogue with its predecessors.[4]

Exactly seventy years after Brooks first diagnosed the division of American life into a narrow Lowbrow practice and a rootless Highbrow culture, Robert Bellah and his associates announced that they had discovered a division between "utilitarian" and "expressive" individualism. The utilitarian culture of the workplace, they charge, has corrupted the public realm by viewing it as a sphere of technical expertise and bureaucratic organization. Expressive individualism, with its therapeutic cant of "personal growth" and "alternative life-styles," has eroded personal relationships by reducing all choices to matters of private whim, which require no justification by a common set of moral standards. Like MacIntyre, they condemn "the bifurcation of the contemporary world into a realm of the organizational in which ends are taken to be given and are not available for rational scrutiny and a realm of the personal in which judgment and debate are central factors, but in which no rational social resolution of issues is available."[5]

Between the dictates of administrative rationality and the shallow pluralism of the emotivist self there exists no middle ground of cultural practices to ground public and private behavior in an understanding of the good life. The authors of *Habits of the Heart* believe that the dual reign of these two realms of modern experience has prevented the establishment of a true American community, in which "the individual self finds its fulfillment in relationships with others in a society organized through public dialogue." With MacIntyre, they hold that a coherent community life and a secure sense of selfhood require a return to the Aristotelian language of civic friendship, in which public and private lives converge in a common devotion to the good. Such a project cuts against the grain of contemporary political discourse, they argue, because it rejects the usual debates between free-market conservatives and liberal defenders of the welfare state as irrelevant to the greater tasks of civic reconstruction and moral renewal. "What matters at this stage," MacIntyre concludes, "is the construction of local forms of community within which civility and the intellectual and moral life can be sustained through the new dark ages which are already upon us."[6]

These contemporary studies in communitarian thought directly recall the Young Americans' early critique of the cultural schism within industrial life. What is even more surprising, however, is that they also recall the Young Americans' difficulties in formulating genuine alternatives to the culture of industrialism. Bellah and his associates invoke a new civic language that lacks any specific political content. There are no conflicts within society or within the human psyche, in their view, that a new language cannot resolve. MacIntyre's book ends—as so many of Mumford's did, after 1940—with a vision of a collective spiritual withdrawal comparable to that made by the early Christians during the late Roman Empire. In both cases, the call to a common culture founders on the same two issues that presented the Young Americans with such difficulties: the relationship between moral and civic renewal and the politics of industrial society; and the predicament of a tradition-based criticism in an age that has broken its ties to traditions. Jeffrey Stout accurately notes the "terminal wistfulness" of this communitarian critique of modern culture and politics. "Denouncing its age, it implicitly announces its own impotence, escaping despair, if at all, only by gesturing weakly toward the future or the past."[7]

The challenge facing Bourne, Brooks, Frank, and Mumford in the 1910s, 1920s, and 1930s was how to envision a project of cultural and moral renewal that engaged modern conditions while simultaneously calling them into question. At their best, the Young Americans heightened the tensions within modern society in an effort to stimulate awareness of the need for their transcendence. Thus Bourne's understanding of personality, Brooks's craft ideal of culture and selfhood, Frank's early aesthetics, and Mumford's theories of symbolic interaction and cultural citizenship all sought to foster a creative tension between the claims of spirit and society, culture and practice, self and community. In Mumford's best work, Bourne's vision of "the good life of personality lived in the environment of the Beloved Community" found its fullest expression. Throughout the 1920s, at least, Mumford tried to preserve an uneasy fit between the self and society, even within the most beloved of communities: the friction between consciousness and the objective world alone gave meaning to life in a public language of forms and symbols. That language heightened the community's resources for reflection and critical thought. It made the social and natural environment accessible to the imagination and gave a home to the individual's longings for self-transcendence in the public world of culture. For Mumford, symbolic communication demonstrated the ability of men and women to participate freely in creating new bonds of association and mutual aid—to act, in other words, as citizens of their own culture. The dialogue of cultural expression played a role in his criticism analogous to that of scientific method in Dewey's pragmatism. In both cases, cultural form was inseparable from political content. Like Dewey's public realm of experiment and education, Mumford's dialogue of symbolic interaction viewed the Beloved Community as an ongoing, reciprocal process of individual and civic regeneration. There was no distinction, for either man, between the method of public inquiry and the values inherent in a good life. Democratic ends inhered in the means citizens used to articulate their conception of the common good.

The obvious problem with this theory of cultural and political change is its vagueness about questions of power. Mumford's theory of symbolic interaction preserved the promise of Deweyan pragmatism from its tendency to idealize scientific technique and industrial organization. His moral realism about the limits of selfhood in the late 1920s was an essential corrective to theories of personal growth that promoted a boundless sense of self, as in the mystical strain of communitarianism that mesmerized Brooks and Frank. But Mumford never fully addressed the ways in which power reproduces itself through language. Nor did he consider the potential for self-deception inherent in any effort at self-definition through cultural forms. Like Bellah and MacIntyre in the 1980s, Mumford counterposed the logic of language and cultural representation to that of bureaucratic rationality without considering how closely the two might be intertwined in modern societies. He did not inquire whether the issues of power at stake in creating new communities could be resolved through culture alone. The current discussion about culture and democratic renewal arrives at the same critical impasse that Mumford reached more than a half-century ago.

What Mumford and the other Young Americans can offer their successors is their incisive critique of the industrial division of labor, their belief in shoring up the cultural foundations of citizenship, and their recognition that personal growth is possible only through participation in a common civic culture. With Morris and Dewey, they shared a deep antagonism to the destruction of craftsmanship and practical knowledge that attended the rise of the factory system. The ideal of craft as a culture of conscious experience was the point at which the traditions of Deweyan pragmatism and Morrisite radicalism met, and it was at this juncture that the Young Americans launched their own indictment of modern culture. A resurgent public philosophy cannot ignore their case for the revival of craftsmanship as a central element of any program for cultural renewal. The Young Americans' defense of craft returns the critique of modern culture to the social and political arrangements of advanced industrial societies. Their analysis makes the recovery of a common civic life dependent upon the reintegration of art and labor in new forms of creative work. It demands the democratization of work as well as the democratization of culture.

Those concerned about the waning commitment to public life in a consumer culture can still benefit from the vision of democratic self-realization articulated by Dewey and the Young Americans at the start of this century. Their attempts to foster a "culture of personality" linking personal growth to participation in the making and remaking of civic identity should in no way be mistaken for a therapeutic gospel of accommodation to existing industrial realities. On the contrary, their joining of civic and self-renewal remains a powerful indictment of modern bureaucratic institutions and an important restatement of the republican tradition's understanding of citizenship. A politics based on such premises begins with the recognition that much of what passes for self-absorption in a private realm devoted to consumption is in fact a search for moral meaning and selfhood that our public institutions either refuse to acknowledge or make impossible. It insists on the public roots of the frustrations most people experience as purely private dissatisfactions. A politics of democratic self-realization seeks to repair the damage done to our civic culture by promoting a common discourse about our ills and our aspirations.

The fundamental lesson of the Young Americans' analysis of industrial culture is that the creation of personal identity, the reconstruction of a public language, and the enrichment of practical activity must proceed together. Only then will the desire for self-realization find fulfillment in the durable artifacts of a common culture. "The craftsman perfects his art," writes Richard Bernstein, "not by comparing his product to some 'ideal' model, but by the cumulative results of experience— experience which benefits from tried and tested procedures, but always involves risk and novelty." The work of the Young Americans remains of essential value to those crafting a future Beloved Community because it challenges us to make the renewal of creative experience the means and end of a democratic politics. Their criticism provides no recipes for community, no prescriptions for personality. Instead, like the assembled lore of a living craft, it subverts the hubris of the present, reminds us of the ways past cultures have ordered human experience, and opens up the future to our capacity for innovation.[8]

Notes

Introduction

1. Randolph Bourne, "Trans-national America," in *The Radical Will: Randolph Bourne Selected Writings, 1911–1918*, ed. Olaf Hansen (New York: Urizen Books, 1977), p. 264.
2. Waldo Frank, "The Seven Arts," *Golden Goose* 3 (1951): 20.
3. See R. Jackson Wilson, *In Quest of Community: Social Philosophy in the United States, 1860–1920* (New York: Oxford University Press, 1968); Jean B. Quandt, *From the Small Town to the Great Community: The Social Thought of Progressive Intellectuals* (New Brunswick: Rutgers University Press, 1970); and John L. Thomas, *Alternative America: Henry George, Edward Bellamy, Henry Demarest Lloyd and the Adversary Tradition* (Cambridge, Mass.: Harvard University Press, 1983). See also the treatment of early twentieth-century communitarian theorists of American cultural pluralism in Everett H. Akam, "Pluralism and the Search for Community" (Ph.D. dissertation, University of Rochester, 1989). H. Stuart Hughes, *Consciousness and Society: The Reorientation of European Social Thought, 1890–1930*, rev. ed. (New York: Vintage Books, 1977), p. 39.
4. William M. Sullivan, *Reconstructing Public Philosophy* (Berkeley and Los Angeles: University of California Press, 1986), pp. 157, 158.
5. Charles Taylor, *Hegel and Modern Society* (Cambridge: Cambridge University Press, 1979), p. 71.
6. Walter Rauschenbusch, *Christianity and the Social Crisis*, ed. Robert D. Cross (New York: Harper & Row, 1964), p. 44. Two significant steps in this direction are James T. Kloppenberg, *Uncertain Victory: Social Democracy and Progressivism in European and American Thought, 1870–1920* (New York: Oxford University Press, 1986);. and Robert B. Westbrook, "John Dewey and American Democracy" (Ph.D. dissertation, Stanford University, 1980).

Chapter 1

1. Waldo Frank, *The Unwelcome Man: A Novel* (New York: Boni and Liveright, 1923), pp. 93–94.

2. Van Wyck Brooks, *An Autobiography* (New York: Dutton, 1965), pp. 13, 11.
3. Waldo Frank, *Memoirs of Waldo Frank*, ed. Alan Trachtenberg (Amherst: University of Massachusetts Press, 1973), p. 4.
4. Richard Wightman Fox and T. J. Jackson Lears, Introduction to *The Culture of Consumption: Critical Essays in American History, 1880–1980* (New York: Pantheon, 1983), p. xiii. See also John Higham, "The Reorientation of American Culture in the 1890s," in Higham, *Writing American History: Essays on Modern Scholarship* (Bloomington: Indiana University Press, 1970), pp. 73–102; and T. J. Jackson Lears, *No Place of Grace: Antimodernism and the Transformation of American Culture, 1880–1920* (New York: Pantheon, 1981), for further discussions of the dissolution of Victorian culture.
5. Frank, *Memoirs*, p. 44.
6. Randolph Bourne, "Old Tyrannies," in *The Radical Will: Randolph Bourne Selected Writings, 1911–1918*, ed. Olaf Hansen (New York: Urizen Books, 1977), pp. 172, 169, 173.
7. See Brooks, *Autobiography*, pp. 63, 5–6, 26; Randolph Bourne, "The Social Order in an American Town," *Atlantic Monthly* 111 (February 1913): 233.
8. Frank, *Memoirs*, p. 4; Lewis Mumford, *Sketches from Life: The Autobiography of Lewis Mumford, The Early Years* (New York: Dial Press, 1982), p. 8; Bourne, "The Social Order in an American Town," p. 229.
9. Daniel Walker Howe, "American Victorianism as a Culture," *American Quarterly* 27 (December 1975): 521.
10. Brooks, *Autobiography*, pp. 11, 14, 15, 12; Frank, *Memoirs*, pp. 4, 11, 29, 12.
11. Van Wyck Brooks, *Opinions of Oliver Allston* (New York: Dutton, 1941), p. 15; Brooks, *Autobiography*, pp. 74, 69, 10–11. See also James Hoopes, *Van Wyck Brooks: In Search of American Culture* (Amherst: University of Massachusetts Press, 1977), pp. 6–7; Raymond Nelson, *Van Wyck Brooks: A Writer's Life* (New York: Dutton, n.d.), pp. 9–10, 26.
12. Brooks, "Diary and Commonplace Book," MS in Van Wyck Brooks Collection, Department of Special Collections, Van Pelt Library, University of Pennsylvania; Brooks, *Autobiography*, pp. 70–71; Brooks, "Enterprise," *Seven Arts* 1 (November 1916): 58. See Hoopes, *Brooks*, pp. 24–26; Nelson, *Brooks*, pp. 12–15.
13. Waldo Frank, "I Discover the New World," in Frank, *In the American Jungle (1925–1936)* (New York: Farrar & Rinehart, 1937), p. 3; Frank, *Memoirs*, p. 17.
14. Frank, *Memoirs*, p. 3.
15. Ibid., pp. 21–22, 30–31.
16. John Adam Moreau, *Randolph Bourne: Legend and Reality* (Washington, D.C.: Public Affairs Press, 1966), pp. 3–5; see also Bruce Clayton, *Forgotten Prophet: The Life of Randolph Bourne* (Baton Rouge: Louisiana State University Press, 1984), pp. 7–9.
17. Moreau, *Randolph Bourne*, p. 13.
18. Mumford, *Sketches from Life*, pp. 3, 25, 34, 31–32, 43, 35. See also Donald L. Miller, *Lewis Mumford: A Life* (New York: Weidenfeld & Nicolson, 1989), chap. 1.
19. Mumford, *Sketches from Life*, pp. 13–14, 18; see Mumford, "The Marriage of Museums," in Mumford, *Findings and Keepings: Analects for an Autobiography* (New York: Harcourt Brace Jovanovich, 1975), pp. 29–36.

20. Van Wyck Brooks, *The Malady of the Ideal* (Philadelphia: University of Pennsylvania Press, 1947).
21. Mumford, *Sketches from Life*, pp. 43, 38, 46–50, 55–56.
22. Ibid., pp. 32, 57; Miller, *Mumford*, p. 19. Miller's first chapter powerfully evokes the grimness of Mumford's childhood and the confining atmosphere of his mother's social routine.
23. Randolph Bourne, "History of a Literary Radical," in *Radical Will*, ed. Hansen, pp. 421–22; Bourne, "The Handicapped," ibid., p. 76; Bourne, *Education and Living* (New York: Century Company, 1917), p. 35; Natalie Bourne Fenninger to Alyse Gregory, 23 May 1948, in Randolph S. Bourne Papers, Rare Book and Manuscript Library, Columbia University.
24. Randolph Bourne, "Fragment of a Novel," in *The History of a Literary Radical*, ed. Van Wyck Brooks (New York: B. W. Huebsch, 1920), pp. 324, 326–28, 332, 333.
25. Ibid., p. 307; Mumford, *Sketches from Life*, pp. 10–12; Bourne, "Fragment of a Novel," pp. 303, 305; Brooks, *Autobiography*, p. 66; Bourne, "The Life of Irony," in *Radical Will*, ed. Hansen, p. 145; see also Christopher Lasch, *The New Radicalism in America (1889–1963): The Intellectual as a Social Type* (New York: Vintage Books, 1965), pp. 113–14.
26. Randolph Bourne, "This Older Generation," in *Radical Will*, ed. Hansen, p. 161; Bourne, "Fragment of a Novel," pp. 321–22.
27. Bourne, "History of a Literary Radical," p. 421; Brooks, *Autobiography*, p. 13.
28. Waldo Frank, *Our America* (New York: Boni and Liveright, 1919), pp. 92, 79, 85.
29. Ibid., pp. 86–87; Frank, Notebook IV (1909–11), in Waldo Frank Collection, Department of Special Collections, Van Pelt Library, University of Pennsylvania.
30. Waldo Frank, "That Israel May Live," in Frank, *The Jew in Our Day* (New York: Duell, Sloan and Pearce, 1944), p. 92; Frank, "Toward an Analysis of the Problem of the Jew," ibid., p. 47; Frank, *Memoirs*, p. 15.
31. Bourne to Prudence Winterrowd, 5 February 1913, in *The Letters of Randolph Bourne: A Comprehensive Edition*, ed. Eric J. Sandeen (Troy, N.Y.: Whitston, 1981), pp. 71–72; Bourne to Henry W. Elsasser, 10 October [1913], ibid., p. 154; Frank, *Memoirs*, p. 32; see Lears, *No Place of Grace*, for a broad treatment of these currents in antimodernist thought.
32. Sigmund Freud, *Civilization and Its Discontents*, trans. James Strachey (New York: Norton, 1961), pp. 11–12, 19. I use the term *the feminine ideal* throughout to refer to the Young Americans' vision of union—rather than the more technical psychoanalytical term, *the ego ideal*—because of the identification of this ideal state with feminine or maternal values in these critics' consciousness. For a discussion of the Freudian concept of the ego ideal that has great relevance to my analysis, see J. Chasseguet-Smirgel, "Some Thoughts on the Ego Ideal: A Contribution to the Study of the 'Illness of Ideality,' " *Psychoanalytic Quarterly* 45 (July 1976): 345–73.
33. See Higham, "The Reorientation of American Culture in the 1890s"; Lears, *No Place of Grace*; and Donald Meyer, *The Positive Thinkers: Religion as Pop Psychology from Mary Baker Eddy to Oral Roberts*, 2d ed. (New York: Pantheon, 1981).
34. Frank, *Unwelcome Man*, p. 371.

35. Ibid., pp. 44, 25.
36. Ibid., pp. 28, 27, 40, 202.
37. Ibid., p. 312.
38. Ibid., pp. 92, 95, 122, 255.
39. Ibid., pp. 259, 205.
40. Ibid., pp. 141–43.
41. Ibid., pp. xi, 357.
42. Frank, *Memoirs*, pp. 5, 7, 6.
43. Ibid., pp. 9, 19, 11.
44. Waldo Frank, *The Rediscovery of Man: A Memoir and a Methodology of Modern Life* (New York: George Braziller, 1958), pp. 256–57; Frank, Notebook IV (1909–11).
45. Quoted in Alan Trachtenberg, "Editor's Preface" to Frank, *Memoirs*, p. vii.
46. Van Wyck Brooks, "A Little Sermon," MS in Brooks Collection.
47. Van Wyck Brooks, "The New Temple of Taste," MS in Brooks Collection.
48. Brooks, *Autobiography*, pp. 241, 243–44.
49. Brooks, "Diary and Commonplace Book." For a discussion of Brooks's poems for Eleanor Stimson, see Hoopes, *Van Wyck Brooks*, p. 19.
50. Brooks, "Diary and Commonplace Book."
51. Ibid.
52. Ibid.; Brooks, "Imaginary Letters," MS in Brooks Collection.
53. Quoted in Nelson, *Van Wyck Brooks*, p. 46.
54. Brooks, "The New Temple of Taste," MS in Brooks Collection.
55. Ibid.; Brooks's "strange adventure" quoted in Nelson, *Van Wyck Brooks*, p. 63.
56. Brooks, "Imaginary Letters."
57. Bourne, "Fragment of a Novel," pp. 338–41.
58. See Randolph Bourne, "The Mystic Turned Radical," in *Youth and Life* (Boston: Houghton Mifflin, 1913), pp. 205–13; Bourne, "History of a Literary Radical," p. 433.
59. Lewis Mumford, "The Sense of Myself," in Mumford, *My Works and Days: A Personal Chronicle* (New York: Harcourt Brace Jovanovich, 1979), p. 39.
60. Frank, *Unwelcome Man*, pp. 167, 169. See, in this regard, Alan Trachtenberg, "Cultural Revisions in the Twenties: Brooklyn Bridge as 'Usable Past,' " in *The American Self: Myth, Ideology, and Popular Culture*, ed. Sam B. Girgus (Albuquerque: University of New Mexico Press, 1981), pp. 58–75. Trachtenberg views this scene in *The Unwelcome Man* more positively than I do here as the first instance of literary efforts at bringing together aesthetic consciousness and technology, a project that culminates in Hart Crane's poem *The Bridge*.
61. Mumford, *Sketches from Life*, pp. 129–30.
62. Ibid., p. 130.

Chapter 2

1. A recent example of the conservative argument, which has parallels in the liberal and Marxist positions I mention, is Aileen Kraditor, *The Radical Persuasion, 1890–1917: Aspects of the Intellectual History and Historiography of Three American Radical Organizations* (Baton Rouge: Louisiana State University Press, 1981).

2. For evidence of the crisis of personal identity prevalent among turn-of-the-century intellectuals and radicals, see Charlotte Perkins Gilman, *The Yellow Wallpaper* (1899; rpt. Old Westbury, N.Y.: Feminist Press, 1973); Christopher Lasch, *The New Radicalism in America (1889–1963): The Intellectual as a Social Type* (New York: Vintage Books, 1965); Neil Coughlan, *Young John Dewey: An Essay in American Intellectual History* (Chicago: University of Chicago Press, 1975); Donald Meyer, *The Positive Thinkers: Religion as Pop Psychology from Mary Baker Eddy to Oral Roberts*, 2d ed. (New York: Pantheon, 1980); Robert B. Westbrook, "John Dewey and American Democracy" (Ph.D. dissertation, Stanford University, 1980); T. J. Jackson Lears, *No Place of Grace: Antimodernism and the Transformation of American Culture, 1880–1920* (New York: Pantheon, 1981); Nick Salvatore, *Eugene V. Debs: Citizen and Socialist* (Urbana: University of Illinois Press, 1982); and T. J. Jackson Lears, "From Salvation to Self-Realization: Advertising and the Therapeutic Roots of the Consumer Culture, 1880–1930," in *The Culture of Consumption: Critical Essays in American History, 1880–1980*, ed. Richard Wightman Fox and T. J. Jackson Lears (New York: Pantheon, 1983), pp. 1–38.

3. Warren I. Susman, *Culture as History: The Transformation of American Society in the Twentieth Century* (New York: Pantheon, 1984), pp. 271–85. Susman's distinction between character and personality recalls David Riesman's well-known contrast of "inner-directed" and "other-directed" character types in Riesman et al., *The Lonely Crowd: A Study of the Changing American Character* (New Haven: Yale University Press, 1961). William Lyon Phelps quoted in Joan Shelley Rubin, "'Information Please!': Culture and Expertise in the Interwar Period," *American Quarterly* 35 (Winter 1983): 504.

4. I expand on this critique of historians' treatment of the therapeutic culture of personality in Casey Blake, "The Young Intellectuals and the Culture of Personality," *American Literary History* 1 (Fall 1989): 510–34.

5. Randolph Bourne, "The Doctrine of the Rights of Man as Formulated by Thomas Paine," in *The Radical Will: Randolph Bourne Selected Writings, 1911–1918*, ed. Olaf Hansen (New York: Urizen Books, 1977), p. 246.

6. Van Wyck Brooks, "The Mission of American Art," *Oracle* 2 (June 1904): 158–59.

7. Ibid., p. 159; Brooks, "A Little Sermon," MS in Van Wyck Brooks Collection, Department of Special Collections, Van Pelt Library, University of Pennsylvania.

8. Van Wyck Brooks, *An Autobiography* (New York: Dutton, 1965), pp. 105, 120. For a discussion of the turn-of-the-century Dante revival and of the Norton circle at Harvard, see Lears, *No Place of Grace*, pp. 155–60, 243–47.

9. Brooks, *Autobiography*, p. 111. I have saved discussion of *The Wine of the Puritans* for the following chapter.

10. Van Wyck Brooks, "The Poet Who Dies Young," 1906, MS in Brooks Collection; Brooks, "The New Temple of Taste," 11 July 1908, MS, ibid.; the second piece from the *Advocate* is cited in James Hoopes, *Van Wyck Brooks: In Search of American Culture* (Amherst: University of Massachusetts Press, 1977), p. 43.

11. Van Wyck Brooks, "Dante and the Literary Temperament," *Harvard Monthly* 42 (March 1906), pp. 15–18.

12. Charles Augustin Sainte-Beuve, "On Sainte-Beuve's Method," in Charles Augustin Sainte-Beuve, *Sainte-Beuve: Selected Essays*, ed. Francis Steegmuller and

Norbert Guterman (New York: Anchor Books, 1963), p. 299; Yeats quoted in Raymond Nelson, *Van Wyck Brooks: A Writer's Life* (New York: Dutton, n.d.), p. 68; Brooks's letter to Eleanor Stimson quoted in Hoopes, *Van Wyck Brooks*, p. 71.

13. Van Wyck Brooks, "Notes on Vernon Lee," *Forum* (April 1911): 449, 454, 455.

14. Van Wyck Brooks, *The Soul: An Essay towards a Point of View* (San Francisco: Privately printed, 1910), p. 12.

15. Ibid., pp. 6–8.

16. Ibid., pp. 7, 12–13.

17. Ibid., pp. 33–34, 10.

18. Ibid., pp. 20, 21.

19. Ibid., p. 35.

20. Ibid., pp. 22, 23.

21. Ibid., pp. 29, 38.

22. Ibid., p. 39.

23. Ibid., p. 40; Hoopes, *Van Wyck Brooks*, p. 79.

24. Van Wyck Brooks, "The Twilight of the Arts," *Poet Lore* 24 (Autumn 1913), pp. 323–24.

25. Ibid., pp. 330, 324.

26. Van Wyck Brooks, *The Malady of the Ideal* (Philadelphia: University of Pennsylvania Press, 1947), pp. 86–87.

27. Ibid., pp. 34, 77.

28. Randolph Bourne, "Youth," in *Radical Will*, ed. Hansen, p. 97; Bourne, *Youth and Life* (Boston: Houghton Mifflin, 1913), p. 291.

29. Olaf Hansen, "Youth and Life: In Search of a Radical Metaphor," in *Radical Will*, ed. Hansen, p. 67.

30. Randolph Bourne, "The Handicapped," in *Radical Will*, ed. Hansen, p. 75; Bourne, *Youth and Life*, pp. 40–41; Bourne, "The Experimental Life," in *Radical Will*, ed. Hansen, p. 152; Bourne, "Youth," p. 101.

31. Bourne, *Youth and Life*, p. 307.

32. Randolph Bourne, "The Dodging of Pressures," in *Radical Will*, ed. Hansen, pp. 126–27, 132.

33. Ibid., p. 115; Bourne, "Youth," p. 105; Bourne, "The Life of Irony," in *Radical Will*, ed. Hansen, pp. 135, 148.

34. Bourne, "The Life of Irony," p. 138.

35. Beulah Amidon to Alyse Gregory, 4 October 1948, in Randolph S. Bourne Papers, Rare Book and Manuscript Library, Columbia University; Bourne to Prudence Winterrowd, 2 March 1913, in *The Letters of Randolph Bourne: A Comprehensive Edition*, ed. Eric J. Sandeen (Troy, N.Y.: Whitston, 1981), pp. 74–75; Bourne, "Some Aspects of Good Talk," *Columbia Monthly* 7 (January 1910), p. 95. Alyse Gregory later recalled of Bourne, "Though he was to so large an extent the leader of his generation in education and politics, his chief interest centered upon personal relationships" (*The Day Is Gone* [New York: Dutton, 1948], p. 135).

36. Bourne to Prudence Winterrowd, 30 June [1913], in *Letters*, ed. Sandeen, pp. 93, 94; Bourne, "The Excitement of Friendship," in *Radical Will*, ed. Hansen, p. 108; Bourne, "The Handicapped," p. 82.

37. For the turn-of-the-century cult of "friendliness" in bureaucratic social rela-

tions, see Robert N. Bellah et al., *Habits of the Heart: Individualism and Commitment in American Life* (Berkeley and Los Angeles: University of California Press, 1985), pp. 118–19; Alasdair MacIntyre, *After Virtue: A Study in Moral Theory*, 2d ed., (Notre Dame: University of Notre Dame Press, 1984), p. 156. See also the discussion of the Aristotelian ideal of friendship in Bellah et al., *Habits of the Heart*, pp. 115–16.

38. Aristotle quoted in Jane J. Mansbridge, *Beyond Adversary Democracy*, rev. ed. (Chicago: University of Chicago Press, 1983), pp. 9, 10.

39. Bourne, "The Doctrine of the Rights of Man as Formulated by Thomas Paine," p. 246.

40. Bourne, "The Handicapped," p. 86; Bourne, "The Life of Irony," p. 148.

41. Bourne, "The Excitement of Friendship," p. 114; Bourne to Alyse Gregory, 16 January 1913, in *Letters*, ed. Sandeen, p. 63.

42. Bourne to Alyse Gregory, 1 June 1913, in *Letters*, ed. Sandeen, p. 87.

43. Bourne to Gregory, 5, 19 January, 13 March 1914, ibid., pp. 200–201, 205, 231–32.

44. Bourne to Gregory, 1 December 1914, ibid., pp. 278–79.

45. Bourne, "The Handicapped," p. 176; Bourne to Alyse Gregory, 24 July 1915, in *Letters*, ed. Sandeen, p. 311. Edward Abrahams has shown how Bourne's determination to maintain his critical independence, even as he sought membership within a group of friends, led to conflicts with the Greenwich Village feminist community. Upon returning to New York from Europe in 1914, Bourne became part of a feminist discussion and consciousness-raising group known as Patchens. Although his break with the group in 1916 resulted largely from personal problems with his old Columbia friend and former roommate Carl Zigrosser and with Zigrosser's wife, Florence King, Bourne recognized that a deeper issue of "personality" was at stake in his inability to remain part of this feminist circle. As he wrote of his discomfort in a pseudonymous article in the *New Republic*, "he would not be a mere social unit" within the group, "shedding satisfaction around" by acquiescing in the views of its dominant members. "He wanted to be always personal, and he would keep on disconcerting his friends by demanding personality of them. He would not let them coalesce into a group and throw bonds of anticipations over him." This argument provides further indication that Bourne's "personal" ideal in friendship and group relations was the very opposite of the affable, accommodating notion of personality that advertisers and therapists advocated as a formula for individual success. See Max Coe [Bourne], "Making One's Contribution," *New Republic* 8 (26 August 1916): 92; Edward Abrahams, "Randolph Bourne on Feminism and Feminists," *Historian* 43 (May 1981): 365–77; and Abrahams, *The Lyrical Left: Randolph Bourne, Alfred Stieglitz, and the Origins of Cultural Radicalism in America* (Charlottesville: University Press of Virginia, 1986), pp. 70–77.

46. Bourne, "The Dodging of Pressures," pp. 123–24.

Chapter 3

1. Randolph Bourne, "In the Mind of the Worker," *Atlantic Monthly* 113 (June 1914): 377, 378, 381–82.

2. Walter Rauschenbusch, *Christianity and the Social Crisis*, ed. Robert D. Cross (New York: Harper & Row, 1964), pp. 313, 182.

3. The differing attitudes toward science and scientific method among the Progressive intelligentsia of the 1910s are described in James A. Nuechterlein, "The Dream of Scientific Liberalism: The *New Republic* and American Progressive Thought, 1914–1920," *Review of Politics* 42 (1980): 167–90; and Mark Pittenger, "Science, Culture and the New Socialist Intellectuals before World War I," *American Studies* 28 (Spring 1987): 73–91. The *New Republic* editors Nuechterlein describes saw scientific method as justification for a politics of expertise and efficient administration from above, whereas the intellectuals Pittenger discusses—most notably William English Walling—exploited the critical aspects of scientific thought to free socialism from its reliance on evolutionary and technocratic thinking. This tension between science as a counsel of elite administration and as a means of liberating individuals' ability to control their own environment runs throughout Progressive social thought in this period. Walter Lippmann's 1914 manifesto, *Drift and Mastery: An Attempt to Diagnose the Current Unrest* (Madison: University of Wisconsin Press, 1985), is probably the best example of this tendency to conflate the technocratic and democratic approaches to science and scientific method.

4. Van Wyck Brooks, *America's Coming-of-Age* (Garden City, N.Y.: Doubleday, 1958), pp. 95–96.

5. For the continuing significance of Catholic thought for Bourne's radicalism, see the posthumously published essay "The Uses of Infallibility," in *The Radical Will: Randolph Bourne Selected Writings, 1911–1918*, ed. Olaf Hansen (New York: Urizen Books, 1977), pp. 494–505, in which Bourne wrote that Cardinal Newman's *Apologia Pro Vita Sua* "in 1917 suggests less a reactionary theology than a subtle and secret sympathy with certain veins of our modern intellectual radicalism" (p. 494).

6. Randolph Bourne, "Socialism and the Catholic Ideal," *Columbia Monthly* 10 (November 1912), pp. 15, 16.

7. Ibid., pp. 11, 14, 15.

8. Ibid., p. 11.

9. Ibid., pp. 17, 18.

10. Ibid., p. 15.

11. Bourne to Alyse Gregory, 11 December 1913, in *The Letters of Randolph Bourne: A Comprehensive Edition*, ed. Eric J. Sandeen (Troy, N.Y.: Whitston, 1981), p. 181; Bourne, "Mon Amie," in *Radical Will*, ed. Hansen, p. 441.

12. Bourne to Arthur Macmahon, 30 January 1914, in *Letters*, ed. Sandeen, p. 216; Bourne, "Mon Amie," pp. 437, 441.

13. On Bourne's reactions to French culture and university life, see *Letters*, ed. Sandeen, pp. 185, 203, 219, 234; Bourne to Henry W. Elsasser, 20 January 1914, and Bourne to Carl Zigrosser, 6 March [1914], ibid., pp. 212, 225; Bourne to Alyse Gregory, 18 March 1914, ibid., p. 237; Bourne to Carl Zigrosser, 20 May 1914, ibid., p. 256; Bourne, "Impressions of Europe, 1913–14," *Columbia University Quarterly* 17 (March 1915): 116, 117; Bourne to Prudence Winterrowd, 23 March 1914, in *Letters*, ed. Sandeen, p. 239. For Waldo Frank's views on the *unanimistes* and the Vieux Colombier, see, among other works, "The Art of the Vieux Colombier," in Waldo Frank, *Salvos: An Informal Book about Books and Plays* (New York: Boni and Liveright, 1924), pp. 119–

67, and Frank's novel *City Block* (Darien, Conn.: By the Author, 1922), which was deeply indebted to Romains's *unanimisme*.

Bourne's praise for the democratic nature of France's national character is in strange contrast to his admiring portrait of Maurice Barrès, the French nationalist whose cultural traditionalism would later influence politicians of the extreme Right. See Bourne, "Maurice Barrès and the Youth of France," *Atlantic Monthly* 114 (September 1914): 394–99. When read in light of the subsequent trajectory of the young Frenchmen influenced by Barrès, Bourne's essay suggests the need for caution in enlisting nationalist notions of tradition, mutuality, and organic culture for a democratic communitarianism. Bourne seemed aware of the potential authoritarianism in Barrès's thought, but he hoped (p. 399) that such tendencies would be leavened with the spirit of William James "and of our divine poet of democracy, Walt Whitman." His essay ends on an overly hopeful note: "A traditionalism, rich and appealing like that of Barrès, but colored by this new social and pragmatic feeling, seems the best of guaranties that the younger generation in France . . . will not go very permanently or very far along the path of obscurantism and reaction."

14. Bourne to Alyse Gregory, 30 July 1914, in *Letters*, ed. Sandeen, p. 263.
15. Bourne to Gregory, 18 March 1914, ibid., p. 238.
16. Bourne, "Socialism and the Catholic Ideal," p. 17; Bourne to Alyse Gregory, 24 July 1915, in *Letters*, ed. Sandeen, p. 312; Bourne, *Education and Living* (New York: Century Company, 1917), p. vi; for information on Croly's recruitment of Bourne for the *New Republic*, see David W. Levy, *Herbert Croly of the New Republic: The Life and Thought of an American Progressive* (Princeton: Princeton University Press, 1985), p. 209.
17. Robert B. Westbrook, "John Dewey and American Democracy" (Ph.D. dissertation, Stanford University, 1980), pp. 36, 37. I wish to acknowledge my tremendous debt to Robert Westbrook for whatever understanding of Dewey's philosophy I have managed to convey in these pages. I thank him for his relentless efforts to educate me on this subject.

One of the great ironies of the intellectual New Left is that a movement that owed so much to Dewey's conception of democracy ended up writing so many mistaken things about Dewey, parodying him as a positivist theorist of a technocratic "corporate liberalism." For examples of this line of argument, see Clarence Karier, "Making the World Safe for Democracy: An Historical Critique of John Dewey's Pragmatic Liberal Philosophy in the Warfare State," *Educational Theory* 27 (Winter 1977): 12–47, and R. Jeffrey Lustig, *Corporate Liberalism: The Origins of Modern American Political Theory, 1890–1920* (Berkeley and Los Angeles: University of California Press, 1982). Much of this critique recalls Max Horkheimer's 1947 portrait of Dewey as a positivist enemy of critical reason in *Eclipse of Reason* (New York: Continuum, 1974). Fortunately, Westbrook's forthcoming book should set the record straight by rehabilitating Dewey as a radical theorist of participatory democracy. For other recent scholarship on pragmatism and Dewey's democratic radicalism corroborating Westbrook's interpretation, see James T. Kloppenberg, *Uncertain Victory: Social Democracy and Progressivism in European and American Social Thought, 1870–1920* (New York: Oxford University Press, 1986); and William M. Sullivan, *Recon-*

structing Public Philosophy (Berkeley and Los Angeles: University of California Press, 1986).

18. Dewey quoted in Westbrook, "John Dewey," p. 17; John Dewey, *Democracy and Education: An Introduction to the Philosophy of Education* (New York: Free Press, 1966), p. 295.

19. Randolph Bourne, "John Dewey's Philosophy," in *Radical Will*, ed. Hansen, p. 334.

20. Even Richard Rorty, who has emphasized the aesthetic and romantic dimensions of Dewey's reconstruction of philosophy in his own writings on pragmatism, acknowledges that "there is . . . another side of Dewey in which philosophy is not vision but something much more specific—a criticism of society following 'the method of science' in the hope of bringing morals and institutions into line with the spirit of science and technology." Rorty's judgment that "Dewey was at his best when he emphasized the similarities between philosophy and poetry, rather than when he emphasized those between philosophy and engineering," was certainly shared by the Young Americans, as I argue in Chapter 5. See Rorty, "Overcoming the Tradition: Heidegger and Dewey," in Rorty, *Consequences of Pragmatism (Essays, 1972–1980)* (Minneapolis: University of Minnesota Press, 1982), p. 56 n. 38.

21. John Dewey, *The School and Society* (Chicago: University of Chicago Press, 1956), pp. 12, 152.

22. Bourne, "John Dewey's Philosophy," p. 332. Although this contradictory conception of reason was always implicit in Dewey's early work, it did not become fully evident until 1920, when he published *Reconstruction in Philosophy*, his sweeping revision and critique of the Western philosophical tradition (Boston: Beacon Press, 1957), especially chapter 2, where he identifies Francis Bacon as a forerunner of his philosophy. Of particular note is his statement that "the office of the new logic" of philosophy after Bacon "would be to protect the mind against itself: to teach it to undergo a patient and prolonged apprenticeship to fact in its infinite variety and particularity: to obey nature intellectually in order to command it practically" (p. 36). When read in conjunction with his exhortations to model social science and philosophy after natural science, this statement cannot fail to make one uneasy about the ambiguities in Dewey's enterprise. The book's recurrent celebrations of scientific technique as an alternative to idealism often threaten to undermine Dewey's masterful insight into rational discourse as the foundation of democratic decision making.

23. See Robert Westbrook, "Lewis Mumford, John Dewey and the 'Pragmatic Acquiescence,' " in *Lewis Mumford: Public Intellectual*, ed. Agatha C. Hughes and Thomas P. Hughes (New York: Oxford University Press, 1990) for a discussion of this critical distinction between adaptation and accommodation in Dewey's thought.

24. Westbrook, "John Dewey," p. 108; Dewey, *School and Society*, p. 18; Bourne, "John Dewey's Philosophy," p. 333.

25. Dewey, *School and Society*, p. 27. See also John Dewey, *The Child and the Curriculum* (Chicago: University of Chicago Press, 1956), pp. 5–8.

26. Dewey, *School and Society*, pp. 132–33. See Alasdair MacIntyre, *After Virtue: A Study in Moral Theory*, 2d ed. (Notre Dame: University of Notre Dame Press, 1984), p. 187: "By a 'practice' I am going to mean any coherent and complex

form of socially established cooperative human activity through which goods internal to that form of activity are realized in the course of trying to achieve those standards of excellence which are appropriate to, and partially definitive of, that form of activity, with the result that human powers to achieve excellence, and human conceptions of the ends and goods involved, are systematically extended." I am indebted to discussions with Richard W. Fox for insight into the connections between Dewey's philosophy and the Aristotelian tradition.

27. Dewey quoted in Westbrook, "John Dewey," p. 107; Dewey, *School and Society*, p. 134.

28. Dewey, *School and Society*, pp. 8, 59. On Deweyan educational reform versus business critics of traditional education, see Raymond E. Callahan, *Education and the Cult of Efficiency* (Chicago: University of Chicago Press, 1962), esp. chap. 6, which describes how business reformers appropriated the language and style employed by William Wirt in the Gary school reform without any of Wirt's democratic content. See also Christopher Lasch, *The World of Nations: Reflections on American History, Politics, and Culture* (New York: Vintage Books, 1972), pp. 256–61, on the convergence of Deweyan thought and efficiency-minded educational reform in the Progressive school movement.

29. Randolph Bourne, "A Moral Equivalent for Universal Military Service," in *War and the Intellectuals: Essays by Randolph S. Bourne, 1915–1919*, ed. Carl Resek (New York: Harper & Row, 1964), p. 146; Bourne to Elsie Clews Parsons, n.d. [1915], in Elsie Clews Parsons Papers, American Philosophical Society, Philadelphia.

30. William James, "The Moral Equivalent of War," in *The Writings of William James*, ed. John J. McDermott (Chicago: University of Chicago Press, 1967), p. 669.

31. Randolph Bourne, "In a Schoolroom," in *Radical Will*, ed. Hansen, pp. 186, 188; Bourne, *Education and Living*, p. 192.

32. Randolph Bourne, "The Cult of the Best," in *Radical Will*, ed. Hansen, pp. 193, 195.

33. Bourne, *Education and Living*, pp. 61, 65; Bourne, "The Cult of the Best," p. 195.

34. Randolph Bourne, "Class and School," in *Radical Will*, ed. Hansen, p. 207; Bourne, *The Gary Schools* (Cambridge, Mass.: MIT Press, 1970), pp. 171–72.

35. Bourne, "A Moral Equivalent for Universal Military Service," p. 145.

36. Van Wyck Brooks, *An Autobiography* (New York: Dutton, 1965), p. 218; Brooks quoted in James Hoopes, *Van Wyck Brooks: In Search of American Culture* (Amherst: University of Massachusetts Press, 1977), pp. 94–95.

37. Van Wyck Brooks, "Harvard and American Life," *Contemporary Review*, 12 December 1908, pp. 610, 618, 613.

38. Ibid., pp. 612, 616, 618. For the critical response to the rise of the modern university by defenders of "liberal culture," see Lawrence R. Veysey, *The Emergence of the Modern University* (Chicago: University of Chicago Press, 1965), chap. 4, and Stow Persons, *The Decline of American Gentility* (New York: Columbia University Press, 1973), chap. 6.

39. Brooks, "Harvard and American Life," p. 611.

40. Van Wyck Brooks, *The Wine of the Puritans*, in *Van Wyck Brooks: The Early Years, A Selection from His Works, 1908–1921*, ed. Claire Sprague (New York: Harper & Row, 1968), p. 9.

41. Ibid., pp. 3, 10, 26, 27.

42. Ibid., p. 6.

43. Ibid., pp. 59, 56.

44. Ibid., p. 59.

45. Brooks, *Autobiography*, pp. 205–6.

46. Raymond Williams, *Culture and Society, 1780–1950* (New York: Harper & Row, 1966), p. xvi. Williams's discussion of the opposition of *culture* and *society* informs much of the following discussion. See also the discussion of these terms in Williams's *Keywords: A Vocabulary of Culture and Society* (New York: Oxford University Press, 1976), pp. 76–82, 243–47. Matthew Arnold, *Culture and Anarchy*, ed. J. Dover Wilson (London: Cambridge University Press, 1961). See, among other passages, p. 202: "Through culture seems to lie our way, not only to perfection, but even to safety. Resolutely refusing to lend a hand to the imperfect operations of our Liberal friends, disregarding their impatience, taunts, and reproaches, firmly bent on trying to find in the intelligible law of things a firmer and sounder basis for future practice than any which we have at present, and believing this search and discovery to be, for our generation and circumstances, of yet more vital and pressing importance than practice itself, we nevertheless may do more, perhaps, we poor disparaged followers of culture, to make the actual present, and the frame of society in which we live, solid and seaworthy, than all which our bustling politicians can do."

47. For an analysis of the tensions between conservative and democratic conceptions of culture in Victorian America, see Alan Trachtenberg, *The Incorporation of America: Culture and Society in the Gilded Age* (New York: Hill & Wang, 1982), chap. 5. See also John Tomsich, *A Genteel Endeavor: American Culture and Politics in the Gilded Age* (Stanford: Stanford University Press, 1971); Persons, *Decline of American Gentility*; and Lewis Perry, *Intellectual Life in America: A History* (New York: Franklin Watts, 1984), chap. 6.

48. See Norman MacKenzie and Jeanne MacKenzie, *The Fabians* (New York: Simon & Schuster, 1977).

49. Morris quoted in Williams, *Culture and Society*, p. 154; William Morris, "Art under Plutocracy," in *Political Writings of William Morris*, ed. A. L. Morton (New York: International Publishers, 1973), p. 70.

50. William Morris, "Communism," in *Political Writings*, ed. Morton, pp. 230, 227.

51. Van Wyck Brooks, *The World of H. G. Wells* (New York: Mitchell Kennerley, 1915), pp. 65, 18.

52. Ibid., pp. 88, 97–98.

53. Ibid., pp. 62, 63, 81, 82. For Belloc's and Chesterton's critique of Fabianism, see Hilaire Belloc, *The Servile State* (Indianapolis: Liberty Classics, 1977), and Margaret Canovan, *G. K. Chesterton, Radical Populist* (New York: Harcourt Brace Jovanovich, 1977).

54. Brooks, *World of H. G. Wells*, pp. 145, 137–38.

55. Ibid., pp. 178, 159.

56. Ibid., pp. 182–84.

57. Morris quoted in E. P. Thompson, *William Morris: Romantic to Revolutionary*, 2d ed. (New York: Pantheon, 1976), p. 809.

58. Randolph Bourne, "Trans-national America," in *Radical Will*, ed. Hansen, p. 264.

59. Brooks, *America's Coming-of-Age*, pp. 63, 78.

60. Bourne, "Trans-national America," pp. 254–55.

61. Ibid., p. 250; Brooks, *America's Coming-of-Age*, pp. 3, 7. The idea that *America's Coming-of-Age* borrowed from Santayana's 1911 critique of the "genteel tradition" is mistaken; more likely, Santayana worked from Brooks's *Wine of the Puritans* in his essay. Santayana even echoed Brooks's language in *Wine*, as in his remark that "the country was new, but the race was tried, chastened, and full of solemn memories. It was an old wine in new bottles" (George Santayana, "The Genteel Tradition in American Philosophy," in Santayana, *The Genteel Tradition: Nine Essays*, ed. Douglas L. Wilson [Cambridge, Mass.: Harvard University Press, 1967], p. 38). Note also the parallels between Santayana's treatment of Whitman (pp. 52–53) and of Mark Twain and American humorists (pp. 51–52) and Brooks's analysis of these writers in *Wine*.

62. Brooks, *America's Coming-of-Age*, p. 16; Bourne, "Trans-national America," p. 251.

63. Bourne, "Trans-national America," p. 264; Brooks, *America's Coming-of-Age*, pp. 59, 62, 64.

64. Brooks, *America's Coming-of-Age*, pp. 82–84.

65. Ibid., pp. 18, 84.

66. Bourne, "Trans-national America," p. 260; Bourne, "The Jew and Trans-national America," in *War and the Intellectuals*, ed. Resek, p. 130; Bourne, "Trans-national America," p. 264.

67. Brooks, *America's Coming-of-Age*, p. 18.

68. Bourne, "Trans-national America," p. 264. For the jeremiad tradition in American Puritanism, see Sacvan Bercovitch, "New England's Errand Reappraised," in *New Directions in American Intellectual History*, ed. John Higham and Paul Conkin (Baltimore: Johns Hopkins University Press, 1979), pp. 85–104. Note especially Bercovitch's dissection of three fundamental elements of the Puritan jeremiad: "first, a precedent from scripture that sets out the communal norms; then, a series of condemnations that detail the actual state of the community; and finally, a prophetic vision that unveils the good things to come, and so explains away the gap between fact and ideal" (p. 90). For an argument about the persistence of this tradition in the work of another twentieth-century American intellectual, see the discussion of Dwight Macdonald's "rhetorical style of the politics of fearful anticipation" in Robert B. Westbrook, "The Responsibility of Peoples: Dwight Macdonald and the Holocaust," in *America and the Holocaust*, ed. Sanford Pinsker and Jack Fischel (Greenwood, Fla.: Penkevill, 1984), p. 55.

Chapter 4

1. Editorial, *Seven Arts* 1 (November 1916): 52. For histories of the *Seven Arts* and its writers, see Claire Sacks, "The *Seven Arts* Critics: A Study of Cultural Nationalism in America, 1910–1930" (Ph.D. dissertation, University of Wisconsin, 1955); Henry May, *The End of American Innocence: A Study of the*

First Years of Our Own Time, 1912–1917 (Chicago: Quadrangle Books, 1959), pp. 322–28; James B. Gilbert, *Writers and Partisans: A History of Literary Radicalism in America* (New York: Wiley, 1968), chap. 1; John S. McCormick, "A Beleaguered Minority: The Young Intellectuals and American Mass Society, 1910–1920" (Ph.D. dissertation, University of Iowa, 1973); Charles L. P. Silet, "*The Seven Arts*: The Artist and the Community" (Ph.D. dissertation, Indiana University, 1973); Arthur Frank Wertheim, *The New York Little Renaissance: Iconoclasm, Modernism, and Nationalism in American Culture, 1908–1917* (New York: New York University Press, 1976), chap. 11; Martin Lloyd Pumphrey, "Art and Leadership in America: The Quest for Synthesis" (Ph.D. dissertation, University of Iowa, 1977); Charles C. Alexander, *Here the Country Lies: Nationalism and the Arts in Twentieth-Century America* (Bloomington: Indiana University Press, 1980), chap. 3; Edward Abrahams, *The Lyrical Left: Randolph Bourne, Alfred Stieglitz, and the Origins of Cultural Radicalism in America* (Charlottesville: University Press of Virginia, 1986).

2. "To the Friends of the Seven Arts," *Seven Arts* 2 (October 1917): 670.

3. The equation of Brooks's and Bourne's criticism with the cultural nationalism of Croly and other Progressives is a feature of Paul F. Bourke's critique of the *Seven Arts* group in "The Status of Politics, 1909–1919: *The New Republic*, Randolph Bourne and Van Wyck Brooks," *Journal of American Studies* 8 (August 1974): 171–202. For similar comparisons of the Young Americans and the Progressive intellectuals at the *New Republic*, see Richard H. Pells, *Radical Visions and American Dreams: Culture and Social Thought in the Depression Years* (New York: Harper & Row, 1973), chap. 1, and James Hoopes, "The Culture of Progressivism: Croly, Lippmann, Brooks, Bourne, and the Idea of American Artistic Decadence," *Clio* 7 (Fall 1977): 91–111. A good counterweight to this argument, which stresses the fundamental divergence between Croly's statist view of national regeneration and Brooks's ideal of cultural renewal, is Peter W. Dowell, "Van Wyck Brooks and the Progressive Frame of Mind," *Midcontinent American Studies Journal* 11 (Spring 1970): 30–44; see also the contrast between Croly and Bourne in Olaf Hansen, "Affinity and Ambivalence," in *The Radical Will: Randolph Bourne Selected Writings, 1911–1918,* ed. Hansen (New York: Urizen Books, 1977), pp. 25–28. Dowell and Hansen confirm Sherman Paul's astute observation that Croly was the "unacknowledged enemy" of Brooks's early work. See Paul, *Repossessing and Renewing: Essays in the Green American Tradition* (Baton Rouge: Louisiana State University Press, 1976), p. 135. Paul's essays remain the most reliable guide to the Young Americans' literary criticism and its relation to American literary history as a whole. On the cosmopolitanism of the *Seven Arts,* see Thomas Bender, *New York Intellect: A History of Intellectual Life in New York City, from 1750 to the Beginnings of Our Own Time* (New York: Knopf, 1987), p. 241; and David A. Hollinger, *In the American Province: Studies in the History and Historiography of Ideas* (Bloomington: Indiana University Press, 1985), p. 59. The cosmopolitan nature of the editorial board may have made the journal's two main gentile writers, Bourne and Brooks, somewhat uneasy, if a 1917 letter by Bourne to Elsie Clews Parsons is any indication. Bourne wrote that Brooks was "dissatisfied there at the Seven Arts. The atmosphere is a queer compound of Jewishness and psychoanalysis, which he finds quite alarming. . . . The 'Seven Arts' has its Freudian

religion and doesn't touch the reformed Puritan strata like Brooks and myself"
(Bourne to Elsie Clews Parsons, 9 May 1917, in Elsie Clews Parsons Papers,
American Philosophical Society, Philadelphia).

4. Waldo Frank, "The Seven Arts," *Golden Goose*, 3, no. 1 (1951): 20. The view
of the Young Americans as "cultural nationalists" is found in Sacks, "The *Seven
Arts* Critics"; Hugh McClellan Potter III, "The Romantic Nationalists of the
1920s" (Ph.D. dissertation, University of Minnesota, 1965); Wertheim, *New
York Little Renaissance*; and Alexander, *Here the Country Lies*. The term *lyrical
left* is used by John P. Diggins to describe the politics of the *Seven Arts*, the
Masses, and the Greenwich Village Renaissance in general. See Diggins, *The
American Left in the Twentieth Century* (New York: Harcourt Brace Jovano-
vich, 1973), chap. 4; and Abrahams, *Lyrical Left*.

5. Randolph Bourne, "The Cult of Convention," *Liberator* 1 (June 1918): 39;
Harold Stearns, *America and the Young Intellectual* (New York: George H.
Doran, 1921), pp. 154–55.

6. Waldo Frank, *Our America* (New York: Boni and Liveright, 1919), p. 9; Van
Wyck Brooks, "Toward a National Culture," *Seven Arts* 1 (March 1917): 547.

7. Frank, *Our America*, p. 232.

8. Van Wyck Brooks, *An Autobiography* (New York: Dutton, 1965), p. 269. (The
remark appears in the second part of Brooks's autobiography, *Days of the Phoe-
nix*, first published in 1957.) James Oppenheim, "The Story of the *Seven Arts*,"
American Mercury 20 (June 1930): 162.

9. Waldo Frank, *Memoirs of Waldo Frank*, ed. Alan Trachtenberg (Amherst: University of Massachusetts Press, 1973), p. 11; William Ernest Hocking to Frank,
8 December 1911, in Waldo Frank Collection, Department of Special Collections, Van Pelt Library, University of Pennsylvania.

10. Waldo Frank, "The Spirit of Modern French Letters," MS in Frank Collection;
Frank, *Memoirs*, p. 48; Frank, Notebook VIII (June 1922–December 1924), in
Frank Collection.

11. Frank, *Memoirs*, p. 68.

12. Waldo Frank, "I Discover the New World," in Frank, *In the American Jungle
(1925–1936)* (New York: Farrar & Rinehart, 1937), pp. 8, 9.

13. Ibid., p. 10.

14. All quotations from Frank, Notebook V (1913–14), in Frank Collection.

15. See, for example, Robert S. Lynd's definition, which he carefully distinguishes
from "the refined sense of *belles lettres* and sophisticated learning." In *Knowledge for What?* Lynd argues for an anthropological conception of culture as "all
the things that a group of people inhabiting a common geographical area do, the
ways they do things and the ways they think and feel about things, their material
tools and their values and symbols" (*Knowledge for What? The Place of Social
Science in American Culture* [Princeton: Princeton University Press, 1967], p.
19). The redefinition of *culture* in the early twentieth century is the subject of
many of the essays in Warren I. Susman, *Culture as History: The Transformation of American Society in the Twentieth Century* (New York: Pantheon, 1984).

16. For early examples of this critique, see Paul Rosenfeld's essay on Brooks in *Port
of New York* (Urbana: University of Illinois Press, 1969), pp. 19–63; Gorham
Munson, "Van Wyck Brooks: His Sphere and His Encroachments," *Dial* 78
(January 1925): 28–42; Harold Stearns, "Van Wyck Brooks: Critic and Cre-

ator," in Stearns, *America and the Young Intellectual*, pp. 24–33; and Edmund Wilson's review of Brooks's *The Pilgrimage of Henry James*, reprinted in *The Portable Edmund Wilson*, ed. Lewis M. Dabney (New York: Penguin, 1983), pp. 125–35. More recently, Charles C. Alexander has repeated this argument in *Here the Country Lies*, p. 37: "Throughout his long critical career Brooks never seemed to make up his mind whether great American artists would be able to transform American society, or whether the transformation of society had to come before there could be great art."

17. Frank's prospectus was reprinted in an unsigned editorial, *Seven Arts* 1 (November 1916): 52–53.

18. Ibid., pp. 55–56.

19. Van Wyck Brooks, "Young America," *Seven Arts* 1 (December 1916): 146–47.

20. Van Wyck Brooks, "Enterprise," *Seven Arts* 1 (November 1916): 59, 58, 60.

21. Van Wyck Brooks, "The Culture of Industrialism," *Seven Arts* 1 (April 1917): 656; Brooks, "The Splinter of Ice," *Seven Arts* 1 (January 1917): 275, 274.

22. Brooks, "Culture of Industrialism," p. 662.

23. Ibid., p. 660; Brooks, "Our Critics," *Seven Arts* 2 (May 1917): 110.

24. Brooks, "Young America," pp. 149–50.

25. Brooks, "Culture of Industrialism," p. 657; Brooks, "Our Awakeners," *Seven Arts* 2 (June 1917): 239.

26. Van Wyck Brooks, *Letters and Leadership*, in Brooks, *America's Coming-of-Age* (Garden City, N.Y.: Doubleday, 1958), pp. 106–7; Brooks, "Toward a National Culture," p. 545.

27. Brooks, "Toward a National Culture," p. 547; Brooks, "Culture of Industrialism," p. 663; Brooks, "Enterprise," p. 59.

28. Brooks, "Culture of Industrialism," pp. 665, 666; Brooks, "Our Critics," p. 113.

29. Alasdair MacIntyre, *After Virtue: A Study in Moral Theory*, 2d ed. (Notre Dame: University of Notre Dame Press, 1984), pp. 222, 223.

30. Brooks, "Our Awakeners," p. 248.

31. Ibid., p. 238.

32. Brooks, "Toward a National Culture," p. 541.

33. Waldo Frank, "Vicarious Fiction," *Seven Arts* 1 (January 1917): 294.

34. Waldo Frank, "Emerging Greatness," *Seven Arts* 1 (November 1916): 73. See Georg Lukács, *The Theory of the Novel*, trans. Anna Bostock (Cambridge, Mass.: MIT Press, 1971).

35. Frank, "Vicarious Fiction," pp. 295–96; Frank, "A Prophet in France," *Seven Arts* 1 (April 1917): 647.

36. Frank, "A Prophet in France," pp. 639, 646, 640.

37. Frank, *Our America*, pp. 141, 144; Sherwood Anderson to Frank, n.d., in Sherwood Anderson Papers, Newberry Library, Chicago; Frank, "Emerging Greatness," p. 74.

38. Frank, *Our America*, p. 184; Frank, *Memoirs*, p. 64.

39. James Oppenheim, Editorial, *Seven Arts* 1 (December 1916): 152–54.

40. Romain Rolland, "America and the Arts," *Seven Arts* 1 (November 1916): 50, 47. In *The Re-discovery of America: An Introduction to a Philosophy of American Life* (New York: Charles Scribner's Sons, 1929), chap. 18, Frank called for the creation of Rolland's "symphonic nation."

41. Frank, *Memoirs*, p. 91; James Oppenheim, Editorial, *Seven Arts* 1 (January 1917): 266, 267; Oppenheim, Editorial, *Seven Arts* 1 (February 1917): 394.
42. James Oppenheim, "Art, Religion and Science," *Seven Arts* 2 (June 1917): 234, 231.
43. James Oppenheim, Editorial, *Seven Arts* 1 (March 1917): 504–5; Oppenheim, Editorial, *Seven Arts* 2 (June 1917): 201; Oppenheim, Editorial, *Seven Arts* 2 (August 1917): 492.
44. Paul L. Rosenfeld, "The American Composer," *Seven Arts* 1 (November 1916): 91, 93–94.
45. Peter Minuit [pseud. Paul Rosenfeld], " '291 Fifth Avenue,' " *Seven Arts* 1 (November 1916): 61–65. Rosenfeld's divergence from Frank's and Brooks's position became even more evident by the early 1920s. By the time he published *Port of New York* in 1924, Rosenfeld believed that Brooks was guilty of repeatedly "drawing an exaggerated picture of the obstacles which surround the aggressive, militant life in America" and of "externalizing problems which are truly internal." This remark complements another, in Rosenfeld's chapter on Stieglitz, in which he absolves American social and cultural conditions of any responsibility for the closing of 291. "It was because of the smallness of the artists that it had to be destroyed," he explained. Rosenfeld's tendency to emphasize the shortcomings of individual artists in recognizing the opportunities of American life was already evident in his contributions to the *Seven Arts*, but it reached a climax of sorts in the epilogue to *Port of New York*. The lyric closing to the collection suggested that Frank's portrait of the estrangement of spirit from New York's urban landscape was now obsolete: "We know it here, our relationship with this place in which we live. The buildings cannot deprive us of it. For they and we have suddenly commenced growing together.... It seems that we have taken root." See Rosenfeld, *Port of New York*, pp. 60, 266, 292.
46. "An American Immigrant," "Following Freedom," *Seven Arts* 2 (September 1917): 548–50.
47. Frank, "Vicarious Fiction," p. 296.
48. "To the Friends of the Seven Arts," p. 670.

Chapter 5

1. Randolph Bourne, "Twilight of Idols," in *The Radical Will: Randolph Bourne Selected Writings, 1911–1918*, ed. Olaf Hansen (New York: Urizen Books, 1977), pp. 337–38. See also Bourne's composite portrait of himself and his friends in "Below the Battle," in *War and the Intellectuals: Essays by Randolph S. Bourne, 1915–1919*, ed. Carl Resek (New York: Harper & Row, 1964), esp. p. 17: "With the outbreak of the Great War, most of his socialist and pacifist theories were knocked flat. The world had turned out to be an entirely different place from what he had thought it. Progress and uplift seemed to be indefinitely suspended." See also "The Disillusionment," in *Radical Will*, ed. Hansen, pp. 396–407, for Bourne's most embittered statement of the war's effects on his youthful idealism.
2. Randolph Bourne, "A War Diary," in *Radical Will*, ed. Hansen, p. 325; Robert Westbrook, "John Dewey and American Democracy" (Ph.D. dissertation, Stanford University, 1980), p. 118. See also Westbrook's treatment of the Bourne-

Dewey debate in "Lewis Mumford, John Dewey and the 'Pragmatic Acquiescence,'" in *Lewis Mumford: Public Intellectual*, ed. Agatha C. Hughes and
Thomas P. Hughes (New York: Oxford University Press, 1990).

3. Paul F. Bourke is right to see the origins of the Young Americans' position in the
English romantic critique of utilitarianism formulated by Carlyle, Arnold, and
Morris. But he misses their synthesis of this tradition with pragmatic principles
when he reduces their critique to "two opposing sets of words and associations:
pragmatism-technique-machinery-means versus poetry-values-quality-of-living-
ends." By ignoring the ways in which Bourne, Brooks, and Frank attempted to
introduce romantic concepts into a pragmatic philosophy of experience, Bourke
is able to portray their position as a retreat from politics. Such an interpretation
obscures the Young Americans' commitment to cultural renewal as a means to
new forms of political and social practice. See Bourke, "The Status of Politics,
1909–1919: *The New Republic*, Randolph Bourne and Van Wyck Brooks,"
Journal of American Studies 8 (August 1974): 193–94.

4. Randolph Bourne, "The War and the Intellectuals," in *Radical Will*, ed. Hansen,
p. 316; John Dewey, "The Future of Pacifism," in *Essays on Philosophy and
Education, 1916–1917: The Middle Works of John Dewey, 1899–1924*, Vol.
10, ed. Jo Ann Boydston (Carbondale: Southern Illinois University Press, 1985),
p. 268; John Dewey, "The Social Possibilities of War," in *Characters and Events:
Popular Essays in Social and Political Philosophy*, Vol. 2, ed. Joseph Ratner
(New York: Henry Holt, 1929), pp. 551–61; Dewey, "The Future of Pacifism,"
p. 268; Bourne, "The War and the Intellectuals," p. 308; Bourne, "A War Diary,"
p. 324; Harold Stearns, *Liberalism in America: Its Origin, Its Temporary Collapse, Its Future* (New York: Boni and Liveright, 1919), p. 181.

5. Bourne, "The War and the Intellectuals," pp. 314, 312.

6. Bourne to Elsie Clews Parsons, 28 May [1917], in Elsie Clews Parsons Papers,
American Philosophical Society, Philadelphia; Waldo Frank, *Our America* (New
York: Boni and Liveright, 1919), pp. 27–28.

7. Bourne, "Twilight of Idols," pp. 343–44.

8. Van Wyck Brooks, "Our Awakeners," *Seven Arts* 2 (June 1917): 242–43.

9. Bourne, "Twilight of Idols," pp. 336, 346; Bourne to Esther Cornell, [September
1917], in *The Letters of Randolph Bourne: A Comprehensive Edition*, ed. Eric J.
Sandeen (Troy, N.Y.: Whitston, 1981), p. 402; Bourne to Agnes de Lima, 6
August [1917], ibid., p. 399.

10. Frank, *Our America*, pp. 20–21. Bourne and Stearns both invoked James's
memory in their polemics against Dewey. See, for example, Bourne, "Twilight of
Idols," p. 338, and Stearns, *Liberalism in America*, pp. 188–89. The latter is
especially interesting as a vindication of pragmatism against its misuse by
Dewey and his followers during the war.

11. Bourne, "A War Diary," pp. 328, 326; Frank, *Our America*, pp. 231–32.

12. Bourne, "A War Diary," p. 328.

13. My discussion of the tension between the Young Americans' role as civic moral-
ists and that of romantic prophets draws on Christopher Lasch's observations
about "the public role of a learned class" in "A Typology of Intellectuals,"
Salmagundi 70–71 (Spring–Summer 1986): 27–32. There Lasch distinguishes
between three ideal types of modern intellectuals: the religious or humanist
intellectual; the Enlightenment rationalist, in either its expert "insider" or radi-

cal "outsider" role; and the romantic rebel. The difficulty with applying this typology directly to the case of the Young Americans lies in their blurring of Lasch's first and third categories of intellectual life in reaction against Enlightenment experts (the prowar liberals) and revolutionaries (the orthodox Left). The issue is further complicated by the relative absence of a traditional humanist-religious intelligentsia in the United States—the subject of much of Brooks's analysis in *America's Coming-of-Age* and his *Seven Arts* essays—which left the Young Americans little ideological or institutional basis for assuming such a position themselves. For similar arguments in defense of the intellectual's vocation as civic conscience, see Russell Jacoby on the "public intellectual" in *The Last Intellectuals: American Culture in the Age of Academe* (New York: Basic Books, 1987); and Michael Walzer's case for the "socially connected" critic in *The Company of Critics: Social Criticism and Political Commitment in the Twentieth Century* (New York: Basic Books, 1988).

It might be useful to conceive of the Young Americans as aspiring "traditional" intellectuals—to use Antonio Gramsci's typology—opposed to the new "organic" intellectuals of bureaucratic industrialism. Gramsci noted "the absence to a considerable degree of traditional intellectuals" in American history, which meant that there existed no cultural force to impede "a massive development, on top of an industrial base, of the whole range of modern superstructures." The Young Americans were certainly in favor of the creation of what Gramsci would later call an "organic" intelligentsia of the working class. Bourne's "transnationalism" was, at least in part, a call for ethnic working-class intellectuals to mediate between immigrant experience and Anglo-Saxon high culture. But their own social backgrounds and their suspicion of the instrumentalization of thought kept the Young Americans from embracing such an "organic" stance themselves. Rather, they hoped to serve as an American equivalent of the European "traditional" intelligentsia and, in the process, lay the foundations for a body of critical insight into modern American life. See Antonio Gramsci, "The Intellectuals," in *Selections from the Prison Notebooks*, ed. and trans. Quintin Hoare and Geoffrey Nowell Smith (New York: International Publishers, 1971), pp. 5–23.

14. Bourne, "The War and the Intellectuals," p. 317; Bourne to Brooks, 27 March 1918, in *Letters*, ed. Sandeen, p. 411.
15. Randolph Bourne, "The Price of Radicalism," in *Radical Will*, ed. Hansen, p. 299.
16. Bourne, "The War and the Intellectuals," p. 317.
17. Walzer, *Company of Critics*, p. 61; Randolph Bourne, "H. L. Mencken," in *Radical Will*, ed. Hansen, p. 474. A letter to Elsie Clews Parsons in July 1918 suggests Bourne's growing doubts about his own place as a critic in the changed climate of wartime America. On one hand, he told Parsons that he was working on his "anti-State philosophy," the political essay posthumously published as "The State." On the other hand, he described how his attempts to write an autobiographical novel were directing his attention away from public events. "The war has practically passed out of my consciousness," he explained, "and, like you, I read the papers almost without emotion" (Bourne to Elsie Clews Parsons, 29 July 1918, in Parsons Papers). This withdrawal into autobiography was a far cry from Bourne's declaration of intellectual independence a year

earlier in "The War and the Intellectuals." At that time he had written Parsons, "I am going to give myself the holy mission of satirizing the war. The only weapon that is safe and effective is ridicule, or at least corrosive irony" (Bourne to Elsie Clews Parsons, n.d. [May 1917], in Parsons Papers). As these letters indicate, Walzer is correct to note Bourne's new tone of bitter despair in 1918 and his fear that his "holy mission" had come to naught.

18. Randolph Bourne, "The History of a Literary Radical," in *Radical Will*, ed. Hansen, pp. 432–33.

19. Bourne to Brooks, 27 March 1918, in *Letters*, ed. Sandeen, pp. 412–13.

20. Ibid., pp. 410, 414.

21. Edmund Wilson, *Letters on Literature and Politics, 1912–1972*, ed. Elena Wilson (New York: Farrar, Strauss and Giroux, 1977), p. 223.; Waldo Frank, *Memoirs of Waldo Frank*, ed. Alan Trachtenberg (Amherst: University of Massachusetts Press, 1973), pp. 81, 88–89. In 1935, he told an alumni representative at Yale that his registration in opposition to the war was "one act of my life with which I am completely satisfied" ("Dear Class Secretary," 30 September 1935, in Waldo Frank Collection, Department of Special Collections, Van Pelt Library, University of Pennsylvania).

22. Brooks to Frank, 27 November 1919, in Frank Collection; Frank, *Memoirs*, p. 99. See the discussion of the magazine's dissolution in Arthur Frank Wertheim, *The New York Little Renaissance: Iconoclasm, Modernism, and Nationalism in American Culture, 1908–1917* (New York: New York University Press, 1976), pp. 219–20.

23. Frank, *Our America*, pp. 232, 230.

24. Ibid., pp. 173, 210.

25. Ibid., pp. 52, 49, 56; see the treatment of Lincoln as "more than an American" in Herbert Croly, *The Promise of American Life* (New York: Capricorn Books, 1964), pp. 89–99.

26. Frank, *Our America*, p. 204.

27. D. H. Lawrence to Frank, 27 July 1917, in Frank Collection.

28. See Frank, *Our America*, chap. 4, "The Land of Buried Cultures"; Frank to Sherwood Anderson, 6 August 1918, in Sherwood Anderson Papers, Newberry Library, Chicago. By contrast, Frank found the Bohemian outpost at Taos "a bit depressing—full of bad artists and currupted [sic] Indians" (Frank, *Our America*, pp. 113–14).

29. Frank to Sherwood Anderson, n.d. [November 1919], 27 November [1919], in Anderson Papers.

30. Frank to Sherwood Anderson, n.d. [November 1919], 27 November [1919], 4 December 1919, ibid.

31. Frank to Sherwood Anderson, 18 December 1919, ibid.

32. Frank to Brooks, 18 December 1919, in Van Wyck Brooks Collection, Department of Special Collections, Van Pelt Library, University of Pennsylvania.

33. Max Weber, "Science as a Vocation," in *From Max Weber: Essays in Sociology*, ed. and trans. H. H. Gerth and C. Wright Mills (New York: Oxford University Press, 1946), p. 155.

34. Bourne to Dorothy Teall, 31 May 1918, in *Letters*, ed. Sandeen, p. 414.

Chapter 6

1. Randolph Bourne, "The State," in *The Radical Will: Randolph Bourne Selected Writings, 1911–1918*, ed. Olaf Hansen (New York: Urizen Books, 1977), p. 367.
2. Randolph Bourne, "The War and the Intellectuals," in *Radical Will*, ed. Hansen, p. 309; Lewis Mumford, untitled essay on the crisis of the socialist left, 1915, MS in Lewis Mumford Collection, Department of Special Collections, Van Pelt Library, University of Pennsylvania.
3. Lewis Mumford, "Patriotism and Its Consequences," *Dial* 66 (19 April 1919): 406.
4. Lewis Mumford, "On the Dial," *New York Review of Books* 2 (20 February 1964): 4. The centrality of organicism in Mumford's thought is the subject of Leo Marx, "Lewis Mumford's Organicist Concept of Technology," in *Lewis Mumford: Public Intellectual*, ed. Agatha C. Hughes and Thomas P. Hughes (New York: Oxford University Press, 1990).
5. Lewis Mumford, *The Story of Utopias* (New York: Viking Press, 1962), p. 17.
6. Alan Trachtenberg, "Mumford in the Twenties: The Historian as Artist," *Salmagundi* 49 (Summer 1980): 34. See also Frank G. Novak, Jr., "Lewis Mumford and the Reclamation of Human History," *Clio* 16 (February 1987): 159–81. See Brooks's comments: "Knowing that others have desired the things we desire and have encountered the same obstacles, and that in some degree time has begun to face those obstacles down and make the way straight for us, would not the creative forces of this country lose a little of the hectic individualism that keeps them from uniting against their common enemies? And would this not bring about, for the first time, that sense of brotherhood in effort and in aspiration which is the best promise of a national culture?" (Van Wyck Brooks, "On Creating a Usable Past," in *Van Wyck Brooks: The Early Years, A Selection from His Works, 1908–1921*, ed. Claire Sprague [New York: Harper & Row, 1968], p. 226).
7. Helen E. Meller, "Patrick Geddes: An Analysis of His Theory of Civics, 1880–1904," *Victorian Studies* 16 (March 1973): 304. Meller's essay is the best summary of Geddes's thought that I know of. See also her fine Introduction in *The Ideal City*, ed. Meller (N.p.: Leicester University Press, 1979). A good anthology of Geddes's writing, including useful biographical materials, is *Patrick Geddes: Spokesman for Man and the Environment*, ed. Marshall Stalley (New Brunswick: Rutgers University Press, 1972). Less helpful as a guide to Geddes's thought is Philip Boardman's biography, *Patrick Geddes, Maker of the Future* (Chapel Hill: University of North Carolina Press, 1944). For Geddes's influence on the young Mumford, see Donald L. Miller, *Lewis Mumford: A Life* (New York: Weidenfeld & Nicolson, 1989), chap. 3; Frank G. Novak, Jr., "Master and Disciple: Selections from the Patrick Geddes–Lewis Mumford Letters," *Horns of Plenty: Malcolm Cowley and his Generation* 2 (Fall 1989): 45–62; Joseph Duffey, "Mumford's Quest: The First Decade," *Salmagundi* 49 (Summer 1980): 61–63; Edy Weber Dow, "Lewis Mumford's First Phase: A Study of His Work as a Critic of the Arts in America" (Ph.D. dissertation, University of Pennsylvania, 1965), pp. 1–34. See also the discussion of Geddes in Rosalind

Williams, "Lewis Mumford as an Historian of Technology in *Technics and Civilization*," in *Lewis Mumford*, ed. Hughes and Hughes.

8. Lewis Mumford, *Technics and Civilization* (New York: Harcourt, Brace, and World, 1962), p. 319.

9. Quoted in Meller, Introduction, *Ideal City*, p. 28.

10. Lewis Mumford, "Patrick Geddes, Insurgent," *New Republic* 60 (30 October 1929): 296.

11. Lewis Mumford, *Sketches from Life: The Autobiography of Lewis Mumford, The Early Years* (New York: Dial Press, 1982), p. 143. In 1915, Mumford noted in the "Random Notes" he kept as a running diary that "Athens during the early sixth century B.C. would have been more to my liking than New York in the twentieth century after Christ. It is true, this would have cut me off from Socrates, who lived in the disappointing period that followed. But then, I might have been Socrates" (Mumford, *Findings and Keepings: Analects for an Autobiography* [New York: Harcourt Brace Jovanovich, 1975], p. 7).

12. Mumford, *Sketches from Life*, p. 196. See also Miller, *Mumford*, pp. 100–106; and Mumford, "The Golden Day Revisited," in Mumford, *The Golden Day: A Study in American Literature and Culture* (Boston: Beacon Press, 1957), p. xiii.

13. Victor Branford and Patrick Geddes, *The Coming Polity: A Study in Reconstruction* (London: Williams and Norgate, 1917), p. 4.

14. Patrick Geddes, *John Ruskin, Economist* (Edinburgh: William Brown, 1884), p. 37; Geddes, *Cities in Evolution: An Introduction to the Town Planning Movement and to the Study of Civics* (London: Williams and Norgate, 1915), p. 93. See also Geddes, *John Ruskin*, pp. 34–35, where Geddes noted "the general correspondence between biological principles on the one hand, and Mr. Ruskin's most 'unpractical' teaching on the other. . . . For it is to be observed if these Darwinians are indeed to draw full consequences from their greatest law—that organism is made by function and environment, then man, if he is to remain healthy and become civilised, must not only aim at the highest standard of cerebral as well as non-cerebral excellence, and so at function healthy and delightful, but must take special hold of his environment; not only at his peril keeping the natural factors of air, water, and light at their purest, but caring only for 'production of wealth' at all, in so far as it shapes the artificial factors, the material surroundings of domestic and civic life, into forms more completely serviceable for the Ascent of Life."

15. Lewis Mumford, "Science and Sanctity," *Commonweal* 4 (9 June 1926): 128; Branford and Geddes, *Coming Polity*, p. 92.

16. See Geddes's discussion in *Cities in Evolution*, chap. 4.

17. Branford and Geddes, *Coming Polity*, p. 212.

18. Ibid., pp. 14, 133; Mumford, *Sketches from Life*, p. 156.

19. Mumford, *Sketches from Life*, pp. 330, 147; Mumford, draft of essay on Cobbett, 3 August 1921, MS in Mumford Collection.

20. On the garden city ideal, see Ebenezer Howard, *Garden Cities of To-morrow*, ed. F. J. Osborn (Cambridge, Mass.: MIT Press, 1965); Robert Fishman, *Urban Utopias in the Twentieth Century: Ebenezer Howard, Frank Lloyd Wright, and Le Corbusier* (New York: Basic Books, 1977), Part 1; Peter Hall, *Cities of Tomorrow: An Intellectual History of Urban Planning and Design in the Twen-*

tieth Century (Oxford: Basil Blackwell, 1988), chaps. 4–5. On the other sources of Mumford's "green" politics, see Pëtr Kropotkin, *Fields, Factories and Workshops, or Industry Combined with Agriculture and Brain Work with Manual Work* (New York: G. P. Putnam's Sons, 1901); Thorstein Veblen, *The Theory of the Leisure Class: An Economic Study of Institutions* (New York: Mentor, 1953); and John P. Diggins, *The Bard of Savagery: Thorstein Veblen and Modern Social Theory* (New York: Seabury Press, 1978).

21. The term *adversary tradition* comes from John L. Thomas's study of late nineteenth-century American producerism, *Alternative America: Henry George, Edward Bellamy, Henry Demarest Lloyd and the Adversary Tradition* (Cambridge, Mass.: Harvard University Press, 1983). See also R. Jeffrey Lustig, *Corporate Liberalism: The Origins of Modern American Political Theory, 1890–1920* (Berkeley and Los Angeles: University of California Press, 1982), chap. 3.

22. See Meller, "Patrick Geddes," p. 302.

23. Ibid., p. 300; Geddes and Branford, *Coming Polity*, p. 31; Patrick Geddes, "Civics: As Applied Sociology I," in *Ideal City*, ed. Meller, p. 85.

24. See Meller, "Patrick Geddes," pp. 301–2, and Mumford, *Sketches from Life*, p. 157, for discussions of Geddes's "thinking machine."

25. Bourne, "The State," p. 360; Bruce Clayton, *Forgotten Prophet: The Life of Randolph Bourne* (Baton Rouge: Louisiana State University Press, 1984), p. 262.

26. Randolph Bourne, "A War Diary," in *Radical Will*, ed. Hansen, p. 321; see also, Bourne, "Below the Battle," in *War and the Intellectuals: Essays by Randolph S. Bourne, 1915–1919*, ed. Carl Resek (New York: Harper & Row, 1964), pp. 15–21; Lewis Mumford, "The Status of the State," *Dial* 67 (26 July 1919): 60.

27. Mumford, "Status of the State," p. 59; Clayton, *Forgotten Prophet*, p. 227.

28. Lewis Mumford, "A Search for the True Community," in *The Menorah Treasury: Harvest of Half a Century*, ed. Leo W. Schwartz (Philadelphia: Jewish Publication Society of America, 1964), pp. 859, 863, 867. See also Mumford, "Status of the State," p. 59; and Mumford, "Wardom and the State," *Dial* 67 (4 October 1919): 304.

29. Harold Stearns, *America and the Young Intellectual* (New York: George H. Doran, 1921), pp. 146–47. See also Lewis Mumford, "The Place of the Community in the School," *Dial* 67 (20 September 1919): 244–46; Mumford, "Reeducating the Worker," *Survey* 47 (7 January 1922): 567–69; Mumford, "Ex Libris," *Freeman* 7 (25 April 1923): 167; Mumford, "The Regional Note," *Freeman* 8 (10 October 1923): 107–8.

30. Mumford, *Story of Utopias*, p. 234.

31. Lewis Mumford, "Contemporary Disillusion: A Dialogue," *Nation* 119 (10 December 1924): 636; Mumford, "The Collapse of Tomorrow," *Freeman* 3 (13 July 1921): 414; Mumford to Patrick Geddes, 6 July 1923, in Mumford, *My Works and Days: A Personal Chronicle* (New York: Harcourt Brace Jovanovich, 1979), p. 110. See also Novak, "Master and Disciple."

32. "I undertook this utopian inquiry," Mumford wrote Brooks, "because it seemed to me necessary to throw a rainbow into the sky at just this moment, if our generation, and the one that is on our heels, were not to become sodden in spirit as a result of the storm through which we've passed" (Mumford to Brooks, 1

August 1922, in *The Van Wyck Brooks–Lewis Mumford Letters: The Record of a Literary Friendship, 1921–1963*, ed. Robert E. Spiller [New York: Dutton, 1970], p. 19).

33. Lewis Mumford, "The Russian Changeling," *Freeman* 3 (27 April 1921): 165.

34. Lewis Mumford, "The American Intelligentsia," *World Tomorrow* 8 (July 1925): 200; Mumford, "If Engineers Were Kings," *Freeman* 4 (23 November 1921): 262; Mumford, "The Adolescence of Reform," *Freeman* 2 (1 December 1920): 273.

35. Mumford, *Findings and Keepings*, p. 206.

36. Mumford, *Story of Utopias*, pp. 193–94, 13–14.

37. Ibid., pp. 212, 209.

38. Ibid., pp. 202, 205, 203, 215.

39. Ibid., p. 221.

40. Ibid., pp. 226, 229.

41. Ibid., pp. 147, 252, 268.

42. Ibid., p. 15.

43. Ibid., pp. 249–50, 6.

44. Ibid., p. 38.

45. Plato, *The Republic*, trans. G. M. A. Grube (Indianapolis: Hackett, 1974), 433a; Mumford, *Story of Utopias*, pp. 41, 51, 43, 50, 53.

46. Mumford, *Story of Utopias*, pp. 169, 234.

47. Miller, *Mumford*, p. 163.

48. Mumford to Brooks, 22 July 1925, in *Brooks-Mumford Letters*, ed. Spiller, p. 30.

49. Lewis Mumford, *Sticks and Stones: A Study of American Architecture and Civilization* (New York: Dover, 1955), pp. 82, 109. See also Mumford's essay "The City," in *Civilization in the United States: An Inquiry by Thirty Americans*, ed. Harold Stearns (New York: Harcourt, Brace, 1922), pp. 3–20, which anticipates many of the arguments of *Sticks and Stones*.

50. Carl Sussman, Preface to *Planning the Fourth Migration: The Neglected Vision of the Regional Planning Association of America*, ed. Sussman (Cambridge, Mass.: MIT Press, 1976), p. x. For the history of the Regional Planning Association of America and its influence on urban planning, see also Roy Lubove, *Community Planning in the 1920's: The Contribution of the Regional Planning Association of America* (Pittsburgh: University of Pittsburgh Press, 1963); and Daniel Schaffer, *Garden Cities for America: The Radburn Experience* (Philadelphia: Temple University Press, 1982). Mumford's germinal statement of RPAA principles, "The Fourth Migration," is reprinted in *Planning the Fourth Migration*, ed. Sussman, pp. 55–64; see also his "Devastated Regions," *American Mercury* 3 (October 1924): 217–20. An excellent concise treatment of Mumford's hopes for the RPAA appears in Thomas P. Hughes, *American Genesis: A Century of Invention and Technological Enthusiasm, 1870–1970* (New York: Viking, 1989), pp. 354–60.

51. Lewis Mumford, "Machinery and the Modern Style," in *Roots of Contemporary American Architecture*, ed. Mumford (New York: Dover, 1972), p. 196. See, in addition to the works noted above, Mumford, "Architecture and the Machine," *American Mercury* 3 (September 1924): 77–80; "Towers," *American Mercury* 4 (January 1925): 193–96; "The Poison of Good Taste," *American*

Mercury 6 (September 1925): 92–94; "The Machine and Its Products," *American Mercury* 10 (January 1927): 64–67; "Modernism for Sale," *American Mercury* 16 (March 1929): 453–55; "Architecture and Catholicism," *Commonweal* 1 (15 April 1925): 623–25; "Decoration and Structure," *Commonweal* 2 (7 October 1925): 532–33; "The Paralysis of Luxury," *Commonweal* 5 (5 January 1927): 237–38; *Architecture* (Chicago: American Library Association, 1926); and the 1928 series "American Architecture Today"—"The Search for 'Something More,' " "Domestic Architecture," and "Monumental Architecture"—reprinted in *Architecture as a Home for Man: Essays for Architectural Record*, ed. Jeanne M. Davern (New York: Architectural Record Books, 1975), pp. 7–42. An excellent analysis of Mumford's architectural criticism and its significance for the importation of the International Style to the United States appears in Miles David Samson, "German-American Dialogues: The Modern Movement before the 'Design Migration,' 1910–1933" (Ph.D. dissertation, Harvard University, 1988), chap. 5.

52. Mumford, *Architecture*, pp. 27–28.
53. Mumford, "Machinery and the Modern Style," pp. 197–98.
54. Mumford, "Domestic Architecture," in Mumford, *Architecture as a Home for Man*, ed. Davern, p. 21; Frank Lloyd Wright, "The Art and Craft of the Machine," in *Roots*, ed. Mumford, pp. 169–85; Mumford, "The Search for 'Something More,' " in Mumford, *Architecture as a Home for Man*, p. 12.
55. Mumford, *Architecture as a Home for Man*, p. 13; Mumford, "Towards a Rational Modernism," *New Republic* 54 (25 April 1928): 297–98.
56. A good summary statement of Mumford's mature aesthetics is "Function and Expression in Architecture," in Mumford, *Architecture as a Home for Man*, pp. 154–60. "By now," he wrote in 1951, "many architects have become aware of a self-imposed poverty: in absorbing the lessons of the machine and in learning to master new forms of construction, they have . . . neglected the valid claims of the human personality. In properly rejecting antiquated symbols, they have also rejected human needs, interests, sentiments, values, that must be given full play in every complete structure. This does not mean, as some critics have hastily asserted, that functionalism is doomed: it means rather that the time has come to integrate objective functions with subjective functions: to balance off mechanical facilities with biological needs, social commitments, and personal values." Though nowhere stated as eloquently or succinctly in his criticism from the 1920s, this opposition of an "organic functionalism" to a "mechanical" architectural modernism is implicit in much of his writing from that decade.
57. Mumford, *Golden Day*, pp. 44–45, xviii–xix. The 1957 Beacon Press paperback edition of *The Golden Day* bears a different subtitle, *A Study in American Literature and Culture*, which obscures the original intention of the work.
58. Mumford to Brooks, 23 December 1925, in *Brooks-Mumford Letters*, ed. Spiller, p. 37; Mumford, *Golden Day*, pp. 92, 94–95, 135.
59. Mumford, *Golden Day*, pp. 58, 46–47.
60. Ibid., pp. 50, 83.
61. Ibid., p. 116. Mumford wrote Brooks that "something like a living synthesis" of Dewey's and Santayana's philosophies "would, for the first time perhaps, embrace the values of science and of humanism." In preparing the first of the lectures that led to *The Golden Day*, he had "found myself enormously helped

by Santayana," adding, "I think it's a mistake to consider the pragmatists the sole spokesmen of the American spirit" (Mumford to Brooks, 22 July 1925, in *Brooks-Mumford Letters*, ed. Spiller, p. 30). Santayana returned the compliment. In a letter to Mumford, he called *The Golden Day* "the best book about America, if not the best American book, that I have read." (This excerpt is reprinted on the front cover of the Beacon Press paperback edition of Mumford's book.) Charles Molesworth examines Mumford's attempt to bring together Dewey and Santayana in his essay "Inner and Outer: The Axiology of Lewis Mumford," in *Lewis Mumford*, ed. Hughes and Hughes.

62. Mumford, *Golden Day*, pp. 57, 55, 64, 65.
63. Ibid., p. 51. See Trachtenberg, "Mumford in the Twenties," pp. 29–42, for an excellent discussion of this issue.
64. John Dewey, "The Pragmatic Acquiescence," *New Republic* 49 (5 January 1927): 187, reprinted in *Pragmatism and American Culture*, ed. Gail Kennedy (Boston: D. C. Heath, 1950), pp. 50, 51, 53.
65. Lewis Mumford, "The Pragmatic Acquiescence: A Reply," *New Republic* 49 (19 January 1927): 250, reprinted in *Pragmatism and American Culture*, ed. Kennedy, pp. 54–56.
66. Mumford, for example, willfully disregarded Dewey's treatment of aesthetic and moral issues in *Experience and Nature*. In a 1926 letter to Victor Branford, he acknowledged that in that book Dewey "admits the damage caused by an overwhelming preoccupation with the physical sciences and invention." But Mumford was quick to qualify this praise, noting that there was no way pragmatism could accommodate an aesthetic theory. "The trouble is that in terms of his philosophy there is no place for art; and his exertions in trying to open up a wedge for it are painful to behold" (Mumford to Victor Branford, 3 March 1926, in Mumford Collection).

One would never know from this letter or from Mumford's other commentaries on Dewey's work in the 1920s the depth of Dewey's interest in questions of values and aesthetics in *Experience and Nature*. Nor would one realize that the central issue of much of the book was the very dialectic between the imagination and the environment that was at the heart of Mumford's interest in Emerson's theory of symbolic form in *The Golden Day*. Like Mumford, Dewey tried to explain how subjective experience was capable of taking concrete form through conscious practice—in particular, artistic practice—and thus remake the given world. As Dewey explained, "Imagination as mere reverie is one thing, a natural and additive event, complete in itself, a terminal object rich and consoling, or trivial and silly, as may be. Imagination which terminates in a modification of the objective order, in the institution of a new object is other than a merely added occurrence. It involves a dissolution of old objects and a forming of new ones in a medium which, since it is beyond the old object and not yet in a new one, can properly be termed subjective" (John Dewey, *Experience and Nature* [New York: Dover, 1958], p. 220). See also Robert Westbrook, "Lewis Mumford, John Dewey and the 'Pragmatic Acquiescence,'" in *Lewis Mumford*, ed. Hughes and Hughes, for a defense of Dewey's treatment of art and other forms of consummatory experience generally and for a critical perspective on Mumford's position in this debate.

Dewey also missed the connections between passages like this one from *Expe-*

rience and Nature and Mumford's theory of symbolic interaction in *The Golden Day*. That neither one of these men was able to recognize their common commitment to the transformative possibilities of the human imagination through cultural expression is perhaps the saddest aspect of their debate in the 1920s.

67. John Dewey, *The Public and Its Problems* (Chicago: Swallow Press, 1954), pp. 155, 142. Paul F. Bourke speculates that the Young Americans' critique of Dewey in the 1910s and 1920s was responsible for this new moral-aesthetic emphasis in his work. See his "Philosophy and Social Criticism: John Dewey, 1910–1920," *History of Education Quarterly* 15 (Spring 1975): 14n. See also Westbrook, "Lewis Mumford, John Dewey and the 'Pragmatic Acquiescence,' " on this point.

68. Mumford, *Golden Day*, p. 143.

Chapter 7

1. Van Wyck Brooks, *The Pilgrimage of Henry James* (New York: Dutton, 1925), p. 152.

2. Lewis Mumford, notes for "A Lecture on 'The Critics,' " 1 May 1927, MS in Lewis Mumford Collection, Department of Special Collections, Van Pelt Library, University of Pennsylvania; Waldo Frank, "For a Declaration of War," in *Salvos: An Informal Book about Books and Plays* (New York: Boni and Liveright, 1924), p. 13.

3. See Brooks's Introduction to Randolph Bourne, *The History of a Literary Radical* (New York: S. A. Russell, 1956), pp. 1–20. (The 1956 edition includes Bourne's political pieces, which Brooks left out of the 1920 collection.) Brooks to Frank, 22 May 1919, in Waldo Frank Collection, Department of Special Collections, Van Pelt Library, University of Pennsylvania; Brooks, "The Literary Life in America," in Brooks, *America's Coming-of-Age* (Garden City, N.Y.: Doubleday, 1958), p. 183.

4. Brooks, *America's Coming-of-Age*, pp. 181, 175, 176.

5. Van Wyck Brooks, "The Influence of William James," in Brooks, *Sketches in Criticism* (New York: Dutton, 1932), p. 37. This volume contains many of Brooks's *Freeman* essays.

6. Brooks, "Max Eastman, Science and Revolution," in *Sketches*, p. 284; Brooks, "The Novels of Upton Sinclair," in Brooks, *Emerson and Others* (New York: Dutton, 1927), p. 215.

7. Brooks, "Mr. Mencken and the Prophets," in *Sketches*, pp. 31–32.

8. Brooks, "The Hero as Artist," in *Sketches*, p. 95.

9. See Brooks, "The Novels of Upton Sinclair," in *Emerson and Others*, pp. 209–17; Brooks, "Max Eastman, Science and Revolution," in *Sketches*, pp. 279–80.

10. "Comment," *Dial* 76 (January 1924): 96; Brooks, "The Parvenu Intellectuals," in *Sketches*, pp. 51–52.

11. Brooks, "Parvenu Intellectuals," p. 53; Brooks, "In Search of a Cause," in *Sketches*," pp. 81–82.

12. Quoted in Raymond Nelson, *Van Wyck Brooks: A Writer's Life* (New York: Dutton, n.d.), p. 131; James Hoopes, *Van Wyck Brooks: In Search of American Culture* (Amherst: University of Massachusetts Press, 1977), p. 129.

13. Brooks quoted in Hoopes, *Van Wyck Brooks*, p. 179.

14. Brooks to Mumford, [April 1924], in *The Van Wyck Brooks–Lewis Mumford Letters: The Record of a Literary Friendship, 1921–1963*, ed. Robert E. Spiller (New York: Dutton, 1970), p. 26.
15. Brooks to Mumford, 12 May 1924, 26 July 1926, 13 September 1925, in *Brooks-Mumford Letters*, ed. Spiller, pp. 27, 40, 33.
16. Van Wyck Brooks, *The Ordeal of Mark Twain* (New York: Dutton, 1920), pp. 46, 44; William Wasserstrom, *The Legacy of Van Wyck Brooks: A Study of Maladies and Motives* (Carbondale: Southern Illinois University Press, 1971), pp. 32–34; Brooks, *The Soul: An Essay towards a Point of View* (San Francisco: Privately printed, 1910), p. 7.
17. Brooks, *Pilgrimage of Henry James*, p. 104.
18. See Hoopes, *Brooks*, pp. 136–37, and Nelson, *Brooks*, pp. 138–39, for discussions of Hart's influence on Brooks. Brooks, *Ordeal of Mark Twain*, pp. 14, 89; Brooks, *Pilgrimage of Henry James*, p. 9.
19. Brooks, *Ordeal of Mark Twain*, p. 195; see also Hoopes, *Brooks*, p. 138, and Nelson, *Brooks*, p. 175, on the parallels between Brooks's and Twain's family lives.
20. Van Wyck Brooks, *An Autobiography* (New York: Dutton, 1965), pp. 432–33, 425. For Bazalgette's importance for Brooks, see Nelson, *Brooks*, pp. 142–43.
21. Brooks, *Pilgrimage of Henry James*, p. 128; Brooks, *Autobiography*, p. 439.
22. Brooks, *Pilgrimage of Henry James*, pp. 135–36.
23. Wilson Carey McWilliams, *The Idea of Fraternity in America* (Berkeley and Los Angeles: University of California Press, 1973), p. 353.
24. Mumford to Brooks, 21 March 1929, in *Brooks-Mumford Letters*, ed. Spiller, p. 60.
25. Van Wyck Brooks, *The Life of Emerson* (New York: Dutton, 1932), pp. 120, 115, 48, 304; McWilliams, *Fraternity*, p. 286. On the threat posed to the artifacts of culture by Emerson's intuitive ideal of expression , see F. O. Matthiessen, *American Renaissance: Art and Expression in the Age of Emerson and Whitman* (New York: Oxford University Press, 1941), pp. 24–26.
26. Brooks, *Life of Emerson*, pp. 44–46, 126, 123–24.
27. Brooks, *Autobiography*, pp. 439, 442–43. In the title of chapter 13 of his *Autobiography*, Brooks describes his period of mental collapse as a "season in hell." See Hoopes, *Brooks*, chap. 7; and Nelson, *Brooks*, chap. 9, on Brooks's illness during this period. See also the penetrating analyses of the significance of Brooks's breakdown for his career in Quentin Anderson, "The Critic and Imperial Consciousness," *New Republic* 152 (17 April 1965): 15–17; and T. J. Jackson Lears, *No Place of Grace: Antimodernism and the Transformation of American Culture, 1880–1920* (New York: Pantheon, 1981), pp. 251–57.
28. Brooks, *Autobiography*, p. 451; Brooks, *The Wine of the Puritans* in *Van Wyck Brooks: The Early Years, A Selection from His Works, 1908–1921*, ed. Claire Sprague (New York: Harper & Row, 1968), p. 56.
29. Waldo Frank, *The Re-discovery of America: An Introduction to a Philosophy of American Life* (New York: Charles Scribner's Sons, 1929), pp. 280, 210.
30. Frank, Notebook VII (September 1918–May 1922), MS in Waldo Frank Collection, Department of Special Collections, Van Pelt Library, University of Pennsylvania.

31. Waldo Frank, "From the Note-Books of Waldo Frank," *S4N* 30–31 (September 1923–January 1924): n.p.
32. Ibid.
33. Frank, Notebook VII; Frank, Notebook VIII (June 1922–December 1924), MS in Frank Collection. On the difficulties of the "mystic way," see Evelyn Underhill, *Mysticism: A Study in the Nature and Development of Man's Spiritual Consciousness* (New York: New American Library, 1974), pp. 169–70, and passim.
34. Frank, Notebook IX (August 1925–December 1928), MS in Frank Collection; Frank, *Virgin Spain: Scenes from the Spiritual Drama of a Great People* (New York: Boni and Liveright, 1926), p. 160; Frank, *Re-discovery of America*, p. 24.
35. Frank, *Virgin Spain*, p. 163; Frank, *Re-discovery of America*, p. 128. See Frank, "No Spirit at All," *New Republic* 43 (24 June 1925): 131–32; Frank, "Seriousness and Dada (An Exchange with Malcolm Cowley)" and "Mr. Mencken, King of the Philistines," in *In the American Jungle (1925–1936)* (New York: Farrar & Rinehart, 1937), pp. 128–35, 135–39.
36. Frank, *Virgin Spain*, p. 285. The need for a modernist successor to Jewish law is a constant theme in Frank's writings on Judaism. See, for example, "Toward an Analysis of the Problem of the Jew," a 1926 essay reprinted in *The Jew in Our Day* (New York: Duell, Sloan and Pearce, 1944), pp. 41–58; and *The Re-discovery of America*, pp. 286–87.
37. Reinhold Niebuhr to Frank, 21 December [ca. 1937], in Frank Collection.
38. Frank, Notebook VIII (June 1922–December 1924).
39. Paul Rosenfeld, "The Novels of Waldo Frank," *Dial* 70 (January 1921): 95–105. See also the perceptive portrait of Frank's personality in Mumford's Introduction to *Memoirs of Waldo Frank*, ed. Alan Trachtenberg (Amherst: University of Massachusetts Press, 1973), pp. xv–xxix, which has informed much of my analysis here.
40. Frank, Notebook IX (August 1925–December 1928), MS in Frank Collection.
41. Ibid.
42. John Dewey, "Three Prefaces to Books by Alexander," in *The Resurrection of the Body: The Writings of F. Matthias Alexander*, ed. Edward Maisel (New York: Dell, 1974), p. 182; Randolph Bourne, "Making Over the Body," *New Republic* 15 (4 May 1918): 28–29. See the exchange of letters between Bourne and Dewey that followed Bourne's review: John Dewey, "Reply to a Reviewer," *New Republic* 15 (11 May 1918): 55; and Bourne, "Other Messiahs," *New Republic* 15 (25 May 1918): 117. The Randolph S. Bourne Papers at the Rare Book and Manuscript Library, Columbia University, contain a draft of a letter to Dewey, dated 28 May 1918, that continued the debate. Bourne criticized Dewey's enthusiasm for "a sort of pragmatic demonstration of your philosophy in the field of the human body." "What I said about the need of a philosophy of conscious desire to supplement a philosophy of conscious control applies equally well to Mr. Alexander's technique as to instrumentalism," he wrote. "That is why it seems to me Mr. A's philosophy-technique strictly needs psychoanalysis or some other philosophy-technique of conscious desire and imagination to work with it." Edward Maisel describes Alexander's career in his Introduction to *Resurrection of the Body*, pp. vii–xlvi.
43. Frank, "The Logic of the Body," in *Salvos*, p. 179; Alexander quoted in Maisel,

Introduction, *Resurrection of the Body*, p. xxxix.

44. Frank, *Re-discovery of America*, pp. 291, 293.

45. See Waldo Frank, *The Rediscovery of Man: A Memoir and a Methodology of Modern Life* (New York: George Braziller, 1958), pp. 427–35, 447–56; Frank, Notebook X (January 1929–July 1931), MS in Frank Collection.

46. Santa Teresa quoted in Underhill, *Mysticism*, p. 91.

47. Lewis Mumford, *Herman Melville* (New York: Literary Guild of America, 1929), pp. 344, 364. See Matthiessen's critique of the biography in *American Renaissance*, pp. xvii, 488–90.

48. Ibid., pp. 184–85, 167, 213–14.

49. Ibid., p. 352. The history of Melville's significance for twentieth-century intellectuals has not, to my knowledge, been written. This is not the place for such a history, but Melville's work—and particularly the story "Billy Budd"—played an analogous role in both Mumford's work and Lionel Trilling's, a decade or more later, in restoring a sense of tragedy to modern liberal thought. See, for example, the discussion of "Billy Budd" in Trilling's 1947 novel *The Middle of the Journey* (New York: Avon Books, 1975), pp. 153–59, which refutes the liberal reading of Billy Budd as an innocent victim of an oppressive society. Melville's importance for Mumford's and Trilling's intellectual development suggests that the rediscovery of Melville's work beginning in the 1920s was partly a response to the ethical shallowness of Progressivism and that the concern with human finitude and the "tragic sense of life" that became a central preoccupation of the American liberal intelligentsia after World War II actually began more than a decade earlier than historians have generally realized. For a similar argument about the early emergence of a tragic sensibility among American intellectuals, see Richard Wightman Fox, "Tragedy, Responsibility, and the American Intellectual, 1925–1950," in *Lewis Mumford: Public Intellectual*, ed. Agatha C. Hughes and Thomas P. Hughes (New York: Oxford University Press, 1990).

50. Quoted in Mumford, *Herman Melville*, p. 318.

51. Ibid., p. 193.

52. Ibid., pp. 362–63.

53. Ibid., pp. 186–87.

Chapter 8

1. Lewis Mumford, *The Story of Utopias* (New York: Viking Press, 1962), p. 15.

2. Frank to V. F. Calverton, 14 August 1930, in V. F. Calverton Papers, Rare Books and Manuscripts Division, New York Public Library, Astor, Lenox and Tilden Foundations; Waldo Frank, *The Re-discovery of America: An Introduction to a Philosophy of American Life* (New York: Charles Scribner's Sons, 1929), pp. 11, 65.

3. Frank, *Re-discovery of America*, pp. 41–42; Frank, "The Machine and Metaphysics," in Frank, *In the American Jungle (1925–1936)* (New York: Farrar and Rinehart, 1937), p. 157.

4. Waldo Frank, "Dawn and Dusk," in *In the American Jungle*, p. 176.

5. Matthew Josephson quoted in Dickran Tashjian, *Skyscraper Primitives: Dada*

and the American Avant-Garde, 1910–1925 (Middletown, Conn.: Wesleyan University Press, 1975), pp. 129–30; Frank, "Seriousness and Dada," in *In the American Jungle*, pp. 129–30.

6. Waldo Frank, "The Drug on the Market," in *In the American Jungle*, p. 55.
7. Waldo Frank, "The New Conquistadores," ibid., pp. 41–45. For the use of anthropological relativism as a resource for cultural criticism, see George E. Marcus and Michael M. J. Fischer, *Anthropology as Cultural Critique: An Experimental Moment in the Human Sciences* (Chicago: University of Chicago Press, 1986), esp. pp. 128–31.
8. Frank, *Re-discovery of American*, p. 70; Waldo Frank, "The Treason of the Intellectuals," *Modern Quarterly* 5 (Spring 1929): 163.
9. Waldo Frank, "The Comedy of Commerce," in *In the American Jungle*, pp. 118–19; Frank, "Jazz and Folk Art," ibid., p. 122. For Adorno's critique of jazz, see Theodor W. Adorno, "Perennial Fashion—Jazz," in Adorno, *Prisms*, trans. Samuel Weber and Sherry Weber (Cambridge, Mass.: MIT Press, 1981), pp. 119–33; and Martin Jay, *The Dialectical Imagination: A History of the Frankfurt School and the Institute of Social Research, 1923–1950* (Boston: Little, Brown, 1970), pp. 185–88. Herbert Marcuse's theory of repressive desublimation in consumer culture appears in *Eros and Civilization: A Philosophical Inquiry into Freud* (New York: Vintage Books, 1955), pp. ix–x, 86, and passim.
10. Waldo Frank, "In Defense of Our Vulgarity," in *In the American Jungle*, p. 111.
11. Waldo Frank, "Valedictory to a Theatrical Season," reprinted in Frank, *Salvos: An Informal Book about Books and Plays* (New York: Boni and Liveright, 1924), p. 103. When he reprinted the essay in this collection, Frank added a postscript (p. 115) admitting "the injustice which this essay does to Mr. Chaplin," adding that Chaplin's "art indeed is a symbol of health in a complexly morbid world." Chaplin discussed his friendship with Frank—and, through Frank, Hart Crane—in Charles Chaplin, *My Autobiography* (New York: Simon and Schuster, 1964), pp. 248–49. Frank, *Our America* (New York: Boni and Liveright, 1919), pp. 214–15; Frank, "Charlie Chaplin," in *Salvos*, pp. 218–19; Frank, "Charles Chaplin," in *In the American Jungle*, pp. 71, 72 n. 1; Frank, *Re-discovery of America*, p. 138.
12. See the treatment of turn-of-the-century communitarians in Jean B. Quandt, *From the Small Town to the Great Community: The Social Thought of Progressive Intellectuals* (New Brunswick: Rutgers University Press, 1970); R. Jackson Wilson, *In Quest of Community: Social Philosophy in the United States, 1860–1920* (New York: Oxford University Press, 1968); and Everett H. Akam, "Pluralism and the Search for Community" (Ph.D. dissertation, University of Rochester, 1989).
13. Frank, *Re-discovery of America*, pp. 156, 257.
14. Ibid., p. 156. See Richard Wightman Fox, "Epitaph for Middletown: Robert S. Lynd and the Analysis of Consumer Culture," in *The Culture of Consumption: Critical Essays in American History, 1880–1980*, ed. Richard Wightman Fox and T. J. Jackson Lears (New York: Pantheon, 1983), pp. 101–41.
15. Alan Trachtenberg, "Cultural Revisions in the Twenties: Brooklyn Bridge as 'Usable Past,'" in *The American Self: Myth, Ideology, and Popular Culture*, ed. Sam B. Girgus (Albuquerque: University of New Mexico Press, 1981), p. 60. See also Robert L. Perry, *The Shared Vision of Waldo Frank and Hart Crane*, Uni-

versity of Nebraska Studies, n.s. 33 (Lincoln: University of Nebraska Press, 1966).

16. Waldo Frank, *America Hispana: A Portrait and a Prospect* (New York: Charles Scribner's Sons, 1931), pp. 348–49.

17. Frank, Notebook XI (June 1932–September 1934), MS in Waldo Frank Collection, Department of Special Collections, Van Pelt Library, University of Pennsylvania.

18. Waldo Frank, *Dawn in Russia: The Record of a Journey* (New York: Charles Scribner's Sons, 1932), pp. 230, 135.

19. Waldo Frank, *Memoirs of Waldo Frank*, ed. Alan Trachtenberg (Amherst: University of Massachusetts Press, 1973), p. 196.

20. Lewis Mumford, "What I Believe," *Forum* 84 (November 1930): 267.

21. Lewis Mumford, *Technics and Civilization* (New York: Harcourt, Brace, and World, 1962), p. 55.

22. Frank, "Dawn and Dusk," p. 177; Genevieve Taggard, "Do You Kill Your Own Hogs Too?" *New Masses* 3 (September 1927): 23. See also Mumford's response to an earlier essay of Taggard's, "That Monster—The Machine," *New Masses* 3 (September 1927): 23.

23. Mumford to Frank, 13 March 1927, in Frank Collection; Mumford to Alfred Stieglitz, 20 July 1933, in Alfred Stieglitz Papers, Collection of American Literature, Beinecke Rare Book and Manuscript Library, Yale University.

24. Mumford, "Preface to Action" (1931), MS in Lewis Mumford Collection, Department of Special Collections, Van Pelt Library, University of Pennsylvania. For a similar contemporary argument about the need for inspirational and even irrational myths in revolutionary politics, see Reinhold Niebuhr, *Moral Man and Immoral Society: A Study in Ethics and Politics* (New York: Charles Scribner's Sons, 1960). Writing in 1932, a year after Mumford composed his "Preface," Niebuhr rejected the idea that education and rational persuasion could create a movement for radical social change without recourse to religious or nonrational myths of perfect justice. "Justice cannot be approximated," he explained, "if it does not generate a sublime madness in the soul" (p. 277).

25. Mumford, "Preface"; Edmund Wilson, "An Appeal to Progressives," *New Republic* 65 (14 January 1931): 238; See also Mumford to Malcolm Cowley, 17 August 1932, Malcolm Cowley Papers, Newberry Library, Chicago; and Mumford's many letters to Frank on communism during the 1930s in the Frank Collection.

26. Mumford, "Preface."

27. Ibid. On 1930s technocratic liberalism, see R. Alan Lawson, *The Failure of Independent Liberalism, 1930–1941* (New York: G. P. Putnam's Sons, 1971), esp. chaps. 1 and 5; Richard H. Pells, *Radical Visions and American Dreams: Culture and Social Thought in the Depression Years* (New York: Harper & Row, 1973), esp. chap. 2; Donald L. Miller, *The New American Radicalism: Alfred M. Bingham and Non-Marxian Insurgency in the New Deal Era* (Port Washington, N.Y.: Kennikat Press, 1979); and Robert B. Westbrook, "Tribune of the Technostructure: The Popular Economics of Stuart Chase," *American Quarterly* 32 (Fall 1980): 387–408.

28. Mumford, *Technics*, pp. 3, 51; Mumford, *The Culture of Cities* (New York: Harcourt, Brace Jovanovich, 1970), p. 133. I have discussed Mumford's books

from the 1930s in Casey Blake, "Lewis Mumford: Values over Technique," *democracy* 3 (Spring 1983): 125–37; "The Ambiguities of Radical Organicism: Waldo Frank's and Lewis Mumford's Critique of Industrial Culture" (paper presented at the Ninth Biennial Convention of the American Studies Association, November 1983); and "The Perils of Personality: Lewis Mumford and Politics after Liberalism," in *Lewis Mumford: Public Intellectual*, ed. Agatha C. Hughes and Thomas P. Hughes (New York: Oxford University Press, 1990). The following discussion draws on these essays. See also Rosalind Williams's superb analysis of the contradictory strains within Mumford's work in this period in "Lewis Mumford as an Historian of Technology in *Technics and Civilization*," ibid.

29. Mumford, *Technics*, pp. 266, 354.
30. Ibid., pp. 386–87. For more critical, and more convincing, treatments of Taylor, Mayo, and the science of human relations in industry, see Harry Braverman, *Labor and Monopoly Capital: The Degradation of Work in the Twentieth Century* (New York: Monthly Review Press, 1974); and David F. Noble, *America by Design: Science, Technology, and the Rise of Corporate Capitalism* (New York: Knopf, 1979).
31. Mumford, *Culture*, pp. 181, 471, 386.
32. Mumford, *Technics*, p. 351, 361, 243–44. See also the discussion of this idea of an "objective" personality in Blake, "Perils of Personality."
33. For one of many possible examples of Mumford's treatment of early Christianity from his later work, see Mumford, *The Conduct of Life* (New York: Harcourt Brace Jovanovich, 1951), pp. 244–92. Frederic J. Osborn to Mumford, 16 January 1942, in *The Letters of Lewis Mumford and Frederic J. Osborn: A Transatlantic Dialogue, 1938–70*, ed. Michael Hughes (Bath: Adams and Dart, 1971), p. 24; Mumford, *The Myth of the Machine*. Vol. 2, *The Pentagon of Power* (New York: Harcourt Brace Jovanovich, 1970), p. 408.
34. James T. Farrell, "The Faith of Lewis Mumford," in *The League of Frightened Philistines and Other Papers* (New York: Vanguard Press, 1945), pp. 109, 127. See also Waldo Frank's exchange with S. D. Schmalhausen, "The Treason of the Intellectuals," and "The Reply Discourteous," in *Modern Quarterly* 5 (Spring 1929): 161–70; V. F. Calverton's exchange with Mumford, "A Challenge to American Intellectuals, a Controversy: The Revolutionary Approach," *Modern Quarterly* 5 (Winter 1930–31): 406–21; Sidney Hook, "The Non-Sense of the Whole," *Modern Quarterly* 5 (Winter 1930–31): 504–13; Meyer Schapiro, "Looking Forward to Looking Backward," *Partisan Review* 5 (July 1938): 12–24; Alfred M. Bingham's review of Mumford's *Men Must Act* in *Common Sense* 8 (March 1939): 27–28; Fleming MacLeish, "The Assault on Liberalism," *Common Sense* 9 (June 1940): 10–13; Richard H. Rovere's review of Mumford's *Faith for Living*, *Common Sense* 9 (October 1940): 26; Sidney Hook, "Metaphysics, War, and the Intellectuals," *Menorah Journal* 28 (Autumn 1940): 327–37; Richard Chase, "The Armed Obscurantist," *Partisan Review* 11 (Summer 1944): 346–48.
35. Frank, *Re-discovery of America*, p. 87.
36. Mumford, *Culture*, p. 302; Jeffrey Stout, *Ethics after Babel: The Languages of Morals and Their Discontents* (Boston: Beacon Press, 1988), p. 264. Stout's theory of a "modest pragmatism" informs much of my discussion here.

37. Mumford, *Culture*, p. 64.
38. Ibid., pp. 228, 215, 475.
39. Ibid., pp. 473–75.
40. Ibid., pp. 382–83. See Clifford Geertz, *Local Knowledge: Further Essays in Interpretive Anthropology* (New York: Basic Books, 1983). See also Michael Walzer, *Spheres of Justice* (New York: Basic Books, 1983), for an attempt to ground a communitarian conception of the public good in an ethnographic account of diverse social practices.
41. Michael Walzer, *The Company of Critics: Social Criticism and Political Commitment in the Twentieth Century* (New York: Basic Books, 1988), p. 22.

Epilogue

1. Lewis Mumford, "The Emergence of a Past," *New Republic* 45 (25 November 1925): 19.
2. Ibid.
3. Joseph R. Starobin to Waldo Frank, 27 June 1957, in Waldo Frank Collection, Department of Special Collections, Van Pelt Library, University of Pennsylvania.
4. See Russell Jacoby, *The Last Intellectuals: American Culture in the Age of Academe* (New York: Basic Books, 1987); and Michael Walzer, *The Company of Critics: Social Criticism and Political Commitment in the Twentieth Century* (New York: Basic Books, 1988). Mark Krupnick discusses the effect of academic specialization on American literary criticism in his Introduction to *Lionel Trilling and the Fate of Cultural Criticism* (Evanston: Northwestern University Press, 1986). Noting the decline of interest in twentieth-century American cultural criticism among younger literary scholars, Krupnick writes: "It would require a book by itself to explain how American graduate schools have produced a generation so knowledgeable about Georg Lukács, Antonio Gramsci, and Walter Benjamin and yet so ignorant of Van Wyck Brooks, Edmund Wilson, and Lionel Trilling" (p. 2). It would require another book to explain why that same generation remains ignorant of figures like Dewey, Morris, and the Young Americans.
5. Robert N. Bellah et al., *Habits of the Heart: Individualism and Commitment in American Life* (Berkeley and Los Angeles: University of California Press, 1985), pp. 32–35, and passim; Alasdair MacIntyre, *After Virtue: A Study in Moral Theory*, 2d ed. (Notre Dame: University of Notre Dame Press, 1984), p. 34.
6. Bellah et al., *Habits of the Heart*, p. 218; MacIntyre, *After Virtue*, p. 263.
7. Jeffrey Stout, *Ethics after Babel: The Languages of Morals and Their Discontents* (Boston: Beacon Press, 1988), p. 232.
8. Richard Bernstein, *Praxis and Action: Contemporary Philosophies of Human Activity* (Philadelphia: University of Pennsylvania Press, 1971), p. 219.

Bibliography

Manuscript Collections

Chicago, Illinois
  Newberry Library.
    Sherwood Anderson Papers.
    Malcolm Cowley Papers.
New Haven, Connecticut
  Beinecke Rare Book and Manuscript Library, Yale University.
  Collection of American Literature.
    Alfred Stieglitz Papers.
New York, New York
  Rare Book and Manuscript Library, Columbia University.
    Randolph S. Bourne Papers.
New York, New York
  Rare Books and Manuscripts Division, New York Public Library.
  Astor, Lenox and Tilden Foundations.
    V. F. Calverton Papers.
Philadelphia, Pennsylvania
  American Philosophical Society.
    Elsie Clews Parsons Papers.
Philadelphia, Pennsylvania
  Department of Special Collections, Van Pelt Library, University of Pennsylvania.
  Van Wyck Brooks Collection.
  Waldo Frank Collection.
  Lewis Mumford Collection.

Works by the "Young American" Critics

Bourne, Randolph. "Autobiographical Chapter." *Dial* 68 (January 1920): 1–21.
———. "The Cult of Convention." *Liberator* 1 (June 1918): 38–39.
———. *Education and Living*. New York: Century Company, 1917.
———. *The Gary Schools*. Cambridge, Mass.: MIT Press, 1970.

_____. *The History of a Literary Radical*. Edited by Van Wyck Brooks. New York: B. W. Huebsch, 1920.

_____. *The History of a Literary Radical and Other Papers*. New York: S. A. Russell, 1956.

_____. "Impressions of Europe, 1913–14." *Columbia University Quarterly* 17 (March 1915): 109–25.

_____. "In the Mind of the Worker." *Atlantic Monthly* 113 (June 1914): 375–82.

_____. *The Letters of Randolph Bourne: A Comprehensive Edition*. Edited by Eric J. Sandeen. Troy, N.Y.: Whitston, 1981.

_____[Max Coe]. "Making One's Contribution." *New Republic* 8 (26 August 1916): 91–92.

_____. "Making Over the Body." *New Republic* 15 (4 May 1918): 28–29.

_____. "Maurice Barrès and the Youth of France." *Atlantic Monthly* 114 (September 1914): 394–99.

_____. "Other Messiahs." *New Republic* 15 (25 May 1918): 117.

_____. *The Radical Will: Randolph Bourne Selected Writings, 1911–1918*. Edited by Olaf Hansen. New York: Urizen Books, 1977.

_____. "Socialism and the Catholic Ideal." *Columbia Monthly* 10 (November 1912): 11–19.

_____. "The Social Order in an American Town." *Atlantic Monthly* 111 (February 1913): 227–36.

_____. "Some Aspects of Good Talk." *Columbia Monthly* 7 (January 1910): 92–97.

_____. *War and the Intellectuals: Essays by Randolph S. Bourne, 1915–1919*. Edited by Carl Resek. New York: Harper & Row, 1964.

_____. *The World of Randolph Bourne*. Edited by Lillian Schlissel. New York: Dutton, 1965.

_____. *Youth and Life*. Boston: Houghton Mifflin, 1913.

Brooks, Van Wyck. *America's Coming-of-Age*. Garden City, N.Y.: Doubleday, 1958.

_____. *An Autobiography*. New York: Dutton, 1965.

_____. *The Confident Years, 1885–1915*. London: Dent, 1952.

_____. "The Culture of Industrialism." *Seven Arts* 1 (April 1917): 655–66.

_____. "Dante and the Literary Temperament." *Harvard Monthly* 42 (March 1906): 15–18.

_____. *Emerson and Others*. New York: Dutton, 1927.

_____. "Enterprise." *Seven Arts* 1 (November 1916): 57–60.

_____. "Harvard and American Life." *Contemporary Review*, 12 December 1908, pp. 610–18.

_____. *The Life of Emerson*. New York: Dutton, 1932.

_____. *The Malady of the Ideal*. Philadelphia: University of Pennsylvania Press, 1947.

_____. "The Mission of American Art." *Oracle* 2 (June 1904): 157–59.

_____. "Notes on Vernon Lee." *Forum* (April 1911): 447–56.

_____. *Opinions of Oliver Allston*. New York: Dutton, 1941.

_____. *The Ordeal of Mark Twain*. New York: Dutton, 1920.

_____. "Our Awakeners." *Seven Arts* 2 (June 1917): 235–48.

———. "Our Critics." *Seven Arts* 2 (May 1917): 103–16.

———. *The Pilgrimage of Henry James.* New York: Dutton, 1925.

———. *Sketches in Criticism.* New York: Dutton, 1932.

———. *The Soul: An Essay towards a Point of View.* San Francisco: Privately printed, 1910.

———. "The Splinter of Ice." *Seven Arts* 1 (January 1917): 270–80.

———. "Toward a National Culture." *Seven Arts* 1 (March 1917): 535–47.

———. "The Twilight of the Arts." *Poet Lore* 24 (Autumn 1913): 322–32.

———. *Van Wyck Brooks: The Early Years, A Selection from His Works, 1908–1921.* Edited by Claire Sprague. New York: Harper & Row, 1968.

———. *The Van Wyck Brooks–Lewis Mumford Letters: The Record of a Literary Friendship, 1921–1963.* Edited by Robert E. Spiller. New York: Dutton, 1970.

———. *The World of H. G. Wells.* New York: Mitchell Kennerley, 1915.

———. "Young America." *Seven Arts* 1 (December 1916): 144–51.

Frank, Waldo. *America Hispana: A Portrait and a Prospect.* New York: Charles Scribner's Sons, 1931.

———. *City Block.* Darien, Conn.: By the Author, 1922.

———. *Dawn in Russia: The Record of a Journey.* New York: Charles Scribner's Sons, 1932.

———. "Emerging Greatness." *Seven Arts* 1 (November 1916): 73–78.

———. "From the Note-Books of Waldo Frank." *S4N* 30–31 (September 1923–January 1924): n.p.

———. *In the American Jungle (1925–1936).* New York: Farrar and Rinehart, 1937.

———. *The Jew in Our Day.* New York: Duell, Sloan and Pearce, 1944.

———. *Memoirs of Waldo Frank.* Edited by Alan Trachtenberg. Amherst: University of Massachusetts Press, 1973.

———. "No Spirit at All." *New Republic* 43 (24 June 1925): 131–32.

———. *Our America.* New York: Boni and Liveright, 1919.

———. "A Prophet in France." *Seven Arts* 1 (April 1917): 638–48.

———. *The Re-discovery of America: An Introduction to a Philosophy of American Life.* New York: Charles Scribner's Sons, 1929.

———. *The Rediscovery of Man: A Memoir and a Methodology of Modern Life.* New York: George Braziller, 1958.

———. *Salvos: An Informal Book about Books and Plays.* New York: Boni and Liveright, 1924.

———. "The Seven Arts." *Golden Goose* 3 (1951): 20–22.

———. "The Treason of the Intellectuals." *Modern Quarterly* 5 (Spring 1929): 161–66.

———. *The Unwelcome Man: A Novel.* New York: Boni and Liveright, 1923.

———. "Vicarious Fiction." *Seven Arts* 1 (January 1917): 294–303.

———. *Virgin Spain: Scenes from the Spiritual Drama of a Great People.* New York: Boni and Liveright, 1926.

Mumford, Lewis. "The Adolescence of Reform." *Freeman* 2 (1 December 1920): 272–73.

———. "The American Intelligentsia." *World Tomorrow* 8 (July 1925): 200–201.

———. *Architecture.* Chicago: American Library Association, 1926.

————. "Architecture and Catholicism." *Commonweal* 1 (15 April 1925): 623–25.
————. "Architecture and the Machine." *American Mercury* 3 (September 1924): 77–80.
————. *Architecture as a Home for Man: Essays for Architectural Record*. Edited by Jeanne M. Davern. New York: Architectural Record Books, 1975.
————. "A Challenge to American Intellectuals, a Controversy: The Evolutionary Approach." *Modern Quarterly* 5 (Winter 1930–31): 407–10.
————. "The City." In *Civilization in the United States: An Inquiry by Thirty Americans*, edited by Harold S. Stearns, pp. 3–20. New York: Harcourt, Brace, 1922.
————. "The Collapse of Tomorrow." *Freeman* 3 (13 July 1921): 414–15.
————. *The Conduct of Life*. New York: Harcourt Brace Jovanovich, 1951.
————. "Contemporary Disillusion: A Dialogue." *Nation* 119 (10 December 1924): 636–37.
————. *The Culture of Cities*. New York: Harcourt Brace Jovanovich, 1970.
————. "Decoration and Structure." *Commonweal* 2 (7 October 1925): 532–33.
————. "Devastated Regions." *American Mercury* 3 (October 1924): 217–20.
————. "The Emergence of a Past." *New Republic* 45 (25 November 1925): 18–19.
————. "Ex Libris." *Freeman* 7 (25 April 1923): 167.
————. *Findings and Keepings: Analects for an Autobiography*. New York: Harcourt Brace Jovanovich, 1975.
————. "The Fourth Migration." In *Planning the Fourth Migration: The Neglected Vision of the Regional Planning Association of America*, edited by Carl Sussman, pp. 55–64. Cambridge, Mass.: MIT Press, 1976.
————. *The Golden Day: A Study in American Literature and Culture*. Boston: Beacon Press, 1957.
————. *Herman Melville*. New York: Literary Guild of America, 1929.
————. "If Engineers Were Kings." *Freeman* 4 (23 November 1921): 261–62.
————. *The Letters of Lewis Mumford and Frederic J. Osborn: A Transatlantic Dialogue, 1938–70*. Edited by Michael Hughes. Bath: Adams and Dart, 1971.
————. "The Machine and Its Products." *American Mercury* 10 (January 1927): 64–67.
————. "Modernism for Sale." *American Mercury* 16 (March 1929): 453–55.
————. *The Myth of the Machine*. Vol. 2, *The Pentagon of Power*. New York: Harcourt Brace Jovanovich, 1970.
————. *My Works and Days: A Personal Chronicle*. New York: Harcourt Brace Jovanovich, 1979.
————. "On the Dial." *New York Review of Books* 2 (20 February 1964): 3–5.
————. "The Paralysis of Luxury." *Commonweal* 5 (5 January 1927): 237–38.
————. "Patrick Geddes, Insurgent." *New Republic* 60 (30 October 1929): 295–96.
————. "Patriotism and Its Consequences." *Dial* 66 (19 April 1919): 406–7.
————. "The Place of the Community in the School." *Dial* 67 (20 September 1919): 244–46.
————. "The Poison of Good Taste." *American Mercury* 6 (September 1925): 92–94.
————. "The Pragmatic Acquiescence: A Reply." In *Pragmatism and American*

Culture, edited by Gail Kennedy, pp. 54–57. Boston: Heath, 1950.

————. "Reeducating the Worker." *Survey* 47 (7 January 1922): 567–69.

————. "The Regional Note." *Freeman* 8 (10 October 1923): 107–8.

————. "The Russian Changeling." *Freeman* 3 (27 April 1921): 165–66.

————. "Science and Sanctity." *Commonweal* 4 (9 June 1926): 126–28.

————. "A Search for the True Community." In *The Menorah Treasury: Harvest of Half a Century*, edited by Leo W. Schwartz, pp. 129–38. Philadelphia: Jewish Publication Society of America, 1964.

————. *Sketches from Life: The Autobiography of Lewis Mumford, The Early Years*. New York: Dial Press, 1982.

————. "The Status of the State." *Dial* 67 (26 July 1919): 59–61.

————. *Sticks and Stones: A Study of American Architecture and Civilization*. New York: Dover, 1955.

————. *The Story of Utopias*. New York: Viking Press, 1962.

————. *Technics and Civilization*. New York: Harcourt, Brace, and World, 1962.

————. "That Monster—The Machine." *New Masses* 3 (September 1927): 23.

————. "Towards a Rational Modernism." *New Republic* 54 (25 April 1928): 297–98.

————. "Towers." *American Mercury* 4 (January 1925): 193–96.

————. "Wardom and the State." *Dial* 67 (4 October 1919): 303–5.

————. "What I Believe." *Forum* 84 (November 1930): 263–68.

————, ed. *Roots of Contemporary American Architecture*. New York: Dover, 1972.

Oppenheim, James. "Art, Religion and Science." *Seven Arts* 2 (June 1917): 229–34.

[————]. Editorial. *Seven Arts* 1 (November 1916): 52–56.

————. Editorial. *Seven Arts* 1 (December 1916): 152–56.

————. Editorial. *Seven Arts* 1 (January 1917): 265–69.

————. Editorial. *Seven Arts* 1 (February 1917): 390–94.

————. Editorial. *Seven Arts* 1 (March 1917): 504–6.

————. Editorial. *Seven Arts* 2 (June 1917): 199–201.

————. Editorial. *Seven Arts* 2 (August 1917): 489–92.

————. "The Story of the *Seven Arts*." *American Mercury* 20 (June 1930): 156–64.

[————]. "To the Friends of The Seven Arts." *Seven Arts* 2 (October 1917): 670.

Rosenfeld, Paul L. "The American Composer." *Seven Arts* 1 (November 1916): 89–94.

————. "The Novels of Waldo Frank." *Dial* 70 (January 1921): 95–105.

————. *Port of New York*. Urbana: University of Illinois Press, 1966.

————[Peter Minuit]. " '291 Fifth Avenue.' " *Seven Arts* 1 (November 1916): 61–65.

Stearns, Harold. *America and the Young Intellectual*. New York: George H. Doran, 1921.

————. *Liberalism in America: Its Origin, Its Temporary Collapse, Its Future*. New York: Boni and Liveright, 1919.

————, ed. *Civilization in the United States: An Inquiry by Thirty Americans*. New York: Harcourt, Brace, 1922.

Other Primary Sources

Adorno, Theodor W. *Prisms*. Translated by Samuel Weber and Sherry Weber. Cambridge, Mass.: MIT Press, 1981.

Adorno, Theodor, and Max Horkheimer. *Dialectic of Enlightenment*. Translated by John Cumming. New York: Seabury Press, 1972.

Alexander, F. Matthias. *The Resurrection of the Body: The Writings of F. Matthias Alexander*. Edited by Edward Maisel. New York: Dell, 1974.

An American Immigrant [pseud.]. "Following Freedom." *Seven Arts* 2 (September 1917): 548–51.

Anderson, Sherwood. *Winesburg, Ohio*. New York: Viking Press, 1960.

Arnold, Matthew. *Culture and Anarchy*. Edited by J. Dover Wilson. London: Cambridge University Press, 1961.

Belloc, Hilaire. *The Servile State*. Indianapolis: Liberty Classics, 1977.

Bingham, Alfred M. Review of Lewis Mumford, *Men Must Act*. *Common Sense* 8 (March 1939): 27–28.

Branford, Victor, and Patrick Geddes. *The Coming Polity: A Study in Reconstruction*. London: Williams and Norgate, 1917.

Calverton, V. F. "A Challenge to American Intellectuals, a Controversy: The Revolutionary Approach." *Modern Quarterly* 5 (Winter 1930–31): 411–21.

Chaplin, Charles. *My Autobiography*. New York: Simon and Schuster, 1964.

Chase, Richard. "The Armed Obscurantist." *Partisan Review* 11 (Summer 1944): 346–48.

———. *The Democratic Vista: A Dialogue on Life and Letters in Contemporary America*. Garden City, N.Y.: Doubleday, 1958.

"Comment." *Dial* 76 (January 1924): 96–97.

Croly, Herbert. *The Promise of American Life*. New York: Capricorn Books, 1964.

Dewey, John. *Characters and Events: Popular Essays in Social and Political Philosophy*. Vol. 2. Edited by Joseph Ratner. New York: Henry Holt, 1929.

———. *The Child and the Curriculum* and *The School and Society*. Chicago: University of Chicago Press, 1956.

———. *Democracy and Education: An Introduction to the Philosophy of Education*. New York: Free Press, 1966.

———. *Essays on Philosophy and Education 1916–1917*. Vol. 10, *The Middle Works of John Dewey, 1899–1924*. Edited by Jo Ann Boydston. Carbondale: Southern Illinois University Press, 1985.

———. *Experience and Nature*. New York: Dover, 1958.

———. "The Pragmatic Acquiescence." In *Pragmatism and American Culture*, edited by Gail Kennedy, pp. 49–53. Boston: D. C. Heath, 1950.

———. *The Public and Its Problems*. Chicago: Swallow Press, 1954.

———. *Reconstruction in Philosophy*. Boston: Beacon Press, 1957.

———. "Reply to a Reviewer." *New Republic* 15 (11 May 1918): 55.

———. "Three Prefaces to Books by Alexander." In *The Resurrection of the Body: The Writings of F. Matthias Alexander*, edited by Edward Maisel, pp. 169–84. New York: Dell, 1974.

Farrell, James T. *The League of Frightened Philistines and Other Papers*. New York: Vanguard Press, 1945.

Freud, Sigmund. *Civilization and Its Discontents*. Translated by James Strachey. New York: Norton, 1961.

Geddes, Patrick. *Cities in Evolution: An Introduction to the Town Planning Movement and to the Study of Civics.* London: Williams and Norgate, 1915.
———. *John Ruskin, Economist.* Edinburgh: William Brown, 1884.
Gilman, Charlotte Perkins. *The Yellow Wallpaper.* 1899. Reprint. Old Westbury, N.Y.: Feminist Press, 1973.
Gramsci, Antonio. *Selections from the Prison Notebooks.* Edited and translated by Quintin Hoare and Geoffrey Nowell Smith. New York: International Publishers, 1971.
Gregory, Alyse. *The Day Is Gone.* New York: Dutton, 1948.
Hook, Sidney. "Metaphysics, War, and the Intellectuals." *Menorah Journal* 28 (Autumn 1940): 327–37.
———. "The Non-Sense of the Whole." *Modern Quarterly* 5 (Winter 1930–31): 504–13.
Horkheimer, Max. *Eclipse of Reason.* New York: Continuum, 1974.
Howard, Ebenezer. *Garden Cities of To-morrow.* Edited by F. J. Osborn. Cambridge, Mass.: MIT Press, 1965.
James, William. *The Writings of William James.* Edited by John J. McDermott. Chicago: University of Chicago Press, 1967.
Kropotkin, Pëtr. *Fields, Factories and Workshops, or Industry Combined with Agriculture and Brain Work with Manual Work.* New York: G. P. Putnam's Sons, 1901.
Lawrence, D. H. *Studies in Classic American Literature.* New York: Viking Press, 1961.
Lippmann, Walter. *Drift and Mastery: An Attempt to Diagnose the Current Unrest.* Madison: University of Wisconsin Press, 1985.
Lukács, Georg. *The Theory of the Novel.* Translated by Anna Bostock. Cambridge, Mass.: MIT Press, 1971.
Lynd, Robert S. *Knowledge for What? The Place of Social Science in American Culture.* Princeton: Princeton University Press, 1967.
MacLeish, Fleming. "The Assault on Liberalism." *Common Sense* 9 (June 1940): 10–13.
Marcuse, Herbert. *Eros and Civilization: A Philosophical Inquiry into Freud.* New York: Vintage Books, 1955.
Morris, William. *Political Writings of William Morris.* Edited by A. L. Morton. New York: International Publishers, 1973.
Munson, Gorham. *The Awakening Twenties: A Memoir-History of a Literary Period.* Baton Rouge: Louisiana State University Press, 1985.
———. "Van Wyck Brooks: His Sphere and His Encroachments." *Dial* 78 (January 1925): 28–42.
———. *Waldo Frank: A Study.* New York: Boni and Liveright, 1923.
Niebuhr, Reinhold. *Moral Man and Immoral Society: A Study in Ethics and Politics.* New York: Charles Scribner's Sons, 1960.
Plato. *The Republic.* Translated by G. M. A. Grube. Indianapolis: Hackett, 1974.
Rauschenbusch, Walter. *Christianity and the Social Crisis.* Edited by Robert D. Cross. New York: Harper & Row, 1964.
Rolland, Romain. "America and the Arts." *Seven Arts* 1 (November 1916): 47–51.
Rovere, Richard H. Review of Lewis Mumford, *Faith for Living. Common Sense* 9 (October 1940): 26.

Sainte-Beuve, Charles Augustin. *Sainte-Beuve: Selected Essays*. Edited by Francis Steegmuller and Norbert Guterman. New York: Anchor Books, 1963.

Santayana, George. *The Genteel Tradition: Nine Essays*. Edited by Douglas L. Wilson. Cambridge, Mass.: Harvard University Press, 1967.

Schapiro, Meyer. "Looking Forward to Looking Backward." *Partisan Review* 5 (July 1938): 12–24.

Schmalhausen, S. D. "The Reply Discourteous." *Modern Quarterly* 5 (Spring 1939): 167–70.

Stalley, Marshall, ed. *Patrick Geddes: Spokesman for Man and the Environment*. New Brunswick: Rutgers University Press, 1972.

Taggard, Genevieve. "Do You Kill Your Own Hogs Too?" *New Masses* 3 (September 1927): 23–24.

Trilling, Lionel. *The Middle of the Journey*. New York: Avon Books, 1975.

Veblen, Thorstein. *The Theory of the Leisure Class: An Economic Study of Institutions*. New York: Mentor, 1953.

Wasserstrom, William, ed. *Van Wyck Brooks: The Critic and His Critics*. Port Washington, N.Y.: Kennikat Press, 1979.

Weber, Max. "Science as a Vocation." In *From Max Weber: Essays in Sociology*, edited and translated by H. H. Gerth and C. Wright Mills, pp. 129–56. New York: Oxford University Press, 1946.

Wilson, Edmund. "An Appeal to Progressives." *New Republic* 65 (14 January 1931): 234–38.

———. *Letters on Literature and Politics, 1912–1972*. Edited by Elena Wilson. New York: Farrar, Straus and Giroux, 1977.

———. Review of Van Wyck Brooks, *The Pilgrimage of Henry James*. In *The Portable Edmund Wilson*, edited by Lewis M. Dabney, pp. 125–35. New York: Penguin, 1983.

Wright, Frank Lloyd. "The Art and Craft of the Machine." In *Roots of Contemporary American Architecture*, edited by Lewis Mumford, pp. 169–85. New York: Dover, 1972.

Secondary Sources

Aaron, Daniel. *Writers on the Left*. New York: Oxford University Press, 1977.

Abrahams, Edward. *The Lyrical Left: Randolph Bourne, Alfred Stieglitz, and the Origins of Cultural Radicalism in America*. Charlottesville: University Press of Virginia, 1986.

———. "Randolph Bourne on Feminism and Feminists." *Historian* 43 (May 1981): 365–77.

Akam, Everett H. "Pluralism and the Search for Community." Ph.D. dissertation, University of Rochester, 1989.

Alexander, Charles C. *Here the Country Lies: Nationalism and the Arts in Twentieth-Century America*. Bloomington: Indiana University Press, 1980.

Anderson, Quentin. "The Critic and Imperial Consciousness." *New Republic* 152 (17 April 1965): 15–17.

Bellah, Robert N., et al. *Habits of the Heart: Individualism and Commitment in American Life*. Berkeley and Los Angeles: University of California Press, 1985.

Bender, Thomas. *New York Intellect: A History of Intellectual Life in New York*

City, from 1750 to the Beginnings of Our Own Time. New York: Knopf, 1987.

Bercovitch, Sacvan. "New England's Errand Reappraised." In *New Directions in American Intellectual History*, edited by John Higham and Paul Conkin, pp. 85–104. Baltimore: Johns Hopkins University Press, 1979.

Bernstein, Richard. *Praxis and Action: Contemporary Philosophies of Human Activity.* Philadelphia: University of Pennsylvania Press, 1971.

Bittner, William. *The Novels of Waldo Frank.* Philadelphia: University of Pennsylvania Press, 1958.

Blake, Casey. "Aesthetic Engineering." *democracy* 1 (October 1981): 37–50.

――――. "Dissenter in the American Grain." *Commonweal* 113 (5 April 1985): 217–19.

――――. "Lewis Mumford: Values over Technique." *democracy* 3 (Spring 1983): 125–37.

――――. "The Young Intellectuals and the Culture of Personality." *American Literary History* 1 (Fall 1989): 510–34.

Boak, Denis. *Jules Romains.* New York: Twayne Publishers, 1974.

Boardman, Philip. *Patrick Geddes, Maker of the Future.* Chapel Hill: University of North Carolina Press, 1944.

Bourke, Paul F. "Philosophy and Social Criticism: John Dewey, 1910–1920." *History of Education Quarterly* 15 (Spring 1975): 3–16.

――――. "The Status of Politics, 1909–1919: *The New Republic*, Randolph Bourne and Van Wyck Brooks." *Journal of American Studies* 8 (August 1974): 171–202.

Braverman, Harry. *Labor and Monopoly Capital: The Degradation of Work in the Twentieth Century.* New York: Monthly Review Press, 1974.

Bromwich, David. "Literary Radicalism in America." *Dissent* 32 (Winter 1985): 35–44.

Bullert, Gary. "Lewis Mumford: Prophet of the New Age." *South Atlantic Quarterly* 85 (Autumn 1986): 339–50.

Callahan, Raymond E. *Education and the Cult of Efficiency.* Chicago: University of Chicago Press, 1962.

Canovan, Margaret. *G. K. Chesterton, Radical Populist.* New York: Harcourt Brace Jovanovich, 1977.

Carter, Paul J. *Waldo Frank.* New Haven: Twayne Publishers, 1967.

Chapman, Arnold. "Waldo Frank in Spanish America: Between Journeys, 1924–1929." *Hispania* 47 (September 1964): 510–21.

――――. "Waldo Frank in the Hispanic World: The First Phase." *Hispania* 44 (December 1961): 626–34.

Chasseguet-Smirgel, J. "Some Thoughts on the Ego Ideal: A Contribution to the Study of the 'Illness of Ideality.'" *Psychoanalytic Quarterly* 45 (July 1976): 345–73.

Clayton, Bruce. *Forgotten Prophet: The Life of Randolph Bourne.* Baton Rouge: Louisiana State University Press, 1984.

Coben, Stanley, and Lorman Ratner, eds. *The Development of an American Culture.* 2d ed. New York: St. Martin's Press, 1983.

Coughlan, Neil. *Young John Dewey: An Essay in American Intellectual History.* Chicago: University of Chicago Press, 1975.

Crunden, Robert M. *Ministers of Reform: The Progressives' Achievement in American Civilization, 1889–1920.* Urbana: University of Illinois Press, 1982.

Diggins, John P. *The American Left in the Twentieth Century.* New York: Harcourt Brace Jovanovich, 1973.

———. *The Bard of Savagery: Thorstein Veblen and Modern Social Theory.* New York: Seabury Press, 1978.

Dow, Edy Weber. "Lewis Mumford's First Phase: A Study of His Work as a Critic of the Arts in America." Ph.D. dissertation, University of Pennsylvania, 1965.

Dowell, Peter W. "Van Wyck Brooks and the Progressive Frame of Mind." *Midcontinent American Studies Journal* 11 (Spring 1970): 30–44.

Duffey, Joseph. "Mumford's Quest: The First Decade." *Salmagundi* 49 (Summer 1980): 43–68.

Duke, David C. *Distant Obligations: Modern American Writers and Foreign Causes.* New York: Oxford University Press, 1983.

Fairlie, Henry. "A Radical and a Patriot." *New Republic* 188 (2 February 1983): 25–32.

Filler, Louis. *Randolph Bourne.* New York: Citadel Press, 1966.

Fishbein, Leslie. *Rebels in Bohemia: The Radicals of the Masses, 1911–1917.* Chapel Hill: University of North Carolina Press, 1982.

Fishman, Robert. *Urban Utopias in the Twentieth Century: Ebenezer Howard, Frank Lloyd Wright, and Le Corbusier.* New York: Basic Books, 1977.

Forcey, Charles. *The Crossroads of Liberalism: Croly, Weyl, Lippmann, and the Progressive Era, 1900–1925.* New York: Oxford University Press, 1961.

Fox, Richard Wightman, and T. J. Jackson Lears, eds. *The Culture of Consumption: Critical Essays in American History, 1880–1980.* New York: Pantheon, 1983.

Geertz, Clifford. *Local Knowledge: Further Essays in Interpretive Anthropology.* New York: Basic Books, 1983.

Gilbert, James B. *Designing the Industrial State: The Intellectual Pursuit of Collectivism in America, 1880–1940.* Chicago: Quadrangle Books, 1972.

———. *Writers and Partisans: A History of Literary Radicalism in America.* New York: Wiley, 1968.

Green, Martin. *New York 1913: The Armory Show and the Paterson Strike Pageant.* New York: Charles Scribner's Sons, 1988.

Hall, Peter. *Cities of Tomorrow: An Intellectual History of Urban Planning and Design in the Twentieth Century.* Oxford: Basil Blackwell, 1988.

Hawley, Ellis W. *The Great War and the Search for a Modern Order: A History of the American People and Their Institutions, 1917–1933.* New York: St. Martin's Press, 1979.

Higham, John. *Writing American History: Essays on Modern Scholarship.* Bloomington: Indiana University Press, 1970.

Hilfer, Anthony C. *The Revolt from the Village, 1915–1930.* Chapel Hill: University of North Carolina Press, 1969.

Hoeveler, J. David, Jr. *The New Humanism: A Critique of Modern America, 1900–1940.* Charlottesville: University Press of Virginia, 1977.

Hoffman, Frederick J. *Freudianism and the Literary Mind.* 2d ed. Baton Rouge: Louisiana State University Press, 1957.

_____. *The Twenties: American Writing in the Postwar Decade*. Rev. ed. New York: Free Press, 1962.

Hofstadter, Richard. *The Age of Reform from Bryan to F.D.R.* New York: Vintage Books, 1955.

_____. *Anti-Intellectualism in American Life*. New York: Vintage Books, 1963.

Hollinger, David A. *In the American Province: Studies in the History and Historiography of Ideas*. Bloomington: Indiana University Press, 1985.

Hoopes, James. "The Culture of Progressivism: Croly, Lippmann, Brooks, Bourne, and the Idea of American Artistic Decadence." *Clio* 7 (Fall 1977): 91–111.

_____. *Van Wyck Brooks: In Search of American Culture*. Amherst: University of Massachusetts Press, 1977.

Howe, Daniel Walker. "American Victorianism as a Culture." *American Quarterly* 27 (December 1975): 507–32.

Hughes, Agatha C., and Thomas P. Hughes, eds. *Lewis Mumford: Public Intellectual*. New York: Oxford University Press, 1990.

Hughes, H. Stuart. *Consciousness and Society: The Reorientation of European Social Thought, 1890–1930*. Rev. ed. New York: Vintage Books, 1977.

Hughes, Thomas P. *American Genesis: A Century of Invention and Technological Enthusiasm, 1870–1970*. New York: Viking, 1989.

Jacoby, Russell. *The Last Intellectuals: American Culture in the Age of Academe*. New York: Basic Books, 1987.

Jay, Martin. *The Dialectical Imagination: A History of the Frankfurt School and the Institute of Social Research, 1923–1950*. Boston: Little, Brown, 1970.

Joost, Nicholas. "Culture vs. Power: Randolph Bourne, John Dewey, and *The Dial*." *Midwest Quarterly* 9 (Spring 1968): 245–59.

Karrier, Clarence. "Making the World Safe for Democracy: An Historical Critique of John Dewey's Pragmatic Liberal Philosophy in the Warfare State." *Educational Theory* 27 (Winter 1977): 12–47.

_____. *Scientists of the Mind: Intellectual Founders of Modern Psychology*. Urbana: University of Illinois Press, 1986.

Kazin, Alfred. *On Native Grounds: An Interpretation of Modern American Prose Literature*. New York: Harcourt Brace Jovanovich, 1970.

Kloppenberg, James T. *Uncertain Victory: Social Democracy and Progressivism in European and American Social Thought, 1870–1920*. New York: Oxford University Press, 1986.

Kloucek, Jerome W. "Waldo Frank: The Ground of His Mind and Art." Ph.D. dissertation, Northwestern University, 1958.

Kraditor, Aileen. *The Radical Persuasion, 1890–1917: Aspects of the Intellectual History and Historiography of Three American Radical Organizations*. Baton Rouge: Louisiana State University Press, 1981.

Krupnick, Mark. *Lionel Trilling and the Fate of Cultural Criticism*. Evanston: Northwestern University Press, 1986.

Kuhns, William. *The Post-Industrial Prophets: Interpretations of Technology*. New York: Weybright and Talley, 1971.

Lasch, Christopher. *The Agony of the American Left*. New York: Vintage Books, 1969.

———. "Lewis Mumford and the Myth of the Machine." *Salmagundi* 49 (Summer 1980): 4–28.

———. *The New Radicalism in America (1889–1963): The Intellectual as a Social Type.* New York: Vintage Books, 1965.

———. "A Typology of Intellectuals." *Salmagundi* 70–71 (Spring–Summer 1986): 27–32.

———. *The World of Nations: Reflections on American History, Politics, and Culture.* New York: Vintage Books, 1972.

Lawson, R. Alan. *The Failure of Independent Liberalism, 1930–1941.* New York: G. P. Putnam's Sons, 1971.

Lears, T. J. Jackson. *No Place of Grace: Antimodernism and the Transformation of American Culture, 1880–1920.* New York: Pantheon, 1981.

Levy, David W. *Herbert Croly of the New Republic: The Life and Thought of an American Progressive.* Princeton: Princeton University Press, 1985.

Lipow, Arthur. *Authoritarian Socialism in America: Edward Bellamy and the Nationalist Movement.* Berkeley and Los Angeles: University of California Press, 1982.

Lubove, Roy. *Community Planning in the 1920's: The Contribution of the Regional Planning Association of America.* Pittsburgh: University of Pittsburgh Press, 1963.

Lustig, R. Jeffrey. *Corporate Liberalism: The Origins of Modern American Political Theory, 1890–1920.* Berkeley and Los Angeles: University of California Press, 1982.

Lynn, Kenneth S. "The Rebels of Greenwich Village." *Perspectives in American History* 8 (1974): 335–77.

McClay, Wilfred M. "Lewis Mumford: From the Belly of the Whale." *American Scholar* 57 (Winter 1988): 111–18.

McCormick, John S. "A Beleaguered Minority: The Young Intellectuals and American Mass Society, 1910–1920." Ph.D. dissertation, University of Iowa, 1973.

MacIntyre, Alasdair. *After Virtue: A Study in Moral Theory.* 2d ed. Notre Dame: University of Notre Dame Press, 1984.

MacKenzie, Norman, and Jeanne Mackenzie. *The Fabians.* New York: Simon and Schuster, 1977.

McWilliams, Wilson Carey. *The Idea of Fraternity in America.* Berkeley and Los Angeles: University of California Press, 1973.

Mansbridge, Jane J. *Beyond Adversary Democracy.* Rev. ed. Chicago: University of Chicago Press, 1983.

Marcus, George E., and Michael M. J. Fischer. *Anthropology as Cultural Critique: An Experimental Moment in the Human Sciences.* Chicago: University of Chicago Press, 1986.

Matthews, Fred. "Polemical Palefaces and Genteel Redskins: The Debate over American Culture and the Origins of the American Studies Movement." *American Quarterly* 35 (Winter 1983): 543–55.

Matthiessen, F. O. *American Renaissance: Art and Expression in the Age of Emerson and Whitman.* New York: Oxford University Press, 1941.

May, Henry. *The End of American Innocence: A Study of the First Years of Our Own Time, 1912–1917.* Chicago: Quadrangle Books, 1959.

Meller, Helen E. "Patrick Geddes: An Analysis of His Theory of Civics, 1880–

1904." *Victorian Studies* 16 (March 1973): 291–315.

———, ed. *The Ideal City.* N.p.: Leicester University Press, 1979.

Meyer, Donald. *The Positive Thinkers: Religion as Pop Psychology from Mary Baker Eddy to Oral Roberts.* 2d ed. New York: Pantheon, 1980.

Miller, Donald L. *Lewis Mumford: A Life.* New York: Weidenfeld & Nicolson, 1989.

———. *The New American Radicalism: Alfred M. Bingham and Non-Marxian Insurgency in the New Deal Era.* Port Washington, N.Y.: Kennikat Press, 1979.

Moreau, John Adam. *Randolph Bourne: Legend and Reality.* Washington, D.C.: Public Affairs Press, 1966.

Nelson, Elmer S. *Lewis Mumford: A Bibliography, 1914–1970.* New York: Harcourt Brace Jovanovich, 1971.

Nelson, Raymond. *Van Wyck Brooks: A Writer's Life.* New York: Dutton, n.d.

Nilsen, Helge N. "The Status of Waldo Frank in American Letters." *American Studies in Scandinavia* 12 (1980): 27–32.

———. "Waldo Frank and the Idea of America." *American Studies International* 17 (Spring 1979): 27–36.

Noble, David F. *America by Design: Science, Technology, and the Rise of Corporate Capitalism.* New York: Knopf, 1979.

Novak, Frank G., Jr. "Lewis Mumford and the Reclamation of Human History." *Clio* 16 (February 1987): 159–81.

———. "Master and Disciple: Selections from the Patrick Geddes–Lewis Mumford Letters." *Horns of Plenty: Malcolm Cowley and His Generation* 2 (Fall 1989): 45–62.

Nuechterlein, James A. "The Dream of Scientific Liberalism: The *New Republic* and American Progressive Thought, 1914–1920." *Review of Politics* 42 (1980): 167–90.

Ogorzaly, Michael A. "Waldo Frank: A Prophet of Hispanic Regeneration." Ph.D. dissertation, University of Notre Dame, 1982.

Paul, Sherman. *Repossessing and Renewing: Essays in the Green American Tradition.* Baton Rouge: Louisiana State University Press, 1976.

Pells, Richard H. *Radical Visions and American Dreams: Culture and Social Thought in the Depression Years.* New York: Harper & Row, 1973.

Perry, Lewis. *Intellectual Life in America: A History.* New York: Franklin Watts, 1984.

Perry, Robert L. *The Shared Vision of Waldo Frank and Hart Crane.* University of Nebraska Studies, n.s. 33. Lincoln: University of Nebraska Press, 1966.

Persons, Stow. *The Decline of American Gentility.* New York: Columbia University Press, 1973.

Pittenger, Mark. "Science, Culture and the New Socialist Intellectuals before World War I." *American Studies* 28 (Spring 1987): 73–91.

Potter, Hugh. "Paul Rosenfeld: Criticism and Prophecy." *American Quarterly* 22 (Spring 1970): 82–94.

———. "The Romantic Nationalists of the 1920s." Ph.D. dissertation, University of Minnesota, 1965.

Pumphrey, Martin Lloyd. "Art and Leadership in America: The Quest for Synthesis." Ph.D. dissertation, University of Iowa, 1977.

Quandt, Jean B. *From the Small Town to the Great Community: The Social*

Thought of Progressive Intellectuals. New Brunswick: Rutgers University Press, 1970.

Riesman, David, et al. *The Lonely Crowd: A Study of the Changing American Character.* New Haven: Yale University Press, 1961.

Rorty, Richard. *Consequences of Pragmatism (Essays, 1972–1980).* Minneapolis: University of Minnesota Press, 1982.

Rubin, Joan Shelley. *Constance Rourke and American Culture.* Chapel Hill: University of North Carolina Press, 1977.

_____. " 'Information Please!': Culture and Expertise in the Interwar Period." *American Quarterly* 35 (Winter 1983): 499–517.

Sacks, Claire. "The *Seven Arts* Critics: A Study of Cultural Nationalism in America, 1910–1930." Ph.D. dissertation, University of Wisconsin, 1955.

Salvatore, Nick. *Eugene V. Debs: Citizen and Socialist.* Urbana: University of Illinois Press, 1982.

Samson, Miles David. "German-American Dialogues: The Modern Movement before the 'Design Migration,' 1910–1933." Ph.D. dissertation, Harvard University, 1988.

Sandeen, Eric J. "Bourne Again: The Correspondence between Randolph Bourne and Elsie Clews Parsons." *American Literary History* 1 (Fall 1989): 489–509.

Schaffer, Daniel. *Garden Cities for America: The Radburn Experience.* Philadelphia: Temple University Press, 1982.

Shi, David E. *The Simple Life: Plain Living and High Thinking in American Culture.* New York: Oxford University Press, 1985.

Silet, Charles L. P. *"The Seven Arts*: The Artist and the Community." Ph.D. dissertation, Indiana University, 1973.

Sklar, Martin J. "On the Proletarian Revolution and the End of Political-Economic Society." *Radical America* 3 (May–June 1969): 1–41.

Stout, Jeffrey. *Ethics after Babel: The Languages of Morals and Their Discontents.* Boston: Beacon Press, 1988.

Sullivan, William M. *Reconstructing Public Philosophy.* Berkeley and Los Angeles: University of California Press, 1986.

Susman, Warren I. *Culture as History: The Transformation of American Society in the Twentieth Century.* New York: Pantheon, 1984.

Sussman, Carl, ed. *Planning the Fourth Migration: The Neglected Vision of the Regional Planning Association of America.* Cambridge, Mass.: MIT Press, 1976.

Tashjian, Dickran. *Skyscraper Primitives: Dada and the American Avant-Garde, 1910–1925.* Middletown: Wesleyan University Press, 1975.

Taylor, Charles. *Hegel and Modern Society.* Cambridge: Cambridge University Press, 1979.

Thomas, John L. *Alternative America: Henry George, Edward Bellamy, Henry Demarest Lloyd and the Adversary Tradition.* Cambridge, Mass.: Harvard University Press, 1983.

_____. "Lewis Mumford: Regionalist Historian." *Reviews in American History* 16 (March 1988): 158–72.

Thompson, E. P. *William Morris: Romantic to Revolutionary.* 2d ed. New York: Pantheon, 1976.

Tomsich, John. *A Genteel Endeavor: American Culture and Politics in the Gilded Age.* Stanford: Stanford University Press, 1971.

Trachtenberg, Alan. "Cultural Revisions in the Twenties: Brooklyn Bridge as 'Usable Past.'" In *The American Self: Myth, Ideology, and Popular Culture*, edited by Sam B. Girgus, pp. 58–75. Albuquerque: University of New Mexico Press, 1981.

———. *The Incorporation of America: Culture and Society in the Gilded Age.* New York: Hill & Wang, 1982.

———. "Mumford in the Twenties: The Historian as Artist." *Salmagundi* 49 (Summer 1980): 29–42.

Tuttleton, James W. "American Literary Radicalism in the Twenties." *New Criterion* 3 (March 1985): 16–30.

Underhill, Evelyn. *Mysticism: A Study in the Nature and Development of Man's Spiritual Consciousness.* New York: New American Library, 1974.

Veysey, Lawrence R. *The Emergence of the Modern University.* Chicago: University of Chicago Press, 1965.

Walzer, Michael. *The Company of Critics: Social Criticism and Political Commitment in the Twentieth Century.* New York: Basic Books, 1988.

———. *Spheres of Justice.* New York: Basic Books, 1983.

Wasserstrom, William. *The Legacy of Van Wyck Brooks: A Study of Maladies and Motives.* Carbondale: Southern Illinois University Press, 1971.

Weimer, David S. "Anxiety in the Golden Day of Lewis Mumford." *New England Quarterly* 36 (June 1963): 172–91.

Weinstein, James. *The Corporate Ideal in the Liberal State, 1900–1918.* Boston: Beacon Press, 1968.

Wertheim, Arthur Frank. *The New York Little Renaissance: Iconoclasm, Modernism, and Nationalism in American Culture, 1908–1917.* New York: New York University Press, 1976.

Westbrook, Robert B. "John Dewey and American Democracy." Ph.D. dissertation, Stanford University, 1980.

———. "The Responsibility of Peoples: Dwight Macdonald and the Holocaust." In *America and the Holocaust*, edited by Sanford Pinsker and Jack Fischel, pp. 35–68. Greenwood, Fla.: Penkevill, 1984.

———. "Tribune of the Technostructure: The Popular Economics of Stuart Chase." *American Quarterly* 32 (Fall 1980): 387–408.

White, Morton. *Social Thought in America: The Revolt against Formalism.* Boston: Beacon Press, 1957.

Wiebe, Robert H. *The Search for Order, 1877–1920.* New York: Hill & Wang, 1967.

Williams, Raymond. *Culture and Society, 1780–1950.* New York: Harper & Row, 1966.

———. *Keywords: A Vocabulary of Culture and Society.* New York: Oxford University Press, 1976.

Willingham, John R. "The Achievement of Waldo Frank." *Literary Review* 1 (Summer 1958): 465–77.

Wilson, R. Jackson. *In Quest of Community: Social Philosophy in the United States, 1860–1920.* New York: Oxford University Press, 1968.

Wolin, Sheldon. *Politics and Vision: Continuity and Innovation in Western Political Thought.* Boston: Little, Brown, 1960.

Index